LIONS PULLING DOWN GIRAFFE.

London, Hurst & Blackett 1868.

LAKE NGAMI;

OR,

EXPLORATIONS AND DISCOVERIES,

DURING

FOUR YEARS' WANDERINGS IN THE WILDS

OF

SOUTH WESTERN AFRICA.

BY

CHARLES JOHN ANDERSSON.

WITH A MAP, AND NUMEROUS ILLUSTRATIONS
REPRESENTING SPORTING ADVENTURES, SUBJECTS OF NATURAL HISTORY,
DEVICES FOR DESTROYING WILD ANIMALS, &c.

Rediscovery Books

Reproduced by kind permission of the
Royal Geographical Society

Published by
Rediscovery Books Ltd
Unit 10, Ridgewood Industrial Park,
Uckfield, East Sussex,
TN22 5QE England
Tel: +44 (0) 1825 749494
Fax: +44 (0) 1825 765701

This edition © Rediscovery Books Ltd 2007

To find out more about Rediscovery Books
and its range of titles visit
www.rediscoverybooks.com

Published in association with

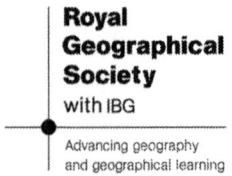

The **Royal Geographical Society with IBG** was founded in 1830 to advance geographical science. Today it supports geographical research, promotes geography in schools and through outdoor learning, in society and to policy makers. Geography connects us to the world's people, places and environments.
The **Rediscovery Books** series allow us to see how previous geographers and travellers understood and recorded the world.

In reprinting in facsimile from the original, any imperfections are inevitably reproduced and the quality may fall short of modern type and cartographic standards.

Printed and bound by Lightning Source

PREFACE.

THE following Narrative of Explorations and Discoveries during four years in the wilds of the South-Western parts of Africa, contains an account of two expeditions in that continent between the years 1850 and 1854. In the first of these journeys, the countries of the Damaras (previously all but unknown in Europe) and of the Ovambo (till now a *terra incognita*) were explored; in the second, the newly-discovered Lake Ngami, was reached by a route that had always been deemed impracticable. It is more than probable that this route (the shortest and best) will be adopted as the one by which commerce and civilization may eventually find their way to the Lake regions.

The first journey was performed in company with Mr. Francis Galton, to whom we are indebted for a work on 'Tropical South Africa;' on the second, the Author was alone, and altogether dependent on his own very scanty resources.

It was suggested to the Author, as regards the first journey, that from the ground having been pre-occupied, it would be best for him to commence where his friend left off. There was some reason for this. But, on mature consideration, he deemed it desirable to start from the beginning; otherwise, he could not have given a connected and detailed account of the regions he visited. Moreover, from the Author having remained two years longer in Africa than Mr. Galton, he has not only been enabled to ascertain the truth respecting much that at first appeared obscure and doubtful, but has had many opportunities of enlarging the stock of information acquired by himself and friend when together. Besides, they were often separated for long periods, during which many incidents and adventures occurred to the Author that are scarcely alluded to in 'Tropical South Africa.' And, lastly, the impressions received by different individuals, even under similar circumstances, are generally found to vary greatly; which, in itself, would be a sufficient reason for the course the Author has decided on pursuing.

As will be seen, the present writer has not only described the general appearance of the regions he visited, but has given the best information he was able to collect of the geological features of the country, and of its probable mineral wealth; and, slight though it may be, he had the gratification of finding that the hints he threw out at the Cape and elsewhere, were acted upon; that mining companies were formed, and that mining operations are now carried on to some extent in regions heretofore considered as utterly worthless.

The Author has also spoken, at some length, of the religion and manners and customs of such of the native tribes (previously all but unknown to Europeans) visited by him during his several journeys. He also noted many of their superstitions; for, too much attention, as it has been truly observed, cannot be paid to the mythological traditions of savages. Considerable discretion is, of course, needful in this matter; as, if every portion were to be literally received, we might be led into grievous errors. Still, by attending to what many might call absurd superstitions, we not only attain to a knowledge of the mental tendencies of the natives, but are made acquainted with interesting facts touching the geographical distribution of men and inferior animals.

Since the different members constituting the brute creation are so intimately connected with the economy of man, and since many of the beasts and birds indigenous to those parts of Africa visited by the Author, are still but imperfectly known, he has thought it advisable to enter largely into their habits, &c.; the rather, as natural history has, from childhood, been his favourite pursuit, and is a subject on which he therefore feels conversant. And though part of what he has stated regarding the rhinoceros, the hippopotamus, the koodoo, the ostrich, and others of the almost incalculable varieties of animals found in the African wilderness, may be known to some inquirers, it is still hoped that the general reader will find matter he has not previously met with.

The larger portion of the beautiful plates to be found in this work (faithfully depicting the scenes described) are by Mr. Wolf— 'the Landseer of animals and vegetation,' to quote the words of the Earl of Ellesmere in a note which his lordship did me the honour to write to me.

The Author has endeavoured in the following pages, faithfully, and in plain and unassuming language, to record his experiences, impressions, feelings, and impulses, under circumstances often peculiarly trying. He lays claim to no more credit than may attach to an earnest desire to make himself useful, and to further the cause of science.

It is more than probable that his career as an explorer and pioneer to civilization and commerce is terminated. Still, he would fain hope that his humble exertions may not be without their fruits.

When he first arrived in Africa, he generally travelled on foot throughout the whole of the day, regardless of heat, and almost scorning the idea of riding on horse-back, or using any other mode of conveyance. Indeed, he was wont to vie with the natives in endurance; but now, owing to the severe hardships he has undergone, his constitution is undermined, and the foundation of a malady has been laid that it is feared he will carry with him to the day of his death Yet, such is the perverseness of human nature, that, did circumstances permit, he would return to this life of trial and privation.

LITHOGRAPHS.

PAGE

1. *Lions pulling down Giraffe.*—Sketched and drawn on Stone by J. WOLF   *To face Title*
2. *Damaras* . . . Sketched by EDM. WALKER, and drawn on Stone by BRANDARD   49
3. *The Lucky Escape* . . Sketched and drawn on Stone by J. WOLF 110
4. *Shooting Trap* . . ,, ,, ,, 126
5. *Ovambo* . . . . Sketched by EDM. WALKER, and drawn on Stone by BRANDARD   196
6. *Unwelcome Hunting Companions* . . . Sketched and drawn on Stone by J. WOLF 213
7. *Coursing Young Ostriches* . ,, ,, ,, 253
8. *Oryx or Gemsbok* . . ,, ,, ,, 279
9. *Chasing the Eland* . . ,, ,, ,, 381
10. *The Approach of Elephants* ,, ,, ,, 414
11. *More Close than Agreeable* ,, ,, ,, 422
12. *Desperate Situation* . . ,, ,, ,, 424
13. *Nakong and Leché* . . ,, ,, ,, 448
14. *The Koodoo* . . . ,, ,, ,, 484
15. *Bayeye* . . . . Sketched by Mr. CHARLES BELL, and drawn on Stone by BRANDARD 502
16. *Harpooning Hippopotamus* Sketched and drawn on Stone by J. WOLF 521

The above Illustrations are lithographed by M. and N. HANHART.

17. *Map.*—Drawn by E. RAVENSTEIN, and lithographed by SCHENCK and MCFARLANE . . . . . *to face* 536

LIST OF WOOD ENGRAVINGS.

		PAGE	
1.	*Malay*	7	⎫ Sketched by the AUTHOR, drawn on wood, and engraved by PEARSON.
2.	*View of Walfisch Bay*	13	⎬
3.	*Hill-Damara Pipe*	80	⎭
4.	*Fan Palm*	165	⎫ Sketched by Major ROBERT GARDEN, drawn on wood, and engraved by DALZIEL.
5.	*Ovambo Pipe*	172	⎭
6.	,, *Dagger and Sheath*	173	⎱ Drawn on wood, and engraved by PEARSON.
7.	,, *Hatchet*	173	⎫ Sketched by the AUTHOR, drawn on wood, and engraved by DALZIEL.
8.	,, *Basket for Merchandize*	174	⎬
9.	*Otjikoto Fountain*	180	⎭
10.	*Interview with King Nangoro*	193	⎬ Sketched by Major ROBERT GARDEN, drawn on wood, and engraved by DALZIEL.
11.	*Ovambo Beer-Cup and Beer-Spoon*	195	⎫ Sketched by the AUTHOR, drawn on wood, and engraved by DALZIEL.
12.	*Ovambo Guitar*	195	⎬
13.	,, *Meat Dish*	199	⎭
14.	,, *Dwelling house and Corn stores*	201	⎫ Sketched by Major ROBERT GARDEN, drawn on wood, and engraved by DALZIEL.
15.	*View in Ondonga*	203	⎭
16.	*Ovambo* Blacksmiths *at work*	204	⎱ Drawn on wood by PALMER, and engraved by PEARSON.
17.	*Damara Grave*	227	
18.	*Jonker Afrikaner*	235	⎫ Sketched by the AUTHOR, drawn on wood, and engraved by DALZIEL.
19.	*Wild Boar's Head*	236	⎭

LIST OF WOOD ENGRAVINGS.

		PAGE	
20.	*Skull of a Bechuana Ox*	317	Sketched by J. Wolf, drawn on wood by Palmer, and engraved by Pearson.
21.	*Dacre's Pulpit*	346	Drawn on wood, and engraved by Dalziel.
22.	*Negro Boy*	351	Drawn on wood by Palmer, and engraved by Pearson.
23.	*Pit-falls*	376	Drawn on wood, and engraved by Dalziel.
24.	*Heads of Rhinoceroses*	386	
25.	*Horns of Rhinoceros Oswellii*	388	
26.	*Fœtus of Rhinoceros Keitloa*	391	Drawn on wood, and engraved by Dalziel.
27.	*The Bechuana Picho*	454	Drawn on wood by Palmer, and engraved by Pearson.
28.	*Ascending the Teoge*	479	
29.	*Tsetse Fly*	489	Drawn on wood, and engraved by Dalziel.
30.	*The Reed Ferry*	497	
31.	*Medal*	516	Drawn on wood by Palmer, and engraved by Pearson.
32.	*Hippopotamus Harpoon*	518	
33.	*The Reed Raft and Harpooners*	520	Drawn on wood, and engraved by Dalziel.
34.	*The Spear*	521	Drawn on wood, and engraved by Pearson.
35.	*Egyptians and Hippopotamus*	523	
36.	*The Spear*	524	Drawn on wood and engraved by Pearson.
37.	„ *Reel*	524	
38.	*The Downfall*	528	Sketched by Mr. Alex. Keiller, drawn on wood by Palmer, and engraved by Pearson.
39.	*Author and Steed broken down*	535	Drawn on wood, and engraved by Dalziel.
40.	*Signal Station at Cape Town*	536	

CONTENTS.

CHAPTER I.
Departure from Sweden—Day Dreams—Fraternal Love—A Tempting Offer—Preparations for Journey to Africa—Departure from England—Arrival at the Cape—Town and Inhabitants—Table Mountain—Curious Legend—Preparation for Journey into the Interior—Departure for Walfisch Bay . . . . 1—12

CHAPTER II.
Arrival at Walfisch Bay—Scenery—Harbour Described—Want of Water—Capabilities for Trade—Fish—Wild Fowl—Mirage—Sand Fountain—The Bush-tick—The Naras—Quadrupeds Scarce—Meeting the Hottentots—Their Filthy Habits—The Alarum—The Turn Out—Death of a Lion—Arrival at Scheppmansdorf—the Place described—Mr. Bam—Missionary Life—Ingratitude of Natives—Missionary Waggons . . . . . . 13—28

CHAPTER III.
Preparations for Journey—Breaking-in Oxen—Departure from Scheppmansdorf—An Infuriated Ox—The Naarip Plain—The Scarlet Flower—The Usab Gorge—The Swakop River—Tracks of Rhinoceros Seen—Anecdote of that Animal—A Sunrise in the Tropics—Sufferings from Heat and Thirst—Arrival at Daviep : great Resort of Lions—A Horse and Mule killed by them—The Author goes in Pursuit—A Troop of Lions—Unsuccessful Chase—Mules' Flesh Palatable . . . . 29—42

CHAPTER IV.
The Gnoo and the Gemsbok—Pursuit of a Rhinoceros—Venomous Fly—Fruit of the Acacia Nutritious—Sun-stroke—Crested Parrot—A Giraffe Shot—Tjobis Fountain—Singular Omelet—Nutritious Gum—Arrival at Richterfeldt—Mr. Rath and the Missions—The Damaras: their Persons, Habits, &c.—Lions Troublesome—Panic—Horse Sickness . . . . . . 43—55

CHAPTER V.

Hans Larsen—His Exploits—He joins the Expedition—How People travel on Ox-back—Rhinoceros Hunt—Death of the Beast—'Look Before You Leap'—Anecdote proving the Truth of the Proverb—Hans and the Lion—The Doctor in Difficulties—Sufferings on the Naarip Plain—Arrival at Scheppmansdorf . 56—64

CHAPTER VI.

Return to Scheppmansdorf—Training Oxen for the Yoke—Sporting—The Flamingo—The Butcher Bird: curious Superstition regarding it—Preparing for Journey—Servants described . 65—72

CHAPTER VII.

Departure from Scheppmansdorf—Cattle refractory at Starting—Tincas —Always Travel by Night—Rhinoceros Hunt—The Author in Danger of a Second Sun-stroke—Reach Onanis—A Tribe of Hill-Damaras settled there—Singular Manner in which these People smoke—Effects of the Weed—The Euphorbia Candelabrum—Remarkable Properties of this Vegetable Poison—Guinea Fowl: the best Manner of shooting them—Meet a Troop of Giraffes—Tjobis Fountain again—Attacked by Lions—Providential Escape—Arrival at Richterfeldt . . . . 73—86

CHAPTER VIII.

A hearty Welcome—We remove the Encampment—An Apparition—Audacity of Wild Beasts—Depriving Lions of their Prey—Excessive Heat—Singular Effects of great Heat—Depart for Barmen—Meet a Troop of Zebras—Their Flesh not equal to Venison—The Missionary's Wail—A Sad Catastrophe—The 'Kameel-doorn'—Buxton Fountain—The Scorpion—Arrival at Barmen . . 87—98

CHAPTER IX.

Barmen—Thunder-storm in the Tropics—A Man Killed by Lightning—Warm Spring—Mr. Hahn: his Missionary Labour; Seed sown in Exceeding Stony Ground—The Lake Omanbondè—Mr. Galton's Mission of Peace—The Author meets a Lion by the way; the Beast bolts—Singular Chase of a Gnoo—'Killing Two Birds with One Stone'—A Lion Hunt—The Author escapes Death by a Miracle—Consequences of shooting on a Sunday . . . 99—111

CHAPTER X.

A Christmas in the Desert—Mr. Galton's Return from the Erongo Mountain—He passes numerous Villages—Great Drought; the

Natives have a Choice of Two Evils—The Hill-Damaras—The Damaras a Pastoral People—The Whole Country Public Property—Enormous Herds of Cattle—They are as destructive as Locusts to the Vegetation—Departure from Richterfeldt—The Author kills an Oryx—The Oxen refractory—Danger of traversing dry Watercourses on the Approach of the Rainy Season—Message from the Robber-Chief Jonker—Emeute amongst the Servants—Depart for Schmelen's Hope . . . . 112—119

CHAPTER XI.

Schmelen's Hope—Scenery—Missionary Station—Raid of the Namaquas—Ingratitude of the Natives—Jonker's Feud with Kahichenè; his Barbarities; his Treachery—Mr. Galton departs for Eikhams—Author's successful Sporting Excursions—He captures a young Steinbok and a Koodoo—They are easily Domesticated—Hyænas very troublesome; several destroyed by Spring-Guns—The latter described—Visit from a Leopard; it wounds a Dog; Chase and Death of the Leopard—The Caracal . . . 120—129

CHAPTER XII.

Wild Fowl abundant—The great Bustard—The Termites—Wild Bees—Mushrooms—The Chief Zwartbooi—Return of Mr. Galton—He makes a Treaty with Jonker—He visits Rehoboth—Misdoings of John Waggoner and Gabriel—Change of Servants—Swarm of Caterpillars—A Reconnoitering Expedition—Thunder-Storm—The Omatako Mountains—Zebra Flesh a God-send—Tropical Phenomenon—The Damaras not remarkable for Veracity—Encamp in an Ant-Hill—Return to Schmelen's Hope—Preparations for visiting Omanbondè . . . . 130—141

CHAPTER XIII.

Depart from Schmelen's Hope—Meeting with Kahichenè—Oxen stolen—Summary Justice—Superstition—Meeting an old Friend—Singular Custom—Gluttony of the Damaras—How they eat Flesh by the Yard and not by the Pound—Superstitious Custom—A Nondescript Animal—The Author loses his Way—Ravages of the Termites—'Wait a bit, if you please'—Magnificent Fountain—Remains of Damara Villages—Horrors of War—Meet Bushmen—Meet Damaras—Difficulties encountered by African Travellers—Reach the Lake Omanbondè—Cruel Disappointment . . 142—159

CHAPTER XIV.

Omanbondè visited by Hippopotami—Vegetation, &c., Described—Game somewhat scarce—Combat between Elephant and Rhinoceros—Advance or Retreat—Favourable Reports of the Ovambo-Land—Resolve to proceed there—Reconnoitre the Country—Depart from Omanbondè—Author shoots a Giraffe—Splendid Mirage—The Fan-Palm—The Guide absconds—Commotion amongst the Natives—Arrive at Okamabuti—Unsuccessful Elephant Hunt—Vegetation—Accident to Waggon—Obliged to proceed on Ox-back—The Party go Astray—Baboon Fountain—Meeting with the Ovambo; their personal Appearance, &c.—Return to Encampment—An Elephant killed—Discover a curious Plant—Immorality—Reflections . . . . . . 160—177

CHAPTER XV.

Depart from Okamabuti—Visit from a Lion—Amulets—Re-visit Baboon Fountain—Otjikoto; a wonderful Freak of Nature; remarkable Cavern—Natives unacquainted with the Art of Swimming—Fish abundant in Otjikoto; frequented by immense Flocks of Doves—Panic of the Ovambo on seeing Birds shot on the Wing—Arrive at Omutjamatunda—A Greasy Welcome—Ducks and Grouse numerous—Author finds himself somewhat 'overdone'—'Salt-Pans'—All 'look blue'—A Second Paradise—Hospitable Reception—Vegetation—People live in Patriarchal Style—Population—Enormous Hogs—Arrive at the residence of the redoubtable Nangoro. 178—191

CHAPTER XVI.

Visit from Nangoro—His extreme Obesity—One must be fat to wear a Crown—His non-appreciation of Eloquence—Singular Effects of Fireworks on the Natives—Cure for making a wry Face—Ball at the Palace—The Ladies very attractive and very loving—Their Dress, Ornaments, &c.—Honesty of the Ovambo—Kindness to the Poor—Love of Country—Hospitality—Delicate Manner of eating—Loose Morals—Laws of Succession—Religion—Houses—Domestic Animals—Implements of Husbandry—Manner of tilling the Ground—Articles of Barter—Metallurgy . . 192—205

CHAPTER XVII.

The River Cunenè—The Travellers are Prisoners at Large—Kingly Revenge—Kingly Liberality—Depart from Odonga—Suffering and consequences resulting from Cold—Return to Okamabuti—Damara

Women murdered by Bushmen—Preparations for Journey—Obtain Guides—Depart from Tjopopa's Werft—Game abundant—Author and three Lions stalk Antelopes in Company—Extraordinary Visitation—The Rhinoceros's Guardian Angel—The Textor Erythrorhynchus—The Amadina Squamifrons; singular Construction of its Nest—Return to Barmen . . . . . 206—216

CHAPTER XVIII.

The Damaras—Whence they came—Their Conquests—The Tide turns—Damara-Land only partially inhabited—Climate—Seasons—Mythology—Religion—Superstitions—Marriage—Polygamy—Children—Circumcision—Bury their Dead—Way they Mourn—Children interred Alive—Burial of the Chief, and Superstitions consequent thereon—Maladies—Damaras do not live long; the cause thereof—Food—Music and Dancing—How they swear—Power of the Chieftain limited—Slothful People—Numerals—Astronomy—Domestic Animals; their diseases . . . . 217—232

CHAPTER XIX.

Despatch a Messenger to Cape-Town—Depart from Barmen—Eikhams—Eyebrecht—Depart from Eikhams—Elephant Fountain—Tunobis—Enormous quanties of Game—Shooting by Night at the 'Skärm'—The Author has several narrow Escapes—Checked in attempt to reach the Ngami—The Party set out on their Return—Reach Elephant Fountain—How to make Soap—Pit-falls—A Night Adventure—Game scarce—Join Hans—The Party nearly poisoned—Arrival at Walfisch Bay—A Tub Adventure—Extraordinary Mortality amongst the Fish—Author narrowly escapes Drowning—Arrival of the Missionary Vessel—Letters from Home—Mr. Galton returns to Europe—Reflections . . . . 233—252

CHAPTER XX.

Capture of Young Ostriches — Natural History of the Ostrich; Where found; description of; Size; Weight; Age; Voice; Strength; Speed; Food; Breeding; Incubation; Cunning; Stones found in Eggs; Chicks; Flesh—Brain in Request amongst the Romans—Eggs highly prized—Uses of Egg-Shells—Feathers an Article of Commerce—Ostrich Parasols—The Bird's destructive Propensities—Habits—Resembles Quadrupeds—Domestication—The Chase—Snares—Ingenious Device—Enemies of the Ostrich.
253—269

CHAPTER XXI.

Sudden Floods—John Allen's Sufferings—Hans and the Author enter into Partnership—Young Grass injurious to Cattle—Depart from Walfisch Bay—Attractive Scenery—Troops of Lions—Extraordinary Proceedings of Kites—Flight of Butterflies—Attachment of Animals to One Another—Arrival at Richterfeldt; at Barmen—Hans' narrow Escape—Self-Possession—Heavy Rains—Runaway Ox; he tosses the Author—Depart from Barmen—Difficulty of crossing Rivers—Encounter great Numbers of Oryxes . 270—278

CHAPTER XXII.

The Oryx; more than one Species—Where found—Probably known in Europe previous to the Discovery of the Passage round Cape-of-Good-Hope—Description of the Oryx—Gregarious Habits—Speed—Food—Water not necessary to its Existence—Will face the Lion—Formidable Horns—Their Use—Flesh—The Chase of this Animal . . . . 279—283

CHAPTER XXIII.

Arrival at Eikhams—Native Dogs; cruelly treated—Jonker Afrikaner—The Author visits the Red Nation; The bad Repute of these People—The Author attacked by Ophthalmia—The Embryo Locust—The 'Flying' Locust; its Devastations—The Locust Bird—Arrival at Rehoboth; The Place described . . 284—294

CHAPTER XXIV.

Return to Eikhams—Ugly Fall—Splendid Landscape—Jonker's Delinquencies—How to manage the Natives—The Ondara—It kills a Man—How his Comrade avenges him—Medical Properties of the Ondara—The Cockatrice—The Cobra-di-capella—The Puff-Adder—The Spitting Snake—The Black Snake—Few Deaths caused by Snakes—Antidotes for Snake Bites—Return to Rehoboth 295—307

CHAPTER XXV.

The Author's Tent takes Fire—He loses everything but his Papers—He is laid on a Bed of Sickness—Want of Medicine, &c.—Reflections—Whole Villages infected with Fever—Abundance of Game—Extraordinary Shot at an Ostrich—A Lion breakfasts on his Wife—Wonderful Shooting Star—Remarkable Mirage—Game and Lions Plentiful—The Ebony Tree—Arrival at Bethany, a Missionary Station—The Trouble of a large Herd of Cattle—A thirsty Man's

Cogitation—Curious Superstition—The Damara Cattle described—
People who live entirely without Water —Cross the Orange River
—Sterile Country . . . . 308—321

CHAPTER XXVI.

Great Namaqua-land—Its Boundaries and Extent—Its Rivers—Nature
of the Country—Vegetation and Climate—Geological Structure—
Minerals—'Topnaars' and 'Oerlams'—Houses—Mythology and
Religion—Tumuli—Wonderful Rock—Curious Legend of the Hare
—Coming of Age—The Witch-Doctor—Amulets—Superstitions—
A Namaqua's Notion of the Sun—Marriage—Polygamy—Children
—Barbarous Practice—Longevity—Singular Customs—Ornaments
—Tattooing—Arms—Idle Habits—Fond of Amusements—Music
and Dancing—Spirits—Mead—Domestic Animals . . 322—336

CHAPTER XXVII.

Leave the Orange River—Arrival at Komaggas—Gardening and Agriculture—The Author starts alone for the Cape—Colony Horses—
Enmity of the Boers to 'Britishers'—Dutch Salutation—The Author
must have been at Timbuctoo, whether or no—He arrives at Cape-Town—Cuts a sorry Figure—Is run away with—A Feast of
Oranges—Ghost Stories—Cattle Auction—Hans and John Allen
proceed to Australia—Preparations for Journey to the Ngami—
Departure from the Cape . . . . . 337—351

CHAPTER XXVIII.

Arrival at Walfisch Bay—Atrocities of the Namaquas—Mr. Hahn—His
Philanthropy—Author departs for Richterfeldt—Shoots a Lion—
Lions unusually numerous—Piet's Performances with Lions—The
Lion a Church-goer—Barmen—Eikhams—Kamapyu's mad Doings
and Consequences thereof—Kamapyu is wounded by other Shafts
than Cupid's—Author visits Cornelius, where he meets Amral and
a Party of Griqua Elephant Hunters—Reaches Rehoboth—Tan's
Mountain—Copper Ore—Jonathan Afrika—A Lion sups on a
Goat—A Lion besieges the Cattle . . . 352—364

CHAPTER XXIX.

Dispatch Cattle to the Cape—Terrible Thunder-Storm—Trees struck by
Lightning—The Nosop River—A Comet—The Author nearly
poisoned—Some of the Men abscond; they return to their Duty—
Babel-like Confusion of Tongues—Game abundant—Author shoots

a Giraffe—Meet Bushmen—Unsuccessful Elephant Hunt—Sufferings from Hunger—Tunobis—Game scarce—Author and Steed entrapped—Pit-falls—The Men turn sulky—Preparations for Departure from Tunobis—Vicious Pack-Oxen—Consequences of excessive Fatigue—The Jackal's Handy-Work—Tracks of Elephants—More Pit-falls—Loss of the Anglo-Saxon Lion and the Swedish Cross—Reach Ghanzé . . . . . . 365—382

CHAPTER XXX.

Ghanzé—Spotted Hyæna—The Rhinoceros—Where found—Several Species—Description of Rhinoceros—Size—Appearance—Age—Strength—Speed—Food—Water—The Young—Affection—Senses—Disposition—Gregarious Habits—Indolence—Domestication—Flesh—Horns—The Chase—Mr. Oswell's Adventures with Rhinoceroses—A Crotchet—Where to aim at the Rhinoceros—Does not bleed externally when wounded—Great numbers slain annually . 383—401

CHAPTER XXXI.

Departure from Ghanzé—Nectar in the Desert—Difficulty in finding Water—Arrive at Abeghan—Unsuccessful Chase—A 'Charm'—How to make the undrinkable drinkable—An Elephant wounded and killed—Bold and courageous Dog—Kobis—Author seized with a singular Malady—Messengers dispatched to the Chief of the Lake Ngami—A large Troop of Elephants—Author kills a huge Male—Lions and Giraffe—Author's hair-breadth Escapes: from a Black Rhinoceros; from a White Rhinoceros; from Two Troops of Elephants—he shoots a Couple of his Adversaries—Where to aim at an Elephant . . . . 402—417

CHAPTER XXXII.

Timbo's Return from the Lake; his Logic; he takes the Law in his own Hands—Calf of Author's Leg goes Astray—A Troop of Elephants—Author is charged by one of them, and narrowly escapes Death—He shoots a White Rhinoceros—He disables a Black Rhinoceros—He is charged and desperately bruised by the latter—He saves the Life of his Attendant, Kamapyu—Author again charged by the Rhinoceros, and escapes Destruction only by the opportune Death of his Antagonist—Reflections—He starts for the Ngami . 418—427

CHAPTER XXXIII.

The Author starts for Kobis—Meets Bechuanas—False Report—Wonderful Race of Men—The Baobob Tree—The Ngami—First Impressions of the Lake—Reflections—Experiences some Disappointment—Reaches the Zouga River and encamps near it—Interview with Chief Lecholètébè—Information refused—Immoderate Laughter—Presents to the Chief—His Covetousness—His Cruelty—Formidable Difficulties—Author permitted to proceed Northwards . 428—439

CHAPTER XXXIV.

The Ngami—When discovered—Its various Names—Its Size and Form—Great Changes in its Waters—Singular Phenomenon—The Teoge River—The Zouga River—The Mukura Mukovanja River—Animals—Birds—Crocodiles—Serpents—Fish . . 440—452

CHAPTER XXXV.

The Batoana—Government—Eloquence—Language—Mythology—Religion—Superstition—The Rain-maker—Polygamy—Circumcision—Burial—Disposition of the Bechuanas—Thievish Propensities—Dress—Great Snuff-takers—Smoking—Occupations—Agriculture—Commerce—Hunting and Fishing . . . 453—473

CHAPTER XXXVI.

Departure for Libèbé—The Canoe—The Lake—Reach the Teoge—Adventure with a Leché—Luxurious Vegetation—Exuberance of Animal Life—Buffaloes—The Koodoo—His Haunts—Pace—Food—Flesh—Hide—Disposition—Gregarious Habits—The Chase.
474—487

CHAPTER XXXVII.

Tsetse Fly—Confined to particular Spots—its Size—Its Destructiveness—Fatal to domestic Animals—Symptoms in the Ox when bitten by the Tsetse . . . . 488—491

CHAPTER XXXVIII.

The Crocodile—An Englishman killed by one of these Monsters—The Omoroanga Vavarra River—Hardships—Beautiful Scenery—Lecholètébè's Treachery—The Reed-ferry . . . 492—497

CHAPTER XXXIX.

The Bayeye—Their Country; Persons; Language; Disposition; lying and pilfering Habits—Polygamy practised amongst the Bayeye—Their Houses; Dress; Ornaments; Weapons; Liquors; Agriculture; Grain; Fruits; Granaries—Hunting—Fishing—Nets—Diseases—The Matsanyana—The Bavicko—Libèbé . 498—506

CHAPTER XL.

Departure from the Bayeye Werft—The Reed-Raft—The Hippopotamus Behemoth or Hippopotamus—Where found—Two Species—Description of Hippopotamus—Appearance—Size—Swims like a Duck—Food—Destructive propensities of the Animal—Disposition—Sagacity—Memory—Gregarious habits—Nocturnal habits—Domestication — Food—Flesh — Hide — Ivory — Medicinal virtues.
507—517

CHAPTER XLI.

The Bayeye Harpoon the Hippopotamus—The Harpoon described—How the Chase of the Hippopotamus is conducted by the Bayeye—How it was conducted by the ancient Egyptians—The Spear used by them—Ferocity of the Hippopotamus—Killed by Guns—Frightful Accident—The Downfall . . . . 518—528

CHAPTER XLII.

Return to the Lake—The Author starts for Namaqua-Land to procure Waggons—Night Adventure with a Lion—Death of the Beast—Sufferings of the Author . . . . . 531—535

LAKE NGAMI.

CHAPTER I.

DEPARTURE FROM SWEDEN — DAY DREAMS—FRATERNAL LOVE — A TEMPTING OFFER — PREPARATIONS FOR JOURNEY TO AFRICA — DEPARTURE FROM ENGLAND—ARRIVAL AT THE CAPE—TOWN AND INHABITANTS—TABLE MOUNTAIN—CURIOUS LEGEND—PREPARATION FOR JOURNEY INTO THE INTERIOR—DEPARTURE FOR WALFISCH BAY.

It was at the close of the year 1849, that I left Gothenbourg, in a sailing vessel, for Hull, at which place I arrived in safety, after a boisterous and somewhat dangerous passage, of about fourteen days' duration. Though a Swede by birth, I am half an Englishman by parentage; and it was with pleasure that I visited, for the second time, a country endeared to me by the ties of kindred and the remembrance of former hospitality.

My stay in England, however, was intended to be only of short duration. I carried with me thither a considerable collection of living birds and quadrupeds, together with numerous preserved specimens of natural history, the produce of many a long hunting excursion amidst the mountains, lakes, and forests of my native country. These I was anxious to dispose of in England, and then proceed in my travels, though to what quarter of the globe, I had scarcely yet determined.

From my earliest youth, my day-dreams had carried me into the wilds of Africa. Passionately fond of travelling, accustomed from my childhood to field sports, and to the study of natural history, and (as I hope I may say with truth) desirous of rendering myself useful in my generation, I earnestly longed to explore some portion of that continent where all my predilections could be fully indulged, and where much still remained in obscurity which might advantageously be brought to light. The expense, however, of such a journey, was, to me, an insurmountable obstacle. I had, therefore, long since given up all idea of making it, and had turned my thoughts northwards to Iceland, a country within my reach, and where I purposed studying the habits and characteristics of the rarer species of birds of the Northern Fauna. While at Hull, accordingly, I consulted some whaling captains on the subject of my enterprise, and had almost completed my arrangements, when a visit to London, on some private affairs, entirely changed my destination.

Before leaving Hull, I witnessed a striking example of that attachment towards each other, so frequently found to exist in the most savage animals. By the kindness of the Secretary, I had been permitted to place my collection in the gardens of the Hull Zoological Society. Amongst others, were two brown bears,—twins—somewhat more than a year old, and playful as kittens when together. Indeed, no greater punishment could be inflicted upon these beasts than to disunite them, for however short a time. Still, there was a marked contrast in their dispositions. One of them was good-tempered and gentle as a lamb, while the other frequently exhibited signs of a sulky and treacherous character. Tempted by an offer for the purchase of the former of these animals, I consented, after much hesitation, to his being separated from his brother.

It was long before I forgave myself this act. On the following day, on my proceeding, as usual, to inspect the collection, one of the keepers ran up to me, in the greatest haste, exclaiming: "Sir, I am glad you are come, for your bear has gone mad!" He then told me that, during the night, the beast had destroyed his den, and was found in the morning roaming wild about the garden. Luckily, the keeper managed to seize him just as he was escaping into the country, and, with the help of several others, succeeded in shutting him up again. The bear, however, refused his food, and raved in so fearful a manner that, unless he could be quieted, it was clear he would do some mischief.

On my arrival at his den, I found the poor brute in a most furious state, tearing the wooden floor with his claws, and gnawing the barricaded front with his teeth. I had no sooner opened the door, than he sprang furiously at me, and struck me repeated blows with his powerful paws. As, however, I had reared him from a cub, we had too often measured our strength together, for me to fear him now; and I soon made him retreat into the corner of his prison, where he remained howling in the most heart-rending manner. It was a most sickening sight to behold the poor creature with his eyes bloodshot, and protruding from the sockets—his mouth and chest white with foam, and his body crusted with dirt. I am not ashamed to confess, that at one time I felt my own eyes moistened. Neither blows nor kind words were of any effect: they only served to irritate and infuriate him; and I saw clearly that the only remedy would be, either to shoot him or to restore him to his brother's companionship. I chose the latter alternative; and the purchaser of the other bear, my kind friend Sir Henry Hunloke, on being informed of the circumstance, consented to take this one also.

Shortly after my arrival in London, Sir Hyde Parker, another valued friend of mine, and 'The King of Fishermen,' introduced me to Mr. Francis Galton, who was then just on the point of undertaking an expedition to Southern Africa; his intention being to explore the unknown regions beyond the boundary of the Cape-of-Good-Hope Colony, and to penetrate, if possible, to the recently-discovered Lake Ngami. Upon finding that I also had an intention of travelling, and that our tastes and pursuits were in many respects similar, he proposed to me to give up my talked-of trip to the far north, and accompany him to the southward; promising, at the same time, to pay the whole of my expenses. This offer awoke within me all my former ambition; and, although I could not be blind to the difficulties and dangers that must necessarily attend such an expedition, I embraced, after some hesitation, Mr. Galton's tempting and liberal proposal.

Preparations for our long and hazardous journey were now rapidly made. An immense quantity of goods of every kind was speedily amassed, intended, partly for barter, and partly for presents to barbarous chiefs. Muskets, long sword-knives, boar-spears, axes, hatchets, clasp-and-strike-light knives, Dutch tinder-boxes, daggers, burning-glasses, compasses, gilt rings (copper or brass), alarums, beads of every size and colour, wolf-traps, rat-traps, old military dresses, cast-off ambassador's uniforms—these, and a host of other articles too various to enumerate, formed our stock-in-trade.

To the above, we added, mostly for our own use, guns and rifles, a vast quantity of ammunition of all kinds, instruments for taking observations, arsenical and other preparations for preserving objects of natural history, writing materials, sketch-books, paints, pencils, canteens, knives, forks, dishes, &c.

It was also deemed advisable that we should take with us boats, for the navigation of Lake Ngami—those used by the natives being unsafe. We, therefore, supplied ourselves with three, each adapted for a specific purpose.

Having thus provided, as far as possible, for all emergences, we transferred ourselves and baggage on board the splendid, but unfortunate ship, the *Dalhousie*.[1] Here we found, to our dismay, in addition to a number of other passengers, several hundred emigrants, destined to the Cape-of-Good-Hope. Instead, however, of these people proving, as we had at first anticipated, a great annoyance, we found that they contributed considerably towards enlivening and diverting us during a long and tedious passage.

I am not, however, about to inflict upon my readers the particulars of our voyage to the Cape. Suffice it to say that, after a few days' delay at Plymouth, we put to sea in half a gale of wind, on the 7th of April, 1850, and experienced, subsequently, the usual vicissitudes of rough and smooth weather. At one time, we were carried by a gentle breeze past the lovely island of Madeira, and so near as to distinguish its pleasant vineyards, and neat, pretty cottages, scattered over the mountain side to the very summit; at another, we were driven so far westward, by gales and adverse winds, as to sight the coast of South America; until, at length, on the night of the 23rd of June, the much wished-for land was descried, and on the following noon we anchored safely in Table Bay,

---

[1] It will doubtless be remembered, that in a gale of wind off the British coast, the *Dalhousie* was thrown on her beam-ends, and foundered in half an hour afterwards, when, with a single exception, every soul on board perished. Out of the several vessels in which I have at different times been a passenger, the *Dalhousie* is the third that has perished shortly after my leaving her!

after a passage of eighty-six days—a time, at least a third longer than the average. How truly welcome to my eyes, as we sailed into the bay, was the fine panoramic view of Cape-Town, with the picturesque Table Mountain rising immediately in the background!

Upon landing, we took up our quarters at Welch's hotel. Our design was to stay a short time at Cape-Town, in order to obtain information respecting our intended route, and to procure whatever was still wanting for our journey. We then proposed to proceed by land northwards, taking the course of the Trans-Vaal river. It will presently be seen, however, that our desires in this respect were entirely frustrated.

To give to an English reader a full description of Cape-Town, would, indeed, be a superfluous task. I fear, also, that, in some respects, I should be found to differ from other travellers.

Cape-Town is generally described as a clean and neat place. With all due deference, I must dissent widely from this opinion. All the streets, for instance, are unpaved, and are, moreover, half-filled with rubbish, swept from the shops and warehouses, until some friendly shower carries it away. Undoubtedly, the town is regularly built, with broad streets, laid out at right angles to each other; but, as almost every person of property resides in the country, few handsome dwelling-houses are to be met with—and by far the greater number are in the Dutch style. Here, however, as everywhere else where the English have obtained firm footing, improvements are very apparent; and, doubtless, now that the colony has obtained its own Legislature, such improvements will become still more visible.

No one can be at Cape-Town for a single day, without being struck by the infinite variety of the human race encountered in the streets: Indians, Chinese, Malays, Caffers, Bechuanas, Hottentots, Creoles, 'Afrikanders,' half-casts of many kinds, negroes of every variety from the east and west coasts of Africa, and Europeans of all countries, form the motley population of the place.

MALAY.

Of all these, with the exception of the Europeans, the Malays are by far the most conspicuous and important. They comprise, indeed, no inconsiderable portion of the inhabitants, and are, moreover, distinguished for their industry and sobriety. Many of them are exceedingly well off, and, not unfrequently, keep their carriages and horses. They profess the Mahomedan religion, and have their own clergy and places of worship. Two-thirds of the week they work hard, and devote the remainder to pleasure, spending much of their time and money on their dress—more especially the women. These latter seldom have any covering for the head; but the men tie round it a red handkerchief, over which they wear an enormous umbrella-shaped straw hat, admirably adapted to ward off the sun's rays, but useless and inconvenient in windy weather.

The Malays are, usually, very honest; but, strange to relate, on a certain day of the year, they exert their ingenuity in purloining their neighbours' poultry, and, Spartan-like, do not consider this dishonourable, provided they are not detected in the fact :—

> 'To be *taken*, to be *seen*,
> *These* have crimes accounted been.'

To be at Cape-Town, without ascending the far-famed Table Mountain, was, of course, not to be thought of. The undertaking, however, is not altogether without danger. On the side of the town, access to the summit is only practicable on foot, and that by a narrow and slippery path; but, on the opposite side, the Table may be gained on horseback, though with some difficulty. The whole mountain side, moreover, is intersected by deep and numerous ravines, which are rendered more dangerous by the dense fogs that, at certain seasons of the year, arise suddenly from the sea.

One fine afternoon, I had unconsciously approached the foot of the mountain, and the top looked so near and inviting, that, though the sun was fast sinking, I determined to make the ascent. At the very outset, I lost the road; but, having been all my life a mountain-climber, I pushed boldly forward. The task, however, proved more difficult than I expected, and the sun's broad disc had already touched the horizon when I reached the summit. Nevertheless, the magnificent panorama that now lay spread before me, amply rewarded me for my trouble. It was, however, only for a very short time that I could enjoy the beautiful scene; darkness was rapidly encroaching over the valley below; and, as in these regions there is but one step from light to darkness, I was compelled to commence the descent, without a moment's delay. I confess that this was not done without some apprehension; for, what with the quick-coming night, and the terrible ravines that lay yawning beneath my feet, the task was anything but agreeable. I found it necessary, for safety, to take off my boots, which I fastened to my waist; and, at length, after much exertion, with hands torn, and trousers almost in rags, I arrived late in the evening at our hotel, where they had begun to entertain some doubt of my safety. As a proof that my fears were not altogether groundless, a short time before this, a young man, who was wandering about the mountain in broad daylight, missed his footing, was precipitated down its sides, and brought in, the next day, a mutilated corpse.

When Europeans first arrived in the Cape Colony, it would appear that almost all the larger quadrupeds indigenous to Southern Africa existed in the neighbourhood of Table Mountain. A curious anecdote is preserved in the archives of Cape-Town, relating to the death of a rhinoceros, which, for its quaintness and originality, is perhaps worthy of record.

Once upon a time—so runs the legend—some labourers employed in a field, discovered a huge rhinoceros, immovably fixed in the quick-sands of the salt river, which is within a mile of the town. The alarm being given, a number of country people, armed with such weapons as were at hand, rushed to the spot with an intention of despatching the monster. Its appearance, however, was so formidable, that they deemed it advisable to open their battery at a most respectful distance. But seeing that all the animal's efforts to extricate itself were fruitless, the men gradually grew more courageous; and approached much nearer. Still, whether from the inefficiency of their weapons, or want of skill, they were unable to make any impression on the tough, and almost impenetrable, hide of the beast. At length, they began to despair, and it was a question if they should not beat a retreat; when an individual, more sagacious than the rest, stepped forward, and suggested that a hole should be cut in the animal's hide, by which means easy access might be had to its vitals; and they could then destroy it at their leisure! The happy device was loudly applauded; and though, I believe, the tale ends here, it may be fairly concluded that, after such an excellent recommendation, success could not but crown their endeavours.

We had now been at Cape-Town somewhat less than a week; and had already added considerably to the stock of articles of exchange, provisions, and other necessaries for our journey. To convey this immense quantity of luggage, we provided ourselves with two gigantic waggons, each represented to hold three or four thousand pounds weight, together with a sort of cart [1] for ourselves.

Mr. Galton bought, also, nine excellent mules, which could be used either for draught or packing; two riding horses; and, in addition to these, he secured about half a dozen dogs, which, if the truth be told, were of a somewhat mongrel description.

Mr. Galton also engaged the needful people to accompany us on our travels, such as waggon-drivers, herdsmen, cooks, &c., in all amounting to seven individuals.

Our preparations being now complete, we were about to set out on our journey, when, to our dismay, we received information which entirely overthrew our plans. It was reported to us that the Boers on the Trans-Vaal river (the very line of country we purposed taking) had lately turned back

---

[1] The term 'cart' in this sense, implies a large, roomy, and *covered* vehicle, capable of holding four or six individuals, and from five hundred to one thousand pounds of baggage. It is usually drawn by six or eight mules or horses.

several traders and travellers, who were on their way northwards, and had, moreover, threatened to kill any person who should attempt to pass through their territories with the intention of penetrating to Lake Ngami. This intelligence, being equally unexpected and unwelcome, we were at a loss on what to decide. On asking the opinion of the Governor of the Cape, Sir Harry Smith, to whose kindness and hospitality we were, on several occasions, indebted, he strongly dissuaded us from attempting the route in question. " The Boers," he said, " are determined men; and, although I have no fear for the safety of your lives, they will assuredly rob you of all your goods and cattle, and thus prevent your proceeding farther." The counsel given us by his Excellency settled the point. We were, however, determined not to be idle; but it was by no means easy to decide on what course to pursue. As the whole of the interior, by which a passage could be obtained to the Lake, was either occupied by the Boers, or served as their hunting-ground, we were compelled to choose between the eastern and western coasts. The former of these, however, was well known to be infected by fevers fatal to Europeans; while the latter presented, for a considerable distance northwards, nothing but a sandy shore, destitute of fresh water and vegetation. The country intervening between the western coast and the Lake, moreover, was represented as very unhealthy.

Whilst in this state of uncertainty, we made the acquaintance of a Mr. M———, who lately had an establishment at Walfisch Bay, on the west coast of Africa, about seven hundred geographical miles north of the Cape. He strongly recommended us to select this place as the starting point for our journey into the interior, which opinion was confirmed by some missionaries whom we met in Cape-Town, and who had a settlement in the neighbourhood of the Bay in question.

This route was ultimately adopted by us; but, as vessels only frequented Walfisch Bay once or twice in the course of every two years, Mr. Galton at once chartered a small schooner, named the *Foam*, the sixth part of the expense of which was defrayed by the missionaries referred to, who were anxious, not only to forward some supplies, but to obtain a passage for a young member of their society, the Rev. Mr. Schöneberg, who was about proceeding on a mission of peace and good-will into Damara-land.

As our plans were now so entirely changed, and as we were about to travel through an almost unknown region, we thought it expedient to disencumber ourselves of whatever could, in any way, be spared. We left, accordingly, at the Cape, amongst other things, two of our boats; taking with us, however, the other, a mackintosh punt, as being light and portable, hoping some day or other to see her floating on the waters of the Ngami.

Our arrangements being finished, and the goods, &c., shipped, we unfurled our sails on the 7th of August, and bade farewell to Cape-Town, where, during our short stay, we had experienced much kindness and hospitality.

CHAPTER II.

ARRIVAL AT WALFISCH BAY—SCENERY—HARBOUR DESCRIBED—WANT OF WATER — CAPABILITIES FOR TRADE — FISH — WILD FOWL — MIRAGE—SAND FOUNTAIN—THE BUSH-TICK—THE NARAS—QUADRUPEDS SCARCE—MEETING THE HOTTENTOTS—THEIR FILTHY HABITS—THE ALARUM—THE TURN OUT—DEATH OF A LION—ARRIVAL AT SCHEPPMANSDORF—THE PLACE DESCRIBED—MR. BAM—MISSIONARY LIFE—INGRATITUDE OF NATIVES—MISSIONARY WAGGONS.

IN the afternoon of the 20th of August, we found ourselves safely anchored at the entrance of Walfisch Bay. From the prevalence of southerly winds, this voyage seldom occu-

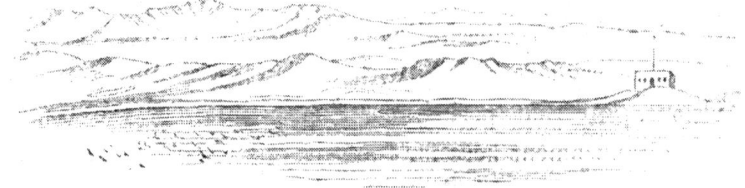

VIEW OF WALFISCH BAY.

pies more than a week; but, on the present occasion, we were double that time performing it.

The first appearance of the coast, as seen from Walfisch

Bay, is little calculated to inspire confidence in the traveller about to penetrate into the interior. A desert of sand, bounded only by the horizon, meets the eye in every quarter, assuming, in one direction, the shape of dreary flats—in another, of shifting hillocks; whilst, in some parts, it rises almost to the height of mountains.

Walfisch Bay has been long known to Europeans, and was once hastily surveyed by Commodore Owen, of the Royal Navy. It is a very spacious, commodious, and comparatively safe harbour, being on three sides protected by a sandy shore. The only winds to which it is exposed, are N. and N.W.; but these, fortunately, are not of frequent occurrence. Its situation is about N. and S. The anchorage is good. Large ships take shelter under the lee of a sandy peninsula, the extremity of which is known to navigators by the name of 'Pelican Point.' Smaller craft, however, ride safely within less than half a mile of the shore.

The great disadvantage of Walfisch Bay is that no fresh water can be found near the beach; but, at a distance of three miles inland, abundance may be obtained, as also good pasturage for cattle. I mention this circumstance, as being essential to the establishment of any cattle-trade in future.

During the time the guano trade flourished on the west coast of Africa, Walfisch Bay was largely resorted to by vessels of every size, chiefly with a view of obtaining fresh provisions. At that period, certain parties from the Cape had an establishment here for the salting and curing of beef. They, moreover, furnished the guano-traders, as, also, Cape Town, with cattle; and had, in addition, a contract with the British Government for supplying St. Helena with live stock. The latter speculation proved exceedingly lucrative for a time, and a profit of many hundred per cent. was said to be realized.

From some mismanagement, however, the contract for St. Helena was thrown up by the Government, and the parties in question were fined a large sum of money for its non-fulfilment. Shortly afterwards, the establishment was broken up, and, for several years, the house and store remained unoccupied. But they are now again tenanted by people belonging to merchants from Cape-Town.

Walfisch Bay affords an easy and speedy communication with the interior. By the late explorations of Mr. Galton and myself, in that quarter, we have become acquainted with many countries previously unknown, or only partially explored, to which British commerce might easily be extended.

Walfisch Bay and the neighbourhood abounds with fish of various kinds: at certain seasons, indeed, it is much frequented by a number of the smaller species of whale, known by the name of 'humpbacks,' which come here to breed. Several cargoes of oil, the produce of this fish, have been already exported.

At the inner part of the harbour, a piece of shallow water extends nearly a mile into the interior, and is separated from the sea, on the west side, by Pelican Point. This lagoon teems with various kinds of fish; and, at low water, many, that have lingered behind, are left sprawling helplessly in the mud. At such times, the natives are frequently seen approaching; and, with a gemsbok's horn, affixed to a slender stick, they transfix their finny prey at leisure. Even hyænas and jackals seize such opportunities to satisfy their hunger.

Walfisch Bay is frequented by immense numbers of water-fowl, such as geese, ducks, different species of cormorants, pelicans, flamingoes, and countless flocks of sand-pipers. But, as the surrounding country is everywhere open, they are difficult of approach. Nevertheless, with a little tact and experience, tolerably good sport may be obtained, and capital rifle-practice at all times. Hardly any of the water-fowl breed here.

Every morning, at daybreak, myriads of flamingoes, pelicans, cormorants, &c., are seen moving from their roosting-places, in and about the bay, and flying in a northerly direction. About noon, they begin to return to the southern portion of the bay, and continue arriving there, in an almost continuous stream, until nightfall.

The way in which the 'duikers' (cormorants and shags) obtain their food is not uninteresting. Instead of hovering over their prey, as the gull, or waiting quietly for it in some secluded spot, like the king-fisher, they make their attacks in a noisy and exciting manner. Mr. Lloyd, in his 'Scandinavian Adventures,' has given a very interesting account of the manner in which the Arctic duck (*harelda glacialis*. Steph.) procures its food; and, as it applies to the birds above named, I cannot do better than quote him on the subject.

"The hareld is a most restless bird," says he, "and perpetually in motion. It rarely happens that one sees it in a state of repose during the day time. The flock—for there are almost always several in company—swim pretty fast against the wind; and the individuals comprising it keep up a sort of race with each other. Some of the number are always diving; and, as these remain long under water, and their comrades are going rapidly a-head in the meanwhile, they are, of course, a good way behind the rest on their re-appearance at the surface. Immediately on coming up, therefore, they take wing, and, flying over the backs of their comrades, resume their position in the ranks, or rather fly somewhat beyond their fellows, with the object, as it would seem, of being the foremost of the party. This fre-

quently continues across the bay, or inlet, until the flock is 'brought up' by the opposing shore, when they generally all take wing and move off elsewhere. * * * *
'Fair play is a jewel,' says the old saw, and so, perhaps, thinks the hareld; for it would really appear as if it adopted the somewhat curious manœuvre just mentioned, to prevent its companions from going over the ground previously."

The day after our arrival, we moved our small craft within half a mile of the shore; and, as soon as she was safely anchored, we proceeded to reconnoitre the neighbourhood. The first thing which attracted our attention, was a mirage of the most striking character and intensity of effect. Objects, distant only a few hundred feet, became perfectly metamorphosed. Thus, for instance, a small bird would look as big as a rock, or the trunk of a tree; pelicans assumed the appearance of ships under canvass; the numerous skeletons and bones of stranded whales, were exaggerated into clusters of lofty houses; and dreary and sterile plains, presented the aspect of charming lakes. In short, every object had a bewildering and supernatural appearance, and the whole atmosphere was misty, tremulous, and wavy. This phenomenon is, at all times, very remarkable; but during the hot season of the year, it is more surprising and deceptive. At an after period, Mr. Galton tried to map the bay, but this mirage frustrated all his endeavours. An object that he had, perhaps, chosen for a mark, became totally indistinguishable when he moved to the next station.

On the beach we found a small house, constructed of planks, in tolerable preservation, which, at high water, was completely surrounded by the sea. This had originally been erected by a Captain Greybourn, for trading purposes, but was now in the possession of the Rhenish Missionary Society.

It was kindly thrown open to our use, and proved of the greatest comfort to us; for, at this season, the nights were bitterly cold, and the dew so heavy, as completely to saturate every article of clothing that was exposed.

We had not been many minutes on shore, when some half-naked, half-starved, cut-throat-looking savages, made their appearance, armed with muskets and assegais. Nothing could exceed the squalid, wretched, and ludicrous aspect of these people, which was increased by a foolish endeavour to assume a martial bearing, no doubt with a view of making an impression on us. Without noticing either their weapons or swaggering air, and in order to disarm suspicion, we walked straight up to them, and shook hands with apparent cordiality. Our missionary friend, Mr. Schöneberg, then explained to them, by signs and gestures, that he wished to have a letter conveyed to Mr. Bam, his colleague, residing at Scheppmansdorf, some twenty miles off, in an easterly direction. It soon became apparent that they were accustomed to similar errands; for, on receiving a small gratuity of tobacco on the spot, with a promise of further payment on their return, they set out immediately, and executed their task with so much dispatch, that, before the dawn of next morning, Mr. Bam had arrived.

In the meantime, we made an excursion to a place called Sand Fountain, about three miles inland. On our way there, we crossed a broad flat, which, in spring tides, is entirely flooded. In spite of this submersion, the tracks of waggons, animals, &c., of several years' standing, were as clear and distinct as if imprinted but yesterday! At Sand Fountain we found another wooden house, but uninhabited, belonging to Mr. D——, a partner of Mr. M——. The natives had taken advantage of the absence of the owner, to injure and destroy the few pieces of furniture left behind; and leaves of books, and panes of window glass, were wantonly strewn about the ground. We next visited the so-called 'fountain,' which was hard by; but, instead of a copious spring—as the name of the place gave us reason to expect—we found, to our dismay, nothing but a small hole, some five or six inches in diameter, and half as many deep; the water, moreover, was of so execrable a quality as to make it totally undrinkable. However, on cleaning away the sand, it flowed pretty freely, and we flattered ourselves that, by a little care and trouble, we might render it fit for use, if not exactly palatable.

After having thus far explored the country, we returned to the vessel. On the following morning, at daybreak, we set about landing our effects, mules, horses, &c., which was not done without some difficulty. As soon as the goods belonging to the missionary should have been removed to Scheppmansdorf, Mr. Bam most considerately promised to assist us with his oxen. In the interval—as there was no fresh water on the beach—we deemed it advisable to remove our luggage, by means of the mules, to Sand Fountain, where we should, at least, be able to obtain water—though bad of its kind—and be better off in other respects.

On the fourth day, the schooner which had conveyed us to Walfisch Bay, set sail for the Cape, leaving us entirely to our own resources on a desert coast; and—excepting the several missionary stations scattered over the country—at several months' tedious journey by land to the nearest point of civilization.

On returning to Sand Fountain, our first care was to sink an old, perforated tar-barrel, in a place dug for the purpose; but instead of improving the quality of the water, it only made matters worse! Fortunately, we had taken the precaution to bring with us from the Cape, a 'copper distiller;' but the water, even thus purified, could only be used for cooking, or making very strong coffee and tea. Strange enough, when the owner of the house resided here, water was abundant and excellent; but the spot where it was obtained, was now hidden from view by an immense sand-hill, which defied digging.

At Sand Fountain we had the full benefit of the sea breeze, which made the temperature very agreeable, the thermometer never exceeding seventy-five degrees in the shade, at noon. The sand, however, was a cruel annoyance, entering into every particle of food, and penetrating our clothes to the very skin. But we were subjected to a still more formidable inconvenience; for, besides myriads of fleas, our encampment swarmed with a species of bush-tick, whose bite was so severe and irritating, as almost to drive us mad. To escape, if possible, the horrible persecutions of these blood-thirsty creatures, I took refuge one night in the cart, and was congratulating myself on having, at last, secured a place free from their attacks. But I was mistaken. I had not been long asleep, before I was awakened by a disagreeable irritation over my whole body, which, shortly became intolerable; and, notwithstanding the night air was very sharp, and the dew heavy, I cast off all my clothes, and rolled on the icy-cold sand, till the blood flowed freely from every pore. Strange as it may appear, I found this expedient serviceable.

On another occasion, a bush-tick, but of a still more poisonous species, attached itself to one of my feet; and, though a stinging sensation was produced, I never thought of examining the part, till one day, when enjoying the unusual luxury of a cold bath, I accidentally discovered the intruder deeply buried in the flesh, and it was only with very great pain that I succeeded in extracting it, or rather its body, for the head remained in the wound. The poisonous effect of its bite was so acrimonious as to cause partial lameness for three following months!

The bush-tick does not confine its attacks to men only, for it attaches itself with even greater pertinacity to the inferior animals. Many a poor dog have I seen killed by its relentless persecutions; and even the sturdy ox has been known to succumb under the poisonous influence of these insects.[1]

Sand Fountain, notwithstanding its disagreeable guests, had its advantages. Almost every little sand-hillock thereabout was covered with a 'creeper,' which produced a kind of prickly gourd (called, by the natives, naras), of the most delicious flavour. It is about the size of an ordinary turnip (a swede), and, when ripe, has a greenish exterior, with a tinge of lemon. The interior, again, which is of a deep orange colour, presents a most cooling, refreshing, and inviting appearance. A stranger, however, must be particularly cautious not to eat of it too freely; as, otherwise, it produces a peculiar sickness, and great soreness of the gum and lips. For three or four months in the year it constitutes the chief food of the natives.

The naras contains a great number of seeds, not unlike a peeled almond in appearance and taste, and being easily separated from the fleshy parts, they are carefully collected, exposed to the sun, dried, and then stored away in little skin bags. When the fruit fails, the natives have recourse to the seeds, which are equally nutritious, and perhaps even more wholesome. The naras may also be preserved by being

---

[1] When a bush-tick is found attached to any part of the body of a man, the simplest, and most effectual, way of getting rid of it, without any disagreeable result, is to anoint the place, to which the insect has fixed itself, with pipe oil. In cases of brute animals, I have found tar to answer the purpose exceedingly well.

boiled. When of a certain consistency, it is spread out into thin cakes, in which state it presents the appearance of brown moist sugar, and may be kept for almost any length of time. These cakes are, however, rather rich and luscious.

But it is not man alone that derives benefit from this remarkable plant, for every animal, from the field-mouse to the ox, and even the feline and canine race, devour it with great avidity. Birds[1] are, also, very partial to it, more especially ostriches, who, during the naras season, are found in great abundance in these parts.

It is in such instances, more especially, that the mind becomes powerfully impressed with the wise provisions of nature, and the great goodness of the Almighty, who, even from the desert, raises good and wholesome sustenance for man and all his creatures.

'——————By his bounteous hand,
God covers earth with food for man and beast,
Insect and bird; yea, the poor creeping worm
Partakes the Creator's bounty.'

In this barren and poverty-stricken country, food is so scarce, that without the naras the land would be all but uninhabitable. The naras serves, moreover, a double purpose; for, besides its usefulness as food, it fixes with wonderful tenacity, by means of its extensive ramifications, the constantly shifting sands; it is, indeed, to those parts what the sand-reed *(ammophila arundinacia)* is to the sandy shores and downs of England.

The naras only grows in the bed of the Kuisip river, in the neighbourhood of the sea. A few plants are to be met with at the mouth of the Orange river, as also, according to

---

[1] I have seen the white Egyptian vulture feed upon it! This is, I believe, with one more exception, the only instance where this class of birds are known to partake of vegetable food.

Captain Messum, in a few localities between the Swakop and the Nourse river.

The general aspect of the country about Sand Fountain is very dreary and desolate. The soil is entirely composed of sand. The vegetation, moreover, is stunted in the extreme, consisting chiefly of the above-mentioned creeper, a species of tamarisk tree (or rather bush), and a few dew-plants. Consequently, the animal world, as might be expected, did not present any great variety. Nevertheless, being an enthusiastic sportsman, and devoted to the study of natural history, I made frequent short excursions into the neighbourhood, on which occasions my spoils consisted for the most part of some exquisitely beautiful lizards, a few long-legged beetles, and some pretty species of field-mice. Once in a time, moreover, I viewed a solitary gazelle in the distance.

A few miles from our encampment, resided a small kraal of Hottentots, under the chief, Frederick, who occasionally brought us some milk and a few goats, as a supply for the larder, in exchange for which they received old soldiers' coats (worth sixpence a-piece), handkerchiefs, hats, tobacco, and a variety of other trifling articles. But they infinitely preferred to beg, and were not the least ashamed to ask for even the shirt on one's back.

These men were excessively dirty in their habits. One fine morning, I observed an individual attentively examining his caross, spread out before him in a sunny and sheltered spot. On approaching him, in order to ascertain the cause of his deep meditation, I found, to my astonishment and disgust, that he was feasting on certain loathsome insects, that cannot with propriety be named to ears polite. This was only one instance out of a hundred that might be named of their filthy customs.

As Frederick, the chieftain, and a few of his half-starved and Chinese-featured followers, were one day intently watching the process of our packing and unpacking divers trunks, I placed alongside of him, as if by accident, a small box-alarum, and then resumed my employment. On the first shrill sound of the instrument, our friend leapt from his seat like one suddenly demented; and during the whole time the jarring notes continued, he remained standing at a respectful distance, trembling violently from head to foot.

As no draught cattle could be obtained in the neighbourhood, nor, indeed, within a less distance than from one hundred and fifty to two hundred miles, Mr. Galton started on an excursion into the interior, with a view of obtaining a supply.

His 'turn-out' was most original, and would have formed an excellent subject for a caricature. From both ends of the cart—with which he made the journey—protruded a number of common muskets, and other articles, intended for barter. The mules harnessed to the vehicle kept up a most discordant concert, viciously kicking out to the right and left. The coachman, bathed in perspiration, kept applying his immense Cape-whip to their flanks with considerable unction; whilst a man, sitting alongside of him on the front seat, abused the stubborn animals with a burst of all the eloquent epithets contained in the Dutch-Hottentot vocabulary. Two sulky goats, tied to the back of the cart, were on the point of strangling themselves in their endeavours to escape. To complete the picture, Galton himself, accompanied by half a dozen dogs of nondescript race, toiled on cheerfully through the deep sand by the side of the vehicle, smoking a common clay pipe.

On my friend's arrival at Scheppmansdorf, however, he found it necessary to adjourn his trip into the interior for a few days.

In the meantime, as Mr. Bam's oxen had arrived at Sand Fountain, I busied myself with conveying the baggage to Scheppmansdorf; but, on account of its great weight and bulk, and the badness of the road, this occupation lasted several days. In the last trip, we had so overloaded the waggons, that, after about three miles, the oxen came to a dead stand-still. The two teams were now yoked to one of the vehicles, and it proceeded on its way without further interruption, whilst I remained alone in charge of the other. It was agreed that some of the men should return with the cattle on the following night; but, on arriving at Scheppmansdorf, they and the oxen were so exhausted, that it was found necessary to give both the one and the other two days' rest. For this delay I was not at all prepared. My small supply of water had been exhausted on the second day, and I began, for the first time in my life, to experience the misery of thirst. I was, however, fortunately relieved from my embarrassing situation by the arrival of a Hottentot, who, for a trifling consideration, brought me an ample supply of water.

At length, all the baggage was safely deposited at Scheppmansdorf, where I rejoined Mr. Galton.

He had not, I found, been many days at that place, when a magnificent lion suddenly appeared one night in the midst of the village. A small dog, that had incautiously approached the beast, paid the penalty of its life for its daring. The next day a grand chase was got up, but the lion, being on his guard, managed to elude his pursuers. The second day, however, he was killed by Messrs. Galton and Bam; and, on cutting him up, the poor dog was found, still undigested, in his stomach, bitten into five pieces.

The natives highly rejoiced at the successful termination of the hunt; for this lion had proved himself to be one of the most daring and destructive ever known, having, in a short time, killed upwards of fifty oxen, cows, and horses. Though he had previously been chased, he had always escaped unscathed, and every successive attack made upon him only served to increase his ferocity.

I regretted much being prevented from taking part in so interesting and exciting an event; but, on the other hand, I felt pleased that my friend had thus early had an opportunity of exercising his skill on one of the most noble and dreaded of the animal creation. My turn was yet to come.

Scheppmansdorf — Roëbank — Abbanhous — as it is indifferently called — was first occupied as a missionary station, in the year 1846, by the Rev. Mr. Scheppman, from whom it takes its name. It is situated on the left bank of the river Kuisip; and immediately behind rise enormous masses and ridges of sand. The Kuisip is a periodical stream, and is dependant on the rains in the interior; but, from the great uncertainty of this supply, and the absorbing nature of the soil, it is seldom that it reaches Walfisch Bay, where it has its estuary. On our arrival, the Kuisip had not flowed for years; but when it does send down its mighty torrent, it fertilizes and changes the aspect of the country to a wonderful degree. Rain falls seldom or never at this place, but thirsty nature is relieved by heavy dews. Fresh water and fuel, however, two of the great necessaries of life, are found in abundance.

Sandy and barren as the soil appears to the eye, portions of it, nevertheless, are capable of great fertility. From time to time, Mr. Bam has cultivated small spots of garden ground in the bed of the river; but although many things thrive exceedingly well, the trouble, risk, and labour were too great to make it worth his while to persevere. A sudden and unexpected flood, the effect of heavy rains in the interior, often lays waste in a few minutes what has taken months to raise.

The principal trees thereabouts are the ana and the giraffe-thorn *(acacia giraffæ)*; and the chief herbage, a species of sand-reed, which is much relished by the cattle when once accustomed to it; but more especially by horses, mules, and donkeys, which thrive and fatten wonderfully on this diet.

During our stay at Scheppmansdorf, we were the constant guests of Mr. and Mrs. Bam, but we felt almost sorry to trespass on a hospitality that we knew they could ill afford; for it was only once in every two years that they received their supplies from the Cape, and then only in sufficient quantities for their own families. The genuine sincerity, however, with which it was offered, over-ruled all scruples.

Mr. Bam had long been a dweller in various parts of Great Namaqua-land.[1] His present residence, however, in this its western portion, was of comparatively recent date. Although he had used every effort to civilize and christianize his small community, all his endeavours had hitherto proved nearly abortive; but as we become acquainted with the character of the Namaquas, who are partially-civilized Hottentots, the wonder ceases; and we discover that they possess every vice of savages, and none of their noble qualities. So long as they are fed and clothed, they are willing enough to congregate round the missionary, and to listen to his exhortation. The moment, however, the food and clothing are discontinued, their feigned attachment to his person and to his doctrines, is at an end, and they do not scruple to treat their benefactor with ingratitude, and load him with abuse.

The missionary is more or less dependent on his own resources. Such assistance as he obtains from the natives is so trivial, and procured with so much trouble, that it is often

---

[1] The southern limit of Great Namaqua-land is, at the present moment, the Orange River. To the north, it is bounded by Damara-land, or by about the twenty-second degree of south latitude.

gladly dispensed with. The good man is his own architect, smith, wheel-wright, tinker, gardener, &c., whilst his faithful spouse officiates as nurse, cook, washerwoman, and so forth. Occasionally, to get the drudgery off their hands, they adopt some poor boy and girl, who, after they have been taught with infinite labour to make themselves useful, and have experienced nothing but kindness, will often leave their protectors abruptly, or, what is nearly as bad, become lazy and indolent.

A Namaqua, it would appear, is not able to appreciate kindness, and no word in his language, as far as I can remember, is expressive of gratitude! The same is the case, as I shall hereafter have occasion to mention, with their northern neighbours, the Damaras, and though a sad, it is, nevertheless, a true picture.

When waggons were first introduced into Great Namaqualand, they caused many conjectures, and much astonishment among the natives, who conceived them to be some gigantic animal possessed of vitality. A conveyance of this kind, belonging to the Rev. Mr. Schmelen, once broke down, and was left sticking in the sand. One day a Bushman came to the owner, and said that he had seen his 'pack-ox' standing in the desert for a long time, with a broken leg; and, as he did not observe it had any grass, he was afraid that it would soon die of hunger unless taken away!

CHAPTER III.

PREPARATIONS FOR JOURNEY — BREAKING-IN OXEN — DEPARTURE FROM SCHEPPMANSDORF—AN INFURIATED OX —THE NAARIP PLAIN—THE SCARLET FLOWER — THE USAB GORGE — THE SWAKOP RIVER — TRACKS OF RHINOCEROS SEEN — ANECDOTE OF THAT ANIMAL — A SUNRISE IN THE TROPICS—SUFFERINGS FROM HEAT AND THIRST— ARRIVAL AT DAVIEP: GREAT RESORT OF LIONS—A HORSE AND MULE KILLED BY THEM — THE AUTHOR GOES IN PURSUIT — A TROOP OF LIONS—UNSUCCESSFUL CHASE—MULES' FLESH PALATABLE.

MR. GALTON had now so far altered his plans, that instead of proceeding up the country, with only one-half of his party, for the purchase of cattle, it was arranged that we should make the journey together. The waggons, and the bulk of our effects, were to be left at Scheppmansdorf, and we were only to take with us some few articles of exchange, a small quantity of provisions, and a moderate supply of ammunition.

Finding, however, that the cart could not conveniently hold all our baggage, though now reduced to the smallest quantity possible, it was resolved to pack a portion on oxen. These animals, on account of their great hardihood, are invaluable in South Africa; the more so, as they can be equally well used for draught, the 'pack,' or the 'saddle.' But as we had no cattle trained for either of these purposes, and only one or two were procurable at the missionary station, we were necessitated, prior to our departure thence, to break in a few. No easy matter, by the by; for oxen are of a wild and stubborn disposition, and it requires months to make them tractable. We were, however, totally at a loss how to set to work.

But fortunately, at this time, Mr. Galton had engaged a Mr. Stewardson, tailor by profession, but now 'jack of all trades,' to accompany us up the country in the capacity of cicerone, &c.; and as this man, from long residence amongst the Hottentots, was thoroughly conversant with the mysteries of ox-breaking, to him, therefore, we deputed the difficult task.

At the end of a 'riem,' or long leather thong, a pretty large noose is made, which is loosely attached to, or rather suspended from, the end of a slight stick some five or six feet in length. With this stick in his hand, a man, under shelter of the herd, stealthily approaches the ox selected to be operated on. When sufficiently near, he places the noose (though at some little distance from the ground) just in advance of the hind feet of the animal; and, when the latter steps into it, he draws it tight. The instant the ox finds himself in the toils, he makes a tremendous rush forward; but, as several people hold the outer end of the 'riem,' he—in sailor language—is quickly 'brought up.' The force of the check is, indeed, such as often to capsize one or more of the men. He now renews his efforts; he kicks, foams, bellows; and his companions, at first startled, return and join in chorus; the men shout, the dogs bark furiously, and the affair becomes at once dangerous and highly exciting. The captured animal not unfrequently grows frantic with rage and fear, and turns upon his assailant, when the only chance of escape is to let go the hold of the 'riem.' Usually he soon exhausts himself by his own exertions, when one or two men instantly seize him by the tail—another thong having also been passed round his horns; and, by bringing the two to bear in exactly opposite directions, or, in other words, by using the two as levers at a right-angle with his body, he is easily brought to the ground. This being once effected, the tail is passed between his legs and held forcibly down over his ribs, and the head is twisted on one side, with the horns fixed in the ground. A short, strong stick, of peculiar shape, is then forced through the cartilage of the nose; and to either end of this stick is attached (in bridle fashion) a thin, tough leathern thong. From the extreme tenderness of the nose, he is now more easily managed; but, if he is still found very vicious, he is either packed in his prostrate position, or fastened with his head to a tree, whilst two or three persons keep the 'riem' tight about his legs, so as to prevent him from turning round, or injuring any person with his feet. For the 'packing,' however, a more common and convenient plan is to secure him between two tame oxen, with a person placed outside each of these animals.

For the first day or two, only a single skin, or empty bag, is put on his back, which is firmly secured with a thong, eighty to ninety feet in length (those employed by the Namaquas, for the same purpose, are about twice as long); but bulk, as well as weight, is daily added; and though he kicks and plunges violently — and sometimes with such effect as to throw off his pack—the ox soon becomes more tractable. Strange enough, those who show the most spirit in the beginning, are often the first subdued. But an ox that lies down, when in the act of 'packing' him, generally proves the most troublesome. Indeed, not one in ten that does so is fit for anything.

I have seen oxen that no punishment, however severe, would induce to rise; not even the application of fire. This would seem a cruel expedient; but when it is remembered that his thus remaining immoveable is entirely attributable to obstinacy, and that a person's life may depend on getting forward, the application of this torture admits of some excuse.

But even when, at last, he has been trained to carry the pack or the saddle, there is another difficulty, scarcely less formidable, to overcome. From the gregarious habits of the ox, he is unwilling either to proceed in advance of the rest, or to remain at any distance behind his comrades; and, if there is no one to lead, the whole troop will instantly come to a stand-still. Only a few can be trained as leaders. Such animals are always selected as have a quick step, and, of themselves, are in the habit of keeping a-head, and apart from the rest of the herd. Oxen of this description, at all times, hold the first rank in a travelling caravan.

At length, after great exertions, and endless delays, we were able to fix upon the day for our departure. Our arrangements were as follows:—On the cart, which was drawn by eight mules, we placed about one thousand pounds, consisting chiefly of guns, presents for chieftains and others, articles for barter, implements of natural history, bedding, &c. Six hundred weight (ammunition and provisions) were besides distributed amongst four 'pack'-oxen, and one mule.

The object of the expedition being entirely for the purpose of obtaining cattle for draught and slaughter, we were given to understand that after about eight to ten days' journey, we should arrive at some native villages, where we might procure any number of beasts required. Our course, as far as we could understand, was to the north-east, and through an exceedingly wild and sterile part of the country.

On the morning of the 19th of September we left Scheppmansdorf. The young cattle proved exceedingly unmanageable; and we had not been on the road many minutes, before a small handsome ox, which from the very beginning had given us much trouble in breaking-in, left the herd and was apparently about retracing his steps to the missionary station. To prevent this, Galton and I endeavoured to head him, on which he set off at a rapid pace. On finding himself hard pressed, however, he suddenly wheeled round and rushed towards my friend at headlong speed. Thinking it merely a demonstration, Mr. Galton remained stationary; but by so doing he nearly lost his life, for the infuriated beast charged home. Fortunately, however, his horn merely grazed my friend's leg, though it inflicted some injury on the shoulder of the horse.

After this little adventure, we continued our route at a pretty quick pace, over a hard, crisp, gravelly country, totally devoid of water, with scarcely a vestige of vegetation.

It was not until about ten o'clock at night, and after having travelled nearly twelve hours, that we reached a small granite rock, at the foot of which we succeeded in obtaining a few pints of very brackish water. Both Mr. Galton and myself were very tired. In order to save the horses, and to give the men an occasional mount, we had walked a considerable part of the way; and after partaking of some coffee, &c., we quickly resigned our weary limbs to sleep.

At break of day we were again stirring; and whilst the men were harnessing the mules, &c., I ascended the rock, where I discovered a most beautiful air-plant in full blossom, of a bright scarlet colour, with the lower part of the interior of the corolla, tinged with lemon.

The sight of such a lovely flower in this dreary and desolate region, excited within me some emotion, and I now fully appreciated the touching expression of Mungo Park, when, having, in a state of complete exhaustion, thrown himself down to die, he discovered at his side a beautiful little moss, and exclaimed—" Can that Being who planted, watered, and brought to perfection in this obscure part of the world, a thing which appears of so small importance, look with unconcern upon the situation and sufferings of a creature formed after his own image?—Surely not!"

Even the mighty Nimrod, Gordon Cumming, whose whole soul one would imagine to be engrossed by lions and elephants, seems to have been struck with equal delight as myself, at the sight of this charming flower: " In the heat of the chase," says he, " I paused spell-bound, to contemplate with admiration its fascinating beauty."

We continued our journey over the same sterile plain (Naarip) till about ten o'clock a.m., when we suddenly entered a narrow and desolate-looking mountain gorge, called Usab, sloping rapidly towards the bed of a periodical river. Here, under the shade of a stunted acacia, Stewardson recommended us to 'outspan;' and, leaving our cook in charge of the cart, we proceeded with the animals at once in search of water.

For more than two miles we continued to follow the gorge, which, as we approached the river, assumed a more gloomy, though perhaps more striking, appearance, being overhung with towering and fantastically-shaped granite rocks. Notwithstanding this, the river—to which the natives give the name of Schwackaup, or Swakop, as Europeans call it —presented a most cheerful and pleasant aspect; for, though not flowing at the time, its moist bed was luxuriantly overgrown with grass, creepers, and pretty ice-plants. The banks on either side were also more or less lined with gigantic reeds, of a most refreshing colour; and above the reeds rose several beautiful trees, such as the acacia, the black-ebony, &c.

Under a projecting rock, a few hundred paces from the spot where we struck upon the river, we discovered a pool of excellent water, where man and beast, in long and copious draughts, soon quenched a burning thirst. This being done, we indulged in a delicious bath, which highly refreshed our fatigued and dusty limbs.

On a lofty and inaccessible rock overhanging the river-bed, I again saw some of those beautiful flowers which in the early morning had caused me so much delight; and, with a well-directed ball, I brought down one almost to my feet.

In the sand we discovered the broad foot-prints of a rhinoceros. From their freshness it was apparent that the monster had visited the river-bed during the preceding night, but all our endeavours to rouse him proved ineffectual.

Whilst still talking about the prospect of soon seeing this singular animal in his native haunts, I remembered a story Mr. Bam had told us, of a wonderful escape he once had from one of these beasts, and which I will endeavour to give in his own words.

"As we entered the Swakop river one day," said he, "we observed the tracks of a rhinoceros; and, soon after unyoking our oxen, the men requested to be allowed to go in search of the beast. This I readily granted, only reserving a native to assist me in kindling the fire and preparing our meal. While we were thus engaged, we heard shouting and firing; and, on looking in the direction whence the noise proceeded, discovered, to our horror, a rhinoceros, rushing furiously at us at the top of his speed. Our only chance of escape was the waggon, into which we hurriedly flung ourselves. And it was high time that we should seek refuge; for the next instant the enraged brute struck his powerful horn into the 'buik-plank' (the bottom boards), with such force as to push the waggon several paces forward, although it was standing in very heavy sand. Most providentially, he attacked the vehicle from behind; for, if he had struck it on the side, he could hardly have failed to upset it, ponderous as it was. From the waggon, he made a dash at the fire, overturning the pot we had placed alongside it, and scattering the burning brands in every direction. Then, without doing any further damage, he proceeded on his wild career. Unfortunately, the men had taken with them all the guns; otherwise, I might easily have shot him dead on the spot. The Damara, however, threw his assegai at him; but the soft iron bent like a reed against his thick and almost impenetrable hide."

The greater part of the afternoon was spent under the shade of some wide-spreading acacias, and in hunting for specimens of natural history. A species of Francolin (*francolinus adspersus*), and one or two pretty kinds of fly-catchers, were amongst the day's spoil.

A little before sunset we returned to the camp; and, as we were to continue our journey on the morrow's dawn, we picketed the mules and horses, and made our encampment as snug as possible. Though the ground was our couch, and the sky our canopy, we slept soundly, and awoke early the next morning, greatly refreshed. We much needed this renewal of our vigour, for the day proved exceedingly trying both to men and cattle.

Once more we were on the Naarip plain; though this time we travelled parallel with the Swakop (which here pursued an easterly course), on the edge of those gloomy rocks through which its deep and turbulent channel has forced its way.

Just as we entered this wild and dreary waste, the sun rose in all its refulgence, converting, as if by magic, the whole of the eastern sky into one mass of the most dazzling light—tinting the distant mountains with a soft vermilion, and causing the dew-bespangled pebbles beneath our feet to sparkle like so many diamonds. He who has not witnessed a sunrise or a sunset in the tropics (rendered the more remarkable by the nearly total absence of twilight), cannot form the least idea of its magnificence and splendour.

But, alas! these sights, so lovely to the eye, are often followed by such intense heats as to be nearly insupportable to the way-worn traveller. We were now in the month of September, and the rays of the sun, at noon, falling almost vertically on our heads, caused a fearfully high state of temperature. The hot sand, moreover, cruelly burnt our feet, and not a breath of wind stirred the glaring and seething atmosphere. To complete our misery, we suffered from the most violent thirst, which our scanty supply of water, half-boiling as it was, could in no way tend to mitigate.

Our poor animals seemed to suffer as much as ourselves. Their gait, protruding tongues, and drooping heads, indicated great distress. Still they toiled on, but slowly and painfully, through the sand, which had now become soft and yielding. Long before we had accomplished the day's stage, one of the mules dropped down from exhaustion, and we were obliged to leave the poor animal to its fate, trusting, however, that when the atmosphere should become a little cooler, it would follow on our track. We dared not stop, nor would delay have been of any avail, for, as far as the eye could reach, neither bush nor blade of grass was to be seen.

In the early morning, I rode one of the horses, but, after a time, observing that some of the men looked jaded and faint, I dismounted, and gave it up to them, proceeding myself on foot during the remainder of the day. Mr. Galton had ridden in advance on the other horse, and, when we met, I was almost speechless from thirst, with my mouth and lips dreadfully parched. Often subsequently have I suffered cruelly from want of water, and for a much longer period than on the present occasion; but never do I remember to have been so much distressed as now; for though, from childhood, accustomed and inured to privations of all kinds, I had not previously experienced the effect of thirst under a tropical sun.

Again we left our cart some little way from the river, and drove the thirsty and weary animals loose to the water, which was, fortunately, not far distant; but, though men and beasts drank to repletion, the water seemed to have lost its property, for our best endeavours to slake our thirst proved unavailing.

The name of the place was Daviep, and it was reported to be a favourite resort of lions, who regularly reared their young in a neighbouring mountain, called Tincas, whence they made predatory excursions. We accordingly lost no time in reconnoitring the ground; but not finding any indications of the presence of lions, or even that they had haunted the place lately, we had little apprehension of their paying us a visit; and as the mules and horses sadly wanted rest and food, we deemed it advisable to leave them to themselves during the night, merely taking the precaution to 'knee-halter' them. We paid dearly, however, for our too easy confidence.

As on our return to the cart in the evening, the mule that had been left behind in the course of the day, had not yet made her appearance, I and Stewardson, each mounting an ox, returned to the spot where she had last been seen. The animal, however, had disappeared; and, finding that her tracks led towards the river, where it would have been next to madness to follow her in the dark, we retraced our steps at once, trusting that instinct, which had made her go in search of water, would also be a guide in seeking her companions.

Early on the following morning, one of the waggon-drivers was dispatched to the river to look after our animals, whilst Mr. Galton and myself followed at our ease; but what was our horror, on entering the bed of the stream, to find that several lions had recently passed and re-passed it in every direction. This, together with the absence of the mules and horses, at once foreboded evil. We were not long left to conjectures; for almost immediately our servant joined us, and said that a mule and a horse had been killed by the lions, and partly devoured. He added, that on his approaching the scene of the catastrophe, he saw five of those beasts feasting on the carcases; but on perceiving him they had retreated with terrible growlings! Instead of his presence having scared the lions from their prey, however, as he asserted, we had reason to believe that so soon as he was aware of them, he immediately hid himself amongst the rocks, and that it was not until emboldened by seeing us he had left his hiding-place. Had it been otherwise, he would have had ample time to give us notice of what had occurred, prior to our leaving the encampment.

Singularly enough, the dead mule was the identical one we had been in search of on the preceding night, and it would appear that it had just rejoined its companions, or was on the point of doing so, when it was attacked and killed. Being a remarkably fine and handsome animal, its loss was much regretted: the horse, moreover, was the best of the two we had brought from the Cape.

On examining the ground, we were glad to find that the other horse and remaining mule, had made good their escape down the bed of the river, though evidently pursued by the lions for some distance. How many of these beasts there really had been, we were unable to ascertain; but they could not have been less than seven or eight.

Having thus far ascertained the fate of the poor animals, we despatched our brave waggon-driver for Stewardson, and the remainder of the men: as also for proper guns and ammunition, as we had determined, if possible, to have our revenge.

On leaving Scheppmansdorf we had, unfortunately, only brought with us three or four small goats as provision for the journey. This scanty supply was now nearly exhausted, and it being uncertain when we should meet with any native village where we could barter for more, we deemed it advisable, in order to provide against contingencies, to lay in a store of mule-flesh and horse-flesh; and though our people seemed horror-stricken at the idea, there was not a second alternative. Whilst waiting the return of the men, we, accordingly, set about cutting off from the slain animals such pieces as had not been defiled by the lions. This being accomplished, we covered the meat with a heap of stones, and the men having arrived, we proceeded in search of the depredators.

But though we beat both sides of the river for a considerable distance, we were unable to discover the beasts. At one time, and when I was quite alone on the inner side of the thick reed-bed that lined the bank, I observed some beautiful 'klip-springers,' or mountain gazelles, and fired both barrels, though, unfortunately, without effect. The report of my gun caused a momentary consternation to Mr. Galton and the men, who imagined that I had fallen in with the lions, while, from the nature of the ground, they would have been unable to render me any assistance.

Being at last obliged to give up the search, two or three of the men on whom we could best depend were sent on the tracks of the scared mules and the remaining horse. After many hours' hard walking they were discovered; but the poor beasts had received such a fright, that it was only with great trouble and exertion that they were secured.

Thinking that the lions would in all probability return during the night, to make an end of what was left of the horse and mule, Galton and I determined to watch for them, and selected for our ambush the summit of a steep rock immediately near one of the carcases.

Shortly after sunset, we proceeded to put our plan into execution; and, having arrived within a short distance of the slain animals, one of the people suddenly exclaimed—"Oh! look at the six bucks!" Imagine our astonishment when, turning our eyes in the direction to which he pointed, we saw, instead of antelopes, six magnificent lions; and this, moreover, on the very rock on which we had purposed ambushing ourselves, and where—as we foolishly imagined—we should have been in perfect security!

On perceiving that they were discovered, the beasts retreated behind the rock; but one or another of them would, nevertheless, steal from its hiding-place occasionally, and take a peep at us.

Contrary to the counsel of Mr. Galton, and others of our party, I now ascended the acclivity where we had last seen the beasts; but, although they were nowhere visible, I had every reason to believe the whole troop was not far distant from the spot where I stood.

To have ambushed ourselves in the rock originally selected, was (from the evidence we had just had of its insecurity) not now to be thought of; and we therefore looked out for a safer place. The only one that offered, however, was a large acacia; but it was more than two hundred yards from either of the carcases, and its stem was so thick and straight, that it was impossible to ascend it. Moreover, total darkness had now succeeded the short twilight; and, however reluctantly, we left the lions in full possession of the field and the remnant of their prey.

On returning to our encampment, we found a waggon had arrived, belonging to Mr. Hahn, a missionary of the Rhenish society, settled amongst the Damaras. The vehicle was on its road to Scheppmansdorf, in order to fetch some goods that had recently arrived from the Cape. The driver civilly supplied us with a few sheep, which, to the great joy of our people, enabled us to dispense with the store of horse-flesh and mule-flesh we had just laid in. We did not, however, throw the meat away altogether, for both Mr. Galton and myself subsequently dined upon it on more than one occasion, and really found it very palatable, more especially that of the horse.

CHAPTER IV.

THE GNOO AND THE GEMSBOK—PURSUIT OF A RHINOCEROS—VENOMOUS FLY—FRUIT OF THE ACACIA NUTRITIOUS—SUN-STROKE—CRESTED PARROT—A GIRAFFE SHOT—TJOBIS FOUNTAIN—SINGULAR OMELET—NUTRITIOUS GUM—ARRIVAL AT RICHTERFELDT—MR. RATH AND THE MISSIONS—THE DAMARAS: THEIR PERSONS, HABITS, ETC.—LIONS TROUBLESOME—PANIC—HORSE SICKNESS.

THE second morning after the adventure with the lions, we continued our journey, alternately on the banks and in the bed of the Swakop. The road was exceedingly heavy, being for the most part composed of loose gravel and fine sand. Stewardson, who had the management of our travelling arrangements, instead of starting us at day-break, or previously, as he ought to have done, did not put the cavalcade in motion until an hour after sunrise. The consequence was, that before we were half through the allotted stage, the sun had reached its zenith, and scorched and harassed us dreadfully.

As yet, with the exception of a few zebras, &c., we had seen no wild animals, though the 'spoor' or track of the gnoo and the gemsbok were frequent enough. This day, however, at a turn of the road, we came suddenly upon a few of the latter, but the sight so fascinated us, that instead of firing, as we might have done, for they were within range, we gazed at them in astonishment.

We passed the night at a fountain called Annis, situated on the side of the river. On the following morning, and at only a few hundred paces from our bivouac, we discovered the tracks of several rhinoceroses. Finding that one of these animals had been drinking in a pool hard by, during the latter part of the night, Galton, Stewardson, and myself, went in search of the beast, the cart following in the bed of the river. But, though we pursued the tracks of the animal, at a pretty rapid pace, for nearly three hours, we were unable to come up with him, and therefore discontinued the chase in despair, and rejoined our caravan.

During the following day, I observed several curious-looking crested parrots of a greyish colour, which screamed discordantly on our approach; but as they always perched on the top of the very highest trees, and kept an excellent look out, I could not possibly get within gunshot.

I met, besides, with a vast number of delicate and pretty butterflies; as, also a wasp-looking fly, of the most brilliant dark blue. Having struck one of these to the ground, I was about to secure it, when it stung me severely in the hand, and in a very few seconds the wounded part began to fester, and swelled to an enormous size, causing the most acute pain.

Whilst following the bed of the river, our mules and cattle fared sumptuously; for, although we found but little grass, there was always an abundance of fine young reeds; but, until animals are accustomed to this diet, it only serves to weaken them. Cattle, however, that are used to this coarse food, soon become fat; and, when killed, prove, contrary to what might be expected, capital eating. When the reeds become somewhat old and dry, they are fired by the natives, and, in a fortnight or three weeks, they have again attained a luxuriant growth.

The pods of a species of acacia *(ana)*, which had dropped from the trees, were, also, much relished by the cattle. Stewardson informed us that when the latter are able to feed on them regularly, they soon become fat. The fruit has an acrid taste, but is not altogether unpalatable.

The wood of this tree, though straight-grained, close, and weighty, is not considered good for implements of husbandry. I have been assured, however, that when the tree is burned down, the quality of the wood is much improved!

Stewardson's habit of starting late had nearly proved fatal to me, for one day, whilst pursuing on foot some interesting birds, I had fallen considerably behind my companions, and, in order to come up with them, I was necessitated to put my best foot forward. The sun's rays (in themselves exceedingly powerful) being reflected from the surrounding barren hills, and the burning sand, made the heat equal to that of an oven.

I had only just caught sight of our party, when I was seized with sudden giddiness, and the horrible idea flashed across my mind that I had received a 'sun-stroke.' Being fully aware of the danger, I collected all my energies, and made the most strenuous efforts to overtake my friend. But the stupor increased every moment, and my voice became so faint, that for a long time I was unable to make myself heard. However, I did at last succeed, and Galton at once rode up to me and placed his horse at my disposal. It was high time, for another minute would probably have proved too late. As it was, I managed with great difficulty to reach a small clump of trees hard by, and tumbling off the animal remained for some time in a state of almost total unconsciousness. When at last I recovered from this stupor, the heat was less, and a gentle breeze having sprung up, I was able slowly to proceed. My head, however, ached intolerably.

The usual result of a *coup-de-soleil*, is known to be either almost instantaneous death, or an affection of the brain for life. In my case, I expected nothing short of the latter infliction. Happily, however, after about several months, daily suffering, I was thoroughly restored; and in time, I could brave heat and fatigue as well as any native.

Having followed the course of the Swakop for some days, we struck into one of its tributaries called Tjobis. At the mouth of this stream we met, for the first time, with a vast number of guinea-fowls, which we afterwards found very common throughout the country. We also made acquaintance with one or two species of toucans; and I succeeded, at last, in obtaining several specimens of the parrot-looking birds of which mention has lately been made. They were the *chizoerhis concolor* of Doctor Smith.

After many hours of fatiguing travel, we met Galton, who had ridden on in advance. His face beamed with delight, whilst announcing to us that he had just killed a fine giraffe. The news was most welcome to every one; for, to say nothing of the prospect of a feast, the heat of the sun, and the heavy nature of the ground, made us all feel exceedingly weary; and we were, therefore, extremely glad of a pretext to take some repose.

The mules were forthwith unharnessed, and all hands were put in requisition to cut up our prize and to 'jerk' the meat; but this proved lean and tough.

The bones, however, of the giraffe contain a great deal of marrow, which, when properly prepared, is eaten with *gusto* by every one; and, even when in a raw state, is sometimes greedily devoured by the natives.

As there was no water where we had 'outspanned,' we were obliged, towards evening, to continue our journey; and when we arrived at 'Tjobis Fountain,' situated in the bed of the Tjobis river, it was already dark.

Here we were at once visited by several Hill-Damaras, of whom more hereafter. On finding that a giraffe had been killed, and that they were at liberty to take what flesh we had left, their joy knew no bounds, and some of them actually returned that same night to the carcase. These men kindly brought us some sweet gum, a kind of coarse stir-about made from the seeds of a species of grass—and a few ostrich-eggs.

Our cook soon made us an excellent omelet from one of the last, and that by a very simple process. A hole is made at one end of the egg, through which is introduced some salt, pepper, &c. The egg is then well shaken, so as thoroughly to mix the white, the yolk, and the several ingredients mentioned. It is then placed in the hot ashes, where it is baked to perfection. An egg thus prepared, although supposed to contain as much as twenty-four of the common fowl egg, is not considered too much for a single hungry individual!

We remained nearly two days at 'Tjobis Fountain,' which gave our animals time to recover a little from their late exhaustion; but, as it was reported to be another favourite resort of lions, and recollecting that we had lately been taught a severe lesson, we took the precaution—as may well be imagined—to secure the horse and the mules during the night. Many zebras came off in the dark to drink, but always absented themselves during the day; and the heat was too intense and harassing for pursuing them at a distance.

The soil continued sandy, as before; but the vegetation

had, notwithstanding, vastly improved; for, instead of naked and desolate plains, the ground was now covered with a profusion of thin grass, dwarfish shrubs, isolated aloes, and one or two species of thorn trees. The latter produced, at this season, an abundance of excellent and nutritious gum, which, though almost as sweet as sugar, might be partaken of in any quantity without the least inconvenience or disagreeable consequence.

In the afternoon of the third day, we took our departure from 'Tjobis fountain,' and, at an early hour on the following morning, found ourselves, once more, in the bed of the Swakop; but here, unfortunately, our mules came to a dead stand-still, and nothing could induce them to proceed any further. Indeed, they were completely knocked up, and we had entirely to thank Stewardson for this misfortune; for had we travelled by night, as we ought to have done, instead of during the hottest part of the day, the poor creatures might have been as fresh as when they left Scheppmansdorf, and we ourselves spared much suffering. It stands to reason that no animal, however hardy, will bear much work or fatigue in the day at this terribly hot season of the year. Fortunately, the missionary station, of Richterfeldt, was now within two hours' ride, and Galton at once pushed on, for the purpose of obtaining assistance. In a short time, six oxen, with attendants, yokes, &c., arrived, and we were able to prosecute our journey without further delay. On reaching the station, we were most kindly and hospitably received by the Rev. Mr. Rath, of the Rhenish society.

Richterfeldt is prettily situated on the bank of the river Swakop, and at the junction of one of its tributaries, the Ommutenna. It is well supplied with fresh water, which is either obtained from a prolific mineral spring, or by digging

DAMARAS.

London, Hurst & Blackett, 1856.

a few inches in the bed of the rivers. There is an abundance of garden ground, which, when properly cultivated and irrigated, is exceedingly productive. Nearly all European vegetables thrive well; wheat grows to perfection, and is of excellent quality; but here, as at Scheppmansdorf, floods, at times, cause sad havoc. The pasturages are extensive and excellent.

Richterfeldt was founded in 1848; and Mr. Rath had consequently not been very long settled there. He had taken up his quarters in a temporary hut, consisting of a mud wall, four feet high, covered over by mat-work and canvass. At the back of his house were three small native villages, composed of about fifty or sixty wretched hovels, and numbering—children included—about two hundred inhabitants. They were all very poor; but a few possessed a small drove of sheep or goats, which they obtained in barter for goods given them by the missionary as recompense for labour, errands, and other services. The currency is iron ware; the regular price for an ox, at this time, was an iron assegai, without the handle; that of a sheep or goat, a certain quantity of iron or copper wire—or two pieces of iron hoop, each five or six inches in length. The Damaras have a perfect mania for copper and iron, but more especially for the latter; and it is strange to see how well a few pieces of polished iron become them, when worn as ornaments.

The Damaras, speaking generally, are an exceedingly fine race of men. Indeed, it is by no means unusual to meet with individuals six feet and some inches in height, and symmetrically proportioned withal. Their features are, besides, good and regular; and many might serve as perfect models of the human figure. Their air and carriage, moreover, is very graceful and expressive. But, though their outward appearance denotes great strength, they can by no means compare, in this respect, with even moderately strong Europeans.

The complexion of these people is dark, though not entirely black; but great difference is observable in this respect. Hence, in their own language, they distinguish between the *Ovathorondu* — the black individuals — and *Ovatherandu*, or red ones. Their eyes are black, but the expression is rather soft.

I never saw any albinos in Damara-land, though such are said to occur amongst the Caffres.

The women are often of the most delicate and symmetrical shape, with full and rounded forms, and very small hands and feet. Nevertheless, from their precarious mode of life, and constant exposure to the sun, &c., any beauty they possess is soon lost; and, in a more advanced age, many become the most hideous of human beings.

Both sexes are exceedingly filthy in their habits. Dirt often accumulates to such a degree on their persons, as to make the colour of their skin totally indistinguishable; while, to complete the disguise, they smear themselves with a profusion of red ochre and grease. Hence the exhalation hovering about them is disgusting in the extreme.

Neither men nor women wear much clothing. Their habiliments consist merely of a skin or two of sheep or goats, with the hair on or off, which they wrap loosely round the waist, or throw across the shoulders. These skins, as with their own limbs, are besmeared with large quantities of red ochre and grease; and, with the wealthier classes, are ornamented with coarse iron and copper beads, of various size.

The men usually go bareheaded; but, in case of cold or rain, they wear a sort of cap, or rather piece of skin, which they can convert into any shape or size that fancy may dictate.

Independently of the skins, the women wear a kind of bodice, made from thousands of little rounded pieces of ostrich egg-shells, strung on threads—seven or eight such strings being fastened together; but I am not sure that it is not more for ornament than real utility. The head-dress of the married women is curious and highly picturesque, being not unlike a helmet in shape and general appearance.

Boys are usually seen in a state of almost absolute nudity. The girls, however, wear a kind of apron, cut up into a number of fine strings, which are sometimes ornamented with iron and copper beads.

Few ornaments are worn by the men, who prefer seeing them on the persons of their wives and daughters. They delight, however, in an amazing quantity of thin leathern 'riems' (forming also part of their dress), which they wind around their loins in a negligent and graceful manner. These 'riems'—which are often many hundred feet in length—serve as a receptacle for their knobsticks, or kieries, their arrows, &c.; but become, at the same time, a refuge for the most obnoxious insects.

The women, when they can afford it, wear a profusion of iron and copper rings—those of gold or brass are held in little estimation—round their waists and ancles.

The weapons of the Damaras are the assegai, the kierie, and the bow and arrow; they have also a few guns.

The head of the assegai consists of iron, and is usually kept well polished; being, moreover, of a soft texture, it is easily sharpened, or repaired, if out of order. The shaft, though, at times, also made of iron, is commonly of wood, the end being usually ornamented with a bushy ox-tail. On account of its great breadth, the assegai is not well adapted for stabbing, and its weight is such that it cannot be thrown to any considerable distance. This weapon, in short, is chiefly used instead of a knife, and, though rather an awkward substitute, it answers the purpose tolerably well.

The kierie is a favourite weapon with the Damaras. They handle it with much adroitness, and kill birds and small quadrupeds with surprising dexterity. Most savage tribes in Southern Africa use this instrument with great advantage and effect. Thus, in speaking of the Matabili, Harris says:—"They rarely miss a partridge or a guinea-fowl on the wing." In an experienced hand, the kierie becomes a most dangerous and effective weapon, as a single well-directed blow is sufficient to lay low the strongest man.

The bow and arrow, on the other hand, though a constant companion, is not, with the Damaras, as effective as it ought to be. They never attain perfection in archery. At ten or a dozen yards, they will shoot tolerably well; but, beyond that distance, they are wretched marksmen.

The Damaras are divided into two large tribes, the *Ovaherero* and the *Ovapantiereu*, of which the former lives nearest to the sea; still, with the exception of a slight difference in the language, they appear to be one and the same people. They may again be divided into rich and poor Damaras,[1] or those who subsist on the produce of their herds; and those who have no cattle, or at least, very few, and who live chiefly by the chase, and what wild fruit and roots they can pick up abroad. These are called *Ovatjimba*, and are looked upon with the utmost contempt by the prosperous classes, who reduce them to a state of slavery, and do not even scruple to take their lives.

But as the Damaras are little known to Europeans, much is to be said of them, and they will require a chapter to

---

[1] To prevent confusion, when speaking hereafter of these people, I shall simply call them Damaras, in contra-distinction to the Hill-Damaras, who are a totally different race of natives.

themselves. I shall, therefore, reserve a more detailed account of their peculiarities, customs, manners, &c., to a later period, when I became better acquainted with them and their country.

In consequence of an unusually severe drought this year, most of the rain-pools in the neighbourhood of Richterfeldt were dried up; but, as spring-water was still to be found at that place, a great number of wild animals nightly congregated there. As usual under such circumstances, the game was followed by troops of lions, who were a constant annoyance to us. To guard against their attacks, we had on our first arrival made a strong fence or enclosure round the camp, but even then we did not feel very secure.

One evening, these beasts were more than usually troublesome. The sun had hardly sunk below the horizon, when they began their terror-striking music, and kept it up without intermission till a late hour, when all became silent. Believing that they had taken themselves off, I sent the men, who had been watching, to sleep. I was, however, deceived; for two hours had hardly elapsed, when, within a very short distance of our encampment, there arose a most horrible roaring, intermingled with the rushing to and fro, the kicking, plunging, and neighing of a troop of zebras, which instantly brought every man to his feet, and the consternation and confusion became indescribable. Some of them rushed about like maniacs, lamenting most piteously that they ever left the Cape. Others convulsively grasped their blankets in their arms, and cried like children; whilst a few stood motionless with fear and anguish depicted in their countenances. It was in vain that I tried to calm their agitation. They seemed fully convinced that their last hour had come, and that they should perish miserably by the fangs of wild beasts.

On going just outside the enclosure, I could distinctly see

the glimmering of lions' eyes, as our small, well-kept bivouac-fire fell full upon them. I sent a ball or two after the intruders, but, as it appeared afterwards, without effect.

The next morning, we found that the zebras had escaped unscathed; and we attributed the unusual anger and ferocity of their pursuers to the disappointment they had experienced in losing their favourite prey.

We had only been a short time at Richterfeldt, when three of our mules, and the remaining horse, were seized with a mortal disease, and in the course of a few hours they all died. Though the loss of the animals was great to us, their death was a god-send to the poor Damaras, who devoured the carcases bodily, and without the least disagreeable result.

The distemper in question is usually known by the vague name of 'paarde-sikte' (the horse-sickness); and, as the cause is totally unknown, no remedy has yet been found efficient to stop it. Throughout Great Namaqua-land it is particularly fatal. Some people attribute this singular disease to poisonous herbs, of which the animals have inadvertently partaken; others, to the dew; and others, again, to the eating the young grass;[1] but all these suppositions are highly improbable, for reasons which it would be unnecessary to enter into here.

Fatal as the disease is to horses, yet, happily, there are places (even in districts where it commits the greatest ravages) that are always exempt from it. And, as these localities are well known to the natives, if one's horse be sent to them prior to the commencement of the sickly season—usually the months of November and December—the animals

[1] A similar notion prevails with regard to that most curious little animal, the lemming (*lemmus norvegicus*, Worm.), on whose mysterious appearance and disappearance so many hypotheses have been unsatisfactorily expended. See Lloyd's "Scandinavian Adventures," vol. ii. chap. v.

invariably escape the malady. The attack of our animals was an unusual exception to this rule, for they fell victims to the disease fully a month prior to the rainy season.

From the Orange river, on the south, and as far north as Europeans have penetrated from the Cape side, this deadly disease is known to prevail, and is one of the greatest drawbacks to successful travelling in South Africa.

CHAPTER V.

HANS LARSEN—HIS EXPLOITS—HE JOINS THE EXPEDITION—HOW PEOPLE TRAVEL ON OX-BACK—RHINOCEROS HUNT—DEATH OF THE BEAST—'LOOK BEFORE YOU LEAP'—ANECDOTE PROVING THE TRUTH OF THE PROVERB — HANS AND THE LION — THE DOCTOR IN DIFFICULTIES—SUFFERINGS ON THE NAARIP PLAIN—ARRIVAL AT SCHEPPMANSDORF.

WHEN at the Cape, we heard much of an individual named Hans Larsen, who was distinguished in a very remarkable degree for courage, energy, perseverance, and endurance. This man was a Dane by birth, and a sailor by profession; but, becoming disgusted with a sea-faring life, had, a few years previously, left his ship, and was now residing somewhere near to Walfisch Bay.

On visiting Mr. Bam, at Scheppmansdorf, that gentleman confirmed to the full all we had been told about Hans, and strongly recommended Mr. Galton to take him into his service. It was not, however, until our arrival at Richterfeldt, where Hans then resided, that we had an opportunity to make his personal acquaintance. Up to a rather recent period, he had been in charge of a herd of cattle; but he was now living independently on the produce of his live-stock and the spoils of the chase.

Hans was a fine specimen of the true Northman—fair complexion, light hair, blue eyes; and, though not above the ordinary stature, he was very muscular and powerfully built. His strength, indeed, almost exceeded belief. One of his feats was to carry an enormous anvil—which no ordinary man could lift from the ground—with as many persons as could possibly cling to it. On one occasion, he had borne from place to place a block of stone, which required ten men to lift on to his shoulders!

In consequence of his great strength and courage, he was much feared by the natives, who, nevertheless, took pleasure in teasing him; but, being of a very quiet disposition, he seldom resented their impertinences. One day, however, when they had carried their jokes somewhat too far, he raised his Herculean fist, and, with a single blow, levelled to the ground the nearest of his tormentors. At first, it was thought that the man was killed; but, fortunately, he was only stunned. On recovering from his stupor, he vowed vengeance; but, unable to carry out his purpose alone, he laid his complaint before the chief of the tribe; and a 'raad,' or counsel, was held. Many were for severe punishment—but, at last, when all the members had spoken, the chief rose and told them that, in his opinion, the offence should be passed over—and that, for the future, it would be better not to molest Hans; for, if they did, they would only fare worse. This advice was felt to be a prudent caution—and from that day forward they ceased to worry the Dane.

Hans was an excellent and indefatigable sportsman, and so successful that, though the country, on his first arrival, literally teemed with rhinoceroses, lions, giraffes, zebras, gnoos, gemsboks, &c., he had all but exterminated them.

To give the reader some idea of the abundance of game and wild beasts, then existing in this part of Africa, I may mention that Hans once shot, with his own hand, no less than nine rhinoceroses in the course of a single day.[1]

Hans ate very little animal food; but, whenever he could afford it, he drank an amazing quantity of tea and coffee. His chief nourishment, however, was thick sour milk, which he swallowed in gallons. It is wonderful how people thrive on this diet, which is the main sustenance of the Damaras, who, as has been already said, are remarkably fine-looking men.

Hans, on the proposal being made to him by Mr. Galton, agreed to accompany us in the capacity of head man; and we were truly fortunate to secure so able and practised a hand. Indeed, from after-experience, it is very doubtful whether we should have been able to get on without him. We had, moreover, found that it would be next to impossible to obtain from the natives, by barter, any considerable number of cattle; and, even had we succeeded, they would have been so wild and unmanageable, that we could not have made use of them for months. Now, as Hans had a small drove of his own, several of which were already broken-in, and the rest more or less tractable, and was willing to part with them at a moderate price, Mr. Galton secured the whole lot without a moment's hesitation, and thus we had overcome a difficulty which had long given us some uneasiness.

Hans had in his employ an English lad, named John Allen, who had also been a sailor, and who, like his master, had left his ship in Walfisch Bay. In the absence of his employer, John had been accustomed to take charge of the cattle and the house; and being an excellent and well-behaved youth, he also was admitted into Mr. Galton's service.

---

[1] His hunting dress, on these occasions, consisted simply of a thick, coarse, blue shirt or blouse, secured, by a belt, round his waist, containing his balls, caps, wadding, &c.

After a few days' rest, it was determined that Hans and myself, together with most of the people, should return to Scheppmansdorf, for the purpose of breaking-in the oxen, and bringing up the waggons and the stores.

Hans presented me with an ox, called 'Spring,' which I afterwards rode upwards of two thousand miles. On the day of our departure, he mounted us all on oxen, and a curious sight it was to see some of the men take their seats who had never before ridden on ox-back. It is impossible to guide an ox as one would guide a horse, for in the attempt to do so you would instantly jerk the stick out of his nose, which at once deprives you of every control over the beast; but by pulling *both* sides of the bridle at the same time, and towards the side you wish him to take, he is easily managed. Your seat is no less awkward and difficult; for the skin of the ox, unlike that of the horse, is loose; and, notwithstanding your saddle may be tightly girthed, you keep rocking to and fro, like a child in a cradle. A few days, however, enables a person to acquire a certain steadiness, and long habit will do the rest.

Ox-travelling, when once a man is accustomed to it, is not so disagreeable as might be expected, particularly if one succeeds in obtaining a tractable animal. On emergences, an ox can be made to proceed at a tolerably quick pace; for though his walk is only about three miles an hour at an average, he may be made to perform double that distance in the same time. Mr. Galton once accomplished twenty-four miles in four hours, and that, too, through heavy sand!

Early one morning we reached Annis Fountain, where, as on a previous occasion, we observed a number of rhinoceros tracks. Leaving the men to take care of the oxen, Hans, Stewardson, and myself selected the freshest 'spoor,' and started off in pursuit; but after several hours' hard walking under a burning sun, we were apparently as far from the quarry as ever, and Stewardson, who was quite knocked up, used his best endeavours to persuade us from proceeding further. We would not listen to him, however, but, allowing him to return to the encampment, continued to toil on, though with but little hope of success.

An hour might have elapsed, after we had thus parted from Stewardson, when I observed in a distant glen a dark object, which, as it excited my suspicion, I instantly pointed out to Hans, who would not believe that it was anything but a large 'boulder.' Nevertheless, we proceeded towards the spot, and I soon saw that the shapeless mass was nothing less than the rhinoceros of which we were in search. Hans, however, who had had frequent opportunities of seeing this animal in all positions, remained sceptical on the point; and it was not till we were within about twenty paces of the beast that his doubts were removed. With noiseless and quickened step, and our guns on the full cock, we made up to the monster, which still gave no signs of life. At last, however, one of us whistled; on which, and with the rapidity of thought, the beast sat up on its haunches, and surveyed us with a curious and sulky look. But it was only a moment; for, before he had time to get on his legs, two well-directed balls laid him prostrate within less than half-a-dozen paces of our feet.

In the pride of success, I somewhat foolishly leaped upon his back, and, African-like, plunged my hunting-knife into the flesh to ascertain if our prize was fat. But whether life was not altogether extinct, or that the sudden access of my weight caused a vibration in the lately-living body, certain it is that I felt the beast move under me, when, as may be supposed, I speedily jumped to the ground again, and made off. Though my apprehensions in this instance were groundless, the following anecdote, related to me by the natives, will show that there is considerable danger in too quickly approaching an apparently dead rhinoceros:—[1]

Some Namaquas had shot one of these animals, as it was rising from its sleep. One of the party, imagining the beast to be dead, straightway went up to it; and (with like object as myself) acted precisely as I had done. The beast, however, had only been stunned; and as soon as he felt the cold steel enter his body, he started to his feet and made off at full speed. This action was so instantaneous, as to prevent the man from dismounting, and the other Namaquas were paralysed with fear. Fortunately, however, after the beast had run forty or fifty paces, he suddenly stopped short and looked round. The favourable opportunity was not lost—for one of the party, more courageous than the rest, instantly fired, and, as good-luck would have it, brought the animal to the ground, with his terror-stricken rider still clinging to his back.

On re-joining our party, Stewardson was not a little surprised at our success, and mortified at his own want of perseverance. The flesh of the rhinoceros was poor, but not unpalatable; and we remained a day at Annis, to cut up and dry part of it as provision for the journey. We also carried away a goodly supply of the beast's hide, for the purpose of converting it into 'shamboks.'[2]

---

[1] Most animals, when shot, or otherwise killed, fall on their sides: but the rhinoceros is often an exception to this rule, at least such is my experience. In nine cases out of ten, of all those I have killed during my wanderings in Africa—and they amount to upwards of *one hundred*—I found them on their *knees*, with the fore part of their ponderous heads resting on the ground.

[2] The 'shambok' (a Dutch term) consists of a strip of the stoutest part of the hide of the rhinoceros, or the hippopotamus. After being stretched on the ground, and when it has acquired a certain stiffness, the stripe is subjected to a severe hammering, for the double purpose of condensing it, and giving it a rounded shape. It is then reduced to the desired size by means of a knife, or plane; and, lastly, a piece of sand-paper, or glass—if at hand—is employed to give it the finishing smoothness

One day, as I was riding with Hans, he pointed out to me a place where he had been attacked by a lion in broad daylight, pulled off his ox, and only escaped death by a miracle.

Not being encumbered by a vehicle, we were now able to hold the course of the Swakop uninterruptedly; but, on arriving at the Usab gorge, it became necessary to leave the river, and to cross the Naarip plain to Scheppmansdorf. From the great length of this stage (fifteen hours' actual travel), and the total absence of water and pasturage, it is necessary to traverse it during the night. As thick fogs and mists, however, are not uncommon here, the traveller is exposed to some risk. It not unfrequently happens that he loses the track—the result of which usually is that, when the day breaks upon him, he finds himself either back at the place from which he started, or in some unknown part of the plain. Instances are narrated of people having remained in this inhospitable desert as long as three days! "Losing the way," as my friend Galton says, "is the rule here, and not the exception; and a person who has crossed the plain without doing so, rather plumes himself upon the feat."

Hans recited to me the particulars of an adventure which happened to an European in this wilderness. During the time Captain Greybourn (to whom allusion has already been made) was established at Walfisch Bay, the medical gentleman who resided with him had occasion to cross the Naarip plain; but, being a total stranger to the country, he engaged a Hottentot as guide. The day proved hot and oppressive, and the wayfarers had not proceeded far, when the doctor felt faint and thirsty. On inquiry of his attendant, whether

and polish. The 'shambok' is exceedingly tough and pliable, will inflict the most severe wounds and bruises, and will last for years. The price of one of these 'whips,' in the colony, varies from eighteen pence to as much as nine or ten shillings.

any water could be obtained, he received a sulky and unsatisfactory answer, and was about to prosecute his journey, when the man thus abruptly addressed him:—

"You've got a very nice hat, sir, which you must give me, or I will not stir another step."

Under ordinary circumstances, to comply with such a request would have been inconvenient; but it was still more annoying in the present instance, exposed, as the doctor was, to a scorching sun. Finding himself, however, entirely at the man's mercy, and seeing nothing but a howling wilderness all around him, he grudgingly gave the hat, hoping to be exempted from further importunity. But he was mistaken in this matter; for he had not proceeded much farther when the Hottentot sat himself quietly down on the sand, complaining bitterly of the immense distance they had yet to perform, adding, with a sly look at the doctor, that he thought his jacket would fit him exactly! The medical gentleman was amazed at the fellow's impudence, and, at first refused this new demand; but, as the man said that unless he received the garment he would leave him to his fate, he was obliged to comply.

In this manner, he gradually divested the chicken-hearted doctor of his apparel; and would, in all probability, not have left him in possession of the shirt on his back, had it not been for the timely arrival of Hans and another European, then on their way to Walfisch Bay. The doctor's story was, of course, soon told, and the rascally Hottentot was not only deprived of his booty, but soundly thrashed into the bargain.

After having given the animals the necessary rest, we set out the next afternoon, about three o'clock, on the last stage for Scheppmansdorf. As the evening was starlight, we proceeded at a brisk pace till about midnight, when there suddenly arose from the sea a gloomy, bitter cold mist, which soon enveloped us in total darkness, and completely saturated every article of our dress. Unfortunately, in the early part of the night, we had purposely left the waggon-track to save a very circuitous part of the road, and we had now nothing to guide us. Still we toiled on as well as we could.

But we had great difficulty in getting the poor Damaras to keep pace with us, who, being naked, suffered extremely. Every ten minutes, they would lie down on the cold sand, perfectly indifferent to the consequences. If we had not used the utmost vigilance in keeping them moving, I am quite convinced that some of them would have perished. Towards morning, the cold became so intense that I was no longer capable of holding the reins, and, therefore, dismounted, and proceeded on foot. Daybreak brought no relief; for the fog still prevented us from ascertaining our position. The instinct of the oxen, however, came to our rescue, and, by giving them their own way, they soon took us safely to our destination.

CHAPTER VI.

RETURN TO SCHEPPMANSDORF — TRAINING OXEN FOR THE YOKE — SPORTING — THE FLAMINGO — THE BUTCHER BIRD: CURIOUS SUPERSTITION REGARDING IT — PREPARING FOR JOURNEY — SERVANTS DESCRIBED.

MR. AND MRS. BAM, and their family, were, I was glad to find, in good health; and, as heretofore, they gave me not only a most kind reception, but placed at my disposal the best of everything which the house afforded.

It is wonderful what habit and association will effect. When I visited Scheppmansdorf in the first instance, I thought it the most dismal spot that human eye ever rested on. But, in the short space of a few weeks, it had almost become endeared to me. I found what Shakespeare calls the "soul of goodness in things evil." Dreariness was softened down into peaceful seclusion; the savage country round about assumed the dignity of primeval nature, fresh from the hand of the Creator; and the solemn and stern night-silence only hushed me into sounder sleep. These feelings, and this trusting repose, mainly originated in the kind ministrations, and unaffected welcome, of sincere friends.

After a day or two's rest, we began the difficult and

laborious task of breaking-in the oxen; but it proved a much more difficult one than I had anticipated. Whilst herded together, these animals looked tame and docile enough; but the instant they felt the lasso round their legs or horns, their character changed completely.

The spirit of Damara cattle is fiery and wild in the extreme, and I have known many an ox which ten strong men were unable to manage. The only remedy in such a case, is to lasso the beast by his legs and horns, and, after having thrown him down, to affix to his neck a heavy iron chain, of sufficient length to trail along the ground. The effect on the animal of this incumbrance is in some instances very remarkable; for, instead of a wild, stubborn and unbending brute, in a short time he is all docility. Indeed, it not unfrequently happens that he becomes too lazy to be of any use.

Whilst at Scheppmansdorf, and whenever I could snatch a moment from my busy life, I never failed to shoulder my gun with a view of obtaining specimens of natural history, or a 'reinforcement for the larder;' and an hour's walk not unfrequently procured me a tolerable share of both. Ducks and geese, though somewhat shy, were by no means uncommon. Quadrupeds, of every description, however, were scarce. Yet I managed, occasionally, to bag a steinbok or a hare.

Almost every morn we were visited by a splendid flock of pelicans, who kept soaring above the place for hours together; now in wide, graceful circles, the next instant in a compact body, sometimes rising into the sky, till they became nearly invisible; then suddenly sinking till they almost touched the earth; when abruptly, as if recollecting that the land was not their proper home, they would resume their airy station. They generally ended by settling near a large reedy fountain; but they were very difficult of approach.

The *lanius subcoronatus*, a species of shrike, first described by Dr. Andrew Smith, I found to be common at Scheppmansdorf; as also the butcher-bird, which, as known, always impales its prey on some thorn or sharp-pointed stick before devouring it. The Cape people call this bird the 'fiscaal,' or magistrate, in consequence of a superstitious belief that it represents amongst the smaller animals what the judge does amongst men. Many even go further, and say that the 'fiscaal' only administers justice on a Friday; probably, from the Dutch court of justice being held in former times on that particular day.

Part of the oxen being at length pretty well trained to the yoke, we made preparations for our departure.

When we left the Cape, the belief was entertained that we should be able to carry thirty or forty hundred-weight on each waggon; but, on taking into account our young and wild cattle, and the sandy and heavy soil through which we should have to pass, we had ere this made up our minds to reduce the quantity to rather less than one-third of this weight, or to about fifteen-hundred pounds. Even this, as will shortly be seen, proved too great. Accordingly, every article was carefully weighed with the steel-yard previously to being stowed away in the waggons.

Before proceeding farther in my narrative, it may be proper to introduce to the reader our travelling establishment, as the character of the several individuals composing it had, by this time, become pretty well developed. And though, amongst our retainers, we had more than one 'black sheep,' and others whom it was exceedingly difficult to keep in order, yet, taking them together, they were, probably, a fair average of the servants likely to be picked up by the African traveller. On an expedition, similar to the one in which we were engaged, I should remark, people cannot be too particular in the selection of their attendants; for, to say nothing of the success of the undertaking, one's personal comfort mainly depends on their good behaviour.

First, in order, was a youth, named Gabriel, a native of the Cape. He had been engaged by Galton chiefly for his smiling face and winning looks; but he proved himself to be the most troublesome of the whole lot. In our journey up the country, he had already exhibited a vindictive temper and quarrelsome disposition, which, at length, broke forth with increased violence. On two separate occasions, he attempted, if I was rightly informed, the lives of his fellow-servants. Upon this atrocity, I spoke to him with earnest reprobation, and trusted that I had produced some effect; when, to my astonishment and mortification, the very next day he was guilty of the same outrage. After a dispute with one of his companions, he rushed upon him with a hatchet, and would, undoubtedly, have cleft his skull had it not been for a Hottentot, who warded off the blow. So little did the young villain think of the crime he had intended to perpetrate, that, upon receiving punishment, he had the impudence to remonstrate, and to ask why he was flogged.

Next, in order, came Abraham Wenzel (a native also, I believe, of Cape-Town), a wheelwright by trade, and by habit a thief. Even before leaving Scheppmansdorf, I received information that he had purloined divers articles from the stores, for which crime he received his due punishment.

Another of our servants was named John Waggoner. This man teased us continually by his sulkiness and reluctance to work, assigning, as a reason, that he had been seized with home-sickness, and that he wished to return immediately to the Cape. Some little time afterwards, he was gratified in his wish; and, as will subsequently be seen, he proved himself the worst scamp of the set. But John performed his fraudulent tricks with so much cleverness, ingenuity, and self-confidence, that, out of mere admiration at his dexterity, I could not refrain from excusing him.

John St. Helena, a relative of the last-mentioned, was born in the Cape-colony, and officiated as our head-waggoner. This man exhibited the most extraordinary disposition; for, though sometimes he would be good-natured, willing, and hard-working, at others he was sulky, ill-tempered, and indolent. At first, I felt much annoyed at his irritable and changeable temper; but I soon found that by interfering, I only made matters worse; and, as he was an 'excellent whip,' it was necessary to put up with and overlook a great deal, as we should have found it almost impossible to replace him in so wild and inhospitable a region. About three years afterwards I employed him again; and, strange to say, he was then the best of servants.

Another of the attendants, John Williams, also a colony man, was a short, stout, merry, mischievous-looking lad, who agreed to serve in any capacity to which he might be competent. He now cooked for the men, assisted in 'inspanning' and leading the oxen, washed clothes—in short, made himself generally useful. Still he was careless, thoughtless, and dirty in his habits; and had not the least idea of husbanding the provisions. The result was, that before we had been many months in the country, our stock of vegetables, coffee, tea, and other necessaries was all but gone.

Our own cook, John Mortar, a native of Madeira, was the very reverse of this. He was careful, frugal, industrious, strictly honest, and deeply attached to his master's interest. His only fault was irritability; but this, in a cook, is always excusable. I had a great regard for poor John, and, I believe the attachment was mutual.

Mortar had been cook to the club in Cape-Town, where

he won golden opinions; but, though he had certainly attained some proficiency in the culinary art, he required a whole grocer's shop to prepare a dinner; and it was some time before he could reconcile himself to make a beef-steak *à la façon sauvage*.

John had a famous way of telling stories; and, like his own dishes, they were very savoury and well-spiced: a tale never degenerated in his hands; and when, in his happier moments, he condescended to open his mind, he never failed to keep his audience in a roar of laughter. He had, moreover, great ambition, and could never bear that any one should interfere with his cooking establishment. The arrival of a batch of natives at his fire, was the signal for a general burst of eloquent abuse; and, if this did not suffice, he had a provoking way of scattering the hot coals and ashes over the naked legs of the poor unsuspecting savages, which, of course, never failed to have the desired effect. I often trembled for John; for his mind was clearly too republican to make any difference between chief and subject; and I was surprised that he never got into a scrape. I suppose, however, the comical manner in which his dangerous experiments were always carried on, served rather to amuse than irritate or provoke.

John lived to return to the Cape, where he became another Gulliver, embellishing his adventures among the savages with marvels which would have done honour to the invention even of Dean Swift.

I now come to the last, but certainly not the least interesting, of the servants. This man's name was Timbo; he was a native of Mazapa, a country far in the interior, lying to the west of the Portuguese settlements, on the east coast of Africa.

When yet a child, Timbo's country was invaded by a

ferocious and powerful tribe of Caffres, who carried off the cattle, and slew many of the inhabitants. Amongst the latter, were his parents; he, himself, escaped to a neighbouring tribe. As this, however, soon after shared a similar fate to his own, he was, for a long time, a 'stranger on the face of the earth.' At last, he was sold as a slave to the Portuguese; but, after a while, effected his escape. His liberty, however, was of short duration, for he was soon re-captured, and put on board a slaver. Fortunately, the vessel fell into the hands of an English cruiser, and Timbo, together with a great number of slaves, was brought to the Cape, and liberated.

Though of a shining, dark complexion, Timbo was a remarkably fine-looking man, and well formed. He bore the reputation of being a complete lady-killer, not only with those of his own colour, but also amongst the European 'fair sex.' He had, therefore, no great difficulty in securing a partner. His choice, however, seems to have been unfortunate; for, on his return, after eighteen months' absence, he found that his faithless spouse had not only deserted him for another, but had also carried off with her nearly the whole of his hard-earned wages. On asking him, one day, whether he had any intention of again marrying, he replied, in his strange *patois*:—"No, maser; me no more marry; women too great rascals in the Kaap!"

But it was not only of a handsome face and good figure that Timbo could boast, for he possessed, in addition, many excellent qualities—such as even temper, generosity, honesty, prudence, industry—and, like our cook, he was sincere in his attachment to the interest of his employer. With Galton and myself he was a great favourite. He possessed, moreover, the most cheerful disposition, and an inexhaustible store of fun. I was, indeed, never tired of listening to his tales, for he told them with such force and simplicity, that it was impossible not to be pleased and amused.

When reproached for anything of which he knew himself to be innocent, he would lay his hand on his breast and say:—" No, maser; me know dat, me tell you." Or— " No, maser; me heart know that, me heart reproach me, and me tell you."

Timbo had a wonderful aptitude for languages; but, though acquainted with many, he spoke none well. Still, his speech was remarkably fluent, and nothing brought it forth with such abundant fervour as when mention was made of his own country. This was like touching an electric rod, and he spoke in ecstasies. No European could take more pride in his native soil than this man did in his; and if the rest of his countrymen resembled him, they must indeed have been a fine race of men, and, undoubtedly, capable of a very high degree of cultivation.

CHAPTER VII.

DEPARTURE FROM SCHEPPMANSDORF—CATTLE REFRACTORY AT STARTING—TINCAS—ALWAYS TRAVEL BY NIGHT—RHINOCEROS HUNT—THE AUTHOR IN DANGER OF A SECOND SUN-STROKE—REACH ONANIS—A TRIBE OF HILL-DAMARAS SETTLED THERE — SINGULAR MANNER IN WHICH THESE PEOPLE SMOKE — EFFECTS OF THE WEED — THE EUPHORBIA CANDELABRUM — REMARKABLE PROPERTIES OF THIS VEGETABLE POISON—GUINEA FOWL: THE BEST MANNER OF SHOOTING THEM—MEET A TROOP OF GIRAFFES—TJOBIS FOUNTAIN AGAIN—ATTACKED BY LIONS — PROVIDENTIAL ESCAPE—ARRIVAL AT RICHTERFELDT.

AFTER only three weeks' stay at Scheppmansdorf, and though our oxen were but partially broken-in, Hans one day informed me that we might set out in safety. Accordingly, the final arrangements were hastily completed; and, on the 13th of November, I once more bade farewell to the place, and its kind, obliging and hospitable inhabitants.

At first starting, and whilst the sand was very deep and yielding, the oxen caused us much trouble; but when we were on the hard and firm Naarip, all went well, and we arrived at the Usab gorge, where we encamped, without farther inconvenience than passing a cold and sleepless night.

The next evening we resumed our journey; but, instead of following the course of the Swakop—which, with our young oxen and heavy waggons, would have been next to impossible—it was deemed advisable that we should still continue on the Naarip—where, though water was scarce, the road was hard and good. Tincas Mountain, which, on our former journey, was to the right, was now, of course, to our left. After about fourteen hours' fatiguing travel, we reached the small river Tincas, where we unyoked, and rested ourselves and the weary oxen until nightfall, when we were again *en route*.

As we had now adopted the plan of travelling during the night, so as not to distress the animals too much, we found it necessary to keep a sharp look-out, both on account of the wild beasts, and for fear of losing our way. The latter was particularly to be guarded against; for, in this land of drought, any considerable deviation from the regular track is not unfrequently followed by serious consequences. Hans and myself were accustomed to keep watch by turns, for we never dared trust to the men; but this night, owing to our previous fatigue, we both unfortunately fell asleep.

When I awoke, I found that we were far out of our proper course, and all the men were snoring in the waggons. However, as it was starlight, and the landmarks very conspicuous, we had not much difficulty in recovering the proper track.

Towards break of day, we unyoked the tired oxen in the bed of a small dry water-course, where we found abundance of excellent grass. The unattached cattle did not join us till late in the afternoon, as the men in charge of them had fallen asleep. Their negligence, however, was excused on account of the good news they brought. It appeared that soon after it was light they discovered a huge rhinoceros, accompanied by a nearly full-grown calf, following in their wake, and that they had only lost sight of the beasts, when within a short distance of our bivouac.

So favourable an opportunity was too tempting to let slip. Having hurriedly partaken of some breakfast, and provided ourselves with a small supply of water, I, Hans, and an attendant, started in pursuit of the animals; and we had not left the camp for much more than an hour when we fell in with their 'spoor.' The beasts themselves, however, could nowhere be seen; and as several tracks crossed each other more than once (the animals having probably been feeding thereabouts), Hans and I took different directions in search of the trail we were to follow. We had hardly parted, when I heard a tremendous crash amongst the bushes; and about a hundred yards in advance, I saw, to my great vexation, the two rhinoceroses going away at full speed. Notwithstanding the distance, and the unfavourable position of the beasts, I fired at the mother; but, though the ball apparently took effect, she in no wise slackened her pace.

Hans did not discharge his gun, because, as he said, the bushes prevented him from having more than a very indistinct view of the beasts.

When I had re-loaded, we gave chase; and, as that part of the plain we had now reached was totally devoid of every kind of vegetation that could obstruct the sight, we easily kept the animals in view. By degrees they slackened their speed; and, in about twenty minutes, abruptly came to a stand-still, curiously regarding me as, having (though unobserved by myself) separated from Hans, I rapidly made up to them. When within fifteen to twenty paces, I halted, took aim at the mother, and pulled the trigger; but, to my great annoyance, my gun missed fire. Whilst in the very act of discharging my second barrel, she wheeled about, and the ball, instead of entering her heart, lodged in her hind quarters, and only tended to quicken her pace.

In the heat of pursuit I had taken no notice of Hans

and our attendant; but now that my attention was no longer exclusively drawn to the rhinoceros, I looked round to ascertain why they had not fired as well as myself, when to my utter astonishment, I saw both of them about half-a-mile in the back-ground, standing motionless and watching my proceedings. On their rejoining me, and in the first burst of indignation, I charged them with cowardice; but Hans immediately drew himself up to his full height, and indignantly, but respectfully, replied as follows :—

"Sir! when you have had my experience, you will never call that man a coward who does not attack a wounded black rhinoceros on an open and naked plain. I would rather," he continued, "face fifty lions than one of these animals in such an exposed situation; for not one in a hundred would take it as quietly as this has done. A wounded black rhinoceros seldom waits to be attacked, but charges instantly; and there would not have been the least chance of saving one's life in an open place like this. Had there been but the smallest bush or stone, I shouldn't have hesitated a moment, for the sight of the rhinoceros is bad, and if there is the least cover it is easy to avoid him. Not many years ago, a great Namaqua chief, who, contrary to the advice of his friends, had fired at a rhinoceros under precisely similar circumstances to yourself, lost his life by his rashness."

I could not but be sensibly aware of the injustice of my accusation, and my own fool-hardiness; yet I then felt but half convinced of the truth of what Hans had told me, and should certainly have acted in the like imprudent manner (as indeed I did on many subsequent occasions) had another opportunity offered. But, after all, Hans was perfectly right; as I am sure every one who has come much in contact with the beast in question will readily admit. Indeed, after the severe lesson which, at an after period, I received from a black rhinoceros, I am free to confess that nothing in the world would ever again induce me wilfully to expose myself in the way just mentioned.

To proceed. After receiving my fire, both mother and calf galloped off as fast as their legs would carry them; but gradually they slackened their pace to a canter, then to a trot, and finally to a walk. By this time, however, they were so far away that, but for the certain knowledge of their identity, we might readily have taken them for stocks or stones. The indistinctness of objects, moreover, even at a moderate distance, was increased by the effects of a most perplexing mirage.

Whilst discussing the propriety of following up the rhinoceroses, we saw them make for an isolated tree—no doubt, with the intention of sheltering themselves from the scorching rays of the sun. This decided us on continuing the chase; and, although already suffering greatly from thirst (our small supply of water having been long exhausted), the hope of ultimate success gave us strength to proceed.

Approaching under cover of some stunted bushes, and when almost certain of closing with the beasts, and putting an end to one or both, I was startled by the report of guns close behind me; and, on turning round, I found that Hans and our man had fired. I never felt more vexed in my life; for we were still a good hundred yards from the animals, and it had been previously agreed that—unless the beasts knew of our presence—we were not to fire until within a very short distance of them. As, however, the evil could not be remedied, I lost no time in firing; but the brutes being fully one hundred and fifty paces from me, I had small hope of inflicting serious injury. That I hit the mother, however, was very certain; for, at the instant of discharging my gun, she bounded like a cat into the air; and Hans, who looked upon this as a sure sign of her being mortally wounded, exclaimed, "Aha, old girl, you are safe!" Annoyed as I was, I could not help smiling, and ironically replied—"To be sure, she is safe enough." And so it proved, for we never saw her or her calf again.

I felt disappointed at our failure, and the chance of a feast; and was, moreover, sorry for the poor rhinoceros; for, though she was lost to us, I felt certain it was only to die a lingering death at a distance. From experience, indeed, I should say that a similar fate awaits a large portion of birds and animals, that escape us after being badly wounded.

Under ordinary circumstances, I would certainly have continued the pursuit; but this was now impossible. We could not reach our encampment under many hours, and we suffered painfully from thirst; while, owing to severe and continued exertions under a burning sun, I was attacked by torturing headache. Long before we could reach the waggons, I experienced precisely the same feelings as when I received a sun-stroke. Knowing that a renewal of the same infliction would in all probability prove fatal, I still toiled on; yet, at last, the faintness and exhaustion became so overpowering, that, regardless of danger, I threw myself on a small flat rock —so heated by the sun, that I was unable to hold my hand on it for a moment; and even the limbs protected by my dress were almost blistered. I then urged Hans to proceed as quickly as possible, in order that, if he found I did not immediately follow, he might send me some water.

Hans had not long been gone, however, when the rock became so intolerably hot that, stupified as I was, I found it necessary to rise from it; when, with a faltering step, and in a state of almost total unconsciousness, I made for the waggons, which I reached in safety, just as Hans was about to dispatch a man to me with an ample supply of water. My apprehensions, however, had been vain. A few hours' rest and quiet gradually restored me.

The oppressive heat under which I had suffered so severely, had also made the cattle very thirsty, and they refused to eat the dry and sun-burnt grass. As soon, therefore, as the air became a little cooler, we pushed on to Onanis, where we arrived somewhat late in the evening. Notwithstanding the darkness, and the risk of being attacked by lions, which sometimes swarm here, we were obliged to supply our cattle with water; and, as we had to dig for it in the bed of a small periodical stream hard by, it was close on midnight before we could think of refreshment or sleep.

Onanis is the permanent residence of a kraal of very poor Hill-Damaras,[1] who subsist chiefly upon the few wild roots which their sterile neighbourhood produces. Most of them, however, manage to raise a little tobacco, for which they have a perfect mania, and which, moreover, they value nearly as much as the necessaries of life.

They also cultivate 'dacka,' or hemp, not, as with us, for its fibre, but for the sake of the young leaves and seeds, which they use as a substitute for tobacco, and which is of the most intoxicating and injurious character. It not unfrequently happens, indeed, that those who indulge too freely in the use of this plant, are affected by disease of the brain.

The manner in which the Hill-Damaras smoke, is widely different either from Hindu, Mussulman, or Christian. Instead of simply inhaling the smoke, and then immediately letting it escape, either by the mouth or nostril, they *swallow*

---

[1] The proper name of these people is *Haukoin*, which literally means 'real men.' By the Namaquas they are styled *Ghou-Damop* or *Daman*—a term not sufficiently decorous for translation. The name Hill-Damaras is that by which they are best known, and being really very appropriate to their habits and mode of living, I shall retain it throughout the course of this narrative.

it deliberately. The process is too singular to be passed over without notice.

HILL-DAMARA PIPE.

A small quantity of water is put into a large horn—usually of a koodoo—three or four feet long. A short clay pipe, filled either with tobacco or 'dacka,' is then introduced, and fixed vertically into the side near the extremity of the narrow end, communicating with the interior by means of a small aperture. This being done, the party present place themselves in a circle, observing deep silence; and, with open mouths, and eyes glistening with delight, they anxiously abide their turn. The chief man usually has the honour of enjoying the first pull at the pipe. From the moment that the orifice of the horn is applied to his lips, he seems to lose all consciousness of everything around him, and becomes entirely absorbed in the enjoyment. As little or no smoke escapes from his mouth, the effect is soon sufficiently apparent. His features become contorted, his eyes glassy and vacant, his mouth covered with froth, his whole body convulsed, and, in a few seconds, he is prostrate on the ground. A little water is then thrown over his body, proceeding, not unfrequently, from the mouth of a friend; his hair is violently pulled, or his head unceremoniously thumped with the hand. These somewhat disagreeable applications usually have the effect of restoring him to himself in a few minutes. Cases, however, have been known where people have died on the spot, from over-charging their stomachs with the poisonous fumes.

The Ovaherero use tobacco in a similar manner as just described, with this difference only—that they inhale the smoke simply through short clay-pipes without using water to cool it, which, of course, makes it all the more dangerous.

The first time we were present at a smoking bout we were disgusted and frightened; but, from its being of every-day occurrence, we at length became somewhat reconciled to it—as also to many other unpleasant sights and customs.

Instead of the naked and barren Naarip, the country had now begun to assume a more pleasing appearance; for, though everything looked dry and parched at this season, there was no want of vegetation. Besides a variety of shrubs and stunted bushes, the periodical watercourses were marked by the handsome black-stemmed mimosa, and other species of the acacia family. The hill sides, also, were in many places covered with the graceful, but poisonous *euphorbia candelabrum*.

The Ovaherero tip their arrows with this vegetable poison; and the Hill-Damaras introduce it in a liquid state into pools where wild beasts are known to drink; and the flesh of any animal thus destroyed is perfectly wholesome. But its most remarkable property is, that whilst it invariably kills the *white* rhinoceros, it is freely and harmlessly partaken of by the *black* species, whether the plant itself be eaten, or a solution of it drunk. The juice of the *euphorbia candelabrum* has a milk-white appearance, and is very gummy, with an acrid taste.

The wild bee is occasionally known to extract its food from the flowers and the juice of this cactus. In such a case the honey becomes more or less poisonous. Mr. Moffat mentions an instance of his party suffering much pain and inconvenience from having partaken of such honey. They felt as if their throats had been on fire.

In seasons when rain falls abundantly, Onanis becomes one of the finest grazing localities throughout Namaqua-land, and is capable of sustaining many hundred head of cattle for several months together. The hills then afford a variety of shrubs and bushes, of which goats and sheep are fond. The surrounding plains are covered with fine grass, and a species of yellow flower, much relished by the cattle.

This district used to be one of Hans' favourite camping places; for, besides the abundant and excellent pasture grounds, it was largely resorted to by game of all kinds, and is still frequented by the lion, the gemsbok, the giraffe, the zebra, the gnoo, the rhinoceros, and several other animals.

We were to have resumed our journey on the following night; but, in the interval, Hans' right hand and arm had suddenly, and from some unknown cause, swelled in a most alarming manner. In consequence of this mishap, we found it necessary to devote another day to rest.

On the evening of our arrival at Onanis, we had started an immense number of guinea-fowls near the water; and, thinking it a favourable opportunity to replenish our exhausted larder, I slung a double-barrelled gun across my shoulder, and immediately started off; but, though I soon found the birds, they were so wild that for a long time I could not get within range of them. At last, after having chased them about the rocks till I was nearly tired, they scattered themselves amongst the stones, and lay so close, that, unless I almost trod upon them, they would not rise. With a steady pointer, I believe the whole flock might easily have been killed, and, as it was, I made a very large bag.

The flesh of the wild guinea-fowl—that of the young at least—is tender and well-flavoured; and their eggs are excellent. The speed of this bird is almost incredible. On even ground a man is no match for it. Where the country is well wooded, the best plan to shoot them is with a 'cocker,' or other dog, that challenges freely to them when 'treed;'— for whilst the birds are intently watching his movements, they may easily be approached within gun-shot. With a small pea-rifle this sort of sport is particularly amusing.

Early on the afternoon of the second day, Hans having now partially recovered, we started from Onanis; and, with the exception of a short stoppage, for the purpose of preparing some coffee, and to allow the cattle to take a few mouthfuls of grass, we travelled throughout the whole night.

Soon after daylight, we discovered a numerous troop of giraffes. The country, however, was open, and unfavourable for stalking; and, before we could get within range, they were off. The speed of these animals is by no means inconsiderable, more especially on gently rising ground. In such a locality, and from their being very long-winded, a tolerably swift horse is seldom able to overtake them under less than two or three miles. It is one of the most curious sights imaginable to see a troop of these animals at full speed, balancing themselves to and fro in a manner not easily described, and whisking, at regular intervals, from side to side, their tails, tufted at the end, while their long and tapering necks, swaying backwards and forwards, follow the motion of their bodies.

On account of the many short turns, the hilly nature of the ground in places, and the unusual length of the waggons, we anticipated considerable difficulty in the course of this stage. But we got safely through it without accident of any kind, and arrived at Tjobis Fountain about nine o'clock.

We left this place the evening of the same day; and, with the exception of resting for an hour or two by the way, we pushed on throughout the night.

At daybreak, and just as we reached the Swakop, we

were suddenly startled by the most tremendous roaring of lions, which, evidently, were close at hand. In a few moments afterwards, two of those magnificent beasts—male and female—emerged from the bushes at about one hundred and fifty paces a-head of us. On perceiving the cavalcade, they gave another terrific roar, of so angry a nature as to cause the greatest consternation amongst the cattle. Those attached to the foremost waggon, wheeled round instantaneously; and, before it was possible to prevent them, ran right into the midst of the aftermost team, and I expected every moment to see the vehicles capsized or smashed to atoms.

What with the bellowing of the oxen, the shouting and screaming of the men, the smashing and breaking of yokes, &c., and the continued roar of the lions, the scene was such as to baffle all description.

The lion, himself, after having approached very near to us, again retreated into the bushes; but the lioness seated herself quietly within less than a hundred yards of the waggons, growling most furiously. Throwing the reins over the saddle of 'Spring,' who, by-the-bye, had nearly unseated me on the first appearance of the lions, I sprang to the ground, and seizing a double-barrelled gun, which I always kept loaded for emergences, I made towards the beast, intending to punish her for her audacity, when Hans imploringly begged me to desist. "For," said he, "if you do not shoot her dead on the spot, she will be down upon us in an instant."

Allowing myself to be guided by his advice, I refrained from firing, but, nevertheless, took up my position within about fifty paces of, and opposite to, the lioness, as well to draw off her attention from the men, and thus enable them to put the cattle and vehicles to rights, as to be in readiness to give her a warm reception, should she think proper to charge.

A short time before we were thus unceremoniously attacked, one of the draught oxen, which had always been very wild, managed to escape from the yoke, and a fleet-footed Damara was left behind to bring him on. In the midst of our confusion, we heard cries of distress and loud shouting behind us; and, on looking round, we saw, to our horror, the lion in full chase as well of the refractory ox as the man, who was trying to keep off his fierce pursuer by violently waving the fire-brand which he carried in his hand.[1] Telling Hans to mind the lioness as well as he could in my absence, I immediately ran to the rescue of the Damara and his charge; but, before I had proceeded far, the ox, catching sight of the remainder of the herd, made a successful dash right across the lion's path, and fortunately re-joined us in safety. The object of the lion was clearly more the beast than the man; for, upon finding himself thus suddenly baffled, he stopped short, and, with a savage look at us, and an angry growl, bounded out of sight as quick as thought; and, by the time I returned to the waggons, the lioness had thought fit to follow her lord's example. Thus, almost without any effort on our side, we were providentially saved from this most extraordinary and dangerous attack.

At the first appearance of the lions, the men took refuge in the waggons, and, long after the danger was over, they trembled violently from fear and apprehension.

As a general rule, a lion, unless previously molested, will seldom attack an ox in the yoke, or when attended by man, but long abstinence makes him desperate.

---

[1] In the nights the Damaras invariably carry a fire-brand, which they hold close to their bodies, in order to shelter themselves, in some degree, from the wind and cold.

After considerable trouble and difficulty, we succeeded in re-arranging the oxen, which had become excessively scared. Two or three hours' further travelling brought us, without other mishap, safe to Richterfeldt, where our hair-breadth escape was listened to with the deepest interest.

We had left Scheppmansdorf—as said—in the afternoon of the 13th of November, and reached our present quarters early on the morning of the 22nd of the same month. The whole of the distance, by road, could not have been much less than one hundred and thirty miles. Having performed this in five stages, and in about the same number of days, our rate of travelling, at an average, had been twenty-five miles daily. Taking into consideration the nature of the ground, the young and half-broken oxen, &c., it may fairly be considered first-rate speed; and our efforts were loudly praised by every one.

CHAPTER VIII.

A HEARTY WELCOME—WE REMOVE THE ENCAMPMENT—AN APPARITION—AUDACITY OF WILD BEASTS—DEPRIVING LIONS OF THEIR PREY—EXCESSIVE HEAT—SINGULAR EFFECTS OF GREAT HEAT—DEPART FOR BARMEN—MEET A TROOP OF ZEBRAS—THEIR FLESH NOT EQUAL TO VENISON—THE MISSIONARY'S WAIL—A SAD CATASTROPHE—THE 'KAMEEL-DOORN'—BUXTON FOUNTAIN—THE SCORPION—ARRIVAL AT BARMEN.

IMMEDIATELY on our arrival at Richterfeldt, we were surrounded by scores of natives, who, with yells, vociferations, clapping of hands, grotesque dances, and so forth, testified their joy at our return. Mr. Rath, moreover, highly complimented us on the dispatch with which we had broken-in the oxen, and performed the journey.

Mr. Galton, I ascertained, had lately departed for Barmen, Mr. Hahn's station. I determined to follow him as soon as I had taken sufficient rest after my fatiguing journey. In the meantime, the waggons were to remain at Richterfeldt till our return to that place.

At first, we pitched our camp in the same spot we had occupied previously to our departure for Scheppmansdorf; but the high palisades that protected it had been destroyed in our absence by the natives, who had carried away the wood for fuel. This, however, was of little consequence, as the old enclosure would now have been too small to contain both the cattle and our cumbersome conveyances. Moreover, as the place was situated in the bed of a periodical stream, a tributary of the Swakop, and, as the rainy season was fast approaching, it would have been imprudent to remain here any length of time. Accordingly, we brought our waggons, &c., to Hans' own kraal, which was near at hand on the bank of the river, as there we should be perfectly secure in case of any sudden inundation.

The day before our removal, the men had asked and obtained permission to spend the evening with Hans at his encampment. Even the dogs had absented themselves, and I was thus left altogether alone. The night, though somewhat warm, was delightfully bright and still. To enjoy the beautiful weather, I had taken my bedding out of the waggon, and placed it on the ground alongside the wheels, facing a small clump of low tamarisk trees, distant not above twenty paces. Being a bad sleeper, I lay awake until a very late hour. All nature was hushed and silent, and the night so calm that I might have heard the falling of a leaf. Suddenly, my attention was drawn to the tamarisk grove, whence proceeded a low, rustling noise like that of some animal cautiously making its way through it. Thinking it probable that a hyæna or a jackal was about to pay me a visit, I sat up in my bed, and seizing my gun, which I invariably kept within reach, I prepared to give the intruder a warm reception. Imagine my surprise, however, when instead of one or other of these skulking animals, a stately lion stood suddenly before me! In an instant my gun was pointed at his breast, but, hoping he would presently turn his broadside towards me, which would have given me a much better chance of destroying him, I refrained from firing.

In this expectation, however, I was disappointed; for, on perceiving the waggons, he retreated a step or two, and, uttering a low growl, vanished the next moment amongst the bushes.

There is something so grand and imposing in the appearance of the king of beasts in his native wilds—more especially when he assumes an attitude of surprise or defiance—that it is impossible not to feel more or less awed in his presence.

On mentioning to Mr. Rath, the following morning, my adventure of the preceding night, he expressed no kind of surprise; for the tamarisk grove in question was often known, he said, to harbour lions and other beasts of prey. He added, moreover, that lions not unfrequently penetrated thence into his garden, and even approached within a few paces of the dwelling-house itself.

Returning somewhat late one very dark night from Mr. Rath's house to our encampment, I was suddenly startled by sounds of the most painful description, not unlike the stifled groanings of a person who is on the point of drowning. It at once struck me that the lions had surprised some unfortunate native whilst lying in ambush near the water for wild animals that came there to drink. Whilst listening in anxious suspense to the wailings in question—which gradually became more and more faint—there reached me from another quarter a confused sound of human voices, and of hurried footsteps. This only tended to confirm my first impression; but, from the impenetrable darkness, I could not ascertain anything with certainty. Being unable, however, to endure the suspense any longer, and regardless of the danger to which I exposed myself, I caught up my fowling-piece, which happened to be loaded with ball, and set out in the direction whence the wailings—now fast dying away—proceeded.

I had not gone very far, however, before I fell in with a number of the natives, who were hastening in the same direction as myself.

My road, for the most part, lay through a dense tamarisk coppice, and it was surprising to me, how I ever managed to thread the labyrinth. The hope of saving human life, however, enabled me to overcome all obstacles. I might have been three or four minutes in the brake, when, on coming to a small opening, I suddenly encountered, and all but stumbled over, a large black mass lying at my feet; whilst, close to my ear, I heard the twang of a bow-string, and the whizzing of an arrow. At the same moment, and within a very few paces of where I stood, I was startled by the terrific roar of a lion, which seemed to shake the ground beneath me. This was immediately followed by a savage and exulting cry of triumph from a number of the natives.

Having recovered from my surprise, I found that the dark object that had nearly upset me was one of the natives stooping over a dead zebra, which the lion had just killed, and then learnt, for the first time, to my great astonishment as well as relief, that the wailings which had caused me so much uneasiness, and which I imagined were those of a dying man, proceeded from this poor animal.[1]

The designs of the natives, who, from the first, I take it, well knew what they were about, was simply to possess themselves of the zebra, in which they had fully succeeded. Whilst some busied themselves in lighting a fire, the rest joined in a sort of war-dance round the carcase, accompanied by the most wild and fantastic gestures, totally disregarding the proximity of the lion, who had only retreated a few

---

[1] I have since had frequent opportunities of hearing the dying groans of the zebra, which in reality greatly resemble the faint gasps and ejaculations of a drowning man. Even the subdued neighings of this animal, when heard from a distance, are of a very melancholy nature.

paces. As the fire began to blaze, indeed, we could distinctly see him pacing to and fro amongst the bushes on the edge of the river's bank.

He, moreover, forcibly reminded us of his presence by cruelly lacerating a small dog belonging to one of the party, which had incautiously approached him too closely. By a slight touch of his murderous paw he ripped up its body from head to foot; but, notwithstanding its entrails dragged on the ground, the poor creature managed to crawl to our fire, where it breathed its last in the course of a few seconds. It was a most touching sight to see the faithful animal wagging its tail in recognition of its master, who was trying to replace the intestines, and to stop the flow of blood.

The savage features of the natives, which received an unnaturally wild character as the glare of the half-blazing fire fell full upon them; the dying dog, with his wild master stooping despondingly over him; the mutilated carcase of the zebra; and the presence of the lion, within a few paces of us, presented one of the most striking scenes it was ever my fortune to witness.

Expecting every moment that the lion would make a dash at us, I stood prepared to receive him. More than once, indeed, I levelled my gun at him, and was on the point of pulling the trigger; but being now sufficiently acquainted with the character of the animal to know that if I did not shoot him on the spot, the attempt would probably prove the death signal to one or other of us, I refrained from firing.

Contrary to my expectation, however, he allowed us to cut up and to carry away the entire zebra without molesting us in any way. During the process, the natives occasionally hurled huge burning brands at the beast;[1] but these, instead

[1] I have been told that on a similar occasion to the present, a lion was so injured by the flaming missiles thrown at him, that he was found shortly afterwards dead of his wounds.

of driving him to a distance, had only the effect of making him the more savage.

Similar attempts to deprive the lion of his prey are of frequent occurrence in the interior of Africa. Indeed, it is no unusual thing to find a number of natives residing near such pools of water as are frequented by antelopes, other wild animals, and their constant attendant, the lion, subsisting almost altogether in this way, or on carcases which the lion has not had time to devour before the return of day, when it is his habit to retire to his lair.

But it is not always that the attempt to deprive the lion of his prey succeeds as well as in the instance just mentioned. Generally speaking, indeed, if he is famishing with hunger, he turns upon his assailants, and many a man has thus lost his life. One often meets with individuals, either mutilated, or bearing dreadful scars, the result of wounds received in such encounters.

The heat had by this time become almost insupportable, and it was only with great inconvenience that a person could move about after the sun was a few hours above the horizon. Even the cattle were dreadfully distressed. As early as eight o'clock in the morning they would leave off grazing, in order to seek shelter under some tree or bush against the scorching rays of the sun.

Every afternoon regularly at two o'clock, we had a strong breeze from the westward. Strange to say, however, this, though coming from the sea, instead of cooling the atmosphere, only tended to increase its oppressiveness. We experienced precisely the same sensation as when standing before the mouth of a heated oven. The quicksilver rose to such a height as almost to make us doubt our own eyes. Even at Scheppmansdorf, which is situated less than twenty miles as the crow flies from the sea, and where there is almost always a refreshing breeze—the thermometer, at noon, in an airy situation, and in the shade, rises, for many days together, to 110 degrees of Fahrenheit!

In consequence of the fiery state of the atmosphere, every article of horn or wood shrank and contracted most surprisingly. Even the gun-stocks, made of the best English walnut, lost an eighth of an inch of their original solidity. The ink dried in the pen almost the instant it left the stand.[1]

Our waggons, moreover, which on leaving Scheppmansdorf, were in excellent order, were now quite infirm. The spokes and the tires became loose and the felloes and naves exhibited large gaps and fissures. To save them, however, as much as possible, we set about making a shed of reeds and rushes, strongly bound together by cords and light-wooden sticks.

As soon as this was finished, I began my preparations for visiting Galton at Barmen; and, as Mr. Schöneberg was also anxious to make the acquaintance of Mr. Hahn, his intended colleague, it was agreed that we should travel together. On the day appointed, we set out, mounted on oxen, and accompanied by a Hottentot as guide and interpreter. Besides his native tongue, this man spoke Dutch and Damara fluently. One or two natives were also engaged to drive, and to assist in packing, the oxen.

---

[1] Captain Sturt, who in his explorations in Australia, seems to have experienced the same heat in even a greater degree, says—

"The mean of the thermometer for the months of December, January, and February, had been 101, 104, and 105 degrees respectively, in the shade. Under its effects, every screw in our boxes had been drawn, and the horn handles of our instruments, as well as our combs, were split into fine laminæ. The lead dropped out of our pencils and our signal rockets were entirely spoiled; our hair, as well as the wool on the sheep, ceased to grow, and our nails had become brittle as glass. The flour lost more than eight per cent. of its original weight, and the other provisions in still greater proportion." In another part of his narrative, this enterprising explorer mentions the quicksilver once to have risen to 132 degrees in the shade, the thermometer being placed in the fork of a tree, five feet from the ground!

As usual, I rode 'Spring,' and Mr. Schöneberg an ox lent to him by Mr. Rath; but, unfortunately, the latter animal turned very vicious, and before we had proceeded many hundred yards, I saw my friend pitched, head foremost, into the moist bed of the Swakop. On rising from his uncomfortable berth, the Rev. gentleman looked very blank and crest-fallen; and nothing could again induce him to re-mount the brute. Being, however, anxious to prosecute the journey, I made him an offer of my own ox, which was gratefully accepted.

After this little mishap, all went on well for a while. Unfortunately, however, in an unguarded moment, I, too, was doomed to be 'un-oxed,' to the great delight and amusement of my companion. Confiding in his superior skill in managing a refractory ox, our guide now generously exchanged with me. Notwithstanding his boasting, he was as unfortunate as ourselves, for, in the course of half an hour, he had twice bitten the dust. Nothing daunted, however, he mounted a third time, and ultimately succeeded in convincing the animal that he was determined to be master.

In the course of the day, we suddenly came upon a troop of zebras. Quickly dismounting, I took a running shot at them, as they were disappearing in the brushwood, and had the good fortune to bring a fine male dead to the ground. Immediately 'off-saddling,' we helped ourselves to the best parts of the meat, leaving the rest to one of our Damaras, who thought a 'tuck-out' of flesh—as Hans would have called it—preferable to a wearisome journey to Barmen.

The flesh of the zebra, or 'wild horse,' as the Dutch call it, is eatable, but by no means good; for, besides possessing a very strong odour and peculiar flavour, it has a very oily taste. With plenty of pepper and salt, however, a steak is not to be despised by the hungry traveller.

The heat, throughout the day, had been terrific. Before the sun had well disappeared behind the mountains, between which we travelled, Mr. Schöneberg was completely knocked up, and we were obliged to encamp for the night. Each of us carried a small tin water-can; but, instead of having it filled, as I did, with the pure liquid, Mrs. Rath had kindly, but unwisely, provided her friend with a mixture of water, sugar, and cinnamon. This, as may be supposed, only served to increase his thirst.

We had hardly finished removing the packs and saddles from our tired steeds, before the poor missionary threw himself despondingly on the ground, exclaiming — "Ah! Mr. Andersson, if we were to tell people in Europe what we suffer here, none would believe us." I could not help smiling at this burst of despair; for, though from the heat the day had been distressing enough, we had by no means suffered either from want of water or food. Poor Mr. Schöneberg! he was totally unfit for the hardships he must necessarily encounter in the African deserts. Indeed, not many weeks afterwards, he all but perished from his inability to endure thirst for a short period.

The next morning at daybreak we were again in the saddle. Our course was northerly, and a little by east; and the greater part of the road lay some distance from the Swakop, which, at one point, forced its way through a narrow, picturesque and bold gorge.

In one place we passed at the foot of 'Scheppman's mountain,' so called from a melancholy event which occurred here a few years ago. A missionary named Scheppman had made the ascent to obtain a view of the surrounding country; but, in descending, the cock of his gun was caught by a bough, and the contents were lodged in one of his legs. After having suffered agonies for a few days, he expired, and the hill has ever since gone by his name.

The vegetation was more rank than in the parts we had previously traversed. In the course of the day, we crossed the dry beds of several large, sandy, and periodical streams, which were all tributaries to the Swakop. The country near these streams was thickly studded with splendid forests of the gigantic and park-like acacia, known to the Dutch as the 'kameel-doorn,' or giraffe thorn *(acacia giraffæ)*. This tree derives its name from its constituting the favourite and principal food of the beautiful cameleopard. On account of its immense size and peculiar growth, having the foliage disposed from the top downwards in umbrella-shaped masses, it is a great ornament to the country; but, strange to say, it is invariably found only in arid districts.

The 'kameel-doorn' is evidently of very slow growth, and requires, probably, many hundred years to arrive at maturity. The grain is therefore very close; and the wood is so heavy, that, after being dried for years, it will sink when thrown into the water. Our northern oak can in no wise be compared with it as regards hardness and solidity. The grain is, however, rather short, and the wood consequently brittle. Notwithstanding this defect, it is very strong, and is extensively used for building-purposes and implements of husbandry. It is, moreover, almost the only wood strong enough for the axle-trees of waggons. Tools of the best materials, however, are indispensable in working it. I have seen many a well-tempered axe and adze blunted and spoiled when brought in contact with it. The outer part of the tree, is of a whitish colour; but the heart is reddish-brown, not unlike mahogany, and capable of a high polish.

It is in the branches of this acacia, mentioned by several South African travellers, that the social gross-beak *(loxia socia)* chiefly constructs its interesting and singular nest.

Through the stupidity and mismanagement of our guide, who apparently knew but little of the road, we missed a watering-place where we were to have halted, and, in consequence, suffered extremely from thirst. Mr. Schöneberg, moreover, had been very unwell during the day; and, when we arrived at the end of the stage—which was not until seven o'clock at night—he was even more fatigued and exhausted than on the preceding evening.

We bivouacked by the side of 'Buxton Fountain,'—so called in honour of the late Sir Thomas Fowell Buxton, from whom and his family, if I am rightly informed, Mrs. Hahn had experienced much kindness. It is a hot spring; and the water, which flows out of a granite rock, is nearly of a boiling temperature, and has a brackish and disagreeable taste.

The soil, moreover, all round this fountain, is impregnated with saline substances. A considerable number of wild animals congregate here nightly, in order to quench their thirst. Lions, also, are at times numerous; but, on this occasion, they did not molest us.

Having partaken of some supper, I was about to resign my weary limbs to repose, when suddenly there issued from a small hole, close to my head, a swarm of scorpions. Their appearance brought me to my feet in an instant; for, though not a particularly nervous man, I am free to confess to a great horror of all crawling things.

During the hot months these animals lie dormant; but, on the approach of the rainy season, they come forth in great numbers. On removing stones, decayed pieces of wood, &c., it is necessary to be very cautious. The instant the scorpion feels himself in contact with any part of the body of a man or beast, he lifts his tail, and, with his horny sting, inflicts a wound, which, though rarely fatal, is still of a very painful nature.[1]

Like the snake, the scorpion is fond of warmth; and it is not uncommon, on awakening in the morning, to find one or two of these horrid creatures snugly ensconced in the folds of the blanket, or under the pillow. On one occasion I killed a scorpion, measuring nearly seven and a half inches in length, that had thus unceremoniously introduced itself into my bed.

The following morning, our guide declared it to be only a few hours' further travelling to Barmen. We, therefore, did not hurry our departure, but took ample time to prepare, and to partake of, a substantial breakfast—consisting of some strong coffee, and steaks of zebra-flesh, simply prepared on the hot embers of our bivouac fire.

We arrived at Barmen just as the family was sitting down to dinner, and Mr. Hahn kindly invited us to join in the ample repast. I was happy to find Mr. Galton in the enjoyment of health and excellent spirits; and he seemed delighted at our safe and speedy return.

---

[1] "The black, or rock scorpion," says Lieutenant Patterson, "is nearly as venomous as any of the serpent tribe. A farmer, who resided at a place called the Paarle, near the Cape, was stung by one in the foot, during my stay in the country, and died in a few hours."

CHAPTER IX.

BARMEN—THUNDER-STORM IN THE TROPICS—A MAN KILLED BY LIGHTNING—WARM SPRING—MR. HAHN: HIS MISSIONARY LABOUR; SEED SOWN IN EXCEEDING STONY GROUND—THE LAKE OMANBONDÈ—MR. GALTON'S MISSION OF PEACE—THE AUTHOR MEETS A LION BY THE WAY; THE BEAST BOLTS—SINGULAR CHASE OF A GNOO—'KILLING TWO BIRDS WITH ONE STONE'—A LION HUNT—THE AUTHOR ESCAPES DEATH BY A MIRACLE—CONSEQUENCES OF SHOOTING ON A SUNDAY.

At a first glance, Barmen has a rather dreary aspect. Hans thought it resembled many of the most desolate parts of Iceland; but, when more closely examined, it is found to be by no means devoid either of interest or beauty. It is situated about three quarters of a mile from the Swakop, and on its right bank. Towards the west, and immediately behind the station, rise irregular masses of low, broken rocks, ending abruptly on one side in a bluff, about one thousand feet high. The whole are covered with a profusion of shrubs, and several species of thorn-trees of the genus acacia, which, during the greater part of the year assume every shade of green. To the eastward, it faces the Swakop, the course of which is conspicuously marked by the handsome black-stemmed mimosa. Beyond this, the view is limited by a noble range of picturesque mountains, rising between six and seven thousand feet above the level of the sea. These receive additional interest from being more or less a continuation of those mighty chains which take their rise a very few miles from Cape-Town—thus extending, in a direct line, about one thousand miles!

Within a stone's-throw of the missionary-house, a turbulent mountain-stream winds its tortuous course. It flows, however, only during heavy rains, when its great fall and violence prove very destructive to the native gardens.

About two years from the period of which I am now writing, I happened to be on a visit to Barmen, on which occasion I witnessed one of those extraordinary phenomena only to be seen to perfection in tropical climes. One afternoon, heavy and threatening clouds suddenly gathered in the eastern horizon; the thunder rolled ominously in the distance; and the sky was rent by vivid lightnings. Knowing, from long experience, its imports, we instantly set about placing everything under shelter that could be injured by the wet. This was hardly accomplished, when large, heavy drops of rain began to descend, and, in a few seconds the sluice-gates of heaven appeared to have opened. The storm did not last above half-an-hour; but this short time was sufficient to convert the whole country into one sheet of water. The noise, moreover, caused by the river and a number of minor mountain-streams, as they rolled down their dark, muddy torrents in waves rising often as high as ten feet, was perfectly deafening. Gigantic trees, recently uprooted, and others in a state of decay, were carried away with irresistible fury, and tossed about on the foaming billows like so many straws. Every vestige of many gardens was swept away; and some of the native huts, which had been imprudently erected too close to the river, shared a similar fate. Indeed, it must have been a miniature deluge.

Wonderful, however, as are the sudden creation of these floods, the very short time they require to disappear is no less striking. An hour's sunshine is sometimes sufficient to transform flooded fields into a smiling landscape.

These commotions of the elements are of frequent occurrence in the tropics, during the rainy season. Soon after Mr. Galton's arrival at Barmen, there was a very heavy thunder-storm. One evening, as he and Mr. Hahn were conversing, they saw a Damara struck dead by lightning, within a hundred yards of where they stood.

Water was abundant at Barmen, and very good. Mr. Hahn had dug a large well in his own garden, which was of very great convenience and comfort, as the water thus obtained was always clean and wholesome. Within a couple of hundred paces of the dwelling-house there were, moreover, two copious fountains. One of these was a warm spring, the temperature being 157 degrees of Fahrenheit. By means of small channels this spring was made to irrigate a considerable portion of garden land, and was, also, of great use in seasoning timber. To the laundress, besides, it was invaluable. During our stay at Barmen, we indulged freely in the unusual and uncommon luxury of a bath; but it proved somewhat relaxing.

Mr. Hahn was a Russian by birth, but had, for a number of years devoted himself to the service of the German Rhenish Missionary Society, and was now using his best endeavours to convert the natives of this benighted land. At first, he had settled among a tribe of Namaquas, under the powerful robber-chief, Jonker Afrikaner, of whom presently. Finding, however, that these people infinitely preferred to cut the throats of their fellow-creatures, than to listen to his exhortations, and knowing, moreover, that several missionaries had already established themselves throughout various parts of Great Namaqua-land, he thought that he might use his influence to more advantage with the Damaras, amongst whom, therefore, he had pitched his tent. Messrs. Rath and Kolbé were his coadjutors in the good cause.

Seeing that their best endeavours were of little avail without a proper knowledge of the Damara language, they worked hard in order to master it; but the difficulty was immense. At last, by the merest chance, they discovered the key to it; and, from that moment, they made rapid progress, so much so, that, in the course of a few years, Mr. Hahn was able to return to Germany, where he has compiled and published a grammar and dictionary.

On the first appearance of the missionaries in Damaraland, the natives were very reserved, and retired with their cattle into the interior. Being wholly dependent on them for supplies of live-stock, the settlers suffered great hardships and privations. Indeed, on more than one occasion, starvation stared them in the face; and they lived for a long time in a precarious way on such wild animals as their Hottentot servants managed to kill. The Damaras, moreover, probably judging others by themselves, conceived the idea that the missionaries had come into the country with some sinister object, and that it would be advisable to frustrate it. Accordingly, they assembled in great numbers within a few miles of Barmen, for the purpose of exterminating the new settlers. Their diabolical intentions were, however, defeated by the counsel of one of their tribe. At the time of which I am now writing, Mr. Hahn and his coadjutors had completely succeeded in pacifying and conciliating the Damaras, and a great number of the poorer classes were now living at the station, where, by a little industry and perseverance, many managed to live in tolerable comfort. The great source of their wealth consisted in the cultivation of tobacco, which here grew to perfection—the leaves of this plant often attaining the size of three feet by two. What they did not consume themselves, was bartered for cattle to their wealthier countrymen.

Here, however, their civilization seemed to be at a standstill. The missionaries were laudably and strenuously exerting themselves in their behalf; but, as yet, they had met with little or no encouragement. To the mind of a Damara, the idea of men visiting them solely from love and charity, is utterly inconceivable. They cannot banish a suspicion that the motives of the stranger must be interested; and they not unfrequently require a bribe in return for any services they may render to the missionary cause. As an instance of the utter failure of religious zeal in these parts, I may mention, that Mr. Hahn, who is liked and respected by the natives, never succeeded, as he himself told me, in converting a single individual! In one instance, however, he imagined that he had made a convert; but, before the individual in question could be finally admitted as a member of the Christian church, it was necessary that he should give satisfactory answers to certain questions. One of these was, whether, according to the usages of Christianity, he would be contented with *one* wife. To this, the man replied, that, though he was very anxious to oblige Mr. Hahn and his friends personally, and to further the objects of the mission in every way possible, yet his conscience would not permit him to make so great a sacrifice as that required.

The wealthy Damaras were even more indifferent to spiritual matters than their poorer brethren; and, if they happened to visit any of the stations, it was not for the purpose of hearing the gospel preached, but either in the hope of protection against their enemies, or with a view to business by bartering tobacco, iron ware, and so forth. One exception to this rule was found in the case of the chief Kahichené, who had settled, with part of his tribe, at Schmelen's Hope.

Mr. Galton had not been idle during my absence. Besides collecting much interesting information with regard to the Damaras and the Namaquas, he had ascertained the existence of a fresh-water lake, called Omanbondè. This had the effect of raising our spirits considerably. We had landed at Walfisch Bay with a very vague idea as to our route, and had hitherto felt quite at a loss how to act.

To enable us to reach Omanbondè, it was necessary to pass through Damara-land, which was totally unknown to Europeans. Even the missionaries, who had resided several years on the frontiers, were ignorant of the country beyond a very few miles of their own stations. The Damaras themselves entertained the most extravagant notions of its extent, population, and fertility. The people, however, were known to be inhospitable, treacherous, suspicious, and inimical to strangers. It had always been considered insecure to travel amongst them; but more particularly so at this time, since their southern neighbours, the Namaquas, attracted by their vast herds, had lately made several extensive raids upon them, killing the people, and carrying off large numbers of cattle, sheep, &c. They believed, and with some shew of reason, that every individual of a light complexion was leagued against them. They well knew that the cattle stolen from them by their enemies, the Namaquas, were sold to European traders; and they knew, also, that if by accident or design the cattle belonging to the missionaries, or other white men, were stolen by the thievish people in question, they were always restored on application. This, together with the fact that an European could pass unmolested through the Namaqua territory, strengthened them in the conviction that we were enemies in disguise.

In order, therefore, to calm their excited feelings, to assure them of our friendly and peaceable intentions, and to explain to them the real motive of our journey, Mr. Galton had dispatched messengers to the principal Damara chiefs. He also wrote to Jonker Afrikaner (having previously sent messengers to him while at Richterfeldt), remonstrating with him on the barbarity and injustice of his conduct. Jonker is a leading chieftain amongst the Namaqua-Hottentots. He headed in person the greater part of the marauding expeditions into Damara-land.

Having spent a few days agreeably and usefully at Barmen, we prepared to return to our camp at Richterfeldt; but when the day of departure had arrived, I felt very feverish, and Galton was obliged to prosecute his journey without me. In a short time, however, I was able to follow.

On riding briskly along early one morning, I observed, as I thought, a solitary zebra a few hundred yards in advance. Instantly alighting, and leaving 'Spring' to take care of himself, I made towards the quarry, gun in hand, under cover of a few small trees. Having proceeded for some distance, I peeped cautiously from behind a bush, when I found, to my astonishment, that the animal which I had taken for a zebra was nothing less than a noble lion. He was quietly gazing at me. I must confess I felt a little startled at the unexpected apparition; but, recovering quickly from my surprise, I advanced to meet him. He, however, did not think fit to wait till I was within proper range, but turned tail, and fled towards the Swakop. Hoping to be able to come to close quarters with him, I followed at the top of my speed, and was rapidly gaining ground on the brute, when suddenly, with two or three immense bounds, he cleared an open space, and was the next moment hidden from view among the thick reeds that here lined the banks of the river. Having no dogs with me, all my efforts to dislodge him from his stronghold proved unavailing. Whilst still lingering about the place, I came upon the carcase of a gnoo, on which a troop of lions had apparently been feasting not many minutes previously. Undoubtedly my somewhat dastardly friend had been one of the party.

In the afternoon of the same day that I reached Richterfeldt, a very exciting and animating chase took place. A gnoo had been slightly wounded by a Hottentot servant of Mr. Rath. The natives, who had watched the whole affair from the station, immediately gave chase to the animal. Finding itself hard pressed, the gnoo, in its fright, took refuge in the village, where it was quickly hemmed in on all sides. Every woman and child had turned out to witness its destruction, whilst the men were vociferously contending about the right to the carcase. Assegais and arrows, moreover, were whizzing thick round our ears, and I had considerable difficulty in making my way through this scene of confusion to the poor gnoo, which I found at bay in the middle of Mr. Rath's sheep kraal, not twenty feet from his own dwelling. It was pierced with two assegais, and the blood flowed in streams down its panting and foaming sides.

Though the gnoo is but a comparatively small animal, its high fore-quarters, its coarse and shaggy mane, and its buffalo head, gives it a very imposing and formidable appearance. It was impatiently stamping and striking the ground with its fore-feet, and its looks seemed to bid defiance to us all.

At some risk, on account of the immense concourse of people assembled, I put a ball through the animal's shoulders, which at once ended its sufferings. A few minutes more—nay, rather seconds—there was not a vestige to be seen of it. Indeed, it was literally torn to pieces by the natives.

On paying my respects, later in the evening, to Mr. and

Mrs. Rath, I was politely informed that the penalty for shooting the gnoo was a goat. This being explained, I found to my surprise that the ball had passed clean through the antelope, and had struck dead a goat belonging to these worthy people.

The day previously to my reaching the encampment, Mr. Galton had started on an excursion to the westward. His object was chiefly to procure cattle from the natives, for we had not yet succeeded in obtaining a sufficiency of animals. He was also anxious to see and explore Erongo, a mountain famous at once for its peculiar formation, and as a stronghold of that curious race, the Hill-Damaras. Mr. Galton was accompanied by Hans, who had already visited the place, and a few other servants. On his return from Erongo, we were to start, with the waggons, up the country.

One day, when eating my humble dinner, I was interrupted by the arrival of several natives, who, in breathless haste, related that an *ongeama*, or lion, had just killed one of their goats close to the mission station (Richterfeldt), and begged of me to lend them a hand in destroying the beast. They had so often cried 'wolf,' that I did not give much heed to their statements; but, as they persisted in their story, I at last determined to ascertain its truth. Having strapped to my waist a shooting-belt, containing the several requisites of a hunter—such as bullets, caps, knife, &c., I shouldered my trusty double-barrelled gun (after loading it with steel-pointed balls), and followed the men.

In a short time, we reached the spot where the lion was believed to have taken refuge. This was in a dense tamarisk brake, of some considerable extent, situated partially on, and below, the sloping banks of the Swakop, near to its junction with the Omutenna, one of its tributaries.

On the rising ground, above the brake in question, were drawn up, in battle array, a number of Damaras and Namaquas, some armed with assegais, and a few with guns. Others of the party were in the brake itself, endeavouring to oust the lion.

But as it seemed to me that the 'beaters' were timid, and, moreover, somewhat slow in their movements, I called them back; and, accompanied by only one or two persons, as also a few worthless dogs, entered the brake myself. It was rather a dangerous proceeding; for, in places, the cover was so thick and tangled as to oblige me to creep on my hands and knees; and the lion, in consequence, might easily have pounced upon me without a moment's warning. At that time, however, I had not obtained any experimental knowledge of the old saying—"A burnt child dreads the fire," and therefore felt little or no apprehension.

Thus I had proceeded for some time; when suddenly, and within a few paces of where I stood, I heard a low, angry growl, which caused the dogs, with hair erect in the manner of hogs' bristle, and with their tails between their legs, to slink behind my heels. Immediately afterwards, a tremendous shout of "Ongeama! Ongeama!" was raised by the natives on the bank above, followed by a discharge of fire-arms. Presently, however, all was still again, for the lion, as I subsequently learnt, after showing himself on the outskirts of the brake, had retreated into it.

Once more I attempted to dislodge the beast; but, finding the enemy awaiting him in the more open country, he was very loth to leave his stronghold. Again, however, I succeeded in driving him to the edge of the brake, where, as in the first instance, he was received with a volley; but a broom-stick would have been equally efficacious as a gun in the hands of these people; for, out of a great number of shot that were fired, not one seemed to have taken effect.

Worn out at length by my exertions, and disgusted beyond measure at the way in which the natives bungled the affair, I left the tamarisk brake, and, rejoining them on the bank above, offered to change place with them: but my proposal, as I expected, was forthwith declined.

As the day, however, was now fast drawing to a close, I determined to make one other effort to destroy the lion, and, should that prove unsuccessful to give up the chase. Accordingly, accompanied by only a single native, I again entered the brake in question, which I examined for some time without seeing anything; but on arriving at that part of the cover we had first searched, and when in a spot comparatively free from bushes, up suddenly sprung the beast within a few paces of me. It was a black-maned lion, and one of the largest I ever remember to have encountered in Africa. But his movements were so rapid, so silent and smooth withal, that it was not until he had partially entered the thick cover (at which time he might have been about thirty paces distant) that I could fire. On receiving the ball, he wheeled short about, and, with a terrific roar, bounded towards me. When within a few paces, he couched as if about to spring, having his head embedded, so to say, between his fore-paws.

Drawing a large hunting-knife and slipping it over the wrist of my right-hand, I dropped on one knee, and, thus prepared, awaited his onset. It was an awful moment of suspense; and my situation was critical in the extreme. Still my presence of mind never for a moment forsook me—indeed, I felt that nothing but the most perfect coolness and absolute self-command, would be of any avail.

I would now have become the assailant; but as—owing to the intervening bushes, and clouds of dust raised by the lion's lashing his tail against the ground—I was unable to see his head, while to aim at any other part would have been madness, I refrained from firing. Whilst intently watching his every motion, he suddenly bounded towards me; but—whether it was owing to his not perceiving me, partially concealed as I was in the long grass—or to my instinctively throwing my body on one side—or to his miscalculating the distance—in making his last spring, he went clear over me, and alighted on the ground three or four paces beyond. Instantly, and without rising, I wheeled round on my knee, and discharged my second barrel; and, as his broadside was then towards me, lodged a ball in his shoulder, which it completely smashed. On receiving my second fire, he made another and more determined rush at me; but, owing to his disabled state, I happily avoided him. It was, however, only by a hair's breadth, for he passed me within arm's length. He afterwards scrambled into the thick cover beyond, where, as night was then approaching, I did not deem it prudent to pursue him.

At an early hour on the next morning, however, we followed his 'spoor,' and soon came to the spot where he had passed the night. The sand here was one patch of blood; and the bushes immediately about were broken, and beaten down by his weight, as he had staggered to and fro in his effort to get on his legs again. Strange to say, however, we here lost all clue to the beast. A large troop of lions that had been feasting on a giraffe in the early morning, had obliterated his tracks; and it was not until some days afterwards, and when the carcase was in a state of decomposition, that his death was ascertained. He breathed his last very near to where we were 'at fault;' but, in prosecuting the search, we had unfortunately taken exactly the opposite direction.

THE LUCKY ESCAPE.

London, Hurst & Blackett, 1856

On our homeward path from the pursuit of the lion, we fell in with a herd of zebras; and, while discharging my gun at them, I accidentally pulled both triggers at once. The piece being very light, and loaded with double charges, the barrel flew out of the stock—the cocks burying themselves deep in the flesh on either side of my nose just under the eyes, and left scars visible to this day. Mr. Rath, on seeing me in this plight, was good enough to say, by way of consolation, that it was undoubtedly a just punishment of Heaven, in consequence of my having carried a gun on a Sunday!

CHAPTER X.

A CHRISTMAS IN THE DESERT—MR. GALTON'S RETURN FROM THE ERONGO MOUNTAIN—HE PASSES NUMEROUS VILLAGES—GREAT DROUGHT; THE NATIVES HAVE A CHOICE OF TWO EVILS — THE HILL-DAMARAS — THE DAMARAS A PASTORAL PEOPLE—THE WHOLE COUNTRY PUBLIC PROPERTY—ENORMOUS HERDS OF CATTLE—THEY ARE AS DESTRUCTIVE AS LOCUSTS TO THE VEGETATION—DEPARTURE FROM RICHTERFELDT—THE AUTHOR KILLS AN ORYX—THE OXEN REFRACTORY—DANGER OF TRAVERSING DRY WATER-COURSES ON THE APPROACH OF THE RAINY SEASON—MESSAGE FROM THE ROBBER-CHIEF JONKER—EMEUTE AMONGST THE SERVANTS—DEPART FOR SCHMELEN'S HOPE.

WE had now been rather more than four months in the country, and Christmas had imperceptibly stolen upon us. Singularly enough, though I kept a journal, I was not aware of the fact until one morning the men came to wish me a 'merry Christmas.' A merry Christmas! alas! there were no merry children—no joyous feast—no Christmas trees or other indication of 'the hallowed and gracious time.' One day was of the same importance to us as another. Moreover, our store of grocery, &c., was too scant to enable our cook to produce us a plum-pudding, or any of those dainty-dishes that even the working-man in civilized countries would be sorry to be without at this season. Fortunately, we had now so accustomed ourselves to 'bush-diet,' that we did not even feel the want of what others might deem to be the necessaries of life. Constant exposure to the fresh-air and perpetual exercise had so greatly increased our appetites, and improved our digestive powers, that though we might not, like the natives, demolish a 'yard' or so of flesh at a meal, we could, nevertheless, play our part at meals as well as any London alderman—in fact, we could eat at all times, and scarcely anything ever came amiss. A draught of water from the pure spring, and a piece of dried meat just warmed in the hot ashes, was as much relished by us, as a glass of sparkling pale ale and a slice of Yorkshire ham would have been in Europe.

In this way we managed to live on cheerfully and agreeably; yet thoughts of home, with all its comforts, and friends dear to memory, would now and then flash across our minds. Such reflections, however, we tried to avoid, as they only served to sadden us.

On the morning of the 26th of December, Galton returned from his excursion to Erongo. He had been suffering from fever, and was right glad to find himself safe back at the encampment. The trip had been rather satisfactory. The chief result of it was an addition of about twenty oxen, and double that number of sheep and goats, to our live-stock. We were now pretty well provided against all emergences—at least, for some time to come. Galton had, moreover, ascended the mountain, with which he expressed himself much struck and pleased. He fully corroborated the story of the natives as to its impregnability, for it was accessible only in one or two places, and these could easily be defended against a whole army by a mere handful of men.

In round numbers, it was about three thousand feet above

the level of the plain, and extended in a straight line upwards of fifteen miles. The vegetation appeared very much the same as elsewhere in Damara-land, but, perhaps, more rank. The wild fig-tree grew rather plentifully among the crevices of the rocks, and the travellers obtained an abundance of the fruit, which was very palatable.

Erongo was only inhabited by Hill-Damaras, under the rule of different petty chiefs. From all accounts, they were possessed of numerous herds of cattle; but my friend only saw their tracks, as the natives were unwilling to sell or to exhibit any of the animals. They waged an exterminating war with the Damaras, who lived in the plains below; and, having seen the party pass unmolested through the territory of their mortal enemies, they were naturally suspicious as to their motive. They probably thought that Mr. Galton had come with a view to spy out and reconnoitre their stronghold, and then to return with reinforcements, in order to carry off their cattle.

Both in going and coming, Galton had passed through several large villages of Damaras, who complained bitterly of the severe drought, which was daily carrying off numbers of their stock. The only place that still afforded grass and water in tolerable abundance, was the country bordering on the river Swakop; but there they feared the Namaquas. However, they had only two alternatives— either to risk being plundered by these unscrupulous people, or to perish, with their cattle, from hunger and thirst. The first of these was thought the least evil of the two, and they were, therefore, gradually approaching the dangerous district. Indeed, several kraals had already been established at Richterfeldt.

Being entirely a pastoral people, the Damaras have no notions of permanent habitations. The whole country is considered public property. As soon as the grass is eaten off, or the water exhausted, in one place, they move away to another. Notwithstanding this, and the loose notions generally entertained by them as to *meum* and *tuum*, there is an understanding that he, who arrives first at any given locality, is the master of it as long as he chooses to remain there, and no one will intrude upon him without having previously asked and obtained his permission. The same is observed even with regard to strangers. Thus the once powerful chief, Kahichenè, was anxious to take up his quarters at Richterfeldt; but, acting on the understanding described, he first dispatched some of his head men to Mr. Rath, to ascertain from him how far he was agreeable to his proposal. The Rev. gentleman replied that their master could do as he liked in this matter, as he, himself, was but a stranger, and, consequently, could not lay any claim to the soil. However, the messengers would not listen to this, and told him that their chief would never think of intruding without having obtained special permission to do so.

At this period, Kahichenè was supposed to be the richest and most potent chieftain throughout the country. His wealth, of course, consisted solely in oxen and sheep. To give some idea of the number he then possessed, I will state that, early on the day after the interview just mentioned had taken place, the first droves began to make their appearance, and continued to arrive, without intermission, till late in the evening of the second day. Moreover, they did not come in files of one or two, but the whole bed and banks of the Swakop were actually covered with one living mass of oxen. And, after all, this was but a small portion of what he really owned. In the space of three short weeks, not a blade of grass or green thing was to be met with for many miles on either side of Richterfeldt. Indeed, a person, unacquainted with the real cause of this desolation, would have been likely to attribute it to the devastating influence of that scourge of Africa—the locust.

Much valuable time had hitherto been lost in obtaining information of the country and the inhabitants, in buying and breaking-in of cattle, and so forth—and this without our having accomplished any considerable distance. We were now in hope, however, of being able to prosecute our journey in earnest, and no time was lost in making the final arrangements for our departure. Our intended route lay to the north of Richterfeldt; but, as the country was said to be very hilly and densely wooded, we deemed it advisable to proceed *viâ* Barmen. As hardly mules enough were left to draw the cart, it was thought best to leave it behind in charge of Mr. Rath, who kindly promised to look after it in our absence. The two waggons were thought sufficiently large to contain ourselves and baggage.

The oxen, which from the beginning had been only partially broken-in, were now—from their long rest—wild, refractory, and unmanageable in the extreme. Before we could effectually secure the two spans (teams) necessary for the waggons, several hours had elapsed; and it was not till late in the afternoon of the 30th of December, 1850, that we were able to bid a final farewell to Richterfeldt, and its obliging inhabitants.

We made but little progress the first day; and when we bivouacked for the night, which was on the right bank of the Swakop, we were only three hours' journey from the missionary station. Indeed, we were obliged to come to an early halt, in consequence of the mules, and some of the oxen, having taken themselves off.

During the night we were serenaded by whole troops of lions and hyænas. One of the latter had the boldness to come within the encampment, and only retreated after an obstinate combat with the dogs. In the bed of the river, moreover, and where our cattle had been drinking during the night, we discovered a spot where a lion had made a dash at a zebra, but his prey had evidently disappointed him.

Next morning, without waiting for the return of the men who had been sent in search of the missing animals, I shouldered my gun and went in advance, in the hope of procuring a few specimens of natural history—as also of meeting with game of some kind or other: nor was I disappointed. At a bend of the river, I suddenly encountered a fine herd of oryxes, or gemsboks, the supposed South African unicorn. As they dashed across my path at double-quick time, and at least one hundred and fifty yards in advance, I fired at the leading animal (which proved a fine full-grown female), and had the satisfaction to see it drop to the shot. On going up to my prize, I found that the ball—a conical one—had passed clean through both shoulders; and this was, perhaps, somewhat remarkable, as the gun-barrel was smooth in the bore. Having carefully removed the skin, with the head attached to it, I set to work to quarter the flesh, which was rather a laborious task.

Though it was winter (January), the day was oppressively hot, and the leafless thorn-trees afforded no shelter against the burning rays of the sun. I suffered excessively from thirst, and, unfortunately, the waggons did not overtake me till after sunset. The Damaras yelled with delight at the sight of the oryx. They had a glorious gorge that night, and the return of daylight found them still at their feast!

With the exception of a heavy thunderstorm, accompanied by a deluge of rain, our journey to Barmen was marked by no further incident worth recording. We reached it in safety on the 9th of January, 1851, after seven days' travel, half of which time would have been sufficient under ordinary circumstances; but we had experienced very considerable difficulties in getting our waggons forward. The oxen pulled well enough so long as the country was level; but the moment they had to face a hill, they came to a stand, and no amount of flogging would induce them to move. When the whip was applied, it only produced a furious bellowing, kicking, tossing of heads, switching of tails, and so forth. On such occasions they would not unfrequently twist themselves entirely round in the yoke, and it often took a whole hour to put them to rights again.

On account of the thick wood, and general ruggedness of the country, the dry beds of periodical watercourses afford the only really practicable road. On the approach of the rainy-season, however, these are not always safe; for, when in imagined security, the traveller may, perhaps, all at once find himself in the midst of a foaming torrent. If the oxen are not well-trained, most serious results are to be dreaded. There are many instances of waggons with their teams having been thus surprised and swept away. Our fears on this head, therefore, were not quieted until we were in full view of the missionary-house at Barmen. Indeed, it was high time; for on the third day of our arrival there, the Swakop sent down its mighty flood.

The first showers of rain, it should be remarked, usually fall as early as September and October, but the rainy-season does not fairly set-in until December and January.

A letter from Jonker Afrikaner was awaiting our arrival, expressing a wish that Mr. Galton, in person, would pay him an early visit, that they might confer together on the affairs of the country. My friend was, at first, a little undecided how to act, as it might only have been a *ruse* of the crafty chief to entrap him. However, as under every circumstance it would be better to know his real intentions than to be kept in constant uncertainty and suspense, he determined, as soon as circumstances permitted, to comply with Jonker's desire.

When we bade farewell to Richterfeldt, it was in the firm conviction that the principal obstacles to the expedition had been removed; but we were sadly mistaken. Under different pretexts, the natives whom we had engaged suddenly refused to proceed any further. Even the man who had first drawn our attention to the lake Omanbondè, and who seemed to be the only one acquainted with it, threatened to leave us. Our Cape servants also became somewhat sulky and discontented. Indeed, two of them, Gabriel and John Waggoner, whom the reader will remember as having already given us some trouble, demanded and obtained their dismissal. Thus circumstanced, it was out of the question to think of immediately carrying our plan into execution. We felt excessively annoyed, and our stock of patience was well-nigh exhausted. Still we did not give up all hope of ultimate success.

Barmen, however, was ill-suited as an encampment; for, though agreeable enough as a residence for ourselves, grass for the cattle was scarce and distant. Mr. Hahn advised us to push on to Schmelen's Hope, situated at about fifteen miles to the northward, where, inasmuch as there had not been any natives dwelling of late, we should find abundance of pasturage. Accordingly, we acted on his suggestion, and in the afternoon of the 13th of January were established at that place.

CHAPTER XI.

SCHMELEN'S HOPE — SCENERY — MISSIONARY STATION — RAID OF THE NAMAQUAS — INGRATITUDE OF THE NATIVES — JONKER'S FEUD WITH KAHICHENÈ; HIS BARBARITIES; HIS TREACHERY — MR. GALTON DEPARTS FOR EIKAMS — AUTHOR'S SUCCESSFUL SPORTING EXCURSIONS — HE CAPTURES A YOUNG STEINBOK AND A KOODOO — THEY ARE EASILY DOMESTICATED — HYÆNAS VERY TROUBLESOME; SEVERAL DESTROYED BY SPRING-GUNS — THE LATTER DESCRIBED — VISIT FROM A LEOPARD; IT WOUNDS A DOG; CHASE AND DEATH OF THE LEOPARD — THE CARACAL.

SCHMELEN'S HOPE is picturesquely situated on the right bank of the Little Swakop and just at the confluence of one of its tributaries, the banks of which were lined with majestic trees of the mimosa and the acacia family. Some of these were now in full bloom, and presented an interesting and beautiful appearance. Heavy showers of rain, moreover, having lately fallen, the grateful earth acknowledged the tribute by rapidly sending forth her boundless store of aromatic herbs and plants—

"Herbs for man's use of various power,
That either food or physick yield."

The whole aspect of the country changed as if by magic, and

I gazed on the altered features of the landscape in rapture and amazement. It strongly reminded me of the Psalmist's words—

> "His rains from heaven parch'd hills recruit,
> That soon transmit the liquid store,
> Till earth is burden'd with her fruit,
> And Nature's lap can hold no more."

Schmelen's Hope *(Schmelen's Vervachtung)* is so called, partly on account of its advanced position, and partly in honour of its founder, the Rev. Mr. Schmelen, who, by all accounts, was one of the most gifted and most enterprising of missionaries that ever set foot on African soil. For a time, this station was occupied by Mr. Hahn; and, recently, by his colleague, Mr. Kolbé. About the time that we landed at Walfisch Bay, however, the latter had found it necessary to beat a precipitate retreat, in consequence of an attack upon the station by a party of Namaquas.

Shortly after Mr. Kolbé's settlement at Schmelen's Hope, he was joined by Kahichenè—of whom mention has been made in the foregoing pages—and a considerable number of his tribe. They continued to live here in the most unsuspecting security. The missionary-cause made considerable progress, and hopes were really entertained that Damara-land might eventually be civilized. The golden visions of a happy future for this unfortunate country were, however, speedily dispersed by the sudden appearance of a party of Namaquas, under the immediate command of Jonker Afrikaner. By this band, a great number of the natives were massacred; a considerable booty of cattle was carried off; and Kahichenè, himself, had a hair-breadth escape. Just as he was making good his retreat, he was observed and followed by a mounted Namaqua. On finding himself hard pressed, and that it was impossible to avoid his pursuer, the chief turned quickly round, and the next instant, with a poisoned arrow, laid the man dead at his feet.

Many acts of great cruelty were perpetrated on this occasion, of which the following may be cited. Several Damaras had taken refuge on the summit of an isolated rock, eighty or ninety feet in height. As soon as the Namaquas perceived them, they coolly seated themselves round the base; and, whenever any of the poor fellows peeped forth from their hiding-places, they were shot down like so many crows. Mr. Galton and myself visited the spot soon after our arrival at Schmelen's Hope, and saw the bleached bones of the victims scattered about; but we were unable to ascertain the exact number of people killed, as the jackals and hyænas had carried away and demolished many parts of the skeletons.

Though no direct attack was made on the missionary station, on this occasion, Mr. Kolbé, nevertheless, considered it would be imprudent to remain there any longer. Accordingly, packing the most valuable of his goods on his waggon, he hurriedly departed for Barmen.

A few days afterwards, some fugitive Damaras returned to the place of their misfortunes, and, on finding the house abandoned, they were base enough to despoil it of its contents. Moreover, what they could not themselves use, they wantonly destroyed or scattered about on the ground. On our arrival at Schmelen's Hope, therefore, we found nothing remaining but the mere shell of the house. This, though simply constructed of clay, and thatched with reeds, was rather neatly executed, and had apparently, at one time, been the exterior of a comfortable dwelling.

Water was obtained from a large pool or vley, which, however, in very arid years, might dry away. About five miles up the Swakop was, moreover, a rather copious fountain, called Okandu, where cattle might drink.

Generally speaking, if they have a chance of obtaining cattle, the Namaquas are not at all nice as to whether they rob friend or foe. On this particular occasion, however, they were supposed to have had an old grudge against Kahichenè and his tribe. Once, as Jonker, and a large party of his followers, were on the way to Walfisch Bay, their provisions failed them; and hearing that Kahichenè, with whom they were then on friendly terms, was in the neighbourhood, they bent their steps towards his kraal. Kahichenè received them civilly, but refused to supply their wants. He, however, advised Jonker to help himself to cattle from another Damara chief, who, he said (though without any kind of foundation), was their mutual enemy. Jonker did not wait to be told twice, but immediately attacked this man's kraal. In the fight that ensued, some of Kahichenè's people were accidentally killed; but he, believing the slaughter had been intentionally perpetrated, made a furious onset on Jonker that very night. As usually happens, however, and, perhaps, in some degree owing to the Damaras having fewer guns than the Namaquas, he was beaten off with very severe loss. Though the affair was afterwards made up between the chiefs, Jonker, in his heart, never forgave Kahichenè's attack upon him, which he looked upon as a breach of faith.

In all the attacks of the Namaquas, the most atrocious barbarities were committed. The men were unmercifully shot down; the hands and the feet of the women lopped off; the bowels of the children ripped up, &c.; and all this to gratify a savage thirst for blood. Many poor creatures have I myself seen dragging out a miserable existence, that had thus been deprived of limbs, or otherwise cruelly mutilated.

Jonker himself would seem to have been callous to all the better feelings of our nature. News having been brought to him on one occasion of the loss of a merchant vessel (somewhere about Cape Cross), he and his men started in search of the wreck. Before reaching it, some of his cattle were stolen, and as the theft was conjectured to have been committed by the Damaras, Jonker sent for the chief of the suspected tribe, received him in a friendly way, and invited him to remain at his camp for the night, in the course of which, however, he caused him to be brutally murdered. Before expiring, the poor fellow requested permission to see his wife and children, but Jonker was inhuman enough to refuse his request. On receiving a denial, the unfortunate man turned towards his slayer, and, wiping the blood from his face, exclaimed—" Since you have dealt thus treacherously by me, and even refused to allow me to see my family, you shall never prosper; and my cattle, which I well know you covet, shall be a curse to you!"

It has been asserted that Jonker once contemplated the extermination of all grown men amongst the Damaras, and of dividing the women, the children, and the cattle amongst his own people, hoping thereby to make his tribe the most powerful in that part of Africa.

On the 16th of January, Mr. Galton started for Eikhams, the residence of Jonker Afrikaner, on his mission of peace. He was accompanied by Hans, John Mortar, and two or three native servants.

Two days later, the mules, though closely watched, managed to elude our vigilance, and make good their escape. Fortunately, they were intercepted at Barmen, whence they were kindly sent back by Mr. Hahn. Not long afterwards, they again went off; but, passing Barmen this time in the night, no one saw them, and, consequently, they were allowed to pursue their course uninterruptedly, and were never re-taken. Strange to relate, these animals (with the exception of two, that were destroyed by lions, in the neighbourhood of Richterfeldt) ultimately found their way back to Scheppmansdorf, having travelled above two hundred miles by themselves!

During Mr. Galton's absence, I managed to beguile the time agreeably and usefully. Indeed, I spent some of my happiest days in this quiet, secluded, and charming spot, in the full enjoyment of unrestrained liberty. The mornings were usually devoted to excursions in the neighbourhood in search of game. Of quadrupeds, we had the giraffe, the gnoo, the gemsbok, the springbok, the koodoo, the pallah, the steinbok, &c.; so that I had no difficulty in keeping the larder pretty well supplied. I also made many an interesting and valuable addition to my collection of specimens of natural history.

One day, a young steinbok was captured, as also a koodoo, and I was fortunate enough to rear both.

With the steinbok, I had very little trouble; a she-goat, whom I deprived of its kid, having taken to it kindly, and become to it a second mother. The koodoo did not give me much more trouble; for, after a few days, during which milk was given to it with a spoon, it would of itself suck from what mothers call a 'feeding-bottle,'[1] and butt and pull away at it, as if it was drawing nourishment from the teats of its dam.

Both the steinbok and the koodoo were very pretty creatures, and, in a short time became very tame and affectionate. Their lively and graceful caperings, and playful frolics, were to us all a source of much amusement. Their

[1] A bottle of any kind, filled with milk, and with a quill (enveloped in linen) inserted in the cork.

end, however, was somewhat tragical—the steinbok died from exhaustion after a severe day's march, and the koodoo, which would have been a valuable addition to the beautiful menagerie in Regent's Park, I was obliged to kill, because we could not obtain a sufficiency of proper food for its maintenance, and had no room in the waggon for its conveyance. It grieved me much to destroy the poor creature, but there was no alternative.

Hyænas, called wolves, by the colonists, were very numerous at Schmelen's Hope, and exceedingly audacious and troublesome. More than once, during dark and drizzling nights, they made their way into the sheep-kraal, where they committed sad havoc. We had several chases after them, but they managed invariably to elude us.

To get rid of these troublesome guests, we placed some spring-guns in their path, and by means of this contrivance compassed the death of several.

The manner in which the spring-gun is set for the hyæna is as follows:—

Two young trees are selected and divested of their lower branches, or, in lieu of such, a couple of stout posts, firmly driven into the ground, will answer the purpose equally well. To these trees, or posts, as the case may be, the gun is firmly lashed in a horizontal position and with the muzzle pointing slightly upwards. A piece of wood about six inches in length—the lever in short—is tied to the side of the gun-stock in such a manner as to move slightly forwards and backwards. A short piece of string connects the trigger with the lower part of the lever. To the upper extremity of the latter, is attached a longer piece of cord, to the outer end of which, after it has been passed through one of the empty ramrod tubes, is tied a lump of flesh, which is pushed over the muzzle of the gun.

SHOOTING TRAP

London, Hurst & Blackett 1856

These matters being arranged, a sort of fence, consisting of thorny bushes, is made around the spot: only one small, narrow opening being left, and that right in front of the muzzle of the gun. A 'drag,' consisting of tainted flesh, or other offal, is then trailed from different points of the surrounding country directly up to the 'toils.'

When the hyæna seizes the bait—which she can only do by gaping across the muzzle of the weapon—and pulls at it, the gun at once explodes, and the chances are a hundred to one that the brains of the beast are scattered far and wide.

During our stay at Schmelen's Hope, we not unfrequently received visits from leopards, by the Dutch erroneously called 'tigers'—under which denomination the panther is also included. But I do not believe that tigers—at least, of the species common to the East Indies—exist on the African continent. The Damaras, however, assert that the real tiger is found in the country; and they once pointed out to Mr. Rath the tracks of an animal, which he declared to me were very different to any he had ever before seen in Africa, and which the natives assured him were those of the animal in question.

One night, I was suddenly awoke by a furious barking of our dogs, accompanied by cries of distress. Suspecting that some beast of prey had seized upon one of them, I leaped, undressed, out of my bed—and, gun in hand, hurried to the spot whence the cries proceeded. The night was pitchy dark, however, and I could distinguish nothing; yet, in the hope of frightening the intruder away, I shouted at the top of my voice. In a few moments, a torch was lighted, and we then discerned the tracks of a leopard, and also large patches of blood. On counting the dogs, I found that 'Summer,' the best and fleetest of our kennel, was missing. As it was in vain that I called and searched for him, I concluded that the tiger had carried him away; and, as nothing further could be done that night, I again retired to rest; but the fate of the poor animal continued to haunt me, and drove sleep away. I had seated myself on the front chest of the waggon, when suddenly the melancholy cries were repeated; and, on reaching the spot, I discovered 'Summer' stretched at full length, in the middle of a bush. Though the poor creature had several deep wounds about his throat and chest, he at once recognized me, and, wagging his tail, looked wistfully in my face. The sight sickened me, as I carried him into the house—where, in time, however, he recovered.

The very next day, 'Summer' was revenged in a very unexpected manner. Some of the servants had gone into the bed of the river to chase away a jackal, when they suddenly encountered a leopard in the act of springing at our goats, which were grazing, unconscious of danger, on the river's bank. On finding himself discovered, he immediately took refuge in a tree, where he was at once attacked by the men. It was, however, not until he had received upwards of sixteen wounds—some of which were inflicted by poisoned arrows—that life became extinct. I arrived at the scene of conflict only to see him die.

During the whole affair, the men had stationed themselves at the foot of the tree—to the branches of which the leopard was pertinaciously clinging—and, having expended all their ammunition, one of them proposed—and the suggestion was taken into serious condsideration—that they should pull him down by the tail!

The poorer of the Damaras, when hard pressed for food, eat the flesh of the leopard, the hyæna, and many other beasts of prey.

The caracal (*felis caracal*), or the wild cat, as it is generally called in these parts, was not uncommon in the neighbourhood of Schmelen's Hope. The fur of this animal is warm and handsome, and is much esteemed by the natives, who convert the skins into carosses, &c.

According to Professor Thunberg—who gives it on the authority of the Dutch boers—the skin of the caracal is also "very efficacious as a discutient when applied to parts affected with cold or rheumatism."

CHAPTER XII.

WILD FOWL ABUNDANT—THE GREAT BUSTARD—THE TERMITES—WILD BEES—MUSHROOMS—THE CHIEF ZWARTBOOI—RETURN OF MR. GALTON—HE MAKES A TREATY WITH JONKER—HE VISITS REHOBOTH—MISDOINGS OF JOHN WACGONER AND GABRIEL—CHANGE OF SERVANTS—SWARM OF CATERPILLARS—A RECONNOITRING EXPEDITION—THUNDER-STORM—THE OMATAKO MOUNTAINS—ZEBRA FLESH A GODSEND—TROPICAL PHENOMENON—THE DAMARAS NOT REMARKABLE FOR VERACITY—ENCAMP IN AN ANT-HILL—RETURN TO SCHMELEN'S HOPE—PREPARATIONS FOR VISITING OMANBONDÈ.

WE never fared better than at Schmelen's Hope. Besides the larger game mentioned, our table was plentifully supplied with geese, ducks, guinea-fowls, francolins, grouse, and so forth. The large bustard (*otis kori*, Burch.), the South African *paauw*, was, moreover, very abundant, but so shy, that to kill it, even with the rifle, was considered a dexterous exploit. One that I shot weighed no less than twenty-eight pounds. I have since repeatedly killed African bustards of this species; but I never saw a second bird that attained more than two-thirds of the weight just specified; usually, they do not exceed fourteen or fifteen pounds. The flesh is very tender and palatable; indeed, to my notion, it is the best-flavoured of all the game birds found throughout this portion of South Africa.

It being now the breeding season, the numerous flocks of guinea-fowls, in the neighbourhood, afforded us a constant supply of fresh eggs, which, as has been said elsewhere, are excellent.

Schmelen's Hope swarmed with termites, or white ants.[1] My ideas of ant-hills were here, for the first time, realized; for some of the abodes of this interesting, though destructive insect, measured as much as one hundred feet in circumference at the base, and rose to about twenty in height! Termites are seldom seen in the day time; but it is not an unusual thing, after having passed a night on the ground, to find skins, rugs, &c., perforated by them in a hundred different places.

In constructing their nests, the termites do not add to them externally, as with the species of ant common to England, but enlarge them from within by thrusting out, so to say, the wall. Their labours are commonly carried on in the dark; and, at early morn, each night's addition to the building may be discovered by its moisture. "They unite," says the 'English Cyclopædia,' "in societies composed each of an immense number of individuals, living in the ground and in trees, and often attacking the wood-work of houses, in which they form innumerable galleries, all of which lead to a central point. In forming these galleries, they avoid piercing the surface of the wood-work, and hence it appears sound, when the slightest touch is sometimes sufficient to cause it to fall to pieces." This is a clear and, I have no doubt, a correct account. I myself have often been astonished

---

[1] For a detailed account of this curious and interesting insect, see Mr. Westwood *(British Cyclopædia)*; Mr. Savage *(Annals of Natural History*, vol. 5, p. 92*)*, &c.

to find huge trees, apparently sound, crumble to pieces on being touched by the hand.

Wild bees very frequently make their nests in the gigantic dwellings of the termites. In some years, bees are very numerous. The disposition of these insects would appear to be unusually quiet and forbearing. Indeed, I never knew a man to be stung by them when robbing their nests. Commonly, these are smoked in the first instance; but just as often (as I myself have many times witnessed) they are fearlessly approached, and plundered by the naked savage without this precaution.

It is another interesting fact in connection with the dwellings of the termites, that during the rainy season, mushrooms grow in great abundance on their sides. In size and flavour, these mushrooms are far superior to any found in Europe. Care, however, must be taken in selecting them, for other fungi of a poisonous nature are almost identical in appearance. Two of the children of one of our Damaras were very nearly killed by eating some of these instead of mushrooms.

On the 6th of February I received a visit from a great Namaqua chieftain named William Zwartbooi, and found him a very agreeable old personage. He had met Mr. Galton not far from Eikhams, who had sent him to Schmelen's Hope to wait his return.

At one time, this chief had robbed and massacred the Damaras in precisely a similar way as Jonker Afrikaner; but, thanks to the exertions of the missionaries, he had been gradually weaned from his evil practices, and was now living on excellent terms with his neighbours.

Jonker and Zwartbooi associated occasionally, but they were by no means well-disposed towards each other. On one occasion, when the latter had expressed displeasure at his friend's inhuman proceedings against the Damaras, Jonker told him, that if he (Zwartbooi) meddled with his affairs, he would pay him such a visit as would put a stop to his devotions and make him cry for quarter.

Within Zwartbooi's territory was a mountain, called Tans *(see map)*, where horses might pasture throughout the year without being exposed to the 'paarde ziekte,' the cruel distemper to which these animals are subject. Almost all the northern Namaquas, Jonker amongst the rest, are in the habit of sending their horses here during the sickly season.

On one occasion, when Jonker was about to make a 'raid' on the Damaras, he sent an express to Zwartbooi for his horses; but this chief having been apprized of the cause for which the steeds were wanted, refused under some pretext to give them up; and, whilst parleying, the favourable opportunity was lost. It seems Jonker never forgave Zwartbooi this act of treachery, as he called it, and determined, let the risk be whatever it might, never again to put himself in another man's power.

Two days after Zwartbooi's arrival at Schmelen's Hope, Mr. Galton returned. He had been successful beyond his most sanguine expectations, for Jonker had not alone formally apologized to Mr. Kolbé for his brutal behaviour at Schmelen's Hope, but had expressed regret at his past conduct, and had faithfully promised for the future to live in peace and amity with the Damaras. Several important regulations had, moreover, been proposed by my friend, and approved of by Jonker and his tribe, with a view of upholding order and justice in the land; but how far they were carried out the sequel will show.

Fresh messengers had also been dispatched to the respective Namaqua and Damara chiefs, with a request that they would attend a general meeting, in order to secure to the country a lasting peace. We could not, however, induce them to do this. The late attacks were too fresh in their memory, to inspire confidence in either party: each distrusted his neighbour.

Jonker gave Mr. Galton much interesting and valuable information regarding the country northwards. He had, himself, made two or three expeditions in that direction, the last of which, as mentioned, was for the purpose of plundering a vessel, reported to have been wrecked off Cape Cross.

In the course of his journey, Mr. Galton visited Rehoboth, a Rhenish missionary station, and the residence of William Zwartbooi. The mission was here conducted by the Rev. Messrs. Kleinschmjdt and Vollmer, and was at this period the most flourishing establishment of the kind in the country.

Here my friend learnt with regret that John Waggoner, who, as the reader may remember, was dismissed at Barmen, had afterwards acted very disgracefully and dishonestly. He began by selling the same sheep to a trader three times over. And, just as Mr. Galton arrived, John had absconded with several head of cattle, stolen from the missionaries and the natives. My friend at once started off in pursuit; but though he followed on his track for a day and a night, he was obliged to return without having been able to overtake him.

Wherever John Waggoner went, he represented himself as Mr. Galton's servant, and affirmed that he was entrusted with despatches of moment for the British Government at the Cape. He added, moreover, that, under such circumstances, they were in duty bound to assist and speed him on his way. The most extravagant reports of our greatness and importance had already been circulated throughout the length and breadth of the land by the natives themselves. This, together with

John's impudent and confident air, produced the desired effect. Horses, cattle, waggons, &c., were everywhere promptly placed at his disposal. Even the missionaries were duped; and John is said to have reached his destination enriched with spoils, in an incredibly short time. His first act, on arriving at the Cape, was to engage himself to a trader, who imprudently advanced him a considerable sum of money, which he coolly pocketed, and then decamped.

Our lad, Gabriel, also marked his road to the Colony with many traits of violence and insolence, but he had neither the cunning nor the impudence of his associate.

Abraham Wenzel, the thief, had again behaved improperly, and Mr. Galton found it necessary to give him his dismissal.

We had thus in a short time lost the services of three men; but, fortunately, through the kindness of our friend, Zwartbooi, we were able to replace them by two others. The first of these was his own henchman, Onesimus, who was a Damaraby birth, but had been captured as a child and brought up amongst the Namaquas. He spoke the language of these two nations most fluently, and understood, moreover, a few words of Dutch. What with his capacity as an interpreter, his even temper and general good behaviour, he became one of the most useful men of our party.

The other man, Phillipus, was also a Damara by birth, but had forgotten his native tongue. He spoke, however, the Namaqua and the Dutch fluently. He was appointed a waggon-driver.

One morning to our surprise, we found the whole ground about our encampment covered with larvæ of a dark-green colour. Whence, or how, they came there was to us quite a mystery. We, at length, conjectured that at some previous period a swarm of locusts, in passing the place, had deposited their ova in the sand, and, now that the green grass began to spring up (which provided them with suitable food), their progeny emerged in the shape of worms.

At the same time many thousand storks appeared, and evidently much relished the rich and abundant repast.

Mr. Galton's successful remonstrances with Jonker had pacified the excited minds of our Damaras. It had inspired them with fresh confidence, and they no longer declined to accompany us. The worst of our Cape servants had been weeded out, and their places filled with useful and competent men. Our stud of draught-oxen, moreover, had been greatly increased, to say nothing of a large supply of live-stock. Matters thus once more looked bright and cheering; and we no longer hesitated to prosecute our journey. Nevertheless, before making the final arrangements, it was deemed advisable to know something of the country immediately in advance of us, and how far it was practicable for waggons. Galton having just returned from an excursion, it was thought only fair that I should undertake to ascertain this point.

Accordingly, I left Schmelen's Hope on the 24th of February, on ox-back, accompanied by Timbo, John St. Helena, and John Allen, perhaps, the three most trustworthy and useful of our servants; as also a few Damaras, who were to serve me as guides and herdsmen.

On the first night, after leaving Schmelen's Hope, we were visited by a terrific thunderstorm, accompanied by a deluge of rain which continued without intermission till four o'clock the next morning.

With my legs drawn up under my chin, and the caross well wrapped round my head, I spent this dreadful night seated on a stone, whilst the men, strange to tell, slept soundly at my feet in a deluge of water. The next day, however, was bright and warm. The earth steamed with the sweet odours of a tropical herbage, and the landscape looked so beautiful and smiling, that I felt my heart leap with joy and gratitude to the Giver of all good. The misery of the night was soon forgotten, and we proceeded cheerfully on our journey.

As we travelled on, we caught a glimpse of the beautiful cones of Omatako, which rise about two thousand feet above the level of the plain. I scarcely remember having ever been more struck or delighted with any particular feature in a landscape, than when these *two* 'Teneriffes' first broke upon my view.

"Then felt I like some watcher of the skies,
When a new planet swims into his ken."

We must have been fifty or sixty miles from these conical mountains; yet there they were as distinct as if we had stood at their base. The immense distance at which objects can be seen in these regions, in a clear atmosphere, is truly marvellous.

By reference to the map, it will be seen that we were now on a high table-land, about six thousand feet above the level of the sea. It is from this plateau that the principal rivers of Damara-land take their rise.

With the exception of a single kraal of impoverished Damaras, we found no inhabitants. On leaving Schmelen's Hope, we had been led to suppose that we should meet with several werfts of wealthy natives, from whom we might obtain, in barter, an unlimited number of cattle. We foolishly enough trusted to this chance, and started with only one day's provision. Game, it is true, we found very abundant; but the animals were very wild, and I was pressed for time, and could not give chase to them. One evening, I fired at a zebra—but, not distinguishing the peculiar sound of the ball when striking the animal (a power of ear acquired by much practice), I supposed I had missed it, and, therefore, did not follow its tracks. On passing, however, nearly by the same place next evening, we found that the animal had been killed, and, excepting the head and part of the neck, was devoured by vultures. The conical ball I used on the occasion, was found loose in the inside of the skeleton. Notwithstanding the defiled state of what was left of the carcase, we hailed it as a perfect god-send. For the two previous days we had been living on zebra-flesh, in a state of decay, which our Damaras had accidentally picked up. Indeed, our guides had absconded from want of food.

One evening, when very much fatigued from the day's march, and suffering cruelly from thirst, our native servants, by way of consolation, entertained us with the following interesting account of their countrymen.

"The Damaras," they said, "are now watching us from a distance; and, as soon as we shall have gone to sleep, they will suddenly fall upon us, and assegai us."

Timbo, John St. Helena, and John Allen, evidently believed them, and looked wretchedly uncomfortable. As for myself—though there certainly was nothing at all improbable in the story—I felt less apprehensive than annoyed, well knowing the bad effect it would have on the timid and superstitious minds of my men.

On the third day, about noon, we reached the northern side of Omatako, where we struck a small periodical river of the same name. To our dismay, however, we found it perfectly dry; and, as we had then already been twenty-four hours without a drop of water, I was afraid to proceed any further. Just as we were about to retrace our steps, the river, to our inexpressible delight, came down with a rush. To those of my readers who are not conversant with the mysteries of a tropical climate, it may appear almost impossible that a dry water-course should in the space of five minutes, and without any previous indication, be converted into a foaming torrent; yet, in the rainy season, this is almost an every-day occurrence. Not a cloud obscured the transparent atmosphere at the time; but, on the preceding night, there had been vivid lightning and heavy thunder in the direction of the source of the river, which sufficiently accounted for the phenomenon.

On this river I saw, for the first time, the gigantic footprints of elephants. The natives told me that these animals come here in great numbers in the winter-time, and, when the water begins to diminish, they return slowly northwards. Hans assured me that their tracks are still to be seen as far south as the river Swakop, close to its embouchure.

From this point we had a very good prospect of the country. Several interesting mountains presented themselves to the view. To the north, the Konyati, Eshuameno, Ia Kabaka, and Omuvereoom, stood out in bold relief. Some of these were similar to that of Erongo, and, like it, inhabited by Hill-Damaras, as also a few Bushmen.

I was particularly anxious to learn something of the country towards the north, in which direction—as before said—our route to Omanbondè lay; but it was in vain that I endeavoured to get anything like correct information from the natives, notwithstanding some had actually been living there. I was excessively annoyed, and imagined that their conflicting accounts were purposely invented to deceive and frighten me; but, as I became more intimate with the Damara character, I found that they lied more from habit than for the mere sake of lying. Indeed, a Damara would believe his own lies, however glaring and startling they might be. Thus, for instance, they informed me that the mountain Omuvereoom, which was distinctly visible, lay ten long days' journey off, and was inhabited by Hill-Damaras and Bushmen, whom they represented as perfect devils; moreover, that the intervening space was entirely destitute of water, and that any one attempting to traverse it would be sure to perish. At a subsequent period, we not only reached this mountain after fourteen hours' travelling, but found an abundance of water; and the natives, instead of being monsters, were the most timid and harmless of human beings.

This, however, is only one of the hundred instances that might be mentioned of the difficulty of eliciting truth from the Damaras. The missionaries had been living for several years at Barmen and Schmelen's Hope, before they were aware of the existence of either 'Buxton' or Okandu fountain; and yet these places were within a very short distance of the stations, and they had made repeated inquiries after springs.

With regard to the distance and situation of Omanbondè, the chief object of our journey, they could not say whether one or ten weeks would be required in order to reach it. One man told Galton that if he started at once for this place, and travelled as fast as he could, he would be an old man by the time he returned.[1]

Returning homewards, we pursued a somewhat different course. The first night, the men, for the sake of variety it is presumed, thought fit to encamp in the middle of an ant-hill! I was absent at the time, and, on returning, all the arrangements had been made for the night. Tired as we were, I could not well think of moving. The result may easily be imagined.

---

[1] This surpasses the graphic answer given to Björn Jernsida (the bear iron-side), a famous Swedish sea-king. When on his way to plunder Rome, he inquired of a wayfaring man what the distance might be. "Look at these shoes," said the traveller, holding up a pair of worn-out iron-shod sandals; "when I left the place you inquire for, they were new; judge then for yourself!"

The next day, in the more open parts of the country, we met with a very great abundance of a kind of sweet berry, about the size of peas, which afforded us a delicious feast.

Early in the morning of the sixth day we found ourselves back at Schmelen's Hope, having been sixty hours on the move, or, at an average, twelve hours daily. Allowing three miles per hour at the lowest estimation, we had gone over a tract of country fully one hundred and eighty miles in extent, the greater part of which, moreover, had been performed on foot. Under ordinary circumstances, we should, perhaps, have thought nothing of the performance; but, what with bad living, previous long rest, and so forth, we were in poor condition for such sudden and severe exertions. Indeed, before we were at the journey's end, both man and beast were completely knocked up.

The object, however, had been gained. We had ascertained that the country, for several days' journey, was tolerably open and traversable for waggons; that grass abounded; and that (the most important point of all) we should be sure of water for ourselves and cattle.

No time was now lost in making ready for a final start. An American, who had long been in Mr. Hahn's service, was about to travel to the Cape by land. Although the journey was supposed to last at least six or seven months, communication was so rare in these parts that we deemed it advisable to benefit by it. Letters were accordingly written to friends and acquaintances, as also despatches for the British Government at the Cape.

CHAPTER XIII.

DEPART FROM SCHMELEN'S HOPE—MEETING WITH KAHICHENÈ—OXEN STOLEN — SUMMARY JUSTICE — SUPERSTITION — MEETING AN OLD FRIEND—SINGULAR CUSTOM—GLUTTONY OF THE DAMARAS—HOW THEY EAT FLESH BY THE YARD AND NOT BY THE POUND—SUPERSTITIOUS CUSTOM—A NONDESCRIPT ANIMAL—THE AUTHOR LOSES HIS WAY—RAVAGES OF THE TERMITES—'WAIT A BIT, IF YOU PLEASE'—MAGNIFICENT FOUNTAIN—REMAINS OF DAMARA VILLAGES —HORRORS OF WAR—MEET BUSHMEN—MEET DAMARAS—DIFFICULTIES ENCOUNTERED BY AFRICAN TRAVELLERS — REACH THE LAKE OMANBONDÈ—CRUEL DISAPPOINTMENT.

ON the morning of the 3rd of March, we left Schmelen's Hope. The alternately rugged and sandy nature of the soil, the embarrassing thorn-coppices, and the stubbornness and viciousness of the oxen, rendered our progress at first very slow and tedious.

On the fifth day, we arrived at a splendid vley, called Kotjiamkombè. From the branches of the trees and bushes which lined the sides of this piece of water, were suspended innumerable graceful and fanciful nests of the well-known weaver-bird species. The rank grasses and reeds afforded shelter to a great variety of water-fowl, some of which were gorgeously plumaged. Here we found Kahichenè waiting to receive us; he had already announced his intention to visit us, and, in order to propitiate our favour, had, a few days previously, forwarded us a present of several head of cattle. The chief was accompanied by about forty of his people, who, taking them as a whole, were the finest body of men I have ever seen before or since. Yet they were *all* arrant knaves. Kahichenè told them as much in our presence; but, strange to say, they were not in the least abashed.

This tribe had, at one time, been the richest, the most numerous, and the most powerful in the country; but what with their own civil broils, and the exterminating wars with the Namaquas, they had gradually dwindled to about twenty-five villages, with, perhaps, ten or fifteen thousand head of horned-cattle.[1]

Notwithstanding Kahichenè, in former days, had committed many depredations against his neighbours, we could not help liking him. In a very short time, he had thoroughly ingratiated himself in our favour. Indeed, he was the only Damara, whether high or low, for whom we entertained any regard. Perhaps, also, his late misfortunes had ensured our sympathy. With the missionaries, Kahichenè had always been a very great favourite, and they looked upon him as the stepping-stone to the future civilization of Damaraland; but we have already seen how far this was realized.

Kahichenè was somewhat advanced in years; but his deportment was dignified and courteous. He was, moreover, truthful and courageous—rare virtues amongst his countrymen. It would have been well had the rest of the nation at all resembled this chief.

---

[1] Previously to my leaving Africa, I learnt that the entire tribe had been broken up.

Kahichenè was, at this period, at variance with a very warlike and powerful tribe of Damaras, under the rule of Omugundè, or rather his son, whom he represented as a man degraded by every vice, and particularly inimical towards strangers. We, of course, made due allowances, as our friend was speaking of his mortal enemy; but the account so terrified our men, that three of them begged to be dismissed, and they could only be persuaded to discontinue their solicitation by our promising them not to pass through the territory of the hostile chief.

On one occasion, some cattle, belonging to Mr. Hahn, had been stolen by a party of Omugundè's men. Remonstrances being made, they were, after a time, returned, but minus their tails, which were cut off by the natives, and kept by them as 'trophies.'

In conflict with Omugundè, several of Kahichenè's children had been killed, and one or two had unfortunately fallen alive into the hands of the enemy. These were kept as prisoners. Only one stripling was now left to solace Kahichenè in his old age. He informed us that he had made up his mind to try to recover his offspring and his property, or to die in the attempt. At first, he appeared anxious for our assistance; but, on mature consideration, he generously refused any interference on our part in his behalf. "For," said he, "when once the war begins, there is no saying when or where it will end. The whole country will be in an uproar; much blood will be shed; and it would involve you in endless difficulties and dangers." He, moreover, strongly endeavoured to persuade us from proceeding northwards at all; but, in that matter, he, of course, failed.

We had only been a short time at Kochiamkombè, when it was discovered that four of our best draught-oxen were stolen by some stranger Damaras. On being informed of this theft, Kahichenè became exceedingly annoyed, and even distressed, as he considered us under his special protection. He immediately dispatched men on their tracks, with strict orders to recover the oxen, and, if possible, to bring back the thieves. They succeeded in re-capturing all the beasts but one, which the natives had slain and eaten. With regard to the fate of the rogues, we could never ascertain anything with certainty. We were, however, strongly inclined to think they were all killed — the more so, as Kahichenè himself told us, that in case of their capture, they ought to be punished with death, and coolly suggested hanging as the most eligible way of ridding the world of such scoundrels. We, of course, took the liberty to remonstrate with the chief upon the severity of this measure; but with little or no effect. Indeed, one man was accidentally found, at a distance from our camp, in a horribly mangled state; and, on being brought to us, he stated, that he himself, together with several of his friends, were driving away the cattle, when they were overtaken by Kahichenè's men, who immediately attacked them with their kieries, and only left them when they thought life was extinct. He had, however, partially recovered; but was completely naked, having, as is usual on similar occasions, been stripped of every article of dress. The exterior of his body was nearly covered with blood. The head was almost double its natural size; indeed, it resembled rather a lump of mashed flesh; no particular feature could be distinguished, and his eyes were effectually hidden from view. The sight altogether was hideous.

Instead of proceeding due north, as was originally proposed, it was found necessary, in order to avoid Omugundè, to make a considerable *détour* to the westward. As Kahichenè with his tribe, was encamped in that direction, he invited us to take his werft by the way, to which we cordially assented. On the day of our departure from Kotjiamkombè, the chief led the way. A branch of a particular kind of wood (having a small, red, bitter berry, not unlike that of the mountain-ash) was trailed before him—a superstitious act thought to be essential in ensuring success during the pending attack against his mortal enemy.

Before reaching the chief's kraal, we passed the foot of a very conspicuous mountain, called Ombotodthu. This elevation is remarkable for its peculiar red stone, which is eagerly sought after by the natives. Having reduced it to powder they mix it with fat, when it is used as an ointment. I was at first struck by its great resemblance to quicksilver ore, and was led to believe that we had really discovered a mine of that valuable mineral. However, on considering the harmless effect it had on the natives, and that, had it been quicksilver, its use would have produced an opposite result, I came to the conclusion that it was simply oxide of iron, which has since been confirmed by analyzation.

On arriving at Kahichenè's werft, we were well received by our host and his tribe, from whom we obtained by barter a few head of cattle. Indeed, we might here have sold all our articles of exchange to great advantage; but this was not thought advisable, as in case of the cattle being lost or stolen, we should have been in a state of complete destitution. Could we, however, have foreseen the future, our tactics would have been different; for, as it afterwards turned out, this was almost the last opportunity we had of providing ourselves with live-stock.

By a strange chance, I accidentally became the owner of a percussion rifle, which had at one time belonged to Hans, but who, years previously, had disposed of it to a Damara. The latter, however, finding that he could not obtain a regular supply of caps, offered to exchange it for a common flint-lock musket. The rifle was a very indifferent and clumsy-looking concern, and had, if I remember rightly, been manufactured by Powell, of London. In justice to the maker, however, I must confess that a man could not possibly wish for a better. Whilst in my possession, many hundred head of large game, to say nothing of a host of bustards, geese, ducks, guinea-fowl, &c., fell to this piece.

Game was abundant in the neighbourhood of Kahichene's kraal, and Hans made several successful shots. Very little, however, of what was killed reached us; for the portion not immediately appropriated by the Damaras, ultimately found its way to them through the medium of our native servants. In Damara-land, the carcases of all animals—whether wild or domesticated—are considered public property; therefore, unless the natives should share their allowances with every stranger that might choose to intrude himself into their company, a withering 'curse' was supposed to befall them. I have seen the flesh of four zebras, that had been shot by our party, brought to the camp, in a single day, and the next morning we could not obtain a steak for our breakfast.

The Damaras are the most voracious and improvident creatures in the world. When they have flesh, they gorge upon it night and day, and in the most disgusting manner, until not a particle is left; and as a consequence, they not unfrequently starve for several days together. But, they are so accustomed to this mode of living, that it has no injurious effect on them.

In this hot climate, unless preventives of some kind were adopted, flesh would, of course, soon become tainted; and as salt, from the difficulty of conveyance, is exceedingly scarce in Damara-land, the following expedient is adopted. As soon as the animal is killed, lumps are indiscriminately cut from the carcase; a knife is plunged into an edge of one of these lumps, and passed round in a spiral manner, till it arrives at the middle, when a string of meat, often ten to twenty feet long, is produced, which is then suspended like festoons, to the branches of the surrounding trees. By cutting the flesh very thin, it soon dries, and may in that state be carried about any length of time. There is considerable waste in this process, as fully one third of the meat thus jerked is lost. On such occasions, the natives take care not to forget their own stomachs. Besides large pots filled with the most delicate morsels, immense coils may be seen frizzling on the coals, in every direction. When half-roasted, they seize one end with their hands, and, applying it to their mouth, they tug away voraciously, not being over particular as to mastication. In this way they soon manage to get through a yard or two, the place of pepper and salt being supplied by ashes attached to the flesh, which ashes are moreover found to be an excellent remedy against bad digestion.

I frequently observed the daughter of Kahichenè's favourite wife sprinkling water over the large oxen as they returned to the werft about noon to quench their thirst. On such occasions she made use of a small branch of some kind of berry-tree, such as that which Kahichenè caused to be trailed after him when wishing to be successful in his attack on Omugundè. In this instance (as they somewhat poetically expressed themselves) the aspersion was supposed, should the cattle be stolen, to have the power of scattering them like drops of water, in order to confuse their pursuers, and to facilitate their return to the owners.

On the 18th of March we were again *en route*. It was with regret that we parted with our friendly and hospitable host. Poor Kahichenè we were doomed never to meet again! A few months after our departure he made an attack on Omugundè; but at the very commencement of the fight, and when everything promised success, his dastardly followers (as he always had predicted) left him. But too proud himself to fly, he fell, mortally wounded, pierced with a shower of arrows.

Being in advance of the waggons, I suddenly came upon an animal, which, though considerably smaller, much resembled a lion in appearance. Under ordinary circumstances, I should certainly have taken it for a young lion; but I had been formerly given to understand that in this part of Africa there exists a quadruped which, in regard to shape and colour, is like the lion, but, in most other respects, totally distinct from it. The beast in question is said to be nocturnal in its habits, to be timid and harmless, and to prey for the most part on the small species of antelopes. In the native language it is called Onguirira, and would, as far as I could see, have answered the description of a puma. As it was going straight away from me, I did not think it prudent to fire.

Immense quantities of game were now observed; but the country was open, and ill-adapted for stalking; and, having no horses, it was difficult to get within range. A few springboks, however, were killed. I also shot a hartebeest; but, having been obliged to leave it for about an hour, I found, on my return, that it had been entirely devoured by vultures; but as they could not manage to eat the bones, our men consoled themselves by sucking them. The flesh of the hartebeest is considered extremely palatable.

The next day we rounded the cones of Omatako; but, to my great astonishment, the river of that name, although running breast high on my visit to it about a fortnight previously, was now perfectly dry. Fortunately, a pool still remained on its left bank.

The estimate of the Damaras as to the distance between the mountains Omatako and Omuvereoom, of which mention was recently made, was now reduced from ten to three long days' journey. These men still said that the intervening country was destitute of water. We dared no longer trust to their conflicting and unsatisfactory accounts; but, in order to enable us to judge, in a measure, for ourselves, Galton rode to the neighbouring mountain, Eshuameno, whence, from its advanced and isolated position, a good view of the country was likely to be obtained. After the absence of a day and a night, he returned with favourable news. By means of a rough triangulation, he had ascertained that Omuvereoom could not possibly be distant above twelve or fourteen hours' travelling. To the north and west of Omuvereoom, the country appeared as one unbounded plain, only covered by brushwood. Eastward, grass and trees were abundant. This, together with a timely fall of rain, at once determined us to make the attempt.

On the morning of our departure, a bitterly cold wind swept over the dreary wastes, and suddenly reminded us of the approach of the winter season. Hitherto, a shirt and a pair of trousers had been enough to protect our bodies; but this day an addition of thick flannel and a warm pea-jacket were found to be insufficient.

One evening, as Hans and myself were giving chase to a troop of giraffes, we were overtaken by darkness, and, in the heat of pursuit, had completely lost our way. Hans being the most experienced of the two, I blindly abandoned myself to his instinct and guidance. After a while, however, it struck me we were actually retracing our steps to Omatako, and I told him so; but he only laughed at my apprehensions. Still, the more I considered the matter, the more I became convinced that we were pursuing a wrong course. In order, therefore, to split the difference, I proposed to Hans that if in about an hour he did not find any indications of our whereabouts, he should permit me to act as 'pilot' for the same space of time; and that if I were equally unsuccessful as himself we should quietly wait for the return of daylight. Hans was sceptical, and, shaking his head, grudgingly gave his consent. His hour having elapsed without gaining the object of our search, I wheeled right round to his great disapproval, and walked as hard as I could in an exactly opposite direction. Singularly enough, only two or three minutes were wanting in completing my hour, when I was suddenly and agreeably surprised to find my foot in the deep track made by the wheels of the waggons. Nothing could have been more fortunate, for I struck it precisely at a right angle. Another half an hour's walk brought us safe back to our bivouac, where, over a substantial dinner, we joked Hans on his singular obstinacy. His pride as a skilful woodsman had received a severe blow; and he would, at intervals, shrug his shoulder and repeat broken sentences of "Well, I am sure! It's too bad!" and so forth.

The day after this little adventure, we continued our journey; and, in the afternoon, found ourselves safe at the foot of the southern extremity of Omuvereoom, and its sister hill, Ia Kabaka, from which it is only separated by a narrow valley. We 'outspanned' at a small vley, where, for the first time, I observed the willow tree—an agreeable reminiscence of my native land. The water, however, was of the most abominable quality, being apparently much frequented by wild animals, who had converted the pool into something like what we see in a farm-yard.

At this place we had a striking instance of the fearful ravages which termites are capable of committing in an incredibly short time. In the early part of the day, after our arrival, Mr. Galton and Hans started, on foot, with the intention of ascending Omuvereoom. In consequence of a sudden and distressing pain in my side, I was unable to accompany them, and, in the hope of obtainining a little ease, made a sort of extempore couch on the ground, covering it with a plaid. On rising after a while, I discovered, to my dismay and astonishment, that my bedding, had been completely cut to pieces by the destructive insects; and yet, when I first laid down, not one was visible.

Early the next morning, we pushed on to a large vley, upwards of a mile in length, the finest sheet of standing water we had yet seen in Damara-land. It was swarming with geese and ducks. The vegetation had a very tropical appearance; several—to us—new trees and plants, without thorns, presented themselves, and we began to flatter ourselves that we had at last passed the boundary-line of those thorny woods, which had so long and pertinaciously harassed us. In this, however, we were disappointed. The very next day we entered a region far worse than any we had yet seen, which, indeed, bade fair to stop us altogether. Our poor cattle were cruelly lacerated, and it was with the utmost difficulty we succeeded in getting the waggons through. I counted no less than seven distinct species of thorny trees and bushes, each of which was a perfect 'Wacht-een-bigte,' or 'Wait a little,' as the Dutch colonists very properly call these tormentors. Few individuals have ever travelled in the more northerly parts of Southern Africa, without being greeted with a friendly salutation of 'Stop a little, if you please;' and fewer still, who have disregarded this gentle hint, ever came away without first paying a forfeit of some part or other of their dress. Indeed, the fish-hook principle on which most of the thorns are shaped, and the strength of each, make them most formidable enemies. At an average, each prickle will sustain a weight of seven pounds. Now, if the reader will be pleased to conceive a few scores of these to lay hold of a man at once, I think it will not be difficult to imagine the consequences. Indeed, on our return to Barmen, after a few months' absence I possessed hardly a decent article of clothing; and had not Mr. Hahn kindly taken pity on my forlorn condition, I am afraid there would soon have been little difference between me and the savages.

In the course of the day, we arrived at a magnificent fountain, called Otjironjuba—the Calabash—on the side of Omuvereoom. Its source was situated fully two hundred feet above the base of the mountain, and took its rise from different spots; but, soon uniting, the stream danced merrily down the cliffs. These cascades, falling to the plain below, flowed over a bed of red gravel. A gigantic fig-tree had entwined its roots round the scattered blocks of stone by the side of Otjironjuba fountain, its wide and shady branches affording a delicious retreat during the heat of the noon-day sun. It bore an abundance of fruit; but it was not yet the season for figs. Several half-ripe ones that I opened contained a large quantity of small ants, and even wasps. Great caution, therefore, is necessary in eating them.

Otjironjuba was, to us, a perfect paradise. We enjoyed it the more on account of the marked contrast it presented to the country we had previously traversed.

At the foot of the mountain, we discovered the remains of a large Hill-Damara kraal. A considerable extent of land had at one time been carefully cultivated, and a few young calabashes and pumpkins were still seen springing up from the parent stock of the preceding season. The day after our arrival one or two natives came to visit us, and no doubt, also, for the purpose of ascertaining who and what we were. We, of course, entertained them well; and, at parting, gave them a few trifling presents, with a request that they would soon return with the remainder of their tribe, in order that we might buy from them some goats, which, from the surrounding evidences, they must have possessed in great numbers. The fresh tracks of a few horned cattle were also to be seen. However, our friends never came back, nor did we encounter any more of the natives.

Whilst sauntering about the place, we stumbled upon several deserted Damara villages; and our native servants now told us that, after the late attack on Schmelen's Hope by Jonker, Kahichenè and his tribe had fled with the remainder of their cattle to this secluded spot; and yet, a short time previously, they had positively asserted that the country was impassable for man and beast! They, moreover, informed us that several bloody fights, or rather massacres, had at that time taken place between the contending parties; and that whenever a man, woman, or child was met, and the deed could be perpetrated with impunity, they were cruelly murdered. These sanguinary outrages were sometimes inflicted, they said, by the Damaras, and at others by the Hill-Damaras.

I climbed to the top of the Omuvereoom, whence I had a very extensive view of the country to the eastward; but, excepting a few periodical water-courses which originated in the sides of the mountain, nothing but an immense unbroken bush was to be seen. It was in vain that I strained my eyes to catch a glimpse of Omanbondè, which we were told lay only about five days' journey hence, and at the northern extremity of Omuvereoom.

Elephants occasionally visited this neighbourhood, and even breed near a fountain somewhat farther to the northward.

After having spent a couple of days very pleasantly at Otjironjuba fountain, we for a short time followed the course of the rivulet which has its rise there; but it was soon lost in a marsh.

On the second day of our departure, we came, unobserved, upon a few Bushmen, engaged in digging for wild roots, and succeeded in capturing a man and woman, whom, with some difficulty, we persuaded to show us the water. The dialect of these people was so different to any we had yet heard, that, notwithstanding our two excellent interpreters, we could with difficulty understand them. However, by a good deal of cross-questioning we managed to make out, that they had both been to Omanbondè, which they called Saresab; that the "water was as large as the sky," and that hippopotami existed there. The man, moreover, said, that he would conduct us to the lake; but this was only a *ruse*, for, in the course of the night, both he and his wife absconded.

Our doubts and anxiety increased as we approached nearer and nearer the inland sea, and all our thoughts were concentrated in the single idea of the lake. The Bushman's story of the water being "as large as the sky," wrought greatly on our expectation.

"Well, Andersson, what should you suppose this lake's greatest length to be, eh?" said Galton. "Surely it cannot cover less than fifteen miles anyhow; and as for its breadth, it is no doubt, very considerable, for the Hottentots declare, that if you look at a man from the opposite shore, he appears no bigger than a crow."

It would have been well for us had we been less sanguine.

As we journeyed on a course somewhat parallel with Omuvereoom, we fell in with a sort of vley river—if river it could be called, since it consisted alternately of dry, open spaces and deep gullies. Both banks of this peculiar watercourse were hemmed in by one vast thorn-jungle, which seemed to defy the passage of man or beast. It was doubly fortunate, therefore, that we met this river, as its sides served as a good and open road, while a plentiful supply of water was afforded by the occasional pools. It was here, at last, that we arrived at some Damara villages, on the fifth day after leaving Otjironjuba. At first, the natives tried to run away ; but we captured a few women, which soon induced the men to return. These people had never before seen a white man ; and our sudden appearance, therefore, created no small astonishment, not to say consternation. But of all our property, nothing amused them more than the sight of a looking-glass. On finding that the mirror faithfully reflected the smallest of their motions or gesticulations, they became convulsed with laughter; and some of them were so excited, as to throw themselves on the ground, pressing their hands against their stomachs. Others would approach with their faces to the glass, as close as they could, then suddenly turn it round, fully expecting somebody at its back. It is a great pity that the Damaras are such unmitigated scoundrels, for they are full of fun and merriment. Give them a "yard of meat," and a bucket of water, and they are the happiest creatures on the face of the earth.

After some parleying, a man agreed to guide us to the lake. An afternoon's farther travelling brought us to a second werft, the captain of which was the jolliest and the most amusing Damara that we ever saw before or since. He mimicked the figure and the actions of the hippopotamus so admirably, that we should never have mistaken the animal, even had we not known a word of the language. He also gave us an amusing and laughable account of the people to the north.

One day more, and the goal of our hopes and anxieties would be realized! We carefully examined our mackintosh punt to see that it was sound, as we fully purposed to spend a few weeks on the shores of Omanbondè, in order to enjoy some fishing and shooting.

By this time, we had lost sight of Omuvereoom, which gradually dwindled into a mere sand-ridge, and was now identified with the plain. The vley river, just mentioned, which had so long befriended us, we also left behind, and were now travelling across a very sandy tract of country. Fortunately, though the bushes were very thick, only a few were thorny. Moreover, their wood, which was quite new to us, was of so brittle a nature that, although trees from five to six inches in diameter repeatedly obstructed our path, our ponderous vehicles crushed them to the ground like so many rotten sticks. An European can form no conception of the impracticable country one has to travel over in these parts, and the immense difficulties that must be surmounted. To give a faint idea of the obstructions of this kind of travelling, we will suppose a person suddenly placed at the entrance of a primeval forest of unknown extent, never trodden by the foot of man, the haunt of savage beasts, and with soil as yielding as that of an English sand-down; to this must be added a couple of ponderous vehicles, as large as the coal-vans met with in the streets of London, only a great deal stouter—to each of which are yoked sixteen or twenty refractory, half-trained oxen. Let him then be told—" Through yonder wood lies your road; nothing is known of it. Make your way as well as you can; but, remember, your cattle will perish, if they do not get water in the course of two or three days."

No greater calamity could possibly befall us, than the breaking of an axletree at a distance from water. Therefore, every time the waggons struck against a tree, or when the wheels mounted on a stone, several feet in height—from which they descended with a crash like thunder—I would pull up abruptly, and hold my breath till all danger was over, when a weight, like that of the nightmare, fell from my mind. However, in the course of time, we became tolerably accustomed to the hazards that beset us, and looked almost with indifference on the dangers which constantly threatened destruction to our conveyances.

About noon on the 5th of April, we were rapidly approaching Omanbondè; but, oh, how were we disappointed! My heart beat violently with excitement. The sleepy motion of the oxen, as they toiled through the heavy sand, being far too slow for my eagerness and excited imagination, I proceeded considerably in advance of the waggons, with about half-a-dozen Damaras, when all at once the country became open, and I found myself on some rising ground, gently sloping towards the bed of what I thought to be a dry watercourse.

"There!" suddenly exclaimed one of the natives—"there is Omanbondè!"

"Omanbondè!" I echoed, almost in despair; "but where, in the name of heaven, is the water?"

I could say no more, for my heart failed me, and I sat down till the waggons came up; when, pointing to the dry river-bed, I told Galton that he saw *the* Lake before him.

"Nonsense!" he replied; "it is only the end or tail of it which you see there."

After having descended into the bed, we continued to travel, at a rapid pace, about a mile in a westerly direction, when, at a bend, we discovered a large patch of green reeds. At this sight, a momentary ray of hope brightened up every countenance; but the next instant it vanished, for we found that the natives were actually searching for *water* amongst the rushes!

The truth at last dawned upon us. We were indeed at Omanbondè—the lake of hippopotami! We all felt utter prostration of heart. For a long while we were unable to give utterance to our feelings. We first looked at the reeds before us, then at each other in mute dismay and astonishment. A dried-up vley, very little more than a mile in extent, and a patch of reeds, was the only reward for months of toil and anxiety!

CHAPTER XIV.

OMANBONDÈ VISITED BY HIPPOPOTAMI—VEGETATION, ETC., DESCRIBED—GAME SOMEWHAT SCARCE—COMBAT BETWEEN ELEPHANT AND RHINOCEROS—ADVANCE OR RETREAT—FAVOURABLE REPORTS OF THE OVAMBO-LAND—RESOLVE TO PROCEED THERE—RECONNOITRE THE COUNTRY—DEPART FROM OMANBONDÈ—AUTHOR SHOOTS A GIRAFFE — SPLENDID MIRAGE—THE FAN-PALM — THE GUIDE ABSCONDS — COMMOTION AMONGST THE NATIVES—ARRIVE AT OKAMABUTÈ—UNSUCCESSFUL ELEPHANT HUNT—VEGETATION—ACCIDENT TO WAGGON —OBLIGED TO PROCEED ON OX-BACK—THE PARTY GO ASTRAY— BABOON FOUNTAIN—MEETING WITH THE OVAMBO; THEIR PERSONAL APPEARANCE, ETC. — RETURN TO ENCAMPMENT — AN ELEPHANT KILLED—DISCOVER A CURIOUS PLANT—IMMORALITY—REFLECTIONS.

Dry as the basin of Omanbondè then was, it, nevertheless, appeared evident that, at no distant period, it had contained a good deal of water. Moreover, there could be but little doubt as to hippopotami having also, at one time, existed there.

On becoming better acquainted with the geography of these regions, we thought we were able to explain the phenomenon satisfactorily. Thus, for instance, from (or to?) the deep trough-shaped basin of Omanbondè leads a peculiar water-course, in an easterly direction, called Omuramba-[1]

---

[1] Omuramba, in the Damara language, signifies a water-course, in the bed of which both *grass* and *water* is to be had.

k'Omanbondè, consisting of a succession of immense gullies, very similar to Omanbondè itself. These (after being in a short time joined by the Omuramba-k'Omatako), we supposed to be connected with some large permanent water, abounding with hippopotami. In seasons when rains are plentiful, these troughs, or gullies, fill, and, no doubt, retain water from one rainy period to another, which enables the animals to travel at their ease to Omanbondè. Indeed, by similar omurambas they have found their way even as far south as Schmelen's Hope. According to Jonker Afrikaner's account, a hippopotamus had taken up its abode at this place, but was at last killed by a sudden inundation of the Swakop. The carcase was washed up at the mouth of the Tjobis, where he saw its remains.

On a first look at Damara-land, an inexperienced person would "as soon expect," as Mr. Galton says, "a hippopotamus to have travelled across the great Sahara, as from Omanbondè to Tjobis." The fact, however, is that this country, after heavy rains, differs as much from its normal state as a sea-beach, when dry and when at spring-tide.

Little or no rain had fallen this year at Omanbondè, and, consequently, it presented a very dreary and uninteresting appearance. In its bed, however, we discovered several wells, which, together with numerous remains of Damara villages, clearly indicated that the so-called lake was, at times, largely resorted to by the natives.

The vegetation remained precisely as hitherto; but the thorn coppices were, if possible, thicker and more harassing. The monotony of the scene was somewhat relieved by clumps of very fine kameel thorn-trees.

Game was rather scarce, yet I managed to bag a few red bucks (pallahs) and koodoos. Tracks of giraffes, rhinoceroses, and elephants were by no means uncommon; but I never had the good fortune to fall in with any of these animals.

Furious battles are said to take place occasionally between the two last-named; and though, of course, strength in the elephant is infinitely superior to the rhinoceros, the latter, on account of his swiftness and sudden movements, is by no means a despicable antagonist. Indeed, instances are known where they have perished together. At Omanbondè, we were told that a combat of this kind occurred not long before our arrival. A rhinoceros, having encountered an elephant, made a furious dash at him, striking his long sharp horn into the belly of his antagonist with such force as to be unable to extricate himself; and, in his fall, the elephant crushed his assailant to death.

In sauntering one day about the neighbourhood of Omanbondè, Galton suddenly found himself confronted by a lion, which seems greatly to have terrified him; and he candidly tells us that, being only armed with a small rifle, he would " much rather have viewed him at a telescopic distance."

As soon as we had somewhat recovered from our bitter disappointment, we began seriously to consider our situation, and to consult on our future plans. Once more we were without a definite object. Should we return, or push boldly forward? At one time my friend entertained thoughts of going no farther; in which case, though it was probable we might reach home in safety, it was very certain we should reap but little credit for what had been done. On the other hand, by continuing to travel northwards, we exposed ourselves to much risk and danger. From experience, we were aware that, to accomplish even a comparatively short distance, in our very slow mode of travelling, months would elapse. In that time, all the pools and vleys which now contained water would probably be dried up. This would be certain destruction to ourselves and cattle. Besides this, our men were disheartened, and wished to return. However, in that respect there would be less difficulty, as they were now nearly as much dependent on us as we on them; inasmuch as a broad tract of wild, inhospitable country separated us from the nearest point of civilization.

From Jonker Afrikaner, and various other sources of information, we had already learnt that, at a considerable distance to the north, there lived a nation called Ovambo, who had much intercourse with the Damaras, with whom they bartered cattle for iron-ware. They were a people, moreover, of agricultural habits, having permanent dwellings, and were reported to be industrious and strictly honest. The Damaras spoke in raptures of their hospitality and friendliness towards strangers; and represented them as a very numerous and powerful nation, ruled by a single chief or king, named Nangoro, who, to their notions, was a perfect giant in size. With regard to the distance to this country, they gave us the same wild, conflicting, and unsatisfactory accounts as those we received about the position of Omanbondè. A variety of circumstances at last induced us, let the consequence be whatever it might, to attempt to reach this interesting land.

As, however, no reliance could possibly be placed on the accounts of the natives with regard to water, character of the country, and so forth, it was deemed advisable, before moving from our present encampment, to make a short exploratory excursion, in order to see and judge for ourselves.

Mr. Galton, accompanied by a few of the men, therefore, rode northward, in order to ascertain if the route we purposed taking was traversable with waggons. On the evening of the third day he returned, being assured of its practicability. He had met with several native villages; and, though his reception there had by no means been very flattering, we determined to proceed without a moment's delay.

None of the Damaras whom we had brought with us from Barmen professed to know anything of the country we were about to explore. The guide, however, whom we had procured a short distance south of Omanbondè, said that he was well acquainted with it, and volunteered to show us the way to the Ovambo, provided his services should be rewarded with a cow-calf. Mr. Galton gladly agreed to his terms; but, unfortunately, as the event proved, paid him his wages in advance.

Early in the morning of the 12th of April, we bade farewell to the inhospitable *shores* of Omanbondè. For a few hours we kept parallel with the Omuramba, when we struck into a more easterly course.

During the day, we saw vast troops of cameleopards; and, just at night-fall, I had the good fortune to kill a fine, full-grown male, which was an acceptable addition to our larder. Before the carcase had time to cool, twenty or thirty men were busy in tearing it to pieces. As usual on such occasions, the Damaras dispensed with sleep, and devoted the night entirely to the enjoyment of the banquet.

The next morning, we witnessed a magnificent mirage. Lakes, forests, hills, &c., burst on the eye and disappeared in rapid succession.

Later in the day, we were gratified by the sight of a large number of palm-trees. This harbinger of a better land was an agreeable surprise, bringing an involuntary smile of satisfaction to every face. We were astonished at the cheerful and refreshing effect a very slight improvement in the landscape had on our spirits. In the distance, these palms seemed, to us, to form an extensive and compact wood; but, on nearer approach, we found the trees grew at long intervals from each other. They were very tall and graceful, each branch having the appearance of a beautiful fan; and when

FAN-PALM.[1]

gently waved by the wind, the effect produced was indescribably pleasing.

This species of palm is, I believe, new to science.[2] It produces fruit about the size of an apple, of a deep-brown

---

[1] The beautiful drawing from which the above woodcut is taken, was kindly placed at my disposal by my esteemed and accomplished friend, Major Garden. It represents the species of fan-palm, or vegetable ivory-palm, found about Natal, and seems in general appearance to correspond with the kind observed by ourselves. In size, however, it is very inferior; for, according to the Major's estimate, it does not much exceed fifteen feet in height, whilst the tree of the parts of which I am now speaking, not unfrequently attains to the altitude of from thirty to fifty feet, and even more.

[2] On his return to England, Mr. Galton presented the Kew Gardens with specimens of the fruit, but, I am told, that every effort to raise plants from it proved abortive.

colour, with a kernel as hard as a stone, and not unlike vegetable ivory. The fruit is said to have a bitter taste; but, farther north (where, as will be presently seen, we found the tree very plentiful), it was very palatable. On account of the great height, and straightness of the trunk, the fruit was very difficult of access. The story our guide told us previously to leaving Barmen, about a tree, the fruit of which was obtainable only by means of "knob-kieries thrown up at it," was now easily comprehended. But we experienced greater difficulty in realizing his other tales—such as the existence of a people who make trees their sole dwellings; whilst others were found without joints to their limbs, who, nevertheless, were able to indulge in the refined custom of feeding each other by means of their toes.

In the afternoon of this day, we reached a Damara village, which had already been visited by Mr. Galton, and camped near to it. Previously to our arrival here, our guide absconded, taking with him, besides the calf my friend had given him as payment, a horse-rug, which he had borrowed from Timbo.

The next morning, just as I was returning to the village from a successful hunt, I observed an unusual commotion amongst the natives, accompanied by the most terrific yelling, passionate vociferations, and brandishing of assegais. The cause of this uproar was at first thought to be an attack by the Bushmen on one of the cattle-posts of the Damaras. However, on investigating the matter more closely, we ascertained that the apprehensions of the Damaras arose from the arrival of some inhabitants of a neighbouring kraal, who had come forcibly to recover a flock of sheep, which the chief had taken possession of under the pretext of 'hunger.'

The news of our arrival had, by this time, spread far and wide; and the Damaras were flocking together from all parts to see the white strangers. Some of them promised to conduct us to their great chief, Tjopopa, who resided at a place called Okamabuti, which was on our way to the Ovambo.

In the course of our journey to Tjopopa, I learnt the history of the father of one of our visitors, who, it would appear, had been a thorough rogue. He professed great friendship towards the Ovambo, whom he allowed freely and peaceably to pass through his territory; but when, on one occasion, they were returning home with a numerous herd of cattle, obtained by barter, he fell suddenly upon them, and deprived them of all their hard-earned gains. When, however, his treacherous conduct became known to Nangoro, he instantly despatched a party in order to punish him, and this was done so effectually that, since that day, no one has ventured to molest the Ovambo in their peaceable and industrious vocation. Indeed, this tribe now commanded a large share of the good-will and respect of the Damaras.

Elephants were said to be numerous to the northward, and the Damaras pointed to some wooded knolls, where they said these animals walked "as thick as cattle." At times, they would suddenly make their appearance in the night in the midst of a village, and drive the inhabitants precipitately from their dwellings.

On the 15th of April, we were again moving; and the very next day we entirely lost sight of the palms, which we did not again see till nearly a whole month's travel had been accomplished.

On the 17th we reached Tjopopa's werft. It was reported that through the instrumentality of his friend, Nangoro, this man became a chief of the first order. Be that as it may, he was now living in very great abundance, though, like many who are well off with regard to worldly possessions, he was avaricious in the extreme. A miser's parsimony always increases in proportion to the enlargement of his property.

Okamabuti may be said to be the northern limit of Damara-land. It is situated at the foot of those wooded knolls, already pointed out to us by the natives as the resort of elephants; indeed, the ground round about bore ample testimony to the destructive propensities of these animals. The place was well supplied with water by a fountain, springing from a limestone bottom.

The morning after our arrival at Okamabuti, we started off on a shooting excursion, in a north-east direction, in search of elephants; but though we discovered their fresh tracks, and followed these for a whole day, we were unable to overtake the beasts. Notwithstanding our failure, we enjoyed the trip extremely. The scenery was novel and highly interesting. At times, we crossed savannahs, where the grass reached above our heads as we sat on the oxen; and, at others, we passed through magnificent forests of straight-stemmed and dark-foliaged timber trees,[1] fit abodes for the most wonderful creatures of animated nature.

A day or two afterwards, a calamity befell us, which we had long dreaded. In order to be near the elephants, that we might hunt them at our leisure, we had determined to move our camp to a fountain a few hours further to the north-east, that was much frequented by these animals. On the morning of our departure, however, before we had pro-

---

[1] These trees consisted chiefly of what in the Cape Colony is termed *Stink-hout*, or stink-wood. It derives its peculiar name from an offensive odour that it exhales, and which it retains until thoroughly seasoned. In the grain and the shading it somewhat resembles walnut, but in external appearance approaches the oak. Indeed, if I am not mistaken, botanists have described it as *quercus Africana*, in which case I believe it to be the only species of that kind known to be indigenous to the African continent. I am told it is by far the best wood in Southern Africa, and seems well adapted for various purposes, such as waggons, gun-stocks, ship-building, &c.

ceeded many hundred paces, our largest waggon came in contact with a stump of a tree, which entirely demolished the foremost axle-tree. Unfortunate as this circumstance could not fail to be, we had, nevertheless, every reason to feel thankful it occurred where it did. The natives, hereabout, had shown themselves well-disposed towards us. Water and pasturage were abundant; and even suitable wood for repairing the damage, was to be found in the immediate neighbourhood.

A few days would, perhaps, have sufficed to make a temporary repair; but, as we had a journey of several months' duration before us, it was necessary to make the work as permanent as possible, and the seasoning of the wood, alone, in such a case, would occupy several weeks. None of us had much experience in carpentry; but Hans was, by far, the most practical hand, and he boldly undertook the task. To postpone our journey to the Ovambo, till our waggons were in order, was now, indeed, out of the question. The season being advanced, every day became of the greatest importance; and therefore, to save time, it was resolved, that we should leave the vehicles behind; and that Galton and myself should prosecute the journey without further delay, by means of pack-and-ride oxen.

Having come to this determination, our first care was to obtain accurate information of the distance, number of watering-places, and so forth; but the Damaras proved true to their nature—for, after having spent several days in cross questioning them, we were just as far from our object as ever. Tjopopa, himself, was very reserved, and would neither provide us with guides, nor give us the least information. He said, however, that he was just expecting a trading caravan, from Ovambo-land; and that, if we remained with him, till its arrival, he doubted not that we should, by the assistance of the individuals composing it, be enabled to reach that country. But no reliance could be placed in a Damara.

Whilst in this dilemma, a man unexpectedly came to offer his services as guide. Without, perhaps, inquiring sufficiently as to whether he was well-acquainted with the road, we accepted with eagerness the proposal, and did not lose a moment in making preparations for the journey. To shorten a long story, suffice it to say, that we set out; but our *guide* almost immediately lost *himself*; and after we had wandered about the hills for several days, suffering the greatest anxiety of mind, to say nothing of physical privations, we were about to retrace our steps to Okamabuti, when we, fortunately, fell in with some bushmen. We had left both our Hottentot interpreters behind; but we managed to explain to them our wants and wishes. With much persuasion, two of them agreed to accompany us to a certain large water in advance, of which the Damaras had made repeated mention. These men desired to spend the night at their own werft, but we had been so often deceived, that in order to secure their services, we determined that only one of them should be allowed to absent himself. The other was to sleep near us; and, as a further security, Galton and myself agreed alternately to keep watch on the fellow through the night.

During our wanderings in the mountains, we stumbled upon a series of wells, which we christened 'Baboon Fountain,' on account of the number of baboons which frequented the place. Its real name was Otjikango.

It was from this point that on the morning of the 2nd of May we took our fresh departure under the guidance of our bushmen friends. We had not, however, been long on the road before we were overtaken by three or four men whom our Damaras at once recognized as natives of Ovambo-land, coming from the very quarter we had just left. They were part of the expected caravan, and I need hardly say that we were delighted at this opportune meeting. Contrary to custom, the men had made a short cut across the hills, and thus we had missed each other. On the Ovambos reaching our encampment, however, and finding strange tracks, and our bivouac-fire still burning, their curiosity was greatly aroused, and they had detached the men whom we now encountered in order to bring us back. We did not much like the idea; yet in hope of obtaining from them a guide, we acquiesced, intending presently to pursue our journey.

The caravan was composed of twenty-three individuals, of a very dark complexion, tall and robust, but remarkably ugly, and scantily attired. Their looks bespoke determination and independence. On acquainting them with our object, and our wish to obtain a guide to conduct us to their country, they not only refused, but became very reserved in their manner. They promised, however, that if we would return with them to Tjopopa's werft, and there wait until they had disposed of their articles of exchange, we were welcome to accompany them home. They assured us, moreover, that any attempt on our part to accomplish the journey alone would be attended with certain destruction; for, even supposing we should find the waters—which were few and far between — their chief, unless previously apprised of our approach, would never receive us. We thought their language bold, and at first laughed at them; but they remained inflexible. Remonstrances were of no avail, and we soon saw that they were a very different style of natives from those with whom we had been accustomed to deal. Moreover, on mature consideration, we thought it only just that they should know something of our character before taking us into the heart of their country. We accordingly made necessity a law, and agreed to their proposal. No sooner had we done so, than they threw off their reserve, and, in a very short time, we became the best of friends.

Mr. Galton made them a present of some meat, which they greatly prized. Their sole diet, on these occasions, was apparently a kind of grain resembling Caffre-corn (*holcus caffrorum*), which they carried in small skin-bags. This grain was either half-boiled, simply steeped in water, or, more commonly, partially crushed, and then converted into a coarse stir-about. They kindly gave us a liberal supply of their homely fare, which we eagerly partook of, being quite tired with the everlasting flesh diet. Our Damaras were also treated with a dish of soaked corn; but, before they were allowed to taste it, they were obliged to undergo the ceremony (why or wherefore I know not) of having a quantity of water spurted into their faces from the mouth of one of the Ovambo. These people invariably made use of salt with their food—a thing never seen amongst the Damaras. As soon as their plain meal was

PIPE.

finished, pipes—of their own manufacture—were produced, and, after a few whiffs, a song was struck up. One man began to chant, and the whole party joined occasionally in chorus. Though somewhat monotonous, the music was not unpleasing.

They were armed with the bow and arrows, the assegai and the knob-kierie; but the two first-named weapons were of smaller dimensions than those used by the Damaras. Their bows, moreover, were constructed from a kind of wood called mohama, which, in its natural state is flat on one side, and thus, in a degree, of the required form.

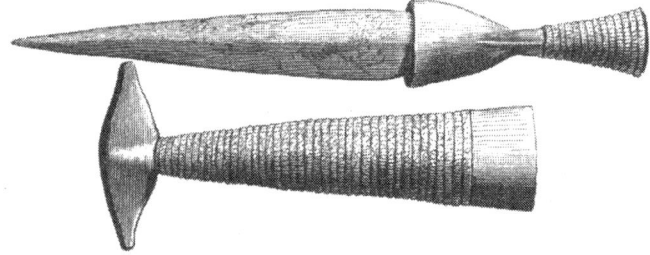

DAGGER AND SHEATH.

The arrows are generally tipped with bone or iron; but they do not often poison them. They carry their quivers under the left arm by means of a strap across the right shoulder. In addition to the weapons mentioned, they have a dagger, protected by a leather sheath tastefully ornamented with thin copper wire.

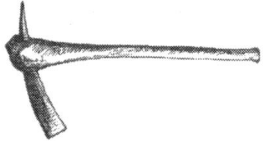

HATCHET.

Carpenter's work is not much practised among the Ovambo. The rude hatchet here represented, is nearly the only mechanic's tool I remember to have seen in their possession.

Their articles of barter were spear-heads, knives, rings, copper and iron beads, &c., but of exceedingly rude workmanship. Indeed, it was to me a constant wonder how they could persuade their neighbours to buy such trash. Yet *all* these things were very dear; an unfinished assegai-blade, or a yard of beads, being the regular price for an ox.

Their merchandize was packed in small square baskets

BASKET FOR MERCHANDIZE.

made out of palm-leaves: these were suspended to both ends of the long, smooth, and elastic pole (of palm wood) that each man bore poised on his shoulder. What with their merchandize, provisions, water, &c., the weight was often very considerable; yet they travelled much faster than ourselves.

They have no idea of making use of oxen for draught, or, perhaps, it would be more correct to say, they value these animals too highly to make use of them for such purposes.

On the 4th of May, we returned to our encampment. Hans and Phillippus had killed an elephant during our absence, which highly delighted the Damaras, who had flocked to the neighbourhood of Okamabuti in very great numbers. We were sorry to find that our cattle, instead of improving in condition by their rest, were fast losing flesh. This we attributed to the grass hereabout, which was bitter tasted, and to change of pasturage in general. The cattle of the natives were accustomed to every variety of herbage, and did not suffer. Sheep, however, failed to thrive here.

Whilst waiting for the return of the Ovambo traders, who, with the exception of their head man, Chikor'onkombè, had now dispersed over the neighbourhood in small bands of two and three, I employed the time in diligently exploring the surrounding country, and ascertaining its natural productions, and was fortunate enough to add many an interesting specimen of insect and bird to my collection.

The natives were unable to comprehend why I thus collected birds and other specimens of natural history; and on an evening, when I returned home, were convulsed with laughter on seeing the contents of my game-bag. This passion of mine (coupled with my name being unpronounceable) caused them to re-christen me 'Karabontera,' or the bird-killer, by which designation I am now universally known throughout the country.

The vegetation at Okamabuti was very rank and luxuriant; but the thorn-jungles still continued to haunt us. The hills were covered with a profusion of creepers, low shrubs, and aromatic herbs. The *euphorbia candelabrum* was particularly abundant.

I discovered a peculiar plant growing on a very large succulent root, protruding about a foot above the soil. It produced two or three immense leaves, with a fruit so closely resembling grapes, that, when I first brought some bunches to our encampment, they were mistaken for such; but they were not eatable—nay, the natives pronounced them to be poisonous.

There was also a tree, yielding an acid fruit, somewhat like an apple, but with a hard kernel similar to that of a plum. In hot weather, this fruit was very refreshing, and not unpalatable.

During our stay at Okamabuti, Tjopopa's aged mother died. The women of the place, according to custom, howled most dismally for a whole day. Great numbers of cattle were killed or sacrificed on this occasion.

Tjopopa would spend whole days at our camp in the most absolute idleness and apathy, teasing us with begging for everything he saw. Like all Damaras, he had a perfect mania for tobacco, and considered no degradation too deep provided he could obtain a few inches of the narcotic weed. He was of an easy and mild disposition, but excessively stingy. We stood greatly in need of live-stock, and took every opportunity to display our most tempting articles of barter in the hope of inducing him to purchase. Brass or gilt ornaments he almost spurned, but cast longing eyes on articles of iron or copper. At last he selected goods to the value of four oxen, with which he quietly walked off. On asking him for payment the following day, he smilingly replied, "Why, between us, there must be no talk of buying and selling. You are going to stop here a long time, and you will want plenty of food: this I will give you."

Knowing the truth of the adage, that 'a bird in the hand is worth two in the bush,' we should infinitely have preferred an immediate settlement to any vague promises. And the end justified our apprehensions. The old rogue took good care neither to pay his debt, nor make us any presents of cattle, of which we stood so much in need. Nay, he even went further. Under pretext of supplying our wants, he induced his people to contribute oxen and sheep, which he was mean enough to keep for his own use.

Our friend Tjopopa was rather a sensual man: he was supposed to have no less than twenty wives—two of whom, I found to my astonishment, were mother and daughter! I have since ascertained that this is by no means an unusual practice amongst this demoralized nation. Moreover, when a chief dies, his surviving wives are transferred to his brother, or to his nearest relation.

It is in vain that poets and philanthropists endeavour to persuade us that savage nations, who have had no previous intercourse with Europeans, are living in a state of the most enviable happiness and purity—where ignorance is virtuous simplicity—poverty, frugality and temperance—and indolence, laudable contempt for wealth. One single day among such people will be sufficient to repudiate these idle notions.

CHAPTER XV.

DEPART FROM OKAMABUTI—VISIT FROM A LION—AMULETS—RE-VISIT BABOON FOUNTAIN—OTJIKOTO ; A WONDERFUL FREAK OF NATURE ; REMARKABLE CAVERN—NATIVES UNACQUAINTED WITH THE ART OF SWIMMING — FISH ABUNDANT IN OTJIKOTO ; FREQUENTED BY IMMENSE FLOCKS OF DOVES — PANIC OF THE OVAMBO ON SEEING BIRDS SHOT ON THE WING — ARRIVE AT OMUTJAMATUNDA — A GREASY WELCOME — DUCKS AND GROUSE NUMEROUS — AUTHOR FINDS HIMSELF SOMEWHAT 'OVERDONE' — 'SALT-PANS' — ALL 'LOOK BLUE'— A SECOND PARADISE — HOSPITABLE RECEPTION—VEGETATION—PEOPLE LIVE IN PATRIARCHAL STYLE—POPULATION—ENORMOUS HOGS—ARRIVE AT THE RESIDENCE OF THE REDOUBTABLE NANGORO.

In conversation with the Ovambo, we learnt that Nangoro's werft was distant at least a fortnight's steady travel. We, therefore, felt anxious for the speedy return of the trading parties, in order that we might prosecute our journey; but they tarried longer than we had expected. By degrees, however, they re-assembled at Tjopopa's werft, having brought about two hundred head of cattle, the result of their trade.

On the 22nd of May, Chikor'onkombè, their leader, announced that everything was in readiness for a start; and, as we ourselves had long been prepared, the caravan set out that very afternoon.

We bivouacked at one of Tjopopa's cattle-posts, only a few hours' journey from Okamabuti, and had just finished dinner, when, all at once, our people rushed towards the fire with cries of "Ongeama!—ongeama!"

And so it was. A lion had, it seems, been crouched in the bush, within twenty paces of our camp, in readiness to spring on the cattle that were scattered about. But as one of the men, who was in search of fuel, had fortunately discovered him, the beast retreated. He was evidently much displeased at being thus foiled, and kept growling in the distance during the remainder of the night. The following morning, on meeting one of the Ovambo, I inquired whether they also had been troubled by the lion, to which he only replied by pointing to a piece of wood—a charm of some kind—hung round his neck, as much as to say :—"Do you think that anything can hurt us, or our cattle, with this in our possession?"

The Damaras have also great faith in amulets, consisting generally of the teeth of lions and hyænas, entrails of animals, pieces of certain kinds of wood, and so forth. Our native servants, indeed, before leaving Okamabuti, had purchased, for a few iron beads, several charms from Tjopopa's favourite wife, and, thus provided, conceived themselves proof against every danger and calamity.

On the 24th, we again found ourselves at Otjikango ("Baboon fountain"). By this time, our caravan was completed, as straggling parties of natives had continued to join us; and we found to our astonishment that, including ourselves, we mustered one hundred and seventy souls. Of this number were no less than seventy or eighty Damara women, bent on various speculations—some in hope of obtaining employment, some to get husbands, and others with a view of disposing of their shell-bodices, spoken of in chapter four. The latter, as we afterwards found, are taken to pieces by the Ovambo women, and worn in strings round the waist. In exchange, the Damaras receive beads, tobacco, corn, &c.

The country between Okamabuti and Otjikango we found well watered with copious springs, and covered with a rank vegetation. Otjikango, itself, being situated in a valley, between high and steep hills, was not unpicturesque. It was well supplied with water, which in several places oozed out of a kind of vley or marsh — in the rainy season, undoubtedly a little lake. We lost no time here; but

OTJIKOTO FOUNTAIN.

were again on the move, at an early hour on the succeeding morning.

After a day and a half travel, we suddenly found ourselves on the brink of Otjikoto, the most extraordinary chasm it was ever my fortune to see. It is scooped, so to say, out of the solid limestone rock; and, though on a thousand times larger scale, not unlike the *Elv-gryta*, one so commonly meets in Scandinavia. The form of Otjikoto is cylindrical; its diameter upwards of four hundred feet, and its depth, as we ascertained by the lead-line, two hundred and fifteen—that is at the sides, for we had no means of plumbing the middle, but had reason to believe the depth to be pretty uniform throughout. To about thirty feet of the brink, it is filled with water.[1]

Otjikoto, "one of the most wonderful of Nature's freaks," is situated at the northern extremity of those broken hills which take their rise in the neighbourhood of Okamabuti, and in the midst of a dense coppice. So effectually is it hidden from view, that a person might pass within fifty paces of it without being aware of its existence. Owing to its steep and rugged sides, cattle have not access to the water; and even a man can only approach this enormous well by means of a steep and slippery footpath. No perceptible difference could be observed in the height of the water; and the Ovambo informed us that, as long as they and their fathers remembered, it had always been the same. It is difficult to imagine how or whence Otjikoto receives its supplies. A spacious cavern, only visible and accessible from the water, may possibly be the grand reservoir.

After gratifying our curiosity, Galton and myself, standing in need of a bath, plunged head-foremost into the profound abyss. The natives were utterly astounded. Before reaching Otjikoto, they had told us, that if a man or beast was so unfortunate as to fall into the pool, he would inevitably perish.

[1] Shortly before reaching 'Baboon Fountain,' I should remark, that, at a place called Orujo, we saw a cavity of a similar kind, though on an infinitely smaller scale. It consisted of a circular-shaped basin in the limestone rock, ninety feet in diameter by thirty in depth. As it was dry at the time, we ascertained that the bottom was flat, or nearly so. In various other places we also met with similar basins, but on a still smaller scale than Orujo.

We attributed this to superstitious notions; but the mystery was now explained. The art of swimming was totally unknown in these regions. The water was very cold, and, from its great depth, the temperature is likely to be the same throughout the year.

We swam into the cavern to which allusion has just been made. The transparency of the water, which was of the deepest sea-green, was remarkable; and the effect produced in the watery mirror by the reflection of the crystallized walls and roof of the cavern, appeared very striking and beautiful. In this mysterious spot, two owls, and a great number of bats, had taken up their abode. On approaching some of the latter, which I saw clinging to the rocks, I found, to my surprise, that they were dead; and had probably been so for many years; at least, they had all the appearance of mummies.

Otjikoto contained an abundance of fish, somewhat resembling perch; but those we caught were not much larger than one's finger. One day we had several scores of these little creatures for dinner, and very palatable they proved.

In the morning and evening, Otjikoto was visited by an incredible number of doves, some of which were most delicately and beautifully marked. On such occasions the wood resounded with their cooing; but when disturbed, as they frequently were, by the invasion of a hawk, the noise caused by their precipitate flight was like that of a sudden rush of wind.

Many bushmen resided near Otjikoto; and, as everywhere else in these regions, they lived on excellent terms with the Ovambo, to whom they brought copper-ore for sale, which they obtained from the neighbouring hills. Indeed, as our acquaintance with the Ovambo increased, we were more and more favourably impressed with their character. They treated all men equally well, and even the so much-despised Hottentots ate out of the same dish, and smoked out of the same pipe, as themselves.

We only stayed a day at Otjikoto. The next morning, after a few hours' travel, we lost sight of all landmarks; and were now making our way through dense thorn-coppices, which harassed and delayed us exceedingly. To say nothing of tearing our clothes to rags, they, now and, then extracted some article from the saddle-bags. Of the regular Ovambo caravan-route, all traces had been obliterated; and we now first began to understand and appreciate the difficulties that would have beset us had we tried to prosecute the journey alone. Indeed, without the most experienced guides, it would have been an utterly hopeless task. The watering-places, moreover, were very few, and scattered over an immense extent of country, which was dreary in the extreme.

Shortly after leaving Otjikoto, and when walking in advance of the caravan, in company with several of the headmen of the Ovambo, in the hope of procuring some specimens of natural history, I suddenly flushed a brace of sand-grouse, both of which I brought to the ground. The effect produced on my companions was ludicrous in the extreme. They looked as if they had received an electric shock, and stood aghast with their mouths wide open. On requesting them to pick up the dead birds, they absolutely refused, and seemed petrified with fear. Their conduct was the more singular, as, on our first meeting, they had given us to understand that, through the Portuguese, with whom they had indirect intercourse, they were well-acquainted with firearms, but that they were not afraid of them, as, by simply blowing in the muzzle, they lost all power.

In the afternoon of the 29th of May we reached Omutjamatunda, the first cattle-post belonging to the Ovambo. On account of this being harvest-time, our friend, Chikor'onkombè, did not expect to find many of his countrymen here; but he was mistaken, for it swarmed with people as well as cattle. The latter I estimated at no less than from three to four thousand.

Immediately on our arrival, we were surrounded by great numbers of inquisitive people, who looked upon the European portion of our party as some *raræ avæ*. They appeared to be gratified at seeing their countrymen safe home again, and expressed much admiration at the fine herd of sleek cattle they had brought with them.

The way of welcoming friends amongst the Ovambo is somewhat singular. In our case, after every one was seated, an immense dish of fresh butter was produced, when the head man of the post besmeared the face and breast of each individual with an abundance of the unction. The ceremony being satisfactorily performed on their own friends and kinsmen, it became evident that they contemplated the same agreeable operation on ourselves. On seeing what was coming, Galton, held out both his hands, and exclaimed—"Oh! for goodness' sake, if the thing is necessary, be it at least moderate!" His request was granted—for he escaped with a brush or two across the face—but it created much jest and mirth amongst the company.

At Omutjamatunda, there is a most copious fountain, situated on some rising ground, and commanding a splendid prospect of the surrounding country. It was a refreshing sight to stand on the borders of the fountain, which was luxuriously over-grown with towering reeds, and sweep with the eye the extensive plain encircling the base of the hill; frequented as it was, not only by vast herds of domesticated cattle, but with the lively springbok and troops of striped zebras. If the monotony of our dreary wanderings had not thus occasionally been relieved, I do not know how we should have borne up against our constant trials and difficulties.

In order to ascertain the proficiency of the Ovambo in archery, we had shooting matches whilst at Omutjamatunda. The result proved that they were inferior in this respect even to the Damaras, who, as already said, are wretched marksmen. The poor despised bushmen beat both tribes out and out in the use of the bow, which, however, is to be expected, since they subsist, in a great measure, by the chase.

During the two days we remained at Omutjamatunda, we amused ourselves with shooting ducks, and birds of the grouse kind. Both were abundant, but more especially the latter, which literally obscured the air with their numbers every morning and evening, when they came to quench their thirst. It is, however, only in the dry season—as in the present instance—that they are observed in such astonishing multitudes. They usually go far in search of food; and, although a pair only may be seen at starting in quest of water, yet, as they draw nearer to the pool, they describe wide and continued circles over it; and thus, by giving time for others to arrive, increase their numbers.

There is a great variety amongst the grouse. Thus, for instance, in the course of a single morning, and in about half-a-dozen discharges, I have bagged grouse of five different species; and I have procured altogether eight or nine; but none of them are good eating. They chiefly live on hard, indigestible seeds, often of an oily substance, which gives to the meat a toughness and an unsavoury flavour. They are best when made into pies.

I have already mentioned that we had one morning been suddenly apprized of the approach of winter by an intensely bleak wind. Since then, the cold had gradually increased, and we suffered much in the night-time. Hitherto, the abundance of fuel we had found everywhere enabled us to keep up a roaring fire, which in some degree shielded us from the night air. At Omutjamatunda, however, dry wood was scarce, because the place was the permanent residence of a great number of natives; and, as a consequence, the cold was painfully disagreeable.

The morning before leaving Omutjamatunda a curious accident occurred to me. On lying down at night alongside a small fire, the air was quite calm; but, towards morning, a strong and cutting wind arose. To protect myself against the chilling blast, I was obliged to pull the blanket over my head, and was thus slumbering in happy ignorance of everything. After a time, an agreeable sensation of warmth and comfort stole over me, and the most exquisite visions floated before my imagination. By degrees, however, this pleasant feeling was converted into uneasiness, and ultimately into absolute pain. I was writhing in agonies. By a violent effort, I roused myself out of the trance, and, starting to my feet, discovered that the coverlet was ignited. A spark had fallen on it, and, being composed of quilted cotton, it had for a long time been slowly smouldering, which accounted for the agreeable feeling I had at first experienced. On the fire coming into contact with my body-linen, however, the lulling sensation was changed into one of torment. Hans had had a similar accident at Schmelen's Hope, on which occasion almost the whole of the skins, &c., spread beneath him, were consumed before he was aware of what had happened. From that day forward, as may be supposed, I always made my bed far away from the fire.

On the last day of May, we were again on the move. Messengers were started in advance to apprise *King* Nangoro of our approach, and to convey to him a few trifling presents. They would probably reach his capital in about two days.

In the course of the first day's journey, we traversed an immense hollow, called Etosha, covered with saline incrustations, and having wooded and well-defined borders. Such places are in Africa designated "salt-pans." The surface consisted of a soft, greenish-yellow, clay soil, strewed with fragments of small sand-stone, of a purple tint. Strange to relate, we had scarcely been ten minutes on this ground, when the lower extremities of ourselves and cattle became of the same purple colour. In some rainy seasons, the Ovambo informed us, the locality was flooded, and had all the appearance of a lake; but now it was quite dry, and the soil strongly impregnated with salt. Indeed, close in shore, this commodity was to be had of a very pure quality.

At night we bivouacked on the southern extremity of a boundless savannah, called Otjihako-tja-Muteya, totally destitute of trees, and even bushes. The natives were unable to give us an idea of its real extent; but, as far as we could learn, it reached to the sea, on the west. Like Etosha, it had distinct and wooded borders.

The second of June will ever be remembered by us. On the afternoon of that day, we first set eye on the beautiful and fertile plains of Ondonga—the country of the Ovambo. Vain would be any attempt to describe the sensations of delight and pleasure experienced by us, on that memorable occasion, or to give an idea of the enchanting panoramic scene that all at once opened on our view. Suffice it to say, that instead of the eternal jungles, where every moment we were in danger of being dragged out of our saddles by the merciless thorns, the landscape now presented an apparently boundless field of yellow corn, dotted with numerous peaceful homesteads, and bathed in the soft light of a declining tropical sun. Here and there, moreover, arose gigantic, wide-spreading, and dark-foliaged timber and fruit trees, whilst innumerable fan-like palms, either singly or in groups, completed the picture. To us it was a perfect elysium, and well rewarded us for every former toil and disappointment. My friend, who had travelled far and wide, confessed he had never seen anything that could be compared to it. Often since have I conjured up to my imagination this scene, and have thought it might not inaptly be compared to stepping out of a hot, white, and shadowless road, into a park, fresh with verdure, and cool with the umbrage cast down by groups of reverend trees.

The first dwelling that lay in our path was that of old Naitjo, one of the chief men of our trading caravan, who, after having feasted us on such fare as the country produced (amongst which was a dish of hot dough, steeped in melted butter), conducted us over his extensive establishment, comprising his harem, his children, granaries, and so forth. Timbo was in ecstasies with the country and its hospitable inhabitants, and declared that it was as like as two peas to his own native land.

Another hour's travel brought us to the residence of our guide, Chikor'onkombè, where we remained two nights and a day to rest our weary animals. Poor creatures! they had had no water for two entire days, and the consequence was that, during the first night, they broke out of the enclosures and strayed far away in search of it.

On the 4th, we again set forward. The aspect of the country was still characterized by the greatest abundance, and the trees became even more numerous.

Nearly all produced edible fruit, though some were not yet ripe. The trees, moreover, were on a grander scale than heretofore. One kind in particular—that mentioned as bearing a fruit somewhat resembling an apple—attained to a most astonishing size. Indeed, the branches of one that we measured, spread over a space of ground one hundred and forty-four feet in diameter, or four hundred and thirty-two in circumference!

The palms growing hereabout—the stems of which, before they began to branch out, often rose to fifty and sixty feet—were, to all appearance, of the same kind as that we had seen about two hundred miles to the southward; but the fruit proved very good. When slightly soaked in water—which, by the by, is the best way of eating it—it tasted precisely like gingerbread.

There appeared to be no roads of any description. Fortunately, however, the harvest had just been completed, or nearly so; and, without damage to the owners, we were therefore enabled to cross the fields as the crow flies.

Two different kinds of grain we found indigenous to this country—viz., the common Caffre-corn, said to resemble the Egyptian 'doura;' and another sort, very small-grained, not unlike canary-seed, and akin, I believe, to the 'badjera' of India. This is the more nutritious of the two; and, when well-ground, produces excellent flour.

The stalk of both these kinds of grain is stout—the thickness of a sugar-cane—some eight or nine feet high, and juicy and sweet to the taste, which has no doubt given rise to a belief in the existence of the sugar-cane in many of the interior parts of Africa. When the grain is ripe, the ear is cut off, and the remainder is left to the cattle, which devour it greedily.

Besides grain, the Ovambo cultivate calabashes, watermelons, pumpkins, beans, peas, &c. They also plant tobacco. When ripe, the leaves and stalks are collected, and mashed together in a hollow piece of wood, by means of a heavy pole. The tobacco is, however, of a very inferior quality; so much so, that our Damaras—who had a mania for the weed—refused to smoke it.

There are no towns or villages in Ovambo-land; but the people, like the patriarchs of old, live in separate families. Each homestead is situated in the middle of a corn-field, and surrounded by high and stout palisades. The natives were obliged to take this precaution in order to guard against the sudden attacks of a neighbouring hostile tribe, which kept constantly harassing them. Once or twice the Ovambo attempted to retaliate, but without success. The tribe just mentioned is the only one with whom this naturally-peaceable people are ever at variance. If not previously provoked, they interfere with no one.

We were anxious to form some sort of estimate of the density of the population; but this was no easy matter. However, by counting the houses in a certain extent of country, and taking the average number of individuals to each, we came to the conclusion that there was about a hundred persons to every square mile.

With the exception of a few cows and goats, no cattle were seen about the dwellings of the natives, yet we knew them to be possessed of vast herds. A general scarcity of water and pasturage in Ondonga compelled them to send the oxen away to distant parts. They also breed hogs, which, from their mischievous propensities, are always sent to a distance during the time of harvest. These animals, they assured us, attain to an enormous size. By all accounts, indeed, they must be perfect monsters. And there can be little doubt of the fact; for captains of vessels, who are accustomed to trade with the natives of the west coast, also speak of a gigantic race of swine.

In the afternoon of the second day after leaving Chikor'onkombè's werft we came in sight of the residence of the redoubtable Nangoro. We were not, however, allowed to enter the royal enclosures, but a clump of trees was pointed out to us as our encamping place.

Whilst arranging our baggage, &c., Chikor'onkombè proceeded to inform his royal master of our arrival, and to state the quantity and quality of the intended presents. Before making his obeisance to his majesty, the eastern custom of taking off the sandals was carefully attended to. On his return he brought a man carrying some fire, with orders to extinguish ours, and to re-light it with that from the king's own hearth.

CHAPTER XVI.

VISIT FROM NANGORO—HIS EXTREME OBESITY—ONE MUST BE FAT TO WEAR A CROWN—HIS NON-APPRECIATION OF ELOQUENCE—SINGULAR EFFECTS OF FIREWORKS ON THE NATIVES—CURE FOR MAKING A WRY FACE—BALL AT THE PALACE—THE LADIES VERY ATTRACTIVE AND VERY LOVING—THEIR DRESS, ORNAMENTS, ETC.—HONESTY OF THE OVAMBO — KINDNESS TO THE POOR — LOVE OF COUNTRY — HOSPITALITY — DELICATE MANNER OF EATING — LOOSE MORALS— LAWS OF SUCCESSION—RELIGION—HOUSES—DOMESTIC ANIMALS— IMPLEMENTS OF HUSBANDRY—MANNER OF TILLING THE GROUND— ARTICLES OF BARTER—METALLURGY.

WE had been nearly three days at Nangoro's capital before its royal occupant honoured our camp with his presence. This unaccountable delay gave us some uneasiness. Yet we could not but surmise that he had been longing to see us during the whole time. I believe it, however, to be a kind of rule with most native princes of note in this part of Africa, to keep strangers waiting, in order to impress them with a due sense of dignity and importance.

If obesity is to be considered as a sign of royalty, Nangoro was 'every inch a king.' To our notions, however, he was the most ungainly and unwieldy figure we had ever seen.

His walk resembled rather the waddling of a duck than the firm and easy gait which we are wont to associate with royalty. Moreover, he was in a state of almost absolute nudity, which

INTERVIEW WITH KING NANGORO.

showed him off to the greatest possible advantage. It appeared strange to us that he should be the only really fat person in the whole of Ondonga. This peculiarity, no doubt is attributable to the custom that prevails in other parts of Africa, viz., that of selecting for rulers such persons only who have a natural tendency to corpulence, or, more commonly, fattening them for the dignity as we fatten pigs.[1]

With the exception of a cow and an ox, Nangoro appeared to appreciate few or none of the presents which Mr. Galton bestowed on him. And as for my friend's brilliant and energetic orations, they had no more effect on the ear of

[1] In speaking of the Matabili, Captain Harris says—"To be fat is the greatest of all crimes; no person being allowed that privilege but the king." Here, then, we have a new kind of lèze-Majesté. According to some of the African tribes, obesity in plebeians is high treason!

royalty, than if addressed to a stock or a stone. It was in vain that he represented to his majesty the advantages of a more immediate communication with Europeans. Nangoro spoke little or nothing. He could not be eloquent because excessive fat had made him short-winded. Like Falstaff, his 'voice was broken.' Any attempt on his part to utter a sentence of decent length, would have put an end to him; so he merely 'grunted' whenever he desired to express either approbation or dissatisfaction.

In common with his men, he was at first very incredulous as to the effect produced by fire-arms. But when he witnessed the depth that our steel-pointed conical balls penetrated into the trunk of a sound tree, he soon changed his opinion, and evidently became favourably impressed with their efficacy. As for the men of his tribe who had not yet seen guns, and who had flocked to the camp to have a look at us, they became so alarmed, that, at the instant of each discharge, they fell flat on their faces, and remained in their prostrate position for some little time afterwards. A few very indifferent fireworks, which we displayed, created nearly equal surprise and consternation.

In another interview with Nangoro, he requested us to shoot some elephants, which were said to abound at no great distance, and which, at times, committed great havoc amongst the corn fields, trampling down what they did not consume. However much we might have relished the proposal under other circumstances, we now peremptorily refused to comply. We reasoned thus:—" Supposing we were successful, Nangoro would not only bag all the ivory—an article he was known to covet and to sell largely to the Portuguese—but he would keep us in Ondonga till all the elephants were shot, or scared away." Neither of these results suited our purpose. The cunning fellow soon had an opportunity of revenging himself on us for this disregard of his royal wish.

BEER-CUP AND BEER-SPOON.

On paying our respects to *his majesty* one day, we were regaled with a prodigious quantity of beer, brewed from grain, and served out of a monster calabash with spoons (made from diminutive pumpkins), in nicely-worked wooden goblets. Being unwell at the time, I was not in a state properly to appreciate the tempting beverage. Nangoro, however, who probably attributed the wry face that I made to the influence of the liquor, suddenly thrust his sceptre, which, by the way, was simply a pointed stick, with great force into the pit of my stomach. I was sitting cross-legged on the ground at the time; but the blow was so violent as to cause me to spring to my feet in an instant. Nangoro was evidently much pleased with his practical joke. As for myself, I sincerely wished him at the antipodes. However, for fear of offending royalty, I choked my rising anger, and re-seated myself with the best grace I could; but I tried in vain to produce a smile.

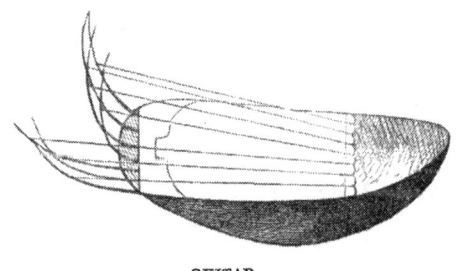

GUITAR.

On another occasion, we attended a ball at the royal

residence. An entertainment of this kind was given every night, soon after dark; but it was the most stupid and uninteresting affair I ever witnessed. The musical instruments were the well-known African tom-tom, and a kind of guitar. We did not join in the dance, but amused ourselves with admiring the ladies. What with their charms, which were by no means inconsiderable, and the wonderful regard they evinced for us, these damsels all but ruined our peace of mind.

The features of the Ovambo women, though coarse, are not unpleasing. When young they possess very good figures. As they grow older, however, the symmetry gradually disappears, and they become exceedingly stout and ungainly. One of the causes of this is probably to be found in the heavy copper ornaments, with which they load their wrists and ancles. Some of the ancle-rings must weigh as much as two or three pounds, and they have often a pair on each leg. Moreover, their necks, waists, and hips are almost hidden from view, by a profusion of shells, cowries, and beads of every size and colour, which sometimes are rather prettily arranged.[1] Another cause of their losing their good looks in comparatively early life, is the constant and severe labour they are obliged to undergo. In this land of industry, no one is allowed to be idle, and this is more especially the case with the females. Work begins at sun-rise and ends at sun-set.

The hair of both men and women is short, crisp, and woolly. With the exception of the crown, which is always left untouched, the men often shave the head, which has the effect of magnifying the natural prominence of the hinder parts of it. The women, on the other hand, not satisfied with

---

[1] These ornaments, together with a narrow and soft piece of skin in front, and another behind of stout hide, constitute the *dress* of the Ovambo *ladies*.

OVAMBO.

London, Hurst & Blackett, 1858.

the gifts nature has bestowed upon them, resort, like the polished ladies of Europe, to artificial exaggerations. They besmear and stiffen the hair with cakes of grease and a vermilion-coloured substance, which, from being constantly added to and pressed upon it, gives to the upper part of the head a broad and flat look. The persons of the women are also profusely besmeared with grease and red-ochre.

Besides ear-rings of beads or shells, the men display but few ornaments. With regard to clothing, both sexes are far more scantily attired than the Damaras. When grown up, they chip the middle tooth in the under-jaw.

The Ovambo, so far as came under our own observation, were strictly honest. Indeed, they appeared to entertain great horror of theft; and said, that a man detected in pilfering, would be brought to the king's residence, and there speared to death. In various parts of the country, a kind of magistrate is appointed, whose duty is to report all misdemeanours. Without permission, the natives would not even *touch* anything; and we could leave our camp free from the least apprehension of being plundered. As a proof of their honesty, I may mention, that, when we left the Ovambo country, the servants forgot some trifles; and such was the integrity of the people, that messengers actually came after us a very considerable distance to restore the articles left behind. In Damara and Namaqua-land, on the contrary, a traveller is in constant danger of being robbed; and, when stopping at a place, it is always necessary to keep the strictest watch on the movements of the inhabitants.

But honesty was not the only good quality of this fine race of men. There was no pauperism in the country. Crippled and aged people, moreover, seemed to be carefully tended and nursed. What a contrast to their neighbours, the Damaras, who, when a man becomes old, and no longer able to shift for himself, carry him into the desert or the forest, where he soon falls a prey to wild beasts, or is left to perish on his own hearth! Nay, he is often knocked on the head, or otherwise put to death.

The Ovambo are very national, and exceedingly proud of their native soil. They are offended when questioned as to the number of chiefs by whom they are ruled. "We acknowledge only one king. But a Damara," they would add, with a contemptuous smile, "when possessed of a few cows, considers himself at once a chieftain."

The people have also very strong local attachments. At an after-period, whilst Mr. Galton was waiting at St. Helena for a ship to convey him to England, he was told—"That slaves were not exported from south of Benguela because they never thrived when taken away, but became home-sick, and died." This, no doubt, refers in part to the Ovambo. Moreover, though people of every class and tribe are permitted to intermarry with them, they are, in such case, never allowed to leave the country.

The Ovambo are decidedly hospitable. We often had the good fortune to partake of their liberality. Their staple food is a kind of coarse stir-about, which is always served hot, either with melted butter or sour milk.

Being once on a shooting excursion, our guide took us to a friend's house, where we were regaled with the above fare. But as no spoons accompanied it, we felt at a loss how to set to work. On seeing the dilemma we were in, our host quickly plunged his greasy fingers into the middle of the steaming mess, and brought out a handful, which he dashed into the milk. Having stirred it quickly round with all his might, he next opened his spacious mouth in which the agreeable mixture vanished as if by magic. He finally licked his fingers and smacked his lips with evident satisfaction, looking at us as much as to say—"That's the trick, my boys!" However unpleasant this initiation might have appeared to us, it would have been ungrateful, if not offensive, to refuse; therefore, we commenced in earnest, according to example, emptying the dish, and occasionally burning our fingers, to the great amusement of our swarthy friends.

MEAT-DISH.

Although generally very rich in cattle, and fond of animal diet, their beasts would seem to be kept rather for show than for food. When an ox is killed, the greater portion of the animal is disposed of by the owner to the neighbours, who give the produce of their ground in exchange.

The morality of the Ovambo is very low, and polygamy is practised to a great extent. A man may have as many wives as he can afford to keep; but, as with the Damaras, there is always one who is the favourite and the highest in rank. Woman is looked upon as a mere commodity—an article of commerce. If the husband be poor, the price of a wife is two oxen and one cow; but should his circumstances be tolerably flourishing, three oxen and two cows will be expected. The chief, however, is an exception to this rule. In his case, the honour of an alliance with him is supposed to be a sufficient compensation. Our fat friend Nangoro had largely benefited by this privilege; for, though certainly far behind the King of Dahomey in regard to the number of wives, yet his harem boasted of one hundred and six enchanting beauties!

In case of the death of the king, the son of his favourite

wife succeeds him; but if he has no male issue by this woman, her daughter then assumes the sovereignty. The Princess Chipanga was the intended successor to Nangoro. My friend thought that his bearded face had made an impression on this amiable lady; but, though experience has since taught us that he was by no means averse to matrimony, he preferred to settle his affections on one of his own fair countrywomen rather than marry the 'greasy negress,' Chipanga—heiress of Ondonga.

We read of nations who are supposed to be destitute of any religious principles whatever. If we had placed reliance on what the natives themselves told us, we should have set down the Ovambo as one of such benighted races. But can there be so deplorable a condition of the human mind? Does not all nature forbid it? Do not the sun, the moon, the stars, the solemn night and cheerful dawn, announce a Creator even to the children of the wilderness? Is it not proclaimed in the awful voice of thunder, and written on the sky by

"————————the most terrible and nimble stroke
Of quick, cross lightning?"

Is it possible that any reasoning creature can be so degraded as not to have some notion, however faint and inadequate, of an Almighty Being? Such a conception is necessarily included, more or less, in all forms of idolatry, even the most absurd and bestial. The indefinable apprehensions of a savage, and his dread of something which he cannot describe, are testimonies that at least he *suspects* (however dimly and ignorantly) that the visible is not the whole. This may be the germ of religion—the first uncouth approaches of 'faith' as the 'evidence of things not seen'—the distant and imperfectly-heard announcement of a God.

May not our incorrect ideas on this head, in reference to

the Ovambo, be attributed to want of time and insufficient knowledge of their language, habits, and shyness in revealing such matters to strangers? When interrogating our guide on the subject of religion, he would abruptly stop us with a "Hush!" Does not this ejaculation express awe and reverence, and a deep sense of his own utter insufficiency to enter on so solemn a theme? The Ovambo always evinced much uneasiness whenever, in alluding to the state of man after death, we mentioned Nangoro. "If you speak in that manner," they said in a whisper, "and it should come to the hearing of the king, he will think that you may want to kill him." They, moreover, hinted that similar questions might materially hurt our interest, which was too direct a hint to be misunderstood. To speak of the death of a king or chief, or merely to allude to the heir-apparent, many savage nations consider equivalent to high treason.

DWELLING-HOUSE AND CORN-STORES.

As already said, the Ovambo surround their dwellings with high palisades, consisting of stout poles about eight or nine feet in height, fixed firmly in the ground, at short intervals from each other. The interior arrangements of these enclosures were most intricate. They comprised the dwelling-houses of masters and attendants, open spaces devoted to amusement and consultation, granaries, pig-sties, roosting-places for fowls, the cattle kraal, and so forth.

Their houses are of a circular form. The lower part consists of slender poles, about two feet six inches high, driven into the ground, and further secured by means of cord, &c., the whole being plastered over with clay. The roof, which is formed of rushes, is not unlike that of a beehive. The height of the whole house, from the ground to the top of the 'hive,' does not much exceed four feet, while in circumference it is about sixteen.

They store the grain in gigantic baskets, generally manufactured from palm leaves, plastered with clay, and covered with nearly the same material and in the same manner as the dwelling-houses. They are, moreover, of every dimension; and by means of a frame-work of wood, are raised about a foot from the ground.

The domestic animals of the Ovambo are the ox, the sheep, the goat, the pig, the dog, and the barn-door fowl. The latter was of a small breed, a kind of bantam, very handsome, and, if properly fed and housed, the hens would lay eggs daily.

The wet season in these latitudes commences about the same period as in Damara-land, that is in October and November. When the first heavy rains are over, the Ovambo begin to sow grain, &c.; but they plant tobacco in the dry time of the year. Both sexes assist in tilling the ground, which, near the surface, consists of a flinty sand-soil. A short distance beneath, blue clay appears. The land must be rich and fertile, as manure is seldom made use of. The only farm-implement we saw in use amongst the Ovambo was a kind of hoe, of very rude workmanship. Instead of cultivating a

VIEW IN ONDONGA.[1]

whole piece of ground, as with us, they simply dig a hole here and there, in which they deposit a handful of corn. When a little above ground, those seedlings which are too thick, are transplanted. The process of reaping, cleaning and grinding, falls almost exclusively on the women. The grain is reduced to flour by means of a stout pole in a kind of mortar, or hollow wooden tube. Whilst the females are thus employed, some of the men attend to the herding of the cattle, and the rest make trading excursions to the neighbouring tribes.

The chief article of export is ivory, which they procure from elephants caught in pitfalls. In exchange for this, they obtain beads, iron, copper, shells, cowries, &c.; and such

[1] The above wood-cut is a view of the country near Nangoro's residence. The huts seen in the distance are those of Bushmen. A great number of these people dwell amongst the Ovambo, to whom they stand in a kind of vassalage and relationship.

articles as they do not consume themselves, they sell to the Damaras. As far as we could learn, they make four expeditions annually into Damara-land; two by the way of Okamabuti, and two by that of Omaruru (*see map*). The return for these several journeys, on an average, would seem to be about eight hundred head of cattle. Since we were in the country, however, it is probable that great changes may have taken place.

Next to their cattle, they prize beads; but though they never refuse whatever is offered to them, there are some sorts that they more especially value, and it is of very great importance to the traveller and the trader to be aware of this, as, in reality, beads constitute his only money, or means of exchange. Thus, throughout Ondonga, large red (oval or cylindrically-shaped), large bluish white, small dark indigo, small black (spotted with red), and red, in general, are more particularly in request.

BLACKSMITHS AT WORK.

The Ovambo have some slight knowledge of metallurgy.

Though no mineral is indigenous to their own country, they procure copper and iron ore in abundance from their neighbours, which they smelt in fireproof crucibles. The bellows employed in heating the iron are very indifferent, and stones serve as substitutes for hammer and anvil. Yet, rude as these implements are, they manage not only to manufacture their own ornaments and farming tools, but almost all the iron-ware used in barter.

CHAPTER XVII.

THE RIVER CUNENÈ — THE TRAVELLERS ARE PRISONERS AT LARGE — KINGLY REVENGE — KINGLY LIBERALITY — DEPART FROM ONDONGA — SUFFERINGS AND CONSEQUENCES RESULTING FROM COLD — RETURN TO OKAMABUTI — DAMARA WOMEN MURDERED BY BUSHMEN — PREPARATIONS FOR JOURNEY — OBTAIN GUIDES — DEPART FROM TJOPOPA'S WERFT — GAME ABUNDANT — AUTHOR AND THREE LIONS STALK ANTELOPES IN COMPANY — EXTRAORDINARY VISITATION — THE RHINOCEROS'S GUARDIAN ANGEL — THE TEXTOR ERYTHRORHYNCHUS — THE AMADINA SQUAMIFRONS; SINGULAR CONSTRUCTION OF ITS NEST — RETURN TO BARMEN.

MANY years previously to our visit to the Ovambo, a French frigate discovered the embouchure of a magnificent river, known as Cunenè, between the seventeenth and eighteenth degrees of south latitude. Other vessels were sent out to explore it, and to ascertain its course, &c., but, strange to say, they searched for it in vain![1]

The discoverers, could not, however, have been mistaken; and as we now approached the latitudes in question, we made inquiries, and soon found that only four days' travel north of Ondonga there existed a river of great size, which, we doubted

[1] Captain Messum, master of a merchant vessel, subsequently informed me that he has seen it.

not, was identical with Cunenè; and further inquiry fully corroborated this supposition. A run-away slave from Benguela, who was living at the time among the Ovambo, informed us that in its upper course (or rather another branch) this river is called Mukuru Mukovanja, but that in its lower course it is designated Cunenè. Moreover, that though of very considerable size, and containing a large volume of water, it does not always find its way directly into the sea. He declared the cause of this to be the formation of sand-banks at its mouth which compels it to take a subterraneous course. Occasionally, however, it breaks through these barriers. This was exceedingly interesting, inasmuch as it explained the cause of its mysterious disappearance.

The Ovambo, themselves, gave us to understand that they often extended their trading excursions to the Cunenè, and even crossed it by means of canoes. The people dwelling on its south bank were called Ovapangari (a few of whom we saw in Ondonga) and Ovabundya. The latter were represented as living among 'many waters,' which we conjectured meant the confluence of some of the branches. The names of several other tribes will be found in the map, all of which seem to be closely allied in language, habits, &c. Indeed, the Damaras designate them all Ovambo, which they apply to people with permanent habitations and agricultural habits.

Our curiosity to see the Cunenè was greatly aroused; though, in order to accomplish this object, it would be necessary to overcome many difficulties. Pleasant as our arrival and stay in Ondonga had generally been, it was in some respects attended with much inconvenience. The freedom we had enjoyed to such perfection amongst the Damaras ceased with our entrance into Ovambo-land. We could hardly stir half a mile from our camp, without having first obtained the permission of our despotic friend, and much less could we think of returning or proceeding. We had left half our party behind us in a savage and inhospitable country, without a sufficiency of provisions. Our own stores were very deficient in animal food. No pasturage was left in Ondonga but corn-stubble, or rather corn-stalks; and of this, as well as of water, the inhabitants were extremely tenacious. The consequence was that the poor cattle daily fell off in condition. We were already two long weeks' journey distant from our camp at Okamabuti, and to undertake an excursion to the Cunenè, and return, would occupy fully another fortnight, making thus, at the very least, a whole month's actual travel. This, we feared, was more than our emaciated cattle were equal to. Yet, notwithstanding all these formidable difficulties, the enterprise was of such great importance, that we determined not to give it up without a struggle. Unless we could obtain the consent and assistance of Nangoro, we were aware that all our efforts would be unavailing. Accordingly, we informed him of our plans, with a request that he would provide us with guides. But he sulkily replied that as we did not choose to kill elephants for him, he could not oblige us in this matter! Under any circumstances, such ungenerous conduct would have been highly vexatious; but, in our situation, we could only submit, and hope it was all for the best; and that which his majesty intended an act of revenge, might in the end be the means of saving ourselves.

Thus frustrated in our plans, and having seen and ascertained everything we could in the country, we at once determined to retrace our steps. However, after what had just fallen from the lips of the chief, it was not without some misgivings, that we waited to know his wishes and intentions with regard to our departure. But there was no cause for anxiety. Having squeezed everything out of us that would have been of any use to him, he was evidently but too well-pleased to see us leave his territory, which would relieve him from the necessity of making us any presents. During our stay in Ondonga, all that this royal miser gave us, was a small basket of flour; though, on our finally leaving his dominion, he ordered one of his "bread-eaters," who accompanied us as guide to the frontier, to levy a tribute of corn on his subjects, for our behoof; but this largess, at the expense of others, came too late, as we had already laid in a sufficient stock of the staff of life, which we had obtained from the natives by barter.

The 13th of June was fixed for our departure. We were not, however, able to get away till two days later. On the 18th we were fairly out of sight of the fertile plains of Ondonga. Nangoro had originally promised to send our old friend Chikor'onkombè back with us; but the fellow abruptly and treacherously deserted us. This proved of great inconvenience; and it was only by exerting all our ingenuity that we ultimately succeeded in finding our way home. As has been already said, there were no land-marks by which we could steer.

The nights had now become bitterly cold. In crossing the Otjihako-tja-Mutenya, we were obliged to bivouac on this bleak and exposed plain without a particle of fuel. What with the piercing wind, and low temperature, it was one of the most trying nights I remember to have spent in Africa. Indeed I hardly ever felt the cold more during the most severe Scandinavian winter. Even the cattle were so exceedingly distressed, that several of our best draught-oxen never thoroughly recovered. Our poor Damaras suffered fearfully; and it was only by huddling themselves together at the bottom of a dried-up well, that they were enabled to keep the least warmth in their bodies. Timbo, however, appeared to be the greatest sufferer. One morning we were amazed at finding his dark, shiny skin suddenly changed into a pale, ashy, grey.

Owing to the scarcity of water at this time of the year, game was rare. Indeed, we only met with animals, such as the giraffe, the koodoo, the gemsbok, the eland, &c., that either wholly, or in great part, can do without water.

On the 1st of July, after about a fortnight's steady travel, we reached our encampment in safety. The two hundred miles of country we had crossed presented, perhaps, as dreary and uninteresting a prospect as can well be imagined.

In our absence, Tjopopa, with his people, left Okamabuti, and removed a few miles further to the westward. Our men followed his example. On approaching the camp, we espied Hans perched in the top of a tree, anxiously looking out for our return. The whole party was almost wild with delight at seeing us safe back, of which they began to despair. They had passed a most dreary time. The natives, though friendly, teazed and annoyed them excessively with begging, and even pilfering; the chief, as not unfrequently happens, having been the most importunate of the whole lot. Moreover, he had not paid his debt, nor would he sell Hans any cattle; and, as there was then very little game in the neighbourhood, they were so pressed for food, that Hans was obliged to reduce the men's allowances very considerably. Our Damara servants lived for some time solely on such birds and small animals as they could kill by means of the dogs. Fortunately, Hans possessed some tobacco; and whilst the natives refused everything else, he was able to obtain a few sheep for this article, which proved a most opportune supply.

Not many days previous to our arrival, eight Damara women had been surprised by the bushmen, and unmercifully put to death. This, however, was not to be wondered at, for the Damaras themselves are always waging an exterminating war on the bushmen. Indeed, they hunt them down, wherever met with, like wild beasts.

Hans had succeeded in repairing the waggon most satisfactorily; and the oxen, though rather lean, were in tolerably good working order. We now determined to turn our faces homewards, without a moment's delay. A very few days were sufficient to enable us to complete the final preparations.

By this time, all the pools of rain-water, which had befriended us on our journey northwards, were dried up, and it would, therefore, have been impossible to retrace our steps by the same route. The Damaras strongly advised us to strike the Omuramba-k'Omatako (*see map*) at a certain point, and, by following its course, they assured us we should find water and pasturage in abundance. One man in particular, who had always shown himself civil and obliging, offered to act as guide the first part of the way. For the remainder, we secured the services of a lad professing to be well acquainted with the country. Having, on so many occasions, been deceived by the natives, we did not much relish the idea of again trusting ourselves to their guidance. However, there was no alternative; and in this instance, to do justice to the men, I must say they not only spoke the truth, but performed their services most satisfactorily.

Without bidding farewell to Tjopopa who throughout had treated us inhospitably, we yoked our oxen on the 5th of July, and, after about three days' travel, arrived in the Omuramba. At this point, the river, (or rather the riverbed) appeared to cease altogether; but the natives declared that it continued to flow towards the Ovatjona or Matjo'na. I have since ascertained that they alluded to the Bechuana country. Hence, we travelled steadily up towards its source. Its bed, which sometimes spread out into a flat, and at others, formed a narrow channel, afforded us always a good and open road. The country on both sides was hemmed in by an apparently endless thorn-coppice. We usually found water daily; at first in pools, but afterwards exclusively in wells, varying in depth from a few feet to as much as forty. These were generally choked-up with sand, and it often occupied us half a day to clean them out. I remember, on one occasion, working hard with a party consisting of about thirty men and women during upwards of twenty hours, before we could obtain a sufficiency of water. It was cold work; for about sunrise the ice was often half an inch thick, and we had no waterproof-boots to protect our feet.

Game now became abundant. We managed to kill sufficient for the table without being obliged to have recourse to our few-remaining live stock. I saw here for the first time that magnificent antelope, the eland.

Beasts of prey were likewise numerous. Indeed, they always follow the larger game. During the nights, we were constantly annoyed by the dismal howlings of the hyænas; and we had some very exciting foot-chases after these animals.

Whilst out hunting early one morning, I espied a small troop of gnoos, quietly grazing at a bend of the river. Cautiously approaching them under shelter of the intervening ground, they suddenly tossed their heads, switched their tails, scraped the earth impatiently with their hoofs, and sniffed the air. I was puzzled how to account for this unusual agitation, as, from my position, I was certain they could not have discovered me. But I had not much time for conjecture; for the next instant I was startled by the growl of some animal close to me. On looking in the direction

UNWELCOME HUNTING COMPANIONS.

London, Hurst & Blackett, 1856.

whence it proceeded, I discovered, to my utter astonishment, two lions and a lioness on the rising ground just above me; and, as it seemed, they also were on the look-out for the gnoos.[1] I instinctively levelled my piece at the head of the nearest of the beasts; but a moment's reflection convinced me that the odds were too great, and I, therefore, thought it best to reserve my fire, so as to be in readiness to receive them, should they charge. After having regarded me for a few seconds, however, they growlingly disappeared behind a sand-hill.

By this time, the gnoos had become aware of the lions, and were making off at the top of their speed. Being anxious to obtain a shot at them I followed on their tracks, but soon found to my dismay, that my three royal friends, with jaws distended and uttering furious growls, were following a course parallel to mine. Though I must confess I did not at all like their looks, as only excessive hunger could have induced them, in broad day, to seek for victims, I nevertheless continued to follow the tracks of the antelopes until they led me into the bush, where I presently lost them, as well as myself.

On first seeing the gnoos, I left my henchman, "Bill," a Damara lad, who carried my spare gun, at some distance behind, with directions to follow on my track according to circumstances. Now that the gnoos were lost to me, I shouted loudly to the youth, and also discharged my gun more than once, but was unable to elicit a reply. Thinking, however, that he might have returned to our encampment (which was at no great distance) I also repaired there. But, "Bill" had not been heard of. The harassing suspicion at once crossed my mind that the lions had eaten him. Without a moment's delay I hurried back to the spot where I had last seen the

[1] The plate facing the page represents two lions observing me, whilst the lioness, not yet aware of my presence, is still eagerly pushing on towards the intended victims.

beasts, but all my endeavours to find the poor fellow were unavailing. What with my anxiety on his account, and my exertions under a broiling sun (for if the weather were frosty at night, it calcined one by day), I was unable to proceed farther, and sat myself down on the ground to wait for the arrival of the waggons, which were now moving forward. Just at this moment, the Damara, to my inexpressible delight, emerged from the bush. His story was soon told. He had, like myself, lost his way, and it was long before he was able to recover the right track.

One morning, as we were about to yoke the oxen, we were amused to see them suddenly start off in every direction, in the wildest confusion, and cutting the most ridiculous capers. The cause of this commotion was the arrival of a large flock of the *buphaga africana*, which alighted on the backs of the cattle for the purpose of feeding on the ticks with which their hides are covered. By means of their long claws and elastic tails, these birds are enabled to cling to and search every part of the beast. It was evident, however, that our oxen had never experienced a similar visitation; no wonder, therefore, that they were taken somewhat a-back at being thus unceremoniously assailed.

The *buphaga africana*, is also a frequent companion of the rhinoceros, to which, beside being of service in ridding him of many of the insects that infest his hide, it performs the important part of sentinel. On many occasions has this watchful bird prevented me from getting a shot at that beast. The moment it suspects danger, it flies almost perpendicularly up into the air, uttering sharp, shrill notes, that never fail to attract the attention of the rhinoceros, who, without waiting to ascertain the cause, almost instantly seeks safety in a precipitate flight. According to Mr. Cumming, these birds also attend upon the hippopotamus.

Another bird (*textor erythrorhynchus*) is also in the habit of feeding upon parasitical insects, but is said to restrict its visits to the buffalo. In the part of Damara-land of which I am now speaking, that animal is unknown; yet the bird was in very great numbers. It appeared to be very social in its habits, living in colonies, and building its nest, which consists of dry sticks, on lofty trees.

We also made acquaintance with a small, sparrow-looking bird, the *amadina squamifrons*, which deserves notice on account of its peculiar and interesting nest. According to Dr. Andrew Smith, this is placed on a small shrub, and is constructed of grass. But in Damara-land and parts adjacent, the materials are of a beautifully soft texture, not unlike sheep's wool. I never could discover the plant from which it was procured. The Hottentots use it as a substitute for gun-wadding, and it is by no means a bad makeshift. The nest is so strongly put together, that one has difficulty in separating it. When the old bird absents itself, it effectually conceals the opening of the nest from view. Even long after I was acquainted with this peculiarity, I was puzzled to find it out. Just above the entrance is a small hollow which has no communication with the interior of the nest, but which, by the uninitiated, is often mistaken for it. In this tube the male bird sits at night.

We occasionally fell in with Damara villages. In our journey northwards, the natives had shown themselves excessively timid and suspicious; but now that they had so many evidences of our peaceful intentions, they approached our camp without the least reserve or hesitation; but we could not induce them to part with any cattle, of which we stood much in need.

On the 26th of July we came in sight of Omatako, and many other well-known hills. On the 3rd of August we found ourselves at Schmelen's Hope; but how different an aspect did it present to that which lived in our memory! When we left it about three months' previously, the country was covered with the most luxuriant vegetation. Since then, the Damaras had been encamping there with their cattle; and we were now unable to obtain sufficient pasturage for our animals. The water, moreover, was all but exhausted.

On the following day, the 4th of August, we continued our journey to Barmen, where we arrived on the afternoon of the same day safe and well.

Thus ended an expedition which, although it might not have been so successful as we had anticipated, was not without its fruits.

CHAPTER XVIII.

THE DAMARAS — WHENCE THEY CAME — THEIR CONQUESTS — THE TIDE TURNS — DAMARA-LAND ONLY PARTIALLY INHABITED — CLIMATE — SEASONS — MYTHOLOGY — RELIGION — SUPERSTITIONS — MARRIAGE — POLYGAMY — CHILDREN — CIRCUMCISION — BURY THEIR DEAD — WAY THEY MOURN — CHILDREN INTERRED ALIVE — BURIAL OF THE CHIEF, AND SUPERSTITIONS CONSEQUENT THEREON — MALADIES — DAMARAS DO NOT LIVE LONG ; THE CAUSE THEREOF — FOOD — MUSIC AND DANCING — HOW THEY SWEAR — POWER OF THE CHIEFTAIN LIMITED — SLOTHFUL PEOPLE — NUMERALS — ASTRONOMY — DOMESTIC ANIMALS ; THEIR DISEASES.

FREQUENT opportunities had by this time been afforded me of observing and studying the physical features of the country, the character of the natives, and their religious rites and customs. Having previously said but little on these subjects, I propose now to give some account of them. Though, from the lying habits of the Damaras, great difficulty has arisen in arriving at the truth, I believe that my statements will not be very wide of the mark. Besides the concurrent testimony of many of the natives, I have had the satisfaction, on comparing my notes with those of the missionaries, to find them agree in the main ; and, as it has been my fate to witness the complete ruin and downfall of the Damaras—who, probably before another century has passed away, will be forgotten—I think that a connected and somewhat detailed description of their history may not be unacceptable to the general reader.

That the Damaras have not resided for any length of time in the country which they now occupy, is quite certain, though whence they came is doubtful. Some of these people point to the north as their original home; others conjecture that they migrated from the north-east.[1] Be this as it may, it would appear quite certain that, about seventy years ago, not a Damara was to be found south of the Kaoko—but that, at some time within this period, they invaded the country, then inhabited by bushmen and Hill-Damaras, the last being in all probability the aborigines. Not having a warlike disposition, the Hill-Damaras were easily subdued, and those who were not killed were made captives. The few that escaped took refuge among the mountains, or other inhospitable and inaccessible regions, where they are still found dragging on a most miserable and degraded existence.

The Damaras were once, undoubtedly, a great nation; but, unlike others which gradually become powerful by the union of a number of smaller tribes under the head of a single chief or king, they have dwindled into an endless number of petty tribes, ruled by as many chiefs.

After their conquest of the country, the Damaras continued to extend themselves, without much opposition, to the east nearly as far as Lake Ngami, and to about the twenty-fourth degree of latitude on the south. At both these points, however, they were checked in their onward career. At first they were attacked by the Matjo'nas, with whom,

---

[1] In my journey to the Lake Ngami, at an after period, I observed whole forests of a species of tree called Omumborombonga, the supposed progenitor of the Damaras. This fact, coupled with our knowledge that all the tribes to the north are more or less conversant with agriculture, of which the Damaras know nothing (having no word in their language for cereal food), and that many of the nations to the east are partly pastoral, would seem to indicate a north-east or east direction as their original home.

from time to time, they had several desperate conflicts; and though they appear to have fought well, they were ultimately obliged to retreat with considerable loss. But it was from the Namaqua-Hottentots that they were destined to experience the greatest reverse, by whom, as will by-and-by be shown, they were finally destroyed or broken up.

About the period of the conquest alluded to, a small tribe of Namaqua-Hottentots had pitched their tents on the banks of the Orange river under the rule of Jonker Afrikaner,[1] who was then a chief of only secondary importance; yet, as his people were possessed of horses and fire-arms, he soon became formidable to his enemies. The territory lying between him and the Damaras was occupied by various tribes of Namaquas, who, on finding themselves hard pressed by the Damaras, sent to Jonker to demand his assistance. This he granted; and, like another Cæsar, "came, saw, and conquered." Indeed, that day sealed the fate of Damara-land. The Namaquas, at first the oppressed, became in their turn the oppressors. In proportion as they grew powerful and successful, the prospect of booty, which the vast herds of sleek cattle so amply afforded them, was the sole object of their inroads upon the Damaras. They appeared to have adopted the motto of the old sea-kings—

"That they should take who have the power,
And they should keep who can."

From my first arrival in the country to the time I left it

---

[1] His father, Christian Afrikaner, once lived within the present boundary of the Cape Colony; but his brother having killed a Dutch farmer, from whom the tribe is said to have suffered much wrong, he and his kindred were obliged to fly the country. He then settled on the banks of the Garib or Orange river, where he soon became famous for his daring and ferocious exploits against his neighbours. In this state of things he was found by the Rev. Mr. Moffat, well-known for his missionary labours in Southern Africa, who, after having experienced much opposition, finally succeeded in converting him to Christianity. At his death, the present Jonker Afrikaner, though an elder brother was still living, assumed the chieftainship, which occasioned a division in the tribe, and was, moreover, the original cause of their migration northward.

—a period of less than four years—the Namaquas had deprived the Damaras of fully one half of their cattle, the other portion having already been taken from them previously to my visit. With the loss of their property, followed that of their independence.

Although a large tract of country is marked on the map as Damara-land, a small portion only is inhabitable. This may also be affirmed of Namaqua-land; and in both cases the disparity arises either from scarcity of water, or the frequency of inextricable jungles of thorn-wood.

Damara-land being situated in the tropic of Capricorn, the seasons are naturally the reverse of those in Europe. In the month of August, when our summer may be said to be at an end, hot westerly winds begin to blow, which quickly parch up and destroy the vegetation. At the same time, whirlwinds sweep over the country with tremendous velocity, driving along vast columns of sand, many feet in diameter, and several hundred in height. At times, ten or fifteen of these columns may be seen chasing each other. The Damaras designate them Orukumb'ombura, or rain-beggars, a most appropriate name, as they usually occur just before the first rains fall.

Showers, accompanied by thunder and vivid lightning, are not unusual in the months of September and October; but the regular rains do not set in till December and January, when they continue, with but slight intermission, till May. In this month and June, strong easterly winds prevail, which are not only disagreeable but injurious to health. The lips crack, and the skin feels dry and harsh. Occasionally, at this time, tropical rains fall, but they do more harm than good, as a sudden cold, which annihilates vegetation, is invariably the result. In July and August, the nights are the coldest, and it is then no unusual thing to find ice half an inch thick. Snow is of rare occurrence.

The Damaras and the Bechuanas have nearly the same notion as to their origin. Thus, the latter believe that the founders of their nation, and the animals of the country, emerged from a cave, whilst the former declare that they sprung from a tree. When men and beasts first burst from the parent tree—so runs the tradition—all was enveloped in profound darkness. A Damara, then lit a fire, which so frightened the zebra, the giraffe, the gnoo, and every other beast now found wild in the country, that they all fled from the presence of man, whilst the domestic animals, such as the ox, the sheep,[1] and the dog, collected fearlessly round the blazing brands.

The tree, from which the Damaras are descended, is to be seen, they say, at a place called Omaruru. But somehow there must be more than one parent tree; for, both in going and coming, we met with several Omumborombongas, all of which the natives treated with filial affection.[2]

The chief deity of the Damaras is called Omukuru. His abode is said to be in the far-north; but it would be somewhat difficult to specify his attributes. Each tribe is supposed to have its own Omukuru, to whom it ascribes all its superstitious habits and customs, peculiarities, &c. The tribe is divided into castes or "eandas." Thus there are Ovakueyuba, those of the sun, or related to the sun, and Ovakuenombura, those related to the rain, &c., each of which has its peculiar rites and superstitions. These, moreover, are derived from the mother, and not from the father. If a man of the Ovakueyuba marries a woman of the Ovakuenombura, their

---

[1] Some Damaras attribute the origin of the sheep to a large stone.
[2] The grain of this tree is so very close, and the wood so exceedingly weighty, that we gave it the name of the 'iron tree.'

offspring adopt the notions, &c., peculiar to the latter, and *vice-versâ*. They cannot account for this division of castes; they merely say it is derived from the "wind." Some religious notions, no doubt, lie at the bottom of this.

Though the Damaras do not profess absolutely to believe in a life hereafter, they have a confused notion of a future state. Thus, they not unfrequently bring provisions to the graves of a deceased friend or relation, requesting him to eat and make merry. In return, they invoke his blessing, and pray for success against their enemies, an abundance of cattle, numerous wives, and prosperity in their undertakings.

The spirits of deceased persons are believed to appear after death, but are then seldom seen in their natural form. They usually assume on such occasions the shape of a dog, having, not unfrequently, the foot of an ostrich. Any individual to whom such an apparition (Otjruru) might appear, especially if it should follow and accost him, is supposed to die soon after.

The Damaras have great faith in witchcraft. Individuals versed in the black art are called Omundu-Onganga, or Omundu-Ondyai, and are much sought after. Any person falling sick is immediately attended by one of these impostors, whose panacea is to besmear the mouth and the forehead of the patient with the ordure of the hyæna, which is supposed to possess particularly healing virtues. The sorcerer, moreover, makes signs and conjurations.

Some very singular superstitions about meat exist among the Damaras. Thus a man will perhaps not eat the flesh of an ox which may happen to be marked with black, white, or red spots. Others refuse to partake of a sheep should it have no horns; whilst some would not touch the meat of draught-oxen, according to the rule of the "eanda" to which he belongs. If meat is offered a Damara, he will accept it; but before he ventures to eat it, he carefully enquires about the colour of the animal, whether it had horns, &c.; and should it prove forbidden food, he will in all probability leave it untouched, even though he might be dying of hunger. Some even carry their scruples so far as to avoid coming in contact with vessels in which such food has been cooked; nay, even the smoke of the fire by which it is prepared is considered injurious. Hence the religious superstitions of these people often expose them to no small amount of inconvenience and suffering.

The fat of particular animals is supposed to possess certain virtues; and is carefully collected and kept in vessels of a peculiar kind. A small portion of this is given in solution with water, to persons who return safely to their homes after a lengthened absence at the cattle-posts. The chief also makes use of it as an unguent for his body.

When an ox accidentally dies at a chief's werft, his daughter (the offspring, probably of his favourite or chief wife) ties a double knot on her leather apron. Should this be neglected, a 'curse' is believed to be the consequence. She also places a piece of wood on the back of the dead animal, praying at the same time for long life, plenty of cattle, &c. This woman is called Ondangere, and is to the Damaras what the vestal was amongst the ancient Romans; for, besides attending to the sacrifices, it is her duty to keep up the 'holy fire' (Omurangere).

Outside the chief's hut, where he is accustomed to sit in the day-time, a fire is always kept burning; but, in case of rain or bad weather, it is transferred to the hut of the priestess, who, should it be deemed advisable to change the site of the village, precedes the oxen with a portion of this consecrated fire, every possible care being taken to prevent it from being extinguished. Should, however, this calamity happen, the whole tribe is immediately assembled, and large expiatory offerings of cattle are made; after which the fire is re-lit in the primitive way—namely, by friction. This again reminds us of the 'holy fire' of the Romans, which, under similar circumstances, could only be re-lit by fire from heaven.

A portion of such fire is also given to the head man of a kraal, when about to remove from that of the chief. The duties of a vestal then devolve on the daughter of the emigrant.

For every wild animal that a young man destroys, his father makes four small oblong incisions on the front of the son's body as marks of honour and distinction. He is, moreover, presented with a sheep or cow. If either of these should produce young ones, they are slaughtered and eaten, but only males are allowed to partake of such food.

The chief of a kraal must always taste the provisions before they can be eaten by the rest of the tribe. Though sweet milk, when boiled, may be freely drunk by the women and children, it is more commonly swallowed in an acid state.

Should a sportsman return from a successful hunt, he takes water in his mouth, and ejects it three times over his feet, as also in the fire of his own hearth.

When cattle are required merely for food, they are suffocated; but if for sacrifices, they are speared to death. On the decease of one of the tribe, they have also the cruel practice of destroying the poor beasts with clubs, which I believe to be a kind of expiatory offering. The flesh of such cattle as are killed on the death of a chief, is principally consumed by his servants.

The women marry at very much the same age as those in Europe; but few ceremonies are connected with this important affair. A girl is sometimes betrothed to a man when yet a child; though, under such circumstances, she remains with her parents till of proper age. The woman, upon being asked in marriage, puts on a helmet-shaped head-dress, kept in readiness for such occasions, and, for a certain time, hides her face by means of a piece of thin, soft skin, attached to the front of the 'casque,' which she can raise or let fall in much the same manner as a curtain.

Polygamy is practised to a great extent, and, as has been said elsewhere, women are bargained for like merchandize, the price varying according to the circumstances of the husband. Yet, though a man may have as many wives as he likes, I never knew one to have more than twenty!—a pretty good supply, however, it must be admitted.

The favourite wife always takes precedence of the rest; and if she should have a son, he succeeds to his father's possessions and authority.

Each wife builds for herself a hut of a semi-circular form, the walls of which consist of boughs, sticks, &c., the whole being plastered over.

Twins are not uncommon with the Damaras. Children are, generally speaking, easily reared. During infancy, sheep's milk constitutes their chief diet. Their heads are more or less deprived of hair; the boys are shaved, but the crown of the head of the girls is left untouched. Even grown-up females follow this custom. To the hair thus left they attach—not very unlike the Ovambo—thin strings, made from some fibrous substance.

All males are circumcised; but no particular period of life is prescribed for this operation, which usually takes place when any event of national interest occurs.

Children are named after great public incidents; but, as they grow up, should any circumstance arise of still greater importance to the community they are re-named; retaining, however, the original appellation. And since there may be no limit to remarkable transactions, it follows that an individual may have more names than any Spanish hidalgo can boast.

Between the age of fifteen and twenty, both sexes chip a wedge-shaped piece of the two centre teeth in the upper jaw, and at a later period they extract entirely from the lower two or three teeth. The first operation is usually performed by means of a piece of iron, a flint, or simply a stone.

The Damaras bury their dead. Immediately after dissolution, the back-bone of the corpse is broken with a stone,[1] and it is then bent together with the chin resting on the knees. Afterwards it is wrapped in ox-hides, and deposited in a hole in the ground dug for the purpose, care being taken to place the face towards the north. This is done, they say, to remind them (the natives) whence they originally came. The Bechuana mode of disposing of the dead is very similar.

Upon the death of one of the tribe, the whole population of the place assemble to deplore the event. The howlings and lamentations on such occasions are most discordant and dreadful. Tears are considered favourable signs, and the more plentifully they fall on the corpse, the better. Two months is the usual period for a son to mourn his father; but the time is modified according to circumstances. The wealthier the deceased, the greater the outward signs of sorrow—a kind of feeling which, at any rate, bears some approximation to that of civilized life. During the season of mourning, the mourner wears a dark-coloured skin cap,

---

[1] I am told that this is not unfrequently done before life is quite extinct! It is, moreover, affirmed, that when the sick man begins to breathe hard, a skin is immediately thrown over his face, which, no doubt, often causes premature death.

conically shaped on the top, with certain ornaments affixed to it. Round the neck is suspended a 'riem,' to the two extremities of which are attached a small piece of ostrich eggshell. In case of the death of a valued friend, the adults will occasionally shave the head completely, and keep it in that state for years.

When a woman in reduced circumstances dies, and leaves a child, it is not unfrequently buried alive with its mother. Mr. Rath was once fortunate enough to be the means of saving a child that was about to be destroyed in this barbarous manner.

DAMARA GRAVE.

After having consigned the remains of a chief to his last resting-place, they collect his arms, war dress, &c., and suspend them to a pole, or to a tree, at the head of the grave. The horns of such oxen as have been killed in commemoration of the occasion, are hung up in like manner—a custom also found among the natives of Madagascar. The tomb consists of a large heap of stones, surrounded by an enclosure of thorn bushes; no doubt to prevent hyænas and other carnivorous animals from extracting the corpse. Sometimes, however, the chief, should he have expressed a wish to that effect, instead of being buried, is placed in a reclining position on a slightly raised platform in the centre of his own hut, which, in such a case, is surrounded by stout and strong palisadings.

When a chief feels his dissolution approaching, he calls his sons to the bedside, and gives them his benediction, which consists solely in wishing them an abundance of the good things of this world.

The eldest son of the chief's favourite wife succeeds his father; and, as soon as the obsequies are over, he quits the desolate spot, remaining absent for years. At last, however, he returns, and immediately proceeds to his parent's grave, where he kneels down, and in a whispering voice tells the deceased that he is there with his family, and the cattle that he gave him. He then prays for long life, also that his herds may thrive and multiply; and, in short, that he may obtain all those things that are dear to a savage. This duty being performed, he constructs a kraal on the identical spot where once the ancestral camp stood; even the huts and the fireplaces are placed as much as possible in their former position. The chief's own hut is always upon the east side of the enclosure.

The flesh of the first animal slaughtered here is cooked in a particular vessel; and, when ready, the chief hands a portion of it to every one present. An image, consisting of two pieces of wood,[1] supposed to represent the household deity, or rather the deified parent, is then produced, and moistened in the platter of each individual. The chief then takes the image, and, after affixing a piece of meat to the upper end of it, he plants it in the ground, on the identical spot where his parent was accustomed to sacrifice. The first pail of milk produced from the cattle is also taken to the grave; a small quantity is poured on the ground, and a blessing asked on the remainder.

Fever and ophthalmia (eye-sickness) are the prevailing maladies. The symptoms in fever are head-ache, pains in the neck and bowels, general weakness, and ague. It makes its appearance about April and May, or when the periodical rains have ceased. Ophthalmia, on the other hand, begins to show itself in September and October, but reaches its maximum when the cold season sets in. The first sensation experienced is as if the pupil of the eye was too large. A gathering of water in the sides and under the eye-lids then ensues. In a short time this fluid becomes scaldingly hot, and, if not quickly and carefully removed, the pain will be intense. The sight is sometimes completely destroyed by this malady. Indeed, one not unfrequently meets with people either totally blind, or minus one eye. Europeans are as liable to these inflictions as the natives. I speak from experience, having myself been a severe sufferer from fever and ophthalmia.

Comparatively few old people are to be met with in Damara-land, for which several reasons may be assigned; such as their cruel civil broils, and their want of compassion for aged and disabled individuals. At times, indeed, they would seem to do all they can to hasten the death of such

---

[1] Each caste has a particular tree or shrub consecrated to it. Of this tree or shrub a couple of twigs or sticks represent the deceased.

sufferers. Some instances of this atrocity have come to my knowledge: one of the most shocking occurred at Barmen.

Finding that a certain poor woman, being nearly blind, was unable to provide for herself, Mr. Hahn took compassion on the helpless creature, and gave her a small quantity of provision almost daily. The brother, finding he could not obtain the same boon, grew jealous of the preference shown to his sister, and secretly resolved to kill her. This he effected by taking her to a spot destitute of water, under the pretext that they were to dig roots, where she was left to her fate. A boy, who accompanied them, asserted, that, on the unnatural brother returning to the place some days afterwards, and finding his sister still lingering, he beat her about the head with his knob-stick until life was extinct.

Milk is the staple food of the Damaras. They eat or drink it out of one and the same dish without its being cleaned, otherwise than occasionally by the tongues of dogs. The people have a notion that if they wash their "bamboos" (pails), the cows would cease to give milk.

With the exception of the spoils of the chase, they destroy but few animals for food. Indeed, unless it be on the occasion of a marriage, a birth, a death, or a circumcision, cattle are rarely killed.

The Damaras are very fond of music and dancing. The only musical instrument known amongst them is the bow (a kind of temporary rude Jews'-harp), from which they contrive to extract a sort of wild melody. By this instrument the performer endeavours (and frequently with much success) to imitate, musically, the motion peculiar to different animals; for example, the awkward gallop of the giraffe, the quick trot of the zebra and the lively caperings of the beautiful springbok.

The dance consists mostly of mimic representations of the actions of oxen and sheep. The dancers accompany their gesticulations by monotonous tunes, and keep time by clapping their hands, and striking the ground with their feet.

As with the Ovambo, the eastern custom of taking off the sandals, before entering a stranger's house, is observed.

The Damaras swear "by the tears of their mothers." This is most touching and beautiful: it elevates the oath to heaven.

Generally speaking, a chief has but nominal power over his subjects. On an attempt to punish heavy offences, the guilty individual often coolly decamps with his cattle, and takes refuge with another tribe. In minor matters, however, from superstitious customs and old habits, the chief is more or less obeyed.

The Damaras are idle creatures. What is not done by the women is left to the slaves, who are either descendants of impoverished members of their own tribe (is not this another approach to *civilization?*) or captured bushmen. The former are seized upon when children, and mostly employed as herdsmen.

The Damaras have numerals up to a hundred; notwithstanding which they are sorely puzzled should the sum exceed the number of fingers. They count like bad poets, who settle their metre by their digits. It is a most amusing sight to witness a group trying to reckon a dozen head of cattle.

Though they give names to many of the heavenly bodies, they have a very absurd conception of their character, rotatory motion, and so forth. Thus, many imagine that the sun which sets at night is different from that which rises in the morning. Like the children who wondered what was done with the old moons, perhaps these savages are equally perplexed to ascertain what becomes of the *old suns*.

The domestic animals indigenous to the country are oxen, sheep, and dogs. The latter greatly resemble those mentioned as existing among the Namaquas; but—be it said to the honour of the Damaras—they take much more care of these associates and companions of man than their southern neighbours. Indeed, I have known them to pay as much as two fine oxen for a dog.

Of the Damara cattle I shall have occasion to speak hereafter. The sheep are (or rather were) plentiful, and the mutton is by no means bad. Though somewhat spare-looking, they furnish good joints when cut up. Skin and offal included, they not unfrequently weigh 100 lbs., and sometimes as much as 110 to 120 lbs. They have large tails like those of the Cape Colony, but they do not arrive at such a formidable size. They have no wool; but a kind of short, glossy hair (lying close to the skin) covers the body. The greatest peculiarity of these animals is their colour, which is of every hue and tint.

Cattle are subject to several diseases. The most common and dangerous is that which affects the throat, and which invariably proves fatal. Cataracts on the eye, frequently followed by blindness and swelling of the feet, are also very common ailments.

Sheep often die from the blood conglomerating in divers places under the skin, which is called the 'blood-sickness.' It is even asserted that man is affected by this disease (sometimes from partaking the flesh of the infected animal), and that the only thing to save him under such circumstances is instantly to cut away the parts affected.

CHAPTER XIX.

DESPATCH A MESSENGER TO CAPE-TOWN—DEPART FROM BARMEN—EIKHAMS—EYEBRECHT—DEPART FROM EIKHAMS—ELEPHANT FOUNTAIN—TUNOBIS—ENORMOUS QUANTITIES OF GAME—SHOOTING BY NIGHT AT THE 'SKARM'—THE AUTHOR HAS SEVERAL NARROW ESCAPES—CHECKED IN ATTEMPT TO REACH THE NGAMI—THE PARTY SET OUT ON THEIR RETURN—REACH ELEPHANT FOUNTAIN—HOW TO MAKE SOAP—PIT-FALLS—A NIGHT ADVENTURE—GAME SCARCE—JOIN HANS—THE PARTY NEARLY POISONED—ARRIVAL AT WALFISCH BAY—A TUB ADVENTURE—EXTRAORDINARY MORTALITY AMONGST THE FISH—AUTHOR NARROWLY ESCAPES DROWNING—ARRIVAL OF THE MISSIONARY VESSEL—LETTERS FROM HOME—MR. GALTON RETURNS TO EUROPE—REFLECTIONS.

THE vessel which brought the missionary stores to Walfisch Bay every second year, was expected in December, and by this opportunity we hoped to be able to return to Europe, or at least to the Cape. In order, however, to ensure a passage, Mr. Galton dispatched a messenger to his banker in Cape-town, to make the needful arrangements. In the mean time, as we had still several months on our hands, Galton resolved to employ the interval in making an excursion to the eastward, partly with the view of penetrating to the Lake Ngami, our original object, and partly to become better acquainted with Great Namaqua-land and its semi-civilized inhabitants. Moreover, the prospect of good sport with the larger game, which every one said we were sure to meet with in abundance, was a further inducement to undertake the journey.

It was arranged that Hans should proceed to Walfisch Bay with one of the vehicles to fetch the remainder of the stores, &c., whilst Galton and myself, with the other waggon, prosecuted our journey to the eastward. A rendezvous having been appointed where Hans was to meet us, we left Barmen in the afternoon of the 12th of August. In about three days we reached Eikhams, the residence, as already said, of Jonker Afrikaner; where my friend, before finally leaving the country, was anxious to settle certain disputes between the native tribes.

Eikhams is very prettily situated on the slope of a hill, bare at the summit, but at its base adorned with very fine groups of mimosas, among which a tributary to the Swakop winds its course. It was the only spot in South Africa where I ever saw anything resembling a twilight. This was produced from the reflection of the setting sun on the peaks of the picturesque mountain-ranges, by which it is almost entirely surrounded.

Eikhams is abundantly supplied with water from three or four copious springs, and, the site of these springs being elevated, the land in the lower ground is easily irrigated. The natives construct gardens, wherein they grow many sorts of vegetables, some of which arrive at perfection. The soil is exceedingly fertile, and seems well suited to the cultivation of tobacco. Taking it as a whole, Eikhams is the prettiest place I ever saw either in Damara-land or Namaqua-land.

About twenty minutes' walk from Eikhams is a bountiful hot-spring. The water, just where it gushes out from the limestone-rock, has a temperature of 194 degrees of Fahrenheit. Mr. Hahn informed me that here, on one occasion, he boiled a piece of meat, and that, though not quite so good as when dressed in the ordinary manner, it was not unpalatable.

Eikhams, as already said, was formerly a Rhenish missionary station. It was founded as far back as 1843 by the Rev. C. H. Hahn, resident at New Barmen in Damara-land. After a time, however, it was given up to the Wesleyan society, which sent Mr. Haddy to reside there. This gentleman erected an excellent dwelling-house, and a most substantial church. For a while, the mission flourished, but was latterly abandoned, and the station is now rapidly falling into decay. This, I am sorry to say, has been the fate of many other institutions of a similar nature in Southern Africa.

JONKER AFRIKANER.

Amongst other gifts, Mr. Galton presented Jonker with a splendid cocked hat and richly-gilt uniform. A court dress, in fact, that had once probably adorned the person of some great man when paying his respects to majesty, and with which the African chief expressed himself highly gratified.

Being desirous of obtaining a likeness of so famous a personage as Afrikaner, I requested him one day to put on this costume, and allow me to take his portrait. He good-naturedly consented to my solicitation, and on the following morning appeared duly apparelled. We rather expected to have a laugh at him, since his gait and figure were somewhat unprepossessing; but we were disappointed. He marched up to his seat with as much ease and dignity as if he were familiar with the usage of courts.

During our stay at Eikhams, we became acquainted with a Mr. Eyebrecht, formerly in the missionary employ, but now Jonker's right-hand man. In addition to excellent English and Dutch, he spoke the Namaqua and the Damara tongues rather fluently. As he was well-acquainted with the country, Mr. Galton secured his services for our tour to the eastward, and he proved of the greatest assistance.

On arriving at Eikhams, Mr. Galton imagined that his business with Jonker would soon be arranged; but in this part of the world expedition is not the order of the day, and we were therefore so long delayed as to prevent our departure until the 30th of August.

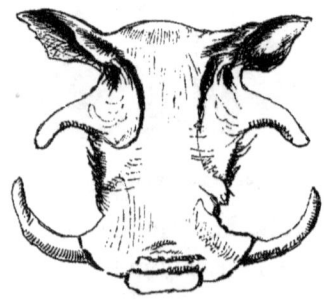

WILD BOAR'S HEAD.

In the course of our journey we encountered a great

number and variety of wild animals, and consequently our larder was well supplied. Indeed, in a few hours, on a certain night, I bagged no less than three hartebeests, two pallahs, and five zebras; and, had I felt inclined, might have shot double this number. We also observed a few wild boars.

After a fortnight's harassing travel, we arrived at Elephant Fountain, formerly a Wesleyan missionary station. It was founded in 1847 by the Rev. Mr. Tindal; but had of late years been abandoned in consequence of a destructive fever, which carried off many of the natives. Even the few Europeans settled there suffered severely. It was situated within the territory of the chief, Amral, who was born and bred in the Cape-Colony; and, if I am not misinformed, was raised to his present dignity partly through missionary influence.

Elephant Fountain is chiefly inhabited by Hill-Damaras, who cultivate extensive gardens of tobacco, &c. Game was abundant thereabouts, but we had not then time to look after it.

From Elephant Fountain, eastward, the country was represented as very sandy and bushy; and, as our oxen were in a very indifferent condition, we determined to leave the waggon behind in charge of John Mortar, the cook, and to prosecute our journey with pack-and-ride oxen. Amral, with a great number of the tribe, expressed a wish to accompany us, chiefly for the sake of the anticipated sport. As we travelled on, we were joined by Lambert, his son, and other Namaquas, with their attendants, till at last our party amounted to several hundred individuals.

After no little inconvenience and misery, on account of the great heat, the terrible drought, and scarcity of pasturage about the few and widely-separated watering-places, we reached Tunobis, or Otjombindè, on the 3rd of October. According to Mr. Galton's observations, this place is situated in latitude 21 deg. 55 min., and 21 deg. 55 min. east longitude.

The bushmen who inhabited these parts declared that the country between here and the Ngami was then impassable, and that any attempt on our part to reach it would be certain destruction to ourselves and cattle. Though we did not altogether credit their story, we felt that, under the circumstances, it would have been highly imprudent to proceed farther.

From a rough calculation, we concluded that we could not be above nine or ten days' journey from the lake; and it was therefore with no little reluctance that we gave up the attempt. However, it was all for the best; and we ought indeed to be grateful to the natives for their truthful information. From after experience, I am quite confident that had we tried to push on that year, nothing could have saved us and our beasts of burden from perishing from thirst. After leaving Tunobis, we should not have met with water for at least three days and a-half of actual travel, besides the necessary delays. To perform this, even with fresh animals, would perhaps have been a thing unheard-of in these regions; but the difficulty was magnified by the state of our cattle, which were now reduced to skeletons. Indeed, even before reaching Tunobis, some of them had been left behind from sheer exhaustion.

I must confess that on first perusing my friend's narrative, I was somewhat startled on coming upon his pleasant assertion that he did not much care about reaching the Lake Ngami. It is true that, when landing at Walfisch Bay, we had but little hope of arriving there; but, at least for my own part, I had always conceived the great goal of our journey to be precisely the Ngami. Moreover, with regard to his supposition that the country hence towards the lake was comparatively open and free from bushes, and that, consequently, a road to it could be traced without the slightest difficulty, I can only say, that shortly after leaving Tunobis—not to mention the scarcity of water—the bush becomes so dense, and the thorns so tormenting, that I found it necessary to make immense *détours*, and even then all our clothes, pack-saddles, &c., were literally torn to ribbons.

The few days that we remained at Tunobis were spent profitably and pleasantly. Besides much interesting information of the country, derived from the bushmen, part of which has since been substantiated, we had abundant shooting. From the absence of water within a distance of two or three days' journey of the place, the number of animals that nightly congregated here to quench their thirst, was truly astonishing.

To give the reader an idea of the immense quantity of game hereabouts, I may mention, that in the course of the few days we remained at Tunobis, our party shot, amongst other animals, upwards of thirty rhinoceroses. One night, indeed, when quite alone, I killed in the space of five hours (independently of other game) no less than eight of those beasts, amongst which were three distinct species. And it is my belief that if I had persevered I might have destroyed double the number.[1] But I never took delight in useless slaughter. In our case—and I think I may say in all cases where I have been concerned in killing a great number of wild beasts—not a pound of flesh was ever wasted; for

---

[1] When we thus shot at night, we generally ensconced ourselves in a 'skärm,' that is, a small circular enclosure, six or eight feet in diameter, the walls (usually consisting of loose stones) being about two feet in height.

what we did not require for our own use, was devoured by the natives.

As another evidence of the enormous quantity of game in this region, I may state that the fountain in question, which was a copious one—nay, apparently inexhaustible—was almost nightly drank dry.

On several occasions, I had narrow escapes from being gored by the horns of these ugly monsters. Thus, one animal, on receiving a mortal wound, charged me with such fury as to carry completely away the fore part of my "skärm," and I only saved my life by throwing myself with great force against the opposite wall, which fortunately gave way.

At another time, I was walking leisurely up to a huge female white rhinoceros, that Mr. Galton had killed during the preceding night, when all at once its calf, about the size of an ox, rushed upon me from behind the carcase. Its movements were so rapid, that I had neither time to get out of its way nor to level my gun, but passing the barrel, like a stick, against its chest, I fired, and, as luck would have it, the ball caused the calf to swerve on one side, and take itself off. A short time afterwards, and at no great distance from our encampment, it was found dead.

Being tired of shooting, and having got all the information we could from the Bushmen, we bent our steps homewards. Our failure in not reaching the Lake Ngami deeply mortified me. Night and day I was haunted by the thought. Taking everything into consideration, I could not help thinking that, under more favourable circumstances, success would crown my endeavours, were I determined to renew the attempt. Accordingly I made up my mind first to see my friend safe from the African shore, and then to return as soon as the rains had fallen.

I communicated my resolve to Mr. Galton, who at once fully entered into my views; and as I had neither oxen nor waggons, he kindly promised to supply me with both; as also with such articles of barter as his own reduced stores afforded.

After nearly a month's absence, we found ourselves safe at Elephant Fountain. Notwithstanding we had been almost solely living on fresh meat during this time, we had only used the one half of a small copper-cap box[1] of salt! I mention the circumstance to show that salt is not strictly necessary to man's existence. Moreover, excepting once or twice at the missionary table, we had not tasted bread for many months. I had so totally forgotten the use of it, that, after our return to Barmen, on being entertained at Mr. Hahn's house, I finished my meal without noticing the piece of bread which was conspicuous enough alongside my plate. Our men grumbled a little at first at being deprived of bread; but they also soon got accustomed to do without it, nor did the least inconvenience arise from its absence. I have always heard that the want of bread and vegetables, is the greatest hardship a man can experience. Be that as it may, the human system—as the above facts demonstrate—is capable of reconciling itself to nearly all conditions and circumstances.

The men left in charge of the waggon were well; but poor John Mortar, the cook, looked pale and thin. On asking him the cause, he pointed to the fire where our food was cooked, and, with something like an oath, exclaimed—"Sir, look at that pot! I have been watching it these seven-and-twenty days and nights, and, after all, I find that my labour is thrown away!"

Shortly after leaving Elephant Fountain, John, it seems,

---

[1] A copper-cap box, for the information of my female readers, is about the size of a pill-box.

had set about making soap, of which our supply was exhausted. Through some mistake, however, he used unslaked lime instead of the alkali obtained in the country from the ash of the native soap-bush. This at once accounted for his failure in regard to the article itself, and his own emaciated appearance.

Game, as has been said, was very abundant near to Elephant Fountain; and, by means of spacious pit-falls, great numbers of wild animals were almost nightly captured. The whole ground in the neighbourhood of Zwart Nosop, which flowed past the place, was literally a succession of pit-falls, and they were so cleverly arranged and well concealed, that it required the utmost caution in walking about. Even people thoroughly acquainted with the locality ran great risk of being precipitated into these dangerous traps.

Lions were numerous, and very daring. From time to time, several of Amral's people, whilst lying in ambush for game at night, had been either carried off or fearfully mangled by these beasts. Finding that I was somewhat incautious, the chief expressed the greatest apprehensions for my safety, more especially as I was usually quite alone.

On one of these occasions, I must confess to having felt rather uncomfortable. I had posted myself in a dense mimosa brake, commanding the approach to the Zwart Nosop river at a point much frequented by wild animals, and flanked by an immense pit-fall. The darkness was deepened by surrounding thick foliage and high river-banks. Indeed, so black was the night that I could not discern even the muzzle of my gun. The gloominess of my solitude was increased by the occasional "Qua-qua!" of the night-heron, which made the succeeding hush more dreary; during which even the falling of leaves, and rustling of insects among dry grass, was hailed as a relief to the oppressive dumbness. To a man in a savage wilderness, and without a companion, silence, especially when combined with utter privation of light, is inexpressibly solemn. It strikes the mind not merely as a negation, but as a threatening presence. It seems ominous. I shall never forget the loneliness and sense of desolation I felt on this occasion. It was past midnight, and still no game appeared.

Suddenly, I fancied I heard the purr and breathing of an animal close behind me; but, as no other indications of any living thing ensued, I attributed the sounds to a heated imagination. All at once, however, the dismal stillness was disturbed by the quick steps of a troop of pallahs, descending the stony slope leading direct to my ambush. Stooping as low as possible, in order to catch their outline, I waited their arrival with my gun on full cock. Nearer and nearer they came, till at last I fancied the leader was on the verge of the pit-fall; but, just at that moment, there was a low, stifled growl, a rush, and then a faint cry as of some dying animal. All was again silent. Though the impenetrable darkness prevented me from seeing anything, I could no longer doubt that I was in the immediate vicinity of a lion. I freely acknowledge that I felt awed, well knowing that were he to attack me, I should be completely at his mercy. My situation was critical in the extreme. Straining eyes and ears to discover the beast's whereabout, I held my breath in fearful suspense, whilst every nerve was strung to the highest pitch. Presently I heard, to my astonishment, the report of a gun within fifty paces of my hiding-place; then a second and a third shot. This made matters worse; for I now became apprehensive that the men, not aware of my presence, might direct their fire towards me. I therefore sprang to my feet, and vociferated—" Who's there ?" " Sir! the lion—the lion!" replied Eyebrecht, for it was no other. The next instant he stood trembling before me. He had, it appeared, been sent by Amral to call me back, but had encountered the beast in his path, and fired in order to frighten him away.

Though I did not exactly comply with the wishes of the chief, I deemed it advisable, after what had passed, to remove to a more open place where I was less likely to be taken by surprise. Early next morning a number of Hottentots came to examine the ground, when, as I had expected, we found the foot-prints of a lion at the very back of my 'skärm,' and scarcely distant the length of the gun-barrel from my own person, where he had evidently been crouching previously to leaping on the pallah (whose cry I had heard in the night), but which, though wounded, had effected its escape. How far the beast intended me mischief is hard to say, but in any case, my position had not been an enviable one.

On our return-journey to Barmen, it rained heavily, and in some places the landscape looked quite revived. Many migratory birds, such as the swallow, the cuckoo, and others, had again made their appearance.

The animals, which during the dry season are compelled to gather round the springs and other permanent waters, were enabled, by the late rains, to scatter themselves over a large extent of country, and were now difficult to find. There can be little doubt that the instinctive power of animals—domesticated as well as wild—is capable of catching the scent of humid winds and green herbage, at a very great distance. Thus I have often seen oxen turn their heads towards the quarter where distant lightning indicated that rain had fallen, and sniff with evident pleasure the breeze produced by colder air. Mr. Moffat, the missionary, mentions an instance where a great number of cattle were entirely lost, solely, as he supposes, from this cause.

"Many years previous to my sojourn in Namaqua-land," says the Reverend gentleman, "Afrikaner thus lost the greater part of his cattle. One evening a strong wind commenced blowing from the north; it smelt of green grass, as the natives expressed it. The cattle not being in folds, started off after dark. The circumstance being unprecedented, it was supposed they had merely wandered out to the common, where they were accustomed to graze; but it was found, after much search, that some thousands of cattle had directed their course to the north. A few were recovered; but the majority escaped to the Damara country, after having been pursued hundreds of miles."

For my own part, I have frequently passed through localities abounding with game; and, re-passing them in a short time, I have found them deserted without any apparent cause. As I proceeded, however, I have discovered them in quite different quarters, and ascertained that the attraction has been the young grass, which was either produced by the moisture of the atmosphere, or from the natives having fired the old grass. The rapidity with which parched and sun-burnt pasturages in tropical climes, are converted by any of these causes into luxuriant savannahs, is incredible, and can only be duly estimated by those who have themselves witnessed such changes.

A stage on this side of Eikhams, we encountered Hans, who had met with a little adventure in the neighbourhood of Scheppman's Mountain, where he had one day unyoked. He had been out in search of game, when on his return he was astonished to observe a number of natives rushing towards the waggon, no doubt with the intention of plundering it, and probably of spearing the men who had it in charge. On seeing Hans approach with a gun, however, they all took to their heels, but some were captured; and after they had undergone a sound drubbing, and been threatened with death should they ever attempt a similar outrage, they were allowed to depart. Not many hours elapsed before these very savages returned to beg for tobacco!

We were sorry to find that our cattle looked thin and miserable. Indeed, Hans had experienced the greatest difficulty in bringing on the waggon. Restored tranquillity had given confidence to the Damaras, who were now flocking in great numbers with their cattle to the banks of the Swakop, the result of which was that every blade of grass was consumed for miles around on both sides of the river. This was indeed sad news, as our route lay precisely through these parts, and our draught animals were by this time in a distressingly exhausted and reduced state. It required some efforts on our side to overcome these difficulties, and we lost no time in retracing our steps. After Mr. Galton had disposed of some of the superfluous goods to the natives, and exchanged the run-away mules to Jonker for cattle, we bade farewell to the hospitable hearth of the missionaries at Barmen and Richterfeldt, and proceeded quickly on our road to Walfisch Bay.

On arriving at the confluence of the Swakop and the Tjobis rivers, we had a narrow escape from being poisoned, as the Hill-Damaras had mixed the juice of the *euphorbia candelabrum* with the stagnant pool-water, for the purpose of killing buffaloes, which were numerous hereabouts. Fortunately, by having gone in advance of our party, in the hope of obtaining a shot at these animals, I discovered the poisoned water (easily detected by its peculiar clay colour) in time to prevent any serious mischief. Some of the dogs partook of it; but having previously taken their fill of clear, pure water, they escaped with a heavy vomiting. At this identical place, Hans had a short time previously found several dead and dying buffaloes that had been poisoned.

The symptoms with men, after imbibing the poison in question—not the least of the many dangers to which the African traveller is almost daily exposed—is generally a fullness of the system, quick pulsation, giddiness, and a violent 'flesh-quake.'

Though our cattle suffered dreadfully from want of pasturage, we reached Walfisch Bay, on the 5th of December, without the loss of a single ox.

The missionary vessel had not yet arrived; but there were two others—a brig and a barque. The master of the first was an Englishman, in search of guano; as also of nitrate of soda, which was reported to exist on this coast. He imagined that he had really found the latter valuable salt, and whispered his discovery to us as a great secret. On examining the specimens in his possession, however, it was found to be nothing more nor less than pieces of common soap! —part, probably, of the cargo of some wrecked vessel. The action of the water had so altered the soap in appearance, that the mistake was really excusable. On learning from us the real nature of his supposed prize, the poor captain, as may be imagined, evinced no little chagrin and disappointment.

The second ship was an American, in search of the sperm whale, which is not unfrequently found in these waters. Our shabby and tattered garments and unshaved faces induced the captain to regard us at first with suspicion, taking us not improbably for outlaws, unfit for other society than savage men and beasts. By degrees, however, his mind, as to our proper character, was set at rest; and we were hospitably entertained on board his ship, which was scrupulously clean and orderly.

The crews of many of the whaling and guano ships who were in the habit of frequenting Walfisch Bay had behaved very outrageously, either by plundering, or wantonly destroying the contents of the temporary store-house. On one occasion they had been amusingly baffled in their dishonest and disreputable practices. At the time of which I am now speaking, the store was tenanted by Mr. Dickson, the trader, who possessed some very fine lion cubs. These a certain captain determined to purloin; and, for that purpose, sent a number of his men in the dead of the night to carry them away. The animals were usually kept in a large tub or barrel; but it so happened that, on the very evening the master had fixed on for the execution of his plan, they had been removed elsewhere; and that Mr. Bassingweight, one of Mr. Dickson's *employés*, had taken up his abode in their old quarters. The sailors entered the building unperceived, and began rapidly to roll the tub away. Mr. Bassingweight at first imagined he was dreaming; but, as the motion became more violent, the thumping of his head against the wooden walls soon brought him to his senses, on which he roared out most lustily. The unexpected and strange noise so terrified the sailors, that they made a precipitate retreat.

The next morning, the captain, having previously had the audacity to possess himself of one of Mr. Dickson's horses, came riding, very drunk, to his house, and in an imperious and impudent tone demanded the cubs to be given up to him. At the same time he thrust an immense dagger through a dish of pancakes, which a servant was busy preparing. Mr. Dickson was not at home; but his wife, who was a shrewd and determined woman, not only refused compliance, but commanded the fellow instantly to dismount, and go about his business. On his hesitating, she unceremoniously pulled him off the horse, and threatened to knock him down if he did not immediately leave the house. Fearing, however, that he might return with his crew during the night to revenge himself, and perhaps take forcible possession of the young lions, she ordered Bassingweight, and another of her servants (having previously primed them with cordials to raise their spirits and courage) to proceed, at dusk, towards the Bay to watch the enemy's movements. Mrs. Dickson's surmise proved correct; for the men had not gone far before they distinguished the clamorous voices of a number of persons who were rapidly approaching them. Squatting behind some sand hillocks they allowed the marauders to come within range, when they fired a shot over their heads, which had the desired effect. Without waiting for further hostility, Jack instantly bolted. Elated by their easy success, Bassingweight and his companion instantly gave chase, and on coming up with the fugitives, a terrible *pele-mêle* fight ensued. Notwithstanding one of the men was almost a giant in strength and stature, the odds were too great, and they were on the point of being overpowered. At this critical moment Bassingweight called loudly for assistance, hoping that some of the natives, who occasionally slept on the beach, might come to the rescue. To their inexpressible relief up rose from among a number of empty barrels, which happened to be ranged along the shore, a bushman. His appearance acted like magic, and instantly turned the cards in their favour; for the sailors, as it was afterwards ascertained, imagining the casks to be savages also, and dreading probably their poisoned arrows, were seized with a panic, and fled precipitately in every direction, some rushing up to their necks in water, whilst others actually fell on their knees begging forgiveness! Unless for the bushman, Bassingweight assured me that himself and companion must have been inevitably killed.

The bay presented at this time a most extraordinary spectacle, the whole being covered with one mass of dead fish. We could only account for so unusual a sight by supposing that an epidemic had occurred amongst them, more especially as it did not appear to be confined to one or two species of the finny tribe, but to all which are indigenous to the coast—the gigantic shark not excepted. In some of the more sheltered spots, the fish lay so deep, that I remember on one occasion to have had some difficulty in forcing my way through in a small mackintosh punt.

As may well be expected, the effluvium arising from such a mass of decomposed matter was offensive and sickening. Whether all the fish died, or the stench drove the survivors away, I am unable to decide; but certain it is that hardly a fish was left in the bay. On our first arrival we captured large quantities by means of a small seine-net, but now all our attempts proved futile.

An incident occurred to me one day which might have been attended with fatal consequences. A cutter had lately arrived from the Cape, the object of the captain being to harpoon the 'humpback' whale, which at this season of the year abounds in the vicinity of Walfisch Bay. I had paid a visit to the craft in the punt mentioned. On my return it came on to blow hard from the land. In calm weather the punt could be managed with great ease; but on account of her flat bottom, and light construction, it was impossible to make head against a stiff breeze. When within a stone's throw of the shore, she became unmanageable, and for the space of fully one hour, all my efforts to propel her were unavailing. At last, finding my strength failing, I made one more desperate effort, and having fortunately succeeded in getting her into shallow water, I leaped over the side and ultimately brought her to a place of safety. My arms were quite paralysed, and for a while I was unable to lift them from my sides. Had the struggle lasted another minute, nothing could have saved me from being blown out into the open sea, and as there was a gale of wind at the time, there can be no doubt as to the result.

On the 31st of December, being then at Scheppmansdorf, I received intelligence that the long-expected missionary vessel had arrived, and that she was to sail in a few days for St. Helena. On the following morning, the first day of the year 1852, a parcel of European letters was handed to me. It was now fully twenty months since I had heard any news of my friends, and I hailed this token of their interest in my behalf with rapture. But, alas!—though I had much to be thankful for—the intelligence was damped by the unexpected tidings of the death of a younger brother. Poor fellow! notwithstanding he and I could never agree during life, I loved him dearly. His last words, uttered in delirium, were said to have been addressed to me, imploring me to come to his assistance. He died at Rio Janeirio of that scourge, the yellow fever. Peace be to his memory! The cholera was also raging in Sweden, and I trembled for the news that might next reach me.

I proceeded immediately to Walfisch Bay to bid farewell to Galton. John Williams, John Mortar, and Timbo were to accompany him to St. Helena, whence they were to be forwarded to Cape-Town. Hans—in himself a host—John Allen, and John St. Helena, agreed to remain with me.

My specimens of natural history, which had been collected with much care and trouble, and which had cost me many a sleepless night, I consigned to Galton's care. They consisted of about five hundred bird-skins, nearly double that number of insects, and a few odds and ends. I also took this opportunity to forward several letters to my European friends.

Galton appeared delighted with the prospect of soon returning to civilized life. Though he had proved himself to be capable of enduring hardships and fatigue as well as any of us, it was evident that he had had enough of it.

The schooner was to have sailed on the 5th of January;

but in consequence of the arrival of "The Grecian" man-of-war, then cruising off the west coast, it was postponed till the next day. As the schooner gradually disappeared from view, I began to feel in full force the loneliness of my situation, and the loss of my friend's company. It would seem that the farther the object of our esteem and regard is separated from us, the better we are able to appreciate its value. Galton's excellent disposition, and even temper, had enabled us to struggle through all difficulties very happily together; and it was, therefore, with sincere regret that I parted from him. I whispered a prayer for his safe return to the bosom of his family. It was heard; for, though the passage proved of long duration, he reached England in safety, after an absence of two years.

Not long subsequently to his return, the Royal Geographical Society, I was happy to learn, bestowed upon him their gold medal, as a reward for his services in the cause of science.

COURSING YOUNG OSTRICHES.

London, Hurst & Blackett, 1856.

CHAPTER XX.

CAPTURE OF YOUNG OSTRICHES—NATURAL HISTORY OF THE OSTRICH; WHERE FOUND; DESCRIPTION OF; SIZE; WEIGHT; AGE; VOICE; STRENGTH; SPEED; FOOD; WATER; BREEDING; INCUBATION; CUNNING; STONES FOUND IN EGGS; CHICKS; FLESH—BRAIN IN REQUEST AMONGST THE ROMANS—EGGS HIGHLY PRIZED—USES OF EGG-SHELLS—FEATHERS AN ARTICLE OF COMMERCE—OSTRICH PARASOLS—THE BIRD'S DESTRUCTIVE PROPENSITIES—HABITS—RESEMBLES QUADRUPEDS—DOMESTICATION—THE CHASE—SNARES—INGENIOUS DEVICE—ENEMIES OF THE OSTRICH.

OSTRICHES are at all times more or less numerous on the Naarip Plain, but more particularly so at this season, on account of the naras (of which, mention was made in the second chapter) being now ripe.

Whilst waiting for the missionary vessel, previously to the departure of Mr. Galton, I made several trips between the Bay and Scheppmansdorf, in order to arrange matters for my intended journey to the Ngami. On one of these occasions I was accompained by my friend. When we had proceeded little more than half the distance, and in a part of the plain entirely destitute of vegetation, we discovered a male and female ostrich with a brood of young ones about the size of ordinary barn-door fowls. This was a sight we had long been looking for, as Galton had been requested by Professor Owen to procure a few craniums of the young of this bird, in order to settle certain anatomical questions. Accordingly, we forthwith dismounted from our oxen, and gave chase, which proved of no ordinary interest.

The moment the parent birds became aware of our intention, they set off at full speed—the female leading the way, the young following in her wake, and the cock, though at some little distance, bringing up the rear of the family-party. It was very touching to observe the anxiety the old birds evinced for the safety of their progeny. Finding that we were quickly gaining upon them, the male at once slackened his pace, and diverged somewhat from his course; but, seeing that we were not to be diverted from our purpose, he again increased his speed, and, with wings drooping so as almost to touch the ground, he hovered round us, now in wide circles, and then decreasing the circumference till he came almost within pistol-shot, when he abruptly threw himself on the ground, and struggled desperately to regain his legs, as it appeared, like a bird that has been badly wounded. Having previously fired at him, I really thought he was disabled, and made quickly towards him. But this was only a *ruse* on his part; for, on my nearer approach, he slowly rose and began to run in an opposite direction to that of the female, who by this time was considerably a-head with her charge.

After about an hour's severe chase, we secured nine of the brood; and though it consisted of about double that number, we found it necessary to be contented with what we had bagged.[1]

On returning to the Bay, however, the next morning in a

---

[1] The lithograph facing this chapter is a faithful representation of the chase described, which took place shortly before sunset.

mule-cart, Mr. Galton again encountered the same birds with the remainder of the family; and, after a short race, captured six more of the chicks.

The ostrich (which, from possessing the rudiments of a gall-bladder, and the absence of wings fit for flight, seems to form a kind of connecting link between the two great families of *mammalia* and *aves*) is an inhabitant of a large portion of Africa, but rarely extends farther east than the deserts of Arabia. Throughout the Indian Archipelago, the family of birds (of which the ostrich is the leading type) is represented by the cassowary; in Australia, by the emeu; in the southern extremity of the western hemisphere, by the rhea; and even in Europe, though somewhat departing from the type, it has its representative in the stately bustard.

Anything like a scientific description of the ostrich would here be out of place; but it may be proper to mention that the lower part of the neck and the body of the mature male bird are of a deep glossy black, intermingled with a few whitish feathers, only visible when the plumage is ruffled. "In the female, the general colour of the feathers is of a greyish, or ashy brown, slightly fringed with white. In both sexes the large plumes of the wings and tail are beautifully white."

The ostrich, when full grown, stands no less than from seven to eight feet, and instances are recorded where individual birds have attained as much as nine. Its weight is proportionate. Judging from what I have experienced in carrying the dead body, it is not less, perhaps, than two or three hundred pounds. Indeed, there are persons who believe that the mature bird, when in prime condition, as a butcher would say, will attain a weight of thirty stone.

I could never obtain any data that would enable me to

form a correct estimate of the age of the ostrich; but it may fairly be concluded that he lives between twenty and thirty years.

The cry of the ostrich so greatly resembles that of a lion, as occasionally to deceive even the natives. It is usually heard early in the morning, and, at times, also at night.

The strength of the ostrich is enormous. A single blow from its gigantic foot (it always strikes forward) is sufficient to prostrate, nay, to kill many beasts of prey, such as the hyæna, the panther, the wild dog, the jackal, and others.

The ostrich is exceedingly swift of foot; under ordinary circumstances out-running a fleet horse: "What time she lifteth up herself on high, she scorneth the horse and its rider." On special occasions, and for a short distance, its speed is truly marvellous—perhaps not much less than a mile in half a minute. Its feet appear hardly to touch the ground, and the length between each stride is not unfrequently twelve to fourteen feet. Indeed, if we are to credit the testimony of Mr. Adanson, who says he witnessed the fact in Senegal, such is the rapidity and muscular power of the ostrich, that, even with two men mounted on his back, he will outstrip an English horse in speed! The ostrich, moreover, is long-winded, if I may use the expression; so that it is a work of time to exhaust the bird.

The food of the ostrich, in its wild state, consists of the seeds, tops and buds of various shrubs and other plants.[1] But it is often difficult to conceive how it can manage to live at all, for one not unfrequently meets with it in regions apparently destitute of vegetation of any kind:

---

[1] At the Zoological Gardens, Regent's Park, where at this moment several of these birds are alive, the ostrich is fed on a mixture of oats, barley, chaff, and cabbage, of which the respective quantities are as follows:—oats, one pint; barley, one pint; chaff, half a gallon; and cabbage, four pounds.

> "A region of emptiness, howling and drear,
>   Which man hath abandoned from famine and fear;
>   Which the ostrich and lizard inhabit alone,
>   With the twilight bat from the old hollow stone;
>   Where grass, nor herb, nor shrub take root,
>   Save poisonous thorns that pierce the foot;
>   And the bitter-melon for food and drink,
>   Is the pilgrim's fare by the salt lake's brink!"

Although the ostrich is undoubtedly capable of undergoing thirst for a considerable period, yet water appears to be indispensable to its existence. In the dry and hot season, I have often observed the same flock drinking almost daily. They swallow the water by a succession of gulps. On such occasions—that is when approaching a spring—they seem quite stupified. Whilst staying at Elephant Fountain, where in a short time I killed eight of these magnificent birds, they made their appearance regularly every day about noon, and although the locality afforded but indifferent shelter, they invariably allowed me to get within range, only retreating step by step.

Like the capercali of Europe, the ostrich has a plurality of wives—from two to six it is said. The breeding season would seem to be somewhat undefined, for I have met with nests in every month from June till October. Each female is represented as laying from twelve to sixteen eggs, and all in one and the same nest, which is simply a cavity scooped out in the sand.

Both male and female assist in hatching the eggs, which are placed upright, in order, it would seem, "that the greatest possible number may be stowed within the space." When about a dozen eggs are laid, the bird, which squats astride over them, with its legs pointed forward, begins to sit. I have observed that on perceiving a man, instead of running away from the nest, it not unfrequently lowers its conspicuous neck till it becomes in a line with the ground, evidently in the hope that it may be passed unnoticed.

During the period of incubation, the ostrich, if an intruder approaches its nest, resorts to various artifices to induce him to withdraw far off.

"One morning," says Professor Thunberg, "as I rode past a place where a hen-ostrich sat on her nest, the bird sprang up and pursued me, with a view to prevent my noticing her young ones, or her eggs. Every time I turned my horse towards her, she retreated ten or twelve paces; but as soon as I rode on she pursued me again."

The period of incubation seems to vary; but on the average, it may be about thirty-eight days. One or more of the females are said to lay meanwhile; but the supernumerary eggs are placed outside the nest, and are supposed to serve as nourishment for the callow brood. If such really be the case, we, in this again, see a wonderful provision of nature, inasmuch as the chicken would be unable to digest the indurated matter furnished by their too-often sterile haunts.

The notion so generally entertained of the ostrich merely depositing her eggs in the sand, and leaving them to be vivified by the sun, arises, probably, from its habit of occasionally quitting the nest in search of food, more especially as it generally does so during the hottest part of the day.

Some travellers affirm that the ostrich not only never sits on her eggs after having once been handled, or even if a man should have passed near the nest, but that she actually destroys them! I, for my part, cannot speak to this point, having, whenever I found an ostrich's nest, usually plundered it at once, thus leaving the bird no opportunity of obeying so strange an instinct.

It seems pretty certain, however, that the ostrich, as with many other birds, is in the habit of deserting her eggs if they be handled. "The slaves," says Professor Thunberg, "always use the precaution not to take away the eggs with their hands (in which case the birds, who perceive it by scent, are apt to quit the spot), but by means of a long stick they rake them out of the nest as fast as the birds lay them."

A peculiarity in regard to the eggs of the ostrich, and, so far as I am aware, confined to the eggs of this bird alone, is mentioned by several African travellers. For example:— "The farmer here likewise informed me," says the author just quoted, "that a stone or two is sometimes found in the ostrich's eggs, which is hard, white, rather flat and smooth, and about the size of a bean. These stones are cut and made into buttons, but I never had the good fortune to see any of them."

Again: "In these eggs," writes Barrow, "are frequently discovered a number of small oval-shaped pebbles, about the size of a marrow-fat pea, of a pale yellow colour, and exceedingly hard. In one egg we found nine, and in another twelve of such stones."

Notwithstanding the number of eggs laid, seldom more than thirty to thirty-five are hatched. Almost as soon as the chicks (which are about the size of pullets) have escaped from the shell, they are able to walk about and to follow the mother, on whom they are dependent for a considerable period. And Nature, with her usual care, has provided the young with a colour and a covering admirably suited to the localities they frequent. The colour is a kind of pepper-and-salt, harmonizing wonderfully with the variegated sand and gravel of the plains, which they are in the habit of traversing. Indeed, when crouching under my very eyes, I have had the greatest difficulty in discerning the chicks. The covering is neither down nor feathers, but a kind of 'prickly external,' which, no doubt, is an excellent protection against injury from the coarse gravel and the stunted vegetation amongst which they dwell.

The flesh of the young ostrich is not unpalatable; but that of the old bird is anything but good. To my notion, it tastes very much like that of the zebra. According to the Mosaic law, the ostrich was denounced as an unclean animal, and the Jews were, consequently, forbidden to eat it. The Arabs of the present day still adhere to this prohibition. Some of the native tribes of Southern Africa, however, are less fastidious, and partake of the flesh with great relish, more especially when fat.

Though people at the present day place little or no value on the ostrich as an article of food, the ancient Romans, who were great epicures, seem to have been of a different opinion. We are told by Vobiscus that the pseudo Emperor Firmus, " equally celebrated for his feats at the anvil and at the trencher, devoured, in his own imperial person, an entire ostrich at one sitting."[1] The brain of this bird was considered a superlative delicacy; and, like everything else with that luxurious nation, it was provided on the most magnificent scale. Thus, according to an ancient testimony, the Emperor Heliogabalus was served at a single feast with the brains of six hundred of these birds.[2]

If the flesh of the ostrich be not much esteemed, its eggs, at all events, are prized in the highest degree by natives and travellers. To say nothing of their flavour, each contains as much as twenty-four of the eggs of the barn-door fowl, and weighs about three pounds.

---

[1] Apicius gives a recipe for the best sauce.

[2] The Romans, as is well known, also introduced large numbers of ostriches into the circus, where they were butchered by the people. We are told that no less than one thousand of these splendid creatures (together with an equal number of the stag, the fallow deer, and the boar tribe) were on one occasion brutally sacrificed to gratify the insatiable thirst for blood of the Roman populace.

From the great size of the ostrich egg it might be supposed that one would be a sufficient meal for any man; but I have known instances where two eggs have been dispatched by a single individual, even when mixed with a quantity of flour and fat. Indeed, Hans and his companion once finished five ostrich eggs in the course of an afternoon!

Even the egg-shell is of considerable value, and is an excellent vessel for holding liquids of any kind. The bushmen have hardly any other. By covering it with a light net-work it may be carried slung across the saddle. Grass, wood, &c., serve as substitutes for corks.

By the monks of Dayr Antonios, we are informed that the Copts (by whom the eggs are looked upon as the emblem of watchfulness, and who suspend them in their churches), pass the cords of their lamps through the shell in order to prevent the rats from coming down and drinking the oil.

The shell of the egg is used medicinally. The Boers, after reducing it to powder, and mixing it with vinegar, give it to cattle afflicted with stranguary, for which disease it is considered a sovereign remedy. The powder itself is said to be an excellent preservative against blindness.

The white wing-feathers[1] of the ostrich (the black ones are used chiefly for mourning) are a considerable article of commerce. The market however is very fluctuating. At the Cape the price varies from one or two guineas sterling, to as much as twelve, for the pound, the latter sum, however, being

---

[1] The plumes, together with the eggs, of the ostrich, are said to have been held in much request with the ancient Egyptians. Indeed, they formed part of the tribute imposed on those of the conquered nations in whose country the bird abounded; and appear to have been used for ornaments as well as for religious purposes. 'The ostrich feather was a symbol of the Goddess of Truth or Justice. It belonged also to the head-dress of Ao; was adopted by Hermes Trismegistus; and worn by the soldiery and the priests on certain religious festivals.' 'In Turkey, the Jannissary who signalized himself in arms had the privilege of empluming his turban; and in the kingdom of Congo the feathers, mixed with those of the peacock, are employed as the ensigns of war and victory.'

only paid for very prime feathers. The thinner the quill, and the longer and more wavy the plume, the more it is prized.[1] Seventy to ninety feathers go to the pound. But although half this number may be obtained from a single bird, only a small portion are of any value. In the pairing season—and it may be at other times—the ostrich, like the turkey-cock, the capercali, and many other birds, is in the habit of drooping its wings, so that the outer feathers trail on the ground, which soon destroys their beauty. The proper time to kill the ostrich for its plumes, is shortly after the moulting season, or in the months of March and April.

The Damaras and the Bechuanas manufacture handsome parasols from the black feathers of the ostrich, which serve as signs of mourning, or are useful for the preservation of the complexion. "It is a beautiful sight," says Harris, "to behold a savage, whose skin, somewhat coarser than the hide of a rhinoceros, might vie in point of colour with a boot, protecting his complexion by the interposition of such an umbrella."

Some of the tribes of Southern Africa are said to employ ostrich-parasols whilst hunting wild animals, with a similar purpose to that of a Spanish bull-fighter who uses a red cloth. Thus, in case of a wounded beast charging a man, the latter, just at the moment he is about to be seized, suddenly thrusts the supports of the nodding plumes into the ground, and, while the infuriated animal is venting its rage on its supposed victim, the native slips unperceived on one side and transfixes his antagonist.

The skin of the ostrich is also said to be held in great request, and forms no inconsiderable article of commerce.

---

[1] Such feathers as have been plucked from the wings of the living bird are said to be preferable to those obtained from the dead ostrich, as being less liable to the attack of worms.

"The whole defensive armour of the Nasamones, inhabitants of Lybia, was manufactured of the birds' thick skin, which, even at the present day, is used as a cuirass by some of the Arab troops."

The ostrich, though usually dwelling far from the haunts of men, occasionally approaches the homestead, and, at such times, causes the Boer considerable damage by trampling down and eating the grain.

The opinion of authors and sportsmen with regard to the ostrich, vary considerably. Some ascribe to it great stupidity, whilst others consider it as possessed of vivacity and much intelligence. Without passing a judgment, I will only mention, that I have seen it exhibit these opposite qualities in no small degree.

In a domesticated state, it is true, the ostrich appears to be a quiet, dull, and heavy-looking bird; but when seen in its native haunts, it is restless, wary, and difficult of approach. From its great stature, and the prominent position of its eyes, its range of vision is naturally considerable, which enables it to discover danger at a considerable distance. This, together with the exposed localities frequented by it, probably accounts for the comparatively few that even the mightiest Nimrods of South Africa can boast of having killed.

What may be the case with the ostrich, in a wild state, is hard to say; but, when in confinement, no bird or other animal demonstrates so little discrimination in the choice of its food; for it then swallows with avidity stones, pieces of wood and iron, spoons, knives, and a variety of other indigestible matters. This strange propensity and apparent obtuseness of taste, obtained for the bird, at an early period, the epithet of 'the iron-eating ostrich:'

"The estridge that will eate
An horshowe so great

> In the steade of meat;
> Such fervent heat
> His stomach doth freat."[1]

Many amusing anecdotes are told of the strange habits of this bird. Once—so runs the story—when the ostrich was still a rare sight in Europe, a woman, on hearing of the arrival of a batch of these birds, and being anxious to obtain a sight of them, hastily shut up her house, taking the key of the door in her hand. No sooner, however, had she arrived on the spot where the birds were kept, than one of them stalked gravely up to the lady, and, snatching the iron instrument out of her hand, deliberately, and to her great horror, swallowed it—*actually shutting her out of her own house!*

"Nothing," says Methuen, in his 'Life in the Wilderness,' when speaking of a female ostrich that came under his immediate notice, "disturbed the ostrich's digestion: dyspepsia was a thing 'undreamt of in its philosophy.' One day, a muscovy duck brought a promising brood of ducklings into the world, and with maternal pride conducted them forth into the yard. Up, with solemn and measured stride, walked the ostrich, and, wearing the most mild, benignant cast of face, swallowed them all, one after the other, like so many oysters, regarding the indignant hissings and bristling plumage of the hapless mother with stoical indifference."

The ostrich is gregarious, and is met with in troops varying from a few individuals to as many as fifty. Singularly enough, it is never known to associate with other birds; but, preferring quadrupeds, is often found in company with the zebra, the springbok, the gnoo, &c. Indeed, in many respects it bears a striking resemblance to four-footed animals; such as in its strong, jointed legs and cloven hoofs; its long, muscular neck; its gruff voice; the absence of the elevated

---

[1] 'The Boke of Philip Sparrow.'

central ridge of the breast bone, so generally characteristic of birds; besides other similarities already mentioned. But, perhaps, when compared with the camel, the affinity becomes still more striking. Both are "furnished with callous protuberances on the chest and on the abdomen, on which they support themselves when at rest; and they both lie down in the same manner." In both the feet and stomach are somewhat similarly constructed; and if we add to this, their capabilities of subsisting on a scanty and stunted vegetation, their endurance of thirst, and their formation in general, which enables ostrich and camel to inhabit and traverse arid and desert regions, the resemblance is by no means so imaginary as one might at first suppose. Indeed, to many of the nations of the East,[1] as well as to the Romans and the Greeks, the ostrich was known by the name of the camel-bird.

The ostrich is easily domesticated, but is sometimes of a vicious disposition. The Rev. Mr. Hahn, if I remember rightly, told me that some of these birds which he kept in confinement for a considerable period, became so mischievous, that, lest they might injure any of the people on the station, he was obliged to kill them.

Several persons have tried to breed from the tame ostrich; but, to the best of my belief, all attempts have hitherto proved abortive. Eggs, however, have been frequently obtained; but the birds never showed any inclination to sit upon them. At the Regent's Park Gardens, moreover, repeated trials have been made to hatch the eggs by artificial means, but without success.

The expedients resorted to in South Africa to capture the ostrich are various. Not unfrequently it is ridden down

[1] Among the people of Persia and Arabia the vulgar belief is said to exist 'that the *shutur-moorg* (the camel-bird) is produced by the union of a camel with a bird!'

by men on horseback. Several hunters take different sides of a large plain, thus hemming the bird in, and chasing it backwards and forwards until its strength is exhausted.

The ostrich is also at times ridden down by a single horseman. Under ordinary circumstances, fleet as the horse may be, this would be impossible. Towards the approach of the rainy season, however, when the days are intolerably hot and oppressive, the giant bird may be seen standing motionless on the plain, with wings spread, and beak wide open; and at such times the capture may be accomplished. Indeed, cases have come under my notice where Namaquas, after a short and spirited chase, have brought the ostrich to a dead stand-still. A blow on the head with a stick or a 'shambok' is then sufficient to despatch it. On similar occasions, however, horses have been known to drop down dead from over-exertion.

When an ostrich finds himself observed, he will often make for some given point—more especially if he be hemmed in near a plain. He is so fully aware that safety is only to be found in the open country, that he always endeavours to gain it. Should the sportsman understand his business, he may easily cut him off; but it requires a keen eye and a practised hand to bring the bird down; for on emergencies like these, its speed, as before said, is truly wonderful.

The Arabs of North Africa are also accustomed to pursue the ostrich on horseback; but instead of trying to overtake the bird at once, it is steadily followed—even for days—without putting it to its speed, until it becomes gradually exhausted, when it falls an easy prey to the persevering hunter.[1]

---

[1] 'When slain, the throat is opened; and a ligature being passed below the incision, several of the hunters raise the bird by the head and feet, and shake and drag him about until they obtain from the aperture nearly twenty pounds of a substance of mingled blood and fat, of the consistence of coagulated oil, which, under the denomi-

In parts of Southern Africa, the ostrich is run down even on foot. I, myself, have seen the bushmen accomplish this exploit on the shores of Lake Ngami. They usually surround a whole troop, and, with shouts and yells, chase the terrified birds into the water, where they are, of course, speedily killed. "We more than once," says Harris, "fell in with a large party of Corannas engaged in an attempt to tire out an ostrich on foot, a feat which they are said sometimes to achieve, knocking him off his legs by *squaling* with a club of rhinoceros horn, fashioned like a hockey stick."

The bushman, however, frequently has recourse to a much simpler plan of circumventing the ostrich. Having found its nest, he removes the eggs to a place of safety, and, ensconcing himself in the empty cavity, awaits the return of the bird, which he generally manages to dispatch with a poisoned arrow.

At other times, the natives lie in wait near pools frequented by ostriches, and shoot them when they come there to quench their thirst. If the gun be loaded with swan-shot instead of ball, and one aims at the necks, several may be killed at a single discharge; but this plan will, of course, never be adopted by the true sportsman.

Ostriches are also not unfrequently captured in snares (similar to those made use of for entangling smaller species of antelopes), but I have quite forgotten whether by the neck or the leg. A long cord, having at one end a noose, is tied to a sapling which is bent down, and the noose pinned to the ground in such a manner that when a bird treads within it, the sapling springs back by its own natural elasticity, suspending the bird or other animal in the air; and it is only released from its suffering by death. Strabo and Oppian

nation of *manteque*, is employed in the preparation of dishes and the cure of various maladies.'—*Harris's Wild Sports.*

make mention of snares being employed by the ancients for the capture of ostriches; either alluring them by stratagem into the toils, or driving them *en masse*, by a brisk pursuit with horses and dogs.

But the most ingenious plan of beguiling the ostrich to its destruction, is that described by Mr. Moffat and others, as practised among the bushmen. The reverend gentleman says :—

"A kind of flat double cushion is stuffed with straw, and formed something like a saddle. All except the under part of this, is covered over with feathers attached to small pegs, and made so as to resemble the bird. The head and neck of an ostrich are stuffed, and a small rod introduced. The bushmen intending to attack game, whitens his legs with any substance he can procure. He places the feathered saddle on his shoulders, takes the bottom part of the neck in his right hand, and his bow and poisoned arrows in his left. Such as the writer has seen were most perfect mimics of the ostrich, and at a few hundred yards' distance it is not possible for the eye to detect the fraud. This *human* bird appears to pick away at the verdure, turning the head as if keeping a sharp look-out, shakes his feathers, now walks, and then trots till he gets within bow-shot; and when the flock runs, from one receiving an arrow, he runs too. The male ostriches will, on some occasions, give chase to the strange bird, when he tries to elude them, in a way to prevent them catching his scent; for when once they do, the spell is broken. Should one happen to get too near in pursuit, he has only to run to windward, or throw off his saddle, to avoid a stroke from a wing, which would lay him prostrate."

But the ostrich has other enemies besides man. Beasts as well as birds are said to seek and devour their eggs with great avidity. According to Sir James Alexander (given on the authority of the natives about the Orange River) when the birds have left their nest in the middle of the day in search of food, " a white Egyptian vulture may be seen soaring in mid air, with a stone between his talons. Having carefully surveyed the ground below him, he suddenly lets fall the stone, and then follows it in rapid descent. Let the hunter run to the spot, and he will find a nest of probably a score of eggs, some of them broken by the vulture."

Again, "the jackal is said to roll the eggs together to break them; whilst the hyæna pushes them off with its nose to break them at a distance."

Nothing of this kind ever came under my notice; though, on the other hand, I have not unfrequently found the bird itself destroyed by lions, panthers, wild dogs, and other beasts.

CHAPTER XXI.

SUDDEN FLOODS—JOHN ALLEN'S SUFFERINGS—HANS AND THE AUTHOR ENTER INTO PARTNERSHIP—YOUNG GRASS INJURIOUS TO CATTLE—DEPART FROM WALFISCH BAY—ATTRACTIVE SCENERY—TROOPS OF LIONS—EXTRAORDINARY PROCEEDINGS OF KITES—FLIGHT OF BUTTERFLIES—ATTACHMENT OF ANIMALS TO ONE ANOTHER—ARRIVAL AT RICHTERFELDT; AT BARMEN—HANS' NARROW ESCAPE—SELF-POSSESSION—HEAVY RAINS—RUNAWAY OX; HE TOSSES THE AUTHOR—DEPART FROM BARMEN—DIFFICULTY OF CROSSING RIVERS—ENCOUNTER GREAT NUMBERS OF ORYXES.

WE were now in the depth of the rainy season. Rain, as already said, rarely falls in the neighbourhood of Walfisch Bay; but the gathering of heavy clouds in the eastern horizon every afternoon, and vivid flashes of lightning accompanied by distant thunder, clearly indicated that the interior of the country had been flooded. We had soon a proof of this in the sudden appearance of the long-dormant Kuisip river—which, now swollen to an unusual height, overflowed its banks, and threatened destruction to everything that opposed its course.

This overflow was equally great in the Swakop, in the lower course of which our cattle were stationed under the charge of John Allen. One fine morning, and without the least previous notice, down came the torrent, and cut him off from the greater number of the animals, which were grazing on the opposite bank. He was an expert swimmer, however; and, boldly plunging into the swollen stream, with difficulty and danger, succeeded in crossing. But no sooner had he gained the bank than the river rushed forward with tenfold velocity, and effectually separated him from the camp. Two days and a night elapsed before the water had sufficiently subsided to enable him to return. The sufferings of the poor lad meanwhile must have been very trying; for he was in a state of complete nudity; and though he had abundance of fuel, he had no means of lighting a fire. Lions and hyænas, moreover, were numerous; and, to add to his misery, the oxen strayed during the night in different directions. In recollecting them the following day, he had to cross the most rugged and jagged rocks and precipices and scorching fields of sands, which severely lacerated and blistered his unprotected feet. Most men, I venture to say, under such circumstances, would have left the cattle to their fate.

As soon as the swollen Kuisip had sufficiently subsided, and the emaciated state of the oxen permitted, I returned from the Bay to Scheppmansdorf. Hans had not been idle during my absence. He had put the waggon in complete order, having replaced the axle-tree (which in our journey from Barmen had received a serious fracture) with a new one, and shortened the tires of the wheels. He had also made a new covering for the vehicle. I too had made considerable progress with regard to the arrangements and preparations for my intended journey. However, on taking a more close survey of my little property, I found that, notwithstanding Mr. Galton had furnished me with a variety of things, I was very deficient in the most important — such as articles for barter, presents for chiefs, instruments for taking observations, provisions, &c. As none of these were procurable by purchase from the vessels then in Walfisch Bay, I was placed in an awkward position. To proceed without ample supplies of all kinds was not advisable; nor did I much relish the idea of returning to the Cape—the nearest point for a refit—since this could only be accomplished by an overland journey of many months' duration, and the consequent loss of an entire season. Yet, after duly weighing the matter, I determined, though with no small regret, to adopt the latter course.

I now entered into partnership with Hans, who, on his side, threw into the general stock, goods, &c., to the amount of about one hundred and fifty pounds sterling.

It was agreed between us that we should barter our waggons, as also every article we could possibly dispense with for cattle, with which we should proceed to the Cape colony, where we understood live-stock always commanded a ready market. When we should have turned the cattle into cash, and provided ourselves with everything needful, we purposed forthwith returning to Walfisch Bay; I, with a view of penetrating to the Lake Ngami, whilst Hans, in my absence, was to trade with the natives. Should he be successful, my share of the profits would materially aid me in following up my geographical explorations, which I was aware, would be attended with considerable expense.

Though our stay at Scheppmansdorf and Walfisch Bay had been of some duration, it was not sufficiently long to enable the oxen to recover their strength. They had not suffered actual want; but the change of pasturage, more especially as the grass was then young and green, instead of benefiting them, had rather tended to deteriorate their condition. Indeed more than half of our best draught-oxen died.

The country being at length in tolerable order for travelling, we once more, on the afternoon of the 26th of January, took our departure from Scheppmansdorf, keeping the same course as on previous occasions. Besides myself and Hans, our party consisted of John Allen, John St. Helena, Phillippus, Onesimus, and a few Damaras.

The effect of the late rains began soon to show itself; for even the barren Naarip was, in places, richly carpeted with grass and flowers; and at every step, the vegetation became more luxuriant. As evening, with its lengthened shadows, began to close upon us, the air was filled with balmy and aromatic scents. One little flower, of a milk-white colour, was particularly sweet and attractive. I could scarcely realize the wonderful change in the landscape, where, less than a month previously, I might have exclaimed:—

> "Still the same burning sun! no cloud in heaven!
> The hot air quivers; and the sultry mist
> Floats o'er the desert with a show
> Of distant waters."

The presence of herds of the beautiful oryx, the lively quagga, and the grotesque gnoo, which looked like

> "Beasts of mixed and monstrous birth,
> Creations of some fabled earth,"

served further to enhance the interest of the scene.

These were glorious times for the lions, who were exceedingly numerous. On passing Tincas and Onanis—both famous strongholds for this animal—we started troops of them amongst the broken ground; but they invariably ran away, and all my efforts to get a shot at them were unavailing.

One day, while refreshing ourselves and cattle in the midst of a scene like that just described, the men being busy cutting up, or 'dressing,' as butchers would say, two fine oryxes, the produce of the morning hunt, we were suddenly surrounded by a cloud of kites. The actions of these birds were most strange. Hovering within a few feet of our heads, they eyed us steadily for awhile, and then took themselves off, as if satisfied. Another batch would now approach so near, that in order to avoid coming in contact with us, they threw themselves on their backs, spreading out their wings and talons, and opening their beaks; whilst one or two actually, with a swoop, snatched the food out of the hands of the natives. It was only after having brought down several with the rifle that the rest thought best to keep at a more respectful distance.[1]

This day, and during the whole of the following, we encountered myriads of lemon-coloured butterflies. Their numbers were so great that the sound caused by their wings resembled the distant murmuring of waves on the sea-shore. They always passed in the same direction as the wind blew, and, as numbers were constantly alighting on the flowers, their appearance at such times was not unlike the falling of leaves before a gentle autumnal breeze.

Every day, at the halting place, we were in the habit of training some oxen to the 'pack' or the saddle. One of the animals particularly captivated my fancy, and I was desirous of having him well broken-in. After a little time, however, I learnt that no person dared any longer to approach the beast. On inquiring the cause, I found that a large ox had taken it under his protection, so to speak, and would allow no one to go near it. Whenever the servants attempted to catch the *protégé*, his protector would rush at them furiously; and my favourite was so well aware of this, that

---

[1] Several well-known Australian explorers make mention of similar occurrences with this identical bird. I have also heard that in India it is no unusual thing to see hawks snatch the food from a person as he travels along.

so soon as he saw any one approaching, he would run directly to his 'father,' as the natives not inaptly styled the big ox. After having personally convinced myself of this singular attachment, and dreading that some serious mischief might ensue, I deemed it prudent to kill my poor pet. For many days, the 'father' appeared inconsolable at his loss. Running wildly about the herd, and smelling first at one and then at the other, he would moan and bellow most piteously. This is another proof of the strong attachment of which the lower animals are capable. I may add that I have frequently seen a sheep, when the butcher has been in the act of killing its comrade, run up to the man, and butt at him most viciously.

On the 5th of February, we found ourselves again at Richterfeldt. Mrs. Rath, I was sorry to find, was suffering grievously from eye-sickness; so much so, that she was unable to bear the least light. Indeed, not long after, the sight of one of her eyes was permanently injured, if not destroyed.

Here I and Hans separated. Whilst he went into Damara-land to trade with the natives, I, myself, proceeded along the Swakop with the waggon. We had only one, the other having already been disposed of at Eikhams. The river was still running breast-high, and we experienced much difficulty in crossing and re-crossing it. One evening, just as we were descending the bank, from which the flood had only lately receded, the vehicle suddenly sank so deep in the mud as almost to hide the fore-wheels. Before we could extricate ourselves—which was a work of many hours —we were obliged to dig a deep trench, and pave it with stones.

In the afternoon of the 11th of February, I reached Barmen, where on the following day I was joined by Hans. He had not been very successful, and, moreover, nearly got into a scrape with the natives. Having one day gone some distance in advance of his small party, he suddenly, at the turn of a hill, came upon some women and children, who, notwithstanding his friendly assurances, ran off in great fright to the werft, which was not far distant, screaming vociferously. The men, thinking that they were about to be attacked by the Namaquas, instantly rushed to arms; and Hans, on coming in view of the village, unexpectedly found himself in the presence of several hundred Damaras, each armed with a huge assegai. Placing his gun against a tree, he walked quietly into the midst of them. His coolness so surprised and amazed them, that the forest of bristling spears, poised in the air ready to strike, were instantaneously lowered. The men, however, continued their yells and shouts for some time, and it was not until his interpreter had arrived, that he was able to set their minds at rest as to his peaceable intentions.

The effect often produced on savages, by the self-possession of a single European, is truly wonderful. If Hans had evinced the smallest sign of fear or hesitation, his fate probably would have been sealed.

I remember, not long after this took place, to have been journeying with fifty or sixty Damaras, accompanied only by my native interpreter, when the chief of the party, next to whom I was walking, turned sharply round and abruptly accosted me in the following manner—"How is it that you venture to go thus alone amongst us? we might easily kill you at any time." Without a moment's hesitation, I replied, "I neither fear you nor any other people, and simply because I never injured you. You, on the other hand, are perpetually robbing and killing your neighbours; and, consequently, you have to dread the revenge of their friends and relations. Besides," I jokingly added, "it is not quite so easy as you may imagine to pull 'three hairs out of a lion's tail.'" This was exactly hitting the nail on the head—for, if they had previously thought my argument good, they were now amazingly pleased with the jest.

We were delayed some little time at Barmen, in consequence of heavy rains that now almost daily deluged the country. It was during this stay that the remarkable thunderstorm occurred—mentioned in a preceding chapter—which caused such havoc among the native gardens.

One day, whilst endeavouring to secure properly a young ox, he broke loose; and, though almost the whole village turned out to assist us, we were unable to re-capture the animal. When an ox thus made off, we usually caused three or four of the steadiest of his comrades to be driven after him, or we put some good runners on his track. By the cattle or the men keeping up a steady pace, they would soon exhaust the refractory animal, and quietly bring him back to the camp. In this instance, Karnarute, perhaps the fleetest man in Damara-land, was sent in pursuit.

Whilst abiding his return, I indulged in a warm bath, and, just as I had finished my ablutions, I observed him coming back with the runaway. As the animal, however, was not proceeding in exactly the required direction, I placed myself in his path, for the purpose of turning him. But as he heeded not my presence, and kept his own course, the result was that he caught me with his horns near the ribs, and pitched me bodily over his back! With the exception of being a good deal shaken, however, I singularly enough escaped unhurt. But one of our native servants was less fortunate; for on trying, like myself, to stay the ox in his headlong career, the poor fellow was thrown to the ground by the exasperated brute, who actually knelt on his body, and in all probability would have killed him, had not the rest of the people come to his assistance. This accident taught us to be more careful in our future proceedings with an over-driven ox.

On leaving Barmen, we were obliged to make a considerable *détour* in order to avoid the 'Great' Swakop, which continued to send down immense torrents of discoloured water. In crossing one of its branches, known as the 'Little' Swakop, our cattle were more than once swept away by the violence of the current, and our waggon had a very narrow escape from being capsized. When half way across the stream it stuck fast, and for upwards of four hours all our efforts to extricate it proved ineffectual. During the whole of this time we were immersed up to our necks, in water, which hourly increased. What with the velocity of the current, the depth of the river, and the looseness of the soil beneath, we were unable to obtain a firm footing; and men, oxen, and dogs were frequently jumbled together in the most awkward confusion. After almost superhuman exertions, having previously been obliged to remove all the heavy things from the vehicle, we succeeded in reaching the shore in safety. Here, again, to our dismay, we found our path barred by immense blocks of stone, and the roughness of the ground in general along the bank. We had no alternative but to retrace our steps, and re-cross the river at a more convenient point, which we successfully accomplished on the following morning, when the water had somewhat subsided.

Hence we travelled about north-east, alternately in the bed and on the banks of a tributary to the Swakop. On reaching the foot of that picturesque chain of mountains extending in a northerly direction from Eikham's towards Schmelen's Hope, where it terminates rather abruptly, we encountered great numbers of the oryx, which afforded us excellent sport.

ORYX OR GEMSBOK.

London, Hurst & Blackett, 1856.

CHAPTER XXII.

THE ORYX; MORE THAN ONE SPECIES — WHERE FOUND — PROBABLY KNOWN IN EUROPE PREVIOUS TO THE DISCOVERY OF THE PASSAGE ROUND CAPE-OF-GOOD-HOPE—DESCRIPTION OF THE ORYX—GREGARIOUS—SPEED—FOOD—WATER NOT NECESSARY TO ITS EXISTENCE—WILL FACE THE LION—FORMIDABLE HORNS—THEIR USE—FLESH—THE CHASE OF THIS ANIMAL.

THREE distinct species of oryxes[1] are recognized by naturalists, ranging over a great extent of the more desert and thinly-peopled districts of Africa. In the northern part of the continent, the type is represented by the leucoryx,[2] which strikingly resembles the oryx or gemsbok *(oryx capensis)*, of which the accompanying drawing is an excellent representation.

The gemsbok (so called by the Dutch, from a supposed resemblance to the chamois of Europe) seems restricted to the central and western parts of Southern Africa, few or none being found in its eastern portion. It was once common within the colony, but what with its shy habits, the constant persecution

---

[1] *Oryx capensis, oryx beisa,* and *oryx leucoryx*.
[2] The numerous engravings of the leucoryx on the sculptures of Egypt clearly indicate that this animal was well known to the nations inhabiting the valley of the Nile. It was chosen as an emblem, but whether as a good or evil symbol is uncertain, though some modern writers seem in favour of the former opinion. The wealthy Egyptians kept a great number of this antelope in a tame state, but it does not appear to have been considered a sacred animal. Indeed, it was indiscriminately sacrificed to the gods, and slaughtered for the table.

it suffers, and the advance of civilization, its numbers are now rapidly decreasing, and few at the present day are to be found within the boundaries of the British territory.

Judging from some ancient coats of arms, it would really seem that the gemsbok was known to Europeans even before the Portuguese discovered the passage round the Cape-of-Good-Hope.[1] We are told that John of Lancaster, the great Duke of Bedford, bore his arms supported by this animal, which is still on the sinister side of the heraldic shield of the present ducal house of Bedford. Amongst various embellishments, which are painted in the Bruges style of the period, in a Prayer-book once the property of John of Lancaster, are found his armorial devices, with the antelope black, whose straight spiral horns, although placed almost at right-angles with the head, are evidently intended for those of the oryx. The animal is adorned with gilded tusks, but in other respects is not ill drawn. It is conjectured that this book was illuminated on the marriage of the Duke of Bedford with Anne, Princess of Burgundy. Be this as it may, it cannot well be later than the period of his death in the year 1435.

The gemsbok is a very remarkable animal, and though possessed of many of those beautiful peculiarities which characterize antelopes, there is something anomalous about him. He has the mane and tail of the horse, the head and colouring of the ass, and the legs and feet of the antelope. The horns are about three feet in length, slightly curved backwards, ringed at the base, and of a shining black colour. Those of the female are somewhat longer than the male's, but of more slender proportions. About one-third of

---

[1] It is possible that heralds became acquainted with this animal, or at least with the leucoryx, through the Crusaders. Or, perhaps, the knowledge was obtained from the Romans, who, according to Martial, had the oryx at their games.

their entire length is hollow, resting on a bony protuberance. When both horns are perfect, and one has a side view of the animal, they appear as one and the same, from which circumstance many believe the gemsbok to be the unicorn[1] of Scripture.

The gemsbok is a truly noble beast. The adult male (about the size of an ass) not unfrequently attains nearly four feet in height at the shoulder, and about ten in extreme length. The general colour of the coat is a 'vinous buff.' The female is very similar in appearance, but slighter in form. The calves are of a reddish cream-colour, which, as they grow up, becomes paler or whitish. They are easily tamed, but sometimes exhibit a vicious and treacherous disposition. Hans more than once domesticated them, and I myself have had the young alive.

The gemsbok may be said to be gregarious in its habits; for though rarely seen together in any great number, it is not often met singly.

Of all the larger quadrupeds of South Africa, with which I can claim acquaintance, the gemsbok is, undoubtedly, the swiftest. Its speed is nearly equal to that of the horse. Unless a man be a 'light weight,' and very well mounted, he has little chance of coming up with it.

The food of the gemsbok consists of grass, succulent plants (often of a very acrid taste), shrubs, &c.

As with several other animals indigenous to Southern Africa, water is not supposed to be essential to the existence of the gemsbok. Gordon Cumming, indeed, tells us "that it never by any chance tastes water." But this, I apprehend, is a mistake; for I have not only seen it, on several occasions, whilst in the very act of drinking, but perfectly well

---

[1] For some curious remarks on the unicorn see Barrow, vol. ii., p. 269 *et seq.*

authenticated instances have come to my knowledge where whole troops of these animals have been discovered either dead or in a dying state near pools purposely poisoned by the natives for the capture of wild animals. The gemsbok, it is true, is found in the most dreary and desolate districts far distant from water:—

> "A region of drought, where no river glides,
> Nor rippling brook with osier'd sides—
> With no reedy pool, nor mossy fountain,
> Nor shady tree, nor cloud-capp'd mountain."

Nevertheless (more especially at early morn) it occasionally frequents the banks of periodical rivers, flanked or bordered by broken ground or hills; and it is to such localities, when pursued, that it flies for refuge.

Though the gemsbok has rarely, if ever, been known to attack man, it is quite capable of defending itself. With its formidable horns, it can strike an object (that is, inflict wounds) in front as well as behind, which, from their pointing backwards, was hardly to be expected. When driven to bay by dogs, it has been seen to place its head between its legs (the tips of its horns, in the while, almost resting on the ground), and to rip open, or toss into the air, such of its assailants as have had the boldness to confront it. In this manner, Hans told me he lost, at different times, the best dogs in his pack.

In open ground, the gemsbok, it is said, will stand on the defensive even against the lion himself. Hans, indeed, knew an instance where a lion and a gemsbok were found lying dead in each other's grasp; the latter having, with his horns, transfixed his assailant! The carcases of the two were discovered before decomposition had taken place. The lion seems to have a great dread of the horns of the gemsbok; for, by all accounts, he rarely ventures to attack except by stealth.

The horns of this animal are used by the natives for a variety of purposes. When polished, they form strong and handsome walking-sticks. The flesh, which is well tasted, is highly prized.

"Owing to the uneven nature of the ground which the oryx frequents," says Gordon Cumming, "its shy and suspicious disposition, and the extreme distances from water to which it must be followed, it is never stalked or driven to an ambush like other antelopes; but is hunted on horseback, and ridden down by a long, severe, tail-on-end chase." This is not exactly correct; for, when on foot, I have killed great numbers of these animals. Moreover, were the option left me, I would rather 'stalk' them than pursue them on horseback. Such was also Hans' experience, who, during his seven years' nomade life in Damara-land, has probably killed more gemsboks than any hunter in Southern Africa. I have also known this animal to be driven into pit-falls.

The gemsbok, as a rule, runs, like the eland, against the wind when pursued.

CHAPTER XXIII.

ARRIVAL AT EIKHAMS — NATIVE DOGS; CRUELLY TREATED — JONKER AFRIKANER — THE AUTHOR VISITS THE RED NATION; THE BAD REPUTE OF THESE PEOPLE — THE AUTHOR ATTACKED BY OPHTHALMIA — THE EMBRYO LOCUST — THE 'FLYING' LOCUST; ITS DEVASTATIONS — THE LOCUST BIRD — ARRIVAL AT REHOBOTH; THE PLACE DESCRIBED.

IN the afternoon of the 20th of February, we drove in to Eikhams during a terrific thunder-storm, drenched to the skin. The deluging rain continued to descend the whole of the ensuing night, and the place on the following morning looked like a foaming torrent. In consequence of this inundation, our ox-gear, and, in short, everything untanned, was completely saturated, and greatly resembled a heap of moist wash-leather.

The starved native dogs had taken advantage of this circumstance, and devoured rather more than two feet of our 'trek-touw.' The curs are of the greatest annoyance to the traveller in Namaqua-land; for, since the owners rarely feed them, they greedily devour almost everything they come across. I have had my powder-flask, 'veld' shoes, and even rifle (the stock of which may have happened to be covered with hide, in order to keep it from cracking), abstracted by them from my side during the night. A person's first impulse, on making the discovery, is to vow vengeance on the head of the thieves; but, on seeing the emaciated state of the poor creatures, in which every rib might be counted, anger is turned into pity—and the uplifted arm, ready to strike the blow, falls to its place.

It has been said, with much truth, by a missionary, that "the Namaquas feed their dogs with stripes." From being constantly kicked and knocked about in the most brutal manner, they gradually become so accustomed to ill-treatment, that flogging produces little or no effect. When struck, they merely shrug up their backs, open their jaws, grin in a ghastly manner, and, if the chastisement be continued, howl most piteously. This, and their skeleton appearance, are enough to sicken a person.

It would be somewhat difficult to determine to what species of the canine race these dogs belong, or from what breed they originally descended. They bear some slight resemblance to those I have seen at the homesteads of the Swedish peasants.[1]

Jonker had removed his werft to some little distance from Eikhams. He invariably did this every year after the rains, in order to save the pasturage for the dry season. I rode over to the village, where I found nearly the whole tribe —women and children, at least—congregated. This was an opportunity I had long desired, since it would enable

[1] Mr. Lichtenstein, when speaking of the bushmen dogs, which may be considered identical with those of the Hottentots, thus writes:—'These dogs, in their size and form, have a striking resemblance to the black-backed fox of Southern Africa, the jackal, as he is falsely called, *canis mesomelas;* so that it seems very probable that the one is really a descendant from the other; only that the properties of the animal are, in the course of time, somewhat changed, from its having been tamed and trained by the hand of man.'

me to form a rough estimate of their number. Jonker and most of the men were absent; but by counting the huts, and taking the average number of individuals to each, I came to the conclusion that the aggregate of Namaquas, capable of carrying arms, did not exceed five hundred. The servants, or rather slaves, on the other hand, consisting of bushmen, Hill-Damaras, and impoverished Damaras, were probably three or four times as numerous. By supposing each man to be possessed of one gun, which is perhaps below the mark, Jonker's tribe possess in round numbers two thousand firelocks. If their courage corresponded to their numerical strength, they might prove a formidable body even to Europeans, but this is fortunately far from being the case.

Jonker was indebted to us several head of cattle, and we were accordingly anxious for his return; but no person could or would, inform us when this was likely to happen. With regard to other inquiries, such as the object and motive of his present journey, the answers were equally unsatisfactory. Nevertheless, the shyness of the natives, when interrogated on these points, coupled with our knowledge that Jonker was accompanied by almost all his warriors, made us suspect that he had gone on a plundering expedition against the Damaras.

After a few days' stay at Eikhams, we directed our steps to a powerful tribe of Namaquas, known as the 'Roode-Natie,' or Red Nation. I had two objects in view for visiting these people, namely, to trade, and to learn something about them and their country. Every one I met, including the missionaries, represented them as the most barbarous and brutal of all the Hottentots in Great Namaqua-land. Only one trader had visited them, and him they treated so shamefully as to discourage others from making a like attempt. I was determined, however, if possible, to ascertain the cause of their evil reputation, and to endeavour to establish friendly relations with them.

My reception was such as to corroborate the ill-reports that had reached my ears. At the first werft we came to, they stole a large quantity of clothing belonging to our servants; but after some trouble, we succeeded in recovering the property. At the next village, they threatened to shoot us on the spot if we did not sell our things at their own terms! Three different times their chief sent to say, that if we attempted to stir without his orders, he would fire upon us. To this insolent message, we quietly replied, that he would have been at liberty to prevent our coming to his werft, but, with regard to our departure, we should consult our own convenience. Finding us determined, and that we were preparing to start, he soon came to terms, and in the most humble manner offered an explanation and apology for his rude conduct, which, under the circumstances, we thought it best to accept.

We were just about to turn our backs upon the Red Nation, when a messenger arrived from Cornelius, the chief, with a civil and pressing invitation to visit him at his kraal. After some little hesitation, we consented, and speedily followed the envoy. On arriving at the werft, prettily situated at the foot of a hill, near the banks of the Kubakop river, which here forced its passage through a very remarkable range of mountains, I immediately called the tribe together, and reproached them for their bad behaviour towards strangers. I, moreover, explained to them the impolicy of such conduct, and how very injurious it would prove to their own interest, since they were entirely dependent on the Cape-Colony for their supplies of arms and ammunition, clothing, and other commodities.

My efforts in bringing about a thorough good understanding were successful. A short time afterwards, indeed, a number of traders, encouraged by my favourable reception, visited these people, and supplied their wants at the same rate as paid by the other Hottentot tribes residing in Great Namaqua-land. Moreover, they have lately admitted a missionary amongst them, and it is to be hoped that through good examples they may ultimately be civilized.

The chief stronghold of the Red Nation is about the Kubakop, but a part of the tribe is settled on the Fish river. Taken as a whole, they possess, probably, the worst portion of the northern part of Great Namaqua-land. They call themselves *Kaikhous*, a word signifying large ridges of hills, in contradistinction to Zwartboi's tribe, the name of which is *Kharikhous*, or small ridges. They look upon Jonker and his people, who are known as 'Oerlam,' not only with jealousy, but with something akin to contempt.

I found but few Damara slaves amongst the Red Nation, which, at first, struck me as singular, for their outrage on the Damaras was, at least, of equal extent to that perpetrated by the rest of the northern Namaquas. I could only explain this by supposing that they killed their prisoners. I afterwards learnt that my conjecture was correct; and that having surrounded a werft, they coolly shot down every soul, women and children not excepted. However, having lately discovered that the Damaras make useful drudges, they have, from interested motives, become less bloody-minded.

Whilst staying with Cornelius, I was attacked by ophthalmia, and for a few days suffered great agonies; but, fortunately, before the disease had arrived at its maximum, it took a favourable turn.

Having succeeded in disposing of the greater part of our goods, we took leave of our host, and bent our steps towards Rehoboth, which was on our road to the Cape. The day after our departure, we met with vast numbers of the larvæ of the locust (*gryllus devastator*, Lich.), commonly called by the Boers, 'voet-gangers,' literally, foot-goers. In some places they might be seen packed in layers several inches in thickness, and myriads were crushed and maimed by our waggon and cattle. Towards night-fall they crawled on to the bushes and the shrubs, many of which, owing to their weight and numbers, were either bowed down to the ground or broken short off. They were of a reddish colour, with dark markings; and, as they hung thus suspended, they looked like clusters of rich fruit. As they hopped along the path and amongst the grass, their appearance was no less curious and striking.

These 'voet-gangers' are justly dreaded by the colonists, as no obstacle seems capable of staying their progress. They are said to cross stagnant pools—ay, even the Orange river—by the leading multitudes throwing themselves heedlessly into the water, where they are drowned, thus affording the survivors a temporary bridge. Fires, which are lighted in their path, in the hope of staying their course, are extinguished by their myriads. "All human endeavours to diminish their numbers," says a recent author, "would appear like attempting to drain the ocean by a pump."

As we travelled on next morning we encountered the locust itself, and in such masses as literally to darken the air.

> "Onward they came, a dark continuous cloud
> Of congregated myriads numberless,
> The rushing of whose wings was as the sound
> Of a broad river, headlong in its course
> Plunged from a mountain summit; or the roar
> Of a wild ocean in the autumn storm,
> Shattering its billows on a shore of rocks."

Our waggon, or any other equally conspicuous object,

could positively not be distinguished at the distance of one hundred paces. In a particular spot, within the circumference of a mile, they had not left a particle of any green thing. The several columns that crossed our path, in the course of the day, must each have been many miles in length and breadth. The noise of their wings was very great—not unlike that caused by a gale of wind whistling through the shrouds of a ship at anchor. It was interesting to witness at a distance the various shapes and forms that these columns assumed, more especially when crossing mountain-ranges. At one time, they would rise abruptly in a compact body, as if propelled by a strong gust of wind; then, suddenly sinking, they would disperse into smaller batallions, not unlike vapours floating about a hill-side at early morn, and when slightly agitated by the breeze. Or they would resemble huge columns of sand or smoke, changing every minute their shape and evolutions.

During their flight, numbers were constantly alighting, an action which has not inaptly been compared to the falling of large snow flakes. It is, however, not until the approach of night that they encamp. Woe to the spot they select as a resting place! When the rising sun again speeds their departure, localities, which on the preceding evening were rich in vegetation, are bare and naked as the Sahara. "When a swarm alights on a garden"—says Mr. Moffat—" or even fields, the crop for one season is destroyed. I have observed a field of young maize devoured in the space of two hours. They eat not only tobacco, and every other vegetable, but also flannel and linen."

From what has been said, it is evident that the husbandman has just reason to be appalled at the approach of this destructive insect. To the poor Bushmen, "the children of the desert," on the other hand, who have neither herds to lose by famine, nor corn-fields to be destroyed by their devastations, their arrival is a cause of rejoicing. Pringle, in his song of the wild Bushman, has the following lines—

> " Yea, even the wasting locust-swarm,
> Which mighty nations dread,
> To me nor terror brings nor harm;
> I make of them my bread."

On the present occasion we found a great number of Hottentots, as also Hill-Damaras, busy collecting the locusts, which was done in a very simple and ingenious manner. Having gathered together large quantities of dry fuel, fires were lighted directly in their path, and as the insects passed over the flames, their wings were scorched, and they fell helplessly to the ground.

They are also collected by cart-loads at night when they have retired to rest; but this plan is occasionally attended with danger. "It has happened that, in gathering them, people have been bitten by venomus reptiles. On one occasion a woman had been travelling several miles with a large bundle of locusts on her head, when a serpent, which had been put into the sack with them, found its way out. The woman supposing it to be a thong dangling about her shoulders, laid hold of it with her hand, and feeling that it was alive, instantly precipitated the bundle to the ground, and fled."

The locusts, after being partially roasted, are eaten fresh, or they are dried in the hot ashes, and then stored away for future emergences. The natives reduce them also to powder, or meal, by means of two stones or a wooden mortar, which powder, when mixed with water, produces a kind of soup or stir-about. I have tasted locusts prepared in various ways, but I cannot say that I have found them very palatable.

But they must contain a vast deal of nourishment, since the poor people thrive wonderfully on them.

Birds of almost every description, more especially storks and kites, are seen devouring them greedily.

The great enemy of the locust, however, is the locust-bird, or the 'spring-haan vogel,' as it is termed by the colonists. This is described as a species of thrush, about the size of a swallow, and is a constant attendant on the insect. It is even said to build its nest and rear its young in the midst of locusts—which, moreover, occasionally prey on each other; for when a locust becomes maimed or crippled, its companions instantly pounce upon and devour it.

The locust which causes such havoc to vegetation in Africa is said to be a different species to that common to Asia—where also, though perhaps not to the same extent, it commits great ravages.

The Cape Colony has been particularly subject to this dreadful scourge, which is invariably followed by famine. The inroads of the locusts are periodical; according to Pringle, about once every fifteen years. In 1808, after having laid waste a considerable portion of the country,[1] they disappeared, and did not return till 1824. They then remained for several years, but in 1830 took their departure.

---

[1] Barrow, who wrote about this period, and who gives a remarkable account of the devastations of these insects, probably alludes to this very circumstance when he says:—
'The present year is the third of their continuance, and their increase has far exceeded that of a geometrical progression whose ratio is a million. For ten years preceding their present visit, the colony had been entirely freed from them. Their last departure was rather singular. All the full-grown insects were driven into the sea by a tempestuous north-west wind, and were afterwards cast upon the beach, where, it is said, they formed a bank of three or four feet high, which extended from the mouth of the Bosjeman's river to that of the Becka, a distance of near fifty English miles; and it is asserted, that when this mass became putrid, and the wind was at south-east, the stench was sensibly felt in several parts of Sneuwberg. * * * The larvæ at the same time were emigrating to the northward. The column of these imperfect insects passed the houses of two of our party, who assured me that it continued moving forward without any interruption, except by night, for more than a month.'

ARRIVE AT REHOBOTH.

The proper home of the locust is yet a mystery. Experience only tells us that they come southwards from the north. They rarely appear in any number except in years of abundance.

Almost every day during several months, we encountered innumerable swarms of these insects; and it was not till we had crossed the Orange river that we fairly lost sight of them.

On the 15th of March we reached Rehoboth, where, as already said, there is a missionary station pertaining to the Rhenish society. Here I had the pleasure of making the acquaintance of the Rev. Messrs. Kleinschmidt and Vollmer. They resided in substantial clay-houses thatched with reeds. The church, in the erection of which Mr. Kleinschmidt had taken a very active part, is a handsome and roomy structure, capable of holding several hundred people. From the disproportionate breadth of the building, however, the roof could not sustain its own weight; and some time previously to my visit, the greater part had fallen down. Divine service, nevertheless, continued to be performed in that portion of the building which remained uninjured.

At this period the station was in a most flourishing condition. But, alas! circumstances have since changed; and it is now a question whether the mission can continue to exist. Should it be abandoned, ten years of unremitted labour and exertion will be entirely lost; and I sadly fear it will break the heart of its founder—the worthy and venerable Kleinschmidt.

Rehoboth is well supplied with good and clear water from a fountain hard by. There is also a copious warm spring flowing from a limestone rock; but the water is looked upon as unwholesome, and only made use of for cattle, washing of clothes, and the seasoning of timber.

The warm spring in question is situated on rising ground, and consequently affords facilities for irrigation; though unfortunately the soil is scanty and unfavourable for gardening. The missionaries, and a few natives, have, by perseverance, succeeded in fertilizing patches of ground which are tolerably productive. Indeed, I have known a fig-tree—certainly not above five or six feet in height—in Mr. Kleinschmidt's garden, to produce a dish of fruit every day for a space of more than three months. The garden-vegetables which thrive best are pumpkins, calabashes, water-melons, &c. The wild gourd, or melon, is also found in great abundance about Rehoboth. When ripe, this fruit is collected by the natives, dried, and stored away for seasons of scarcity.

CHAPTER XXIV.

RETURN TO EIKHAMS—UGLY FALL—SPLENDID LANDSCAPE—JONKER'S DELINQUENCIES—HOW TO MANAGE THE NATIVES—THE ONDARA—IT KILLS A MAN—HOW HIS COMRADE REVENGES HIM—MEDICAL PROPERTIES OF THE ONDARA—THE COCKATRICE—THE COBRA-DI-CAPELLA—THE PUFF-ADDER—THE SPITTING SNAKE—THE BLACK SNAKE—FEW DEATHS CAUSED BY SNAKES—ANTIDOTES FOR SNAKE BITES—RETURN TO REHOBOTH.

LEAVING Hans in charge of the men and cattle, I posted back to Eikhams, a distance of about sixty miles, in the hope of recovering our debt from Jonker; but he had not yet returned. By this time, however, I received positive information that he and his people were engaged in a cattle-lifting foray. To enable me to acquire full details of their proceedings, I set off for Barmen—the head quarter for information as respects Damara-land. Here fugitives arrived daily, bringing tidings of plunder and bloodshed. I felt grieved and angry at Jonker's outrageous behaviour. Only a year before, he had most solemnly promised Mr. Galton never again to molest the Damaras.

Hearing that Kachamaha, the most powerful chief in the country since the death of Kahichenè, resided not far from

Barmen, and that he had been a severe sufferer by the depredations of the Namaquas, I determined to visit him, with a view of ascertaining the extent of his own and his countrymen's losses.

I found Kachamaha's kraal on the steep banks of a periodical stream, one of the largest tributaries of the Swakop. The situation was most picturesque. The wonderful luxuriance of the vegetation, and extreme beauty of the landscape at this season—the thousands of cattle crowding the verdant slopes—the purling stream, which made a music strange to these regions—

> " A noise like of a hidden brook
> In the leafy month of June,
> That to the sleeping woods all night
> Singeth a quiet tune"—

the mimosa (now in full blossom)—the numerous fires on an evening, around which bustling and merry groups of savages were busily preparing their plain 'veld-kost' of wild roots and bulbs—these, and many other signs of abundance, cheerfulness, and content, infused a sensation of tranquil happiness which I had not experienced since my arrival in this sunburnt and unhappy land.

The result of my own and Mr. Hahn's inquiries, was a conviction that Jonker, with his murderous horde, had destroyed in his recent foray upwards of forty werfts or villages; and that the aggregate number of cattle carried off could not have been much short of ten or eleven thousand. One powerful tribe of Damaras had been completely broken up. With regard to the number of people killed, we were unable to ascertain anything with certainty; but we had reason to think that on this occasion it was not considerable.

Having collected all the facts which I thought necessary to convict Jonker of his guilt, I retraced my steps to Eikhams.

Almost immediately after leaving Barmen, I had a very ugly fall from my ox. He was plunging and kicking most viciously; but I succeeded for a time in keeping my seat. Unfortunately, however, all at once both girths gave way, and, after performing a somerset in the air, I came with a violent thump to the ground. I alighted in a sitting position; but, as ill-luck would have it, my left leg came in contact with the stump of a tree, which inflicted a wound fully two inches in depth, and nearly the same in length. In this state I was obliged to ride upwards of one hundred miles; and the consequence was that by the time I reached Rehoboth, what with the heat of the sun, and the jolting of the ox, my limb was alarmingly inflamed. A week's rest, however, restored me, in a degree, to health.

On arriving near Eikhams, I observed almost every hill and dale covered with numerous herds of cattle—the spoils of the last excursion. On my arrival, I requested an immediate interview with the chief. In a day or two, accompanied by twenty of his principal men, he made his appearance. The meeting took place in the old church, where I had established myself, which gave a certain solemnity to the occasion. Eyebrecht and Onesimus acted as interpreters.

Every one being duly seated, and silence obtained, I thus addressed the chieftain:—

"Captain Jonker! when I last saw you, I shook hands with you: it grieves me that I cannot do so to-day; the cause you must be aware of." I then proceeded boldly to accuse him of his late depredations in Damara-land, to which both he and the rest of the audience, listened in the most profound silence.

Having finished my harangue, the cunning chief requested

to be allowed to speak a few words in his defence, which, of course, was granted. He then entered into a very long and cleverly concocted story of the great losses he had sustained at the hands of the Damaras; and that what he had now done was solely in self-defence, or as indemnification for robberies committed on himself. Whatever truth there might have been in his assertion as to preceding outrages, his story, on the present occasion, was one chain of falsehood, and this I clearly proved to him. At last, finding no further excuse, and perceiving that I knew all about his proceedings, he confessed, that, in passing through the country, his men had certainly "taken a few head of cattle; but," added he, "we left plenty after us." The manner in which he thus attempted to get out of the scrape was so ridiculous that I could not help smiling. After a little more parley, the conference broke up.

The Namaquas, however much they may be averse to hear the truth, respect the man who speaks his mind boldly. For this very reason I was never denied a favour or request, if in their power to grant it. The case was similar with Mr. Hahn, who acted on the same principle as myself.

In my dealings with the natives, and more especially with the Namaquas, I made it a rule to treat them civilly, and even deferentially; but I never mixed very freely with them. The moment a person becomes too familiar, they lose all respect for him. The only check he has on their avarice, and safeguard against their treachery, is to exert, as far as possible, a certain moral influence over their minds. This he effects to a certain extent, by showing himself superior to their faults and vices. It might be convenient enough to imitate them in some respects; but, on the whole, it will prove injurious and detrimental to the traveller's interest.

THE ONDARA.

After a short stay at Eikhams, I bade adieu to Jonker, and set off on my return to Rehoboth.

One morning, when crossing a periodical stream, I observed, in its sandy bed, the tracks of an immense serpent, in size, as it would seem, not much inferior to the boa constrictor. I had previously heard that such monsters inhabited this part of Africa,[1] but the natives declared they were poisonous (not characteristic of this family of reptiles), and, consequently, feared them greatly. The Damaras call the serpent in question the Ondara, and said that its chief food was the rock-rabbit (*hyrax capensis*). Mr. Hahn had an opportunity of seeing one of these huge creatures, which had been accidentally killed by the people at Rehoboth. It measured eighteen feet in length.[2]

I was told a very striking story of the Ondara, but I am not at all prepared to vouch for its truth.

Two Hill-Damaras had, it seems, gone in search of honey, and having found a bees' nest in the cleft of a rock, one of them made his way through the confined aperture that led to it, for the purpose of possessing himself of the honeycomb.

[1] Large species of serpents of the python family are known to inhabit many parts of the African continent. Dr. Smith, in his 'Zoology of South Africa,' when speaking of a certain species (*python Natalensis*) found sparingly in the neighbourhood of Natal, thus says:—

'It occasionally attains a very large size, and, according to the natives, individuals have been seen whose circumference was equal to that of the body of a stout man : we have ourselves seen a skin which measured twenty-five feet, though a portion of the tail was deficient. It feeds upon quadrupeds, and for some days after swallowing food it remains in a torpid state, and may then be easily destroyed. The South Africans, however, seldom avail themselves of these opportunities of ridding themselves of a reptile they view with horror, as they believe that it has a certain influence over their destinies; and affirm, that no person has ever been known to maltreat it without, sooner or later, paying for his audacity.'

Mr. Freeman, in 'A Tour in South Africa,' mentions having heard of one of this kind of reptiles being destroyed that actually exceeded this size nearly three times. 'This enormous serpent,' says the rev. gentleman, 'was hanging from the bough of a large tree, and was killed only after a desperate struggle. It measured fifty feet in length. This was ascertained by a number of men lying down at full length by its side. It took nine men to reach from the head to the tail, and was of prodigious girth round the body.'

But he had not long been thus engaged when he discovered a narrow, circular passage, leading, apparently, right through the nest. He told this to his comrade on the outside, who suggested that it was probably caused by a serpent. However, seeing nothing to indicate the reptile's presence, he resumed his labour; and, having secured the honeycomb, was about to withdraw from the aperture, when, to his horror, he saw a huge ondara making towards him. The reptile passed the poor fellow in the first instance, but suddenly turning round, it plunged its murderous fangs into the man's body. The poison was of so virulent a nature as to cause almost instantaneous death. The survivor, witnessing the fate of his friend, fled precipitately. On his way home, however, and when his agitation had subsided, he determined to revenge himself on the reptile, and early the following day he returned to put his plan into execution.

Having seen the serpent leave the aperture in question, he slipped unperceived into it, and quietly awaited the reptile's return. As soon as he observed it approaching, he coolly placed his open hand across the narrowest part of the passage; and, just as the monster's eyes glared within, he grasped it by the throat, and, by striking its head to and fro against the rocks on either side, he soon succeeded in destroying it.

Many Namaquas believe that the ondara possesses certain medicinal virtues; therefore, when they succeed in killing the reptile, its flesh is carefully preserved. If a person falls sick, a portion is either applied externally in the form of an unction, or given to the patient in a decoction.

The natives mention a very singular little snake, about seven or eight inches long, possessing four distinct legs, each provided with toes and nails like a lizard. It is difficult to conceive for what purpose these limbs (which are placed somewhat apart, and rather to the side, as in the seal) have been destined by nature, since they are apparently never used. The motion of this curious creature, which is of a dark slate colour, is said to be that of a perfect snake. Three specimens were brought at different times to Mr. Hahn when at Barmen.

The story of the cockatrice, so common in many parts of the world, is also found amongst the Damaras; but instead of crowing, or rather chuckling, like a fowl when going to roost, they say it bleats like a lamb. It attacks man as well as beast, and its bite is considered fatal. They point to the distant north as its proper home. In Timbo's country it is termed 'hangara,' and is said to attain to twelve feet, or even more, in length, with a beautifully variegated skin. On its head, like the guinea-fowl, it has a horny protuberance of a reddish colour. It dwells chiefly in trees. Its chuckle is heard at night-fall; and people, imagining that the noise proceeds from one of their own domestic fowls that has strayed, hasten to drive it home. But this frequently causes their destruction; for as soon as the cockatrice perceives its victim within reach, it darts at it with the speed of lightning; and if its fangs enter the flesh, death invariably ensues. Timbo informed me that he once saw a dog belonging to his father thus killed. Moreover, the cockatrice, like the wild dog, wantonly destroys more at a time than it can consume.

Notwithstanding the dryness of the soil and the atmosphere between the Orange river and the seventeeth or eighteenth degrees of south latitude, reptiles are rather numerous. Indeed, some parts of Damara-land are so infested by them as to be almost uninhabitable. For my own part, however, I have encountered comparatively few. I never saw the cobra-di-capella, though it does exist in these regions. It is common enough in the colony, and is even met with in the neighbourhood of the Table Mountain.

An acquaintance of mine had a remarkable escape from this reptile. Being passionately fond of botany, he was one day studying the Flora of the so-called 'Cape-flats.' Having discovered a rare plant, he was stooping down to gather it, when up started a cobra immediately beneath his hand. My friend had no time to turn round, but retreated backwards as quickly as his legs would carry him. The serpent, however, was fast gaining ground; and had the chase lasted a few seconds longer, must inevitably have caught him. But just at this critical moment my friend stumbled over an ant-hill and fell to the ground on his back; and whilst in this position, he saw, to his inexpressible relief, the enraged cobra dash furiously past him.

Pringle says that this snake has been known to dart at a man on horse-back, and "with such force as to overshoot its aim." The average length of a full-grown specimen I believe to be about five feet.

The puff-adder (*vipera inflata*) was not uncommon in Namaqua-land and Damara-land. My saddle-ox had an exceedingly narrow escape from being bitten by one. The reptile was lying at length across the path, and I did not discover it until the ox almost trod on it. Any serpent less slow in its movements must have fixed its fangs in the animal. Another time, a woman, the wife of a native servant of mine, found one of these horrid creatures comfortably sleeping in the folds of her skin apron.

Notwithstanding its venomous character, the puff-adder, from its inert, heavy and sluggish habits, is comparatively harmless. The only real danger arises from treading on it. This, however, is not always easy to avoid, since its colour so much resembles the ground.

When about to seize its prey, or attack the enemy, the puff-adder is said to be unable to dart forward, but, on the other hand, to possess the faculty of throwing itself backward with unerring certainty.

Different species of what the Dutch term 'schaap-steker,' or sheep-stinger;[1] 'boom-slang,' or tree-snake; 'ringel-hals,' or ring-throat; 'the spuig-slang,' or spitting-snake;[2] the 'zwart-slang,' or black snake,[3] &c., are also occasionally met with; but none of these are very poisonous. The spuig-slang, however, is much dreaded by the colonist, less for its bite—which, though venomous, is not fatal—but from its peculiar habit of projecting a jet of poison to a distance, of several feet, towards the eyes of any person who may happen to approach its haunts—the result of which is usually loss of sight.

The common people at the Cape have some very singular notions and superstitions about the different reptiles indigenous to the Cape Colony, but more especially with regard to the zwart-slang. Our waggon-driver told us that this snake is very fond of women's milk, and solemnly declared that he had known several instances where it has entered people's dwellings at night, and if it met with a sleeping mother, has dexterously abstracted her milk. I remember a somewhat similar story having been told me by the peasantry of some parts of Sweden, who state that to kill a snake was not alone a duty, but an expiatory sacrifice—since 'seven sins' would be forgiven an individual for each serpent slain by him. Accordingly, in the credulity of my childish days, I was a perfect Thalaba!

Incorrect ideas of the power of the reptile family, coupled with superstitious dread, has no doubt served considerably to exaggerate the fear of snakes. Many, we know, are of the most venomous character; but, as we become better acquainted

---

[1] *Trimerorhinus rhombeatus.*   [2] *Naia haje.*   [3] *Columber canus.*

with the different species, we shall find that by far the greater portion are harmless, or nearly so. The remarkably few cases of death occurring from their bites are a corroboration of this. Moreover, like the rest of lower animals, the most deadly reptile will generally fly at the sight of man. It only exerts its formidable powers of destruction when about to be trampled upon or assailed. Were it otherwise, many of the more humid parts of our globe, where snakes literally swarm, would be uninhabitable. Before setting foot on African soil, my head was full of the dangers to which I should be exposed from them—either when 'treading the maze of the jungle,' or when traversing the endless sand plains. Habit and experience has since taught me to regard snakes with something akin to indifference.

Some of the antidotes in Southern Africa, for the bites of snakes and the stings of poisonous insects, are simple, singular, and striking.

The first point to be attended to is (if it be practicable), to tie a string or ligature tight above the wounded part, so as to prevent the venom spreading.

Cutting away, or applying caustic to the wounded part, if promptly and unhesitatingly done, is also likely to prevent fatal consequences.

Europeans have usually recourse to *eau de luce*, five drops of which is administered to the patient in a glass of water every ten minutes, until the poison is counteracted. *Eau de luce* is also applied externally. Another very good plan, is to scarify with a knife the wound, and then boldly to suck it. Care, however, must be taken that one has no sore about the lips or mouth. Sweet milk, oil, or spirits of hartshorn, must then be applied to the wound. The patient should also be made to drink freely of sweet milk.

In the Cape colony, the Dutch farmers resort to a cruel,

but apparently effective plan to counteract the bad effects of a serpent's bite. An incision having been made in the breast of a living fowl, the bitten part is applied to the wound. If the poison be very deadly, the bird soon evinces symptoms of distress, "becomes drowsy, droops its head, and dies." It is replaced by a second, a third, and more, if requisite. When, however, the bird no longer exhibits any of the signs just mentioned, the patient is considered out of danger. A frog, similarly applied, is supposed to be equally efficacious.

A certain white bean, found in some parts of the colony (designated, somewhat singularly, the gentleman bean), has also been known to cure the bites of serpents, and other poisonous creatures. Thus a Damara woman, who had been stung by a scorpion, was once brought to Mr. Hahn with her whole body very much swollen and inflamed. She was already in such a state as to be unable to walk. He instantly divided one of the beans in question, and applied it to the wound, to which it adhered with such tenacity as only to be removed by force. When the virus was extracted, the bean dropped off of its own accord, and the woman, after a time, thoroughly recovered.

"As an antidote against the bite of serpents," says Thunberg, in his Travels in South Africa, "the blood of the turtle was much cried up, which, on account of this extraordinary virtue, the inhabitants dry in the form of small scales or membranes, and carry about them when they travel in this country, which swarms with this most noxious vermin. Whenever any one is wounded by a serpent, he takes a couple of pinches of the dried blood internally, and applies a little of it to the wound."[1]

And Kolben, when speaking of the cobras (called, by the first colonists, the hair-serpent) says:—

---

[1] Turtle blood is also asserted to be a good remedy against wounds caused by poisoned arrows.

"Some affirm that there is in the head of the hair-serpent a stone, which is a never-failing antidote both against the poison of this and every other sort of serpent. I killed a great many hair-serpents at the Cape, and searched very narrowly the heads of all I killed, in order to find this stone; but I could never discover any such thing. Perhaps, it is only to be found at one season of the year, as are the stones in the heads of crawfish.

"There are in the hands of the Cape Europeans," Kolben goes on to say, "a great many stones called serpent-stones; but they are artificial ones. They are brought from the East Indies, where they are prepared by the Brachmans, who are alone, it seems, possessed of the secret of the composition, and will not let it go out of their own body at any price. I am heartily sorry the secret is not in the Christian world, and that the Brachmans are inflexible in this particular, because those stones are of admirable virtues. I saw one of them tried upon a child at the Cape, who had receiv'd a poisonous bite in one of the arms; but it could not be discover'd from what creature. When the stone was brought, the arm was prodigiously swell'd and inflam'd. The stone being applied to the wound, stuck to it very closely, without any manner of bandage or support, drinking in the poison till it could receive no more; and then it dropt off. The stone was then laid in milk, that it might purge itself of the poison; and it did so presently, the poison turning the milk yellow. The stone, as soon as it was purg'd, was again applied to the wound; and when it had drank in its dose, it was again laid in milk. And this was reiterated till such time as the stone had exhausted all the poison: after which the arm was quickly heal'd."

Mr. Thunberg also tells us that the farmers in the Cape Colony cure the bites of serpents, and of other venomous reptiles, by means of the 'slange-steen,' or snake-stone. "It is imported," he says, "from the Indies, especially from Malabar, and costs several rixdollars. It is convex on one side, of a black colour, with a pale ash-grey speck in the middle, and tubulated, with very minute pores. When thrown into water, it causes bubbles to rise, which is a proof of its being genuine, as it is, also, that if put into the mouth, it adheres to the palate. When it is applied to any part that has been bitten by a serpent, it sticks fast to the wound, and extracts the poison; as soon as it is saturated, it falls off of itself. If it be then put into milk, it is supposed to be purified from the poison it had absorbed, and the milk is said to be turned blue by it. Frequently, however, the wound is scarified with a razor, previously to the application of the stone."

"This antidote," says Barrow, when speaking of the snake-stone, "appears to be, in fact, nothing more than a piece of firm bone of some animal made into an oval shape, and burnt round the edges so as to leave a whitish spot in the middle. The country-people, who purchase this remedy under the idea of its being a stone taken out of the head of a certain species of serpent, were very much astonished on being told that it was only a piece of bone; and the more so, on finding that this substance stood their test of the goodness of the *slange-steen*, which was that of throwing out bubbles on the surface when immersed in water. To the porosity of the bone may be ascribed its healing qualities, if it actually possesses any; for which reason, any other substance made up of capillary tubes, as common sponge, for instance, might perhaps be equally efficacious."

To resume.—Our journey to Rehoboth was unattended with any very remarkable incident, and we reached that place in safety, after an absence of twenty-three days.

CHAPTER XXV.

THE AUTHOR'S TENT TAKES FIRE—HE LOSES EVERYTHING BUT HIS PAPERS—HE IS LAID ON A BED OF SICKNESS—WANT OF MEDICINE, ETC.—REFLECTIONS—WHOLE VILLAGES INFECTED WITH FEVER—ABUNDANCE OF GAME—EXTRAORDINARY SHOT AT AN OSTRICH—A LION BREAKFASTS ON HIS WIFE—WONDERFUL SHOOTING STAR—REMARKABLE MIRAGE—GAME AND LIONS PLENTIFUL—THE EBONY TREE—ARRIVAL AT BETHANY, A MISSIONARY STATION—THE TROUBLE OF A LARGE HERD OF CATTLE—A THIRSTY MAN'S COGITATION—CURIOUS SUPERSTITION—THE DAMARA CATTLE DESCRIBED—PEOPLE WHO LIVE ENTIRELY WITHOUT WATER—CROSS THE ORANGE RIVER—STERILE COUNTRY.

THE old adage, 'Misfortunes never come singly,' was exemplified in my case. The wound in my leg being now nearly healed, we were preparing to leave Rehoboth, when one evening my hut accidentally caught fire, and, being entirely constructed of dry grass and sticks, it was burnt to the ground before anything of moment could be saved. By rushing through the flames, however, I fortunately succeeded in preserving the greater part of my papers and memoranda, which to me were invaluable. I also rescued my saddle; but, in so doing, my clothes took fire, and I had a very narrow escape from being burnt to death. A shirt, a pair of trousers, a cap, and a pair of *under-done* shoes, which had not been long enough at the fire to be thoroughly roasted, were all that was left to me. My situation, consequently, was not very enviable. Through the kindness of Messrs. Kleinschmidt and Vollmer, however, I was once more able to appear decently apparelled.

But I was soon destined to experience a greater calamity. A few stages south of Rehoboth, which we left on the 22nd of April, *en route* to the Cape, and while camped on the banks of the Hountop, I was attacked by intermittent fever, which quickly carried me to the verge of the grave. My sufferings and privations during this period were indeed severe. Regularly every morning at eleven o'clock, I was seized with a violent shivering fit, which lasted three hours. Then came the fever, of almost as long duration, accompanied by racking headache and profuse perspiration. After this, my head was tolerably free from pain; but I was so completely exhausted, that to turn in my bed was a laborious effort. The climate, moreover, at this season, was very trying; for, whilst the days were moderately warm (the thermometer averaging 65° at noon), the nights were piercingly cold and frosty. At sunrise, the ice was from an eighth part of an inch to one inch thick. I became very sensitive to these changes, inasmuch as during the greater part of the illness, I was compelled to sleep in the open air, having previously disposed of our waggons to the natives. What little medicine I once possessed, was consumed in the recent conflagration; and the missionaries—owing to the fever having broken out most alarmingly among themselves and the natives—were unable to spare me any. To add to my misfortunes, no suitable food was procurable. Milk and meat were my only diet. The latter I could not digest, and the former soon became insipid to my taste. The men, it is true, had once the good fortune to surprise an ostrich in its nest, but the eggs were too rich and heavy for my weak stomach.

Up to this period, my busy and roving life had left me but little time for serious reflection. Now, however, that the cares of the world no longer occupied my thoughts, I felt the full force of my lonely situation. During the long and sleepless nights, I was often seized with an indescribable sensation of sadness and melancholy. Death itself I did not fear; but to perish in a foreign land, in the midst of strangers, far away from all I loved, was an idea to which I could hardly reconcile myself. What hand would close my eyes? what mourner would follow my coffin? or what friend would shed a tear on my lonely and distant grave?

I was *alone!* Oh, may the reader never experience the full meaning of that melancholy word!

After upwards of two months of no ordinary sufferings, my strong constitution prevailed, and I was convalescent; but several weeks elapsed before I recovered my usual health and vigour.

John Allen was also seriously ill from the same malady, which had the character of an epidemic; for, in a very short time, it spread like wild-fire throughout the length and breadth of Great Namaqua-land, and vast numbers of people succumbed under it. The disease, indeed, was of so destructive a nature, that it swept off whole villages. In one kraal in particular, all the inhabitants perished, and the cattle were left to take care of themselves.

Fever (the cause of which is unknown) is not common in these parts, and makes its appearance only occasionally.

We had pitched our tent, as already said, near the Hountop river. The country thereabout was a succession of vleys or gullies, then filled with excellent clear water, teeming with water-fowl. Quails, birds of the grouse tribe, and wood-pigeons, were also numerous. Of the larger animals we had the zebra, the springbok, the ostrich, and an occasional oryx and hartebeest; but, from their being much persecuted by the natives, combined with nakedness of the country, they were extremely wary and difficult of approach.

Game of many kinds being thus abundant, it may well be supposed that, as soon as my strength permitted me to carry a gun, I at once took the field, as well for amusement, as for the purpose of replenishing our larder, which was but very ill supplied.

One day I made a capital shot at an ostrich, which, when running at full speed, I brought down at the long distance of two hundred and thirty paces. On a previous occasion I killed one of these splendid birds when upwards of three hundred paces from me.

Another day I had the good fortune to shoot a rhinoceros. He was probably a straggler; for these animals have long since disappeared from the part of the country where we were then encamped—and, indeed, are now very rarely to be met with south of the Kuisip river.

Early one morning, one of our herdsmen came running up to us in great fright, and announced that a lion was devouring a lioness! We thought, at first, that the man must be mistaken; but his story was perfectly true, and only her skull, the larger bones, and the skin, were left. On examining the ground more closely, the fresh remains of a young springbok were also discovered. We therefore conjectured that the lion and lioness being very hungry, and the antelope not proving a sufficient meal for both, they had quarrelled; and he, after killing his wife, had coolly eaten her also. A most substantial breakfast it must have been!

On only one other occasion have I known lions to prey on each other. This was when on my way to Lake Ngami. On a certain night, we had badly wounded a lion. He retreated growlingly into the bush, and immediately after·

wards a whole troop of lions rushed upon their disabled brother and tore him to pieces.

A singular and interesting atmospheric phenomenon occurred at Hountop. Between seven and eight o'clock in the evening of the 24th of June, when reading by the side of my bivouac fire, I was suddenly startled by the whole atmosphere becoming brilliantly—nay, almost painfully—illuminated. On turning to the quarter of the heavens whence this radiance proceeded, I discovered a most magnificent shooting star, passing *slowly*, in an oblique direction, through space, with an immense tail attached to it, and emitting sparks of dazzling light. The fire by which I sat was exceedingly bright, and the moon clear and brilliant; yet they were both totally eclipsed by this immense body of light. Its great beauty and brilliancy might, perhaps, be best realized, by saying that it was like a star of the second or third order when compared to the moon at full.

After a time, the pasturage being nearly exhausted in the neighbourhood of the Hountop, we removed our camp a few miles southward, to another periodical river called the Aamhoup. During our stay here, we observed some very striking and singular horizontal refractions of the air. Once I saw an ostrich walking on the horizon line, whilst its double—clear and well defined—appeared immediately above it. Both the ostrich and its double, moreover, were divided into three different portions by as many different strata of air.

Again: regularly every morning, for *nearly a month*, the projecting ledge of a rock was converted into the semblance of a splendid and embattled castle. As the atmosphere became uniformly heated, the mirage melted away into a soft, watery haze.

In usual refractions, the inverted image of an object

generally appears above the object itself; but occasionally the effect is reversed. Captain Scoresby, the well-known Arctic navigator, once by these means discovered his father's vessel the day before it actually came in sight.

It has long puzzled the learned to account for the mirage. I believe, however, it is now pretty well known to arise from the unequal density and temperature of the lower strata of air.

The abundance of good water and pasturage had enabled our cattle to get into excellent condition; and as the season was now far advanced, and I was sufficiently well to travel, we deemed it necessary to move slowly on towards the Cape-Colony. Accordingly, on the 9th of July, we left our camp on the Aamhoup—a place where we had experienced both misery and happiness.

Our course lay along, and at the foot of, a very picturesque range of table hills, averaging about one thousand feet in height. To the westward were also mountains of a similar nature, but less regular. They were of the trap formation, and consisted chiefly of limestone.

Water continued for a time to be tolerably abundant, but pasturage began soon to fail us. Two causes were to be assigned for this—namely, the devastation of the locusts, and the inferior quality of the soil, which became stony, interspersed here and there with ridges of sand.

Amongst the latter, we encountered herds of gemsboks, and troops of lions following on their scent. The mere sight of the tracks of the latter frightened a friend, with whom I was travelling, almost out of his wits. We were riding in advance of our cattle at the time, and it was with difficulty that I could prevent him from returning with precipitation.

On the 4th of August, we arrived in the neighbourhood

of another Rhenish missionary station, called Bethany. Here we met with the ebony tree, of which I had only before seen a few stragglers in the Swakop river, near the Usab gorge. Hence, on to the Orange river, this tree became more or less abundant; but it was stunted and gnarled. Our bivouac fires usually consisted of its wood.

Whilst Hans and the men were busy preparing our food and camp for the night, I strolled on to the station, which I found deserted by every living creature. Only a short time previously, the Rev. Mr. Knudsen officiated here, but had been obliged to leave on account of some disagreement with the native tribe and its chief, David Christian. It had always been considered as inferior to most of the other missionary stations in this part of Africa; but, what with the absence of the inhabitants, the devastation of the locust which had destroyed every particle of vegetation—and the black and parched appearance of the soil, it now looked wild and dreary in the extreme. The lengthened shadows of evening threw an additional gloom over this once busy scene of cheerful industry. Oh, changes, mysterious and incomprehensible! Surely, God, in his infinite wisdom, will not permit the handy-work of his servants, raised only by years of perseverance, toil, and privations, to perish without some recompense!

Bethany, if I am not mistaken, became a scene of missionary labour as early as 1820. The enterprising and venerable Mr. Schmelen then officiated here, but he found it necessary, after a time, to abandon the place. Subsequently to his departure, it remained deserted for upwards of twenty years, when, in 1843, it was once more tenanted, and this time by Mr. Knudsen, who, in his turn, as seen above, was obliged to move off elsewhere.

After leaving Bethany, water and pasturage became

every day more scarce. All the vleys and pools of rain-water were dried up. The Koanquip river, however, long befriended us, as in its bed we generally managed to obtain a supply of grass and water for our cattle, which now amounted to several hundred head.

But the labour and fatigue of watering the latter was immense. No person who has not been circumstanced as we were, can form the least conception of the trouble, care, and anxiety, that a large drove of cattle occasions. Perhaps, when, after having dug for *twenty consecutive hours* — and this I have done more than once — the water is found insufficient in quantity, or (which is almost as bad) the ground falls in, or the cattle themselves spoil it by their wallowing and excrement.

These native cattle are the most troublesome and disgusting brutes possible; for, after having spoiled the water by their own wildness and wantonness, they rush furiously about, bellowing and moaning. It is enough to discourage the stoutest heart.

When arriving at a place where we supposed water was to be found, the plan usually adopted, in order to guard against the cattle destroying our work, was to send them away to pasture. In the meantime, every available man went speedily to work with such implements as were procurable: spades, wooden troughs, pieces of wood or of bark, were indifferently put in requisition; and even our hands were used with great effect, though not without sustaining injury. Having worked the aperture of sufficient depth and width, it was fenced in by thorn-bushes, leaving only a single entrance. The oxen were then sent for, and allowed to approach singly or in greater number, according to the extent of the water. Sometimes, however, if the nature of the ground did not permit the cattle to have access to the water, a hollow was scooped in the earth, near the edge of the pit, into which (or into a piece of sail-cloth, if at hand) the water was poured by means of small wooden pails, usually denominated 'bamboos.'

Owing to this tedious process, coupled with the slowness with which water filters through sand, and the immense quantity (usually five to six buckets full) that a thirsty ox will drink, and the quarrelsome disposition of the animals themselves—watering four hundred head of cattle will often occupy a whole day or night. And, since a person is in a great degree dependent on his cattle, whether for food, draught, &c., he, himself, must never think of refreshment or rest until their wants have been provided for.

The scarcity of water, and the uncertainty of finding it, in these parched regions, is so great, that, when after a long day's journey the anxiously-looked-for pool is found to be dry, it is almost enough to drive a man mad, especially if he be a stranger to the country, and unaccustomed to traversing the African wilds. One's cogitations at such times are apt to be something to the following effect. "If I advance and do not find water within a certain period, it will be inevitable destruction. To retrace my steps to the last watering-place, is not to be thought of, as, from the distance and the exhausted state of the cattle, it would never be reached. What remains for me but to lie down and die?"

The common people at the Cape entertain a notion, that cattle refrain from feeding only once within the year—namely, on Christmas-eve. Then, it is affirmed, they fall on their knees, and, with closed mouths and half-shut eyes (a sign of placidity), silently thank the Giver of all good things for the grass and water they have enjoyed during the past twelve months. They say, moreover, that a person may witness this act of devotion, by keeping well to leeward and out of sight of the animals.[1]

Our cattle consisted chiefly of the Damara-breed, which, so far as I am aware, differs widely from any found in Europe. They are big-boned, but not particularly weighty; their legs are slender, and they have small, hard, and durable feet. The hair on the body is short, smooth, and glossy, and the extremity of the tail is adorned with a tuft of long, bushy hair, nearly touching the ground. This tuft constitutes the chief ornament of the Damara assegai.

But the horns are the most remarkable feature in the Damara cattle. They are usually placed on the head at an angle of from 45 to 90 degrees, and are at times beautifully arched and twisted, but rarely bend inwards. They are of an incredible length; and one often meets with oxen, the tips of whose horns are from seven to eight feet apart.

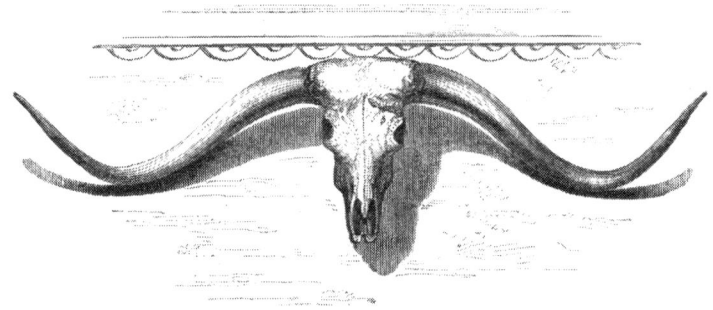

SKULL OF A BECHUANA OX.

The Bechuana cattle (of greater bulk and stouter proportions) seem even to surpass the Damara cattle in this

---

[1] This superstition is common in Devonshire, in the western parts of which it used, till lately, to be affirmed, 'that at twelve o'clock at night on Christmas-eve, the oxen in their stalls are always found on their knees in an attitude of devotion; and that, since the alteration of the style, they continue to do this only on the eve of *old* Christmas-day.' Bravo, oxen!—*(See Brand's 'Popular Antiquities.')*

respect. Amongst many other curious and interesting objects, there is now in the collection of Colonel Thomas Steel, of Upper Brook-street, a perfect cranium of a young Bechuana ox[1], of which the wood-cut is a fair representation. The following are its dimensions:—

Entire length of horns from tip to tip along the curve	13ft.	5in.
Distance (straight) between the tips of the horns	8	8¼
Circumference of horns at the root	1	6½
Breadth of cranium between the eyes	0	9¼
Length ,,	2	2

But I have been told on good authority that in some parts of Africa horns of cattle are found greatly to exceed the above dimensions. The horns, indeed, are of so enormous a size, as seriously to inconvenience the animal. Their length and weight have been known to be so great as to twist the head to one side—one of the horns dragging on the ground, whilst the other pointed upwards.

The Damaras prize their oxen in proportion to the size of their horns. Some African tribes take much pains in forming them of a certain shape. This is effected either by sawing off the tips, splitting them, bending them forcibly when yet tender, and so forth.

The Damara cow is of slender proportions and very wild. Before she can be milked, it is always needful to lash her head to a tree, in like manner as the Laplanders treat their rein-deer, or to tie her hind legs together. The best cow rarely gives more than two or three pints of milk daily; and should her calf die, or be taken from her, she absolutely refuses to give any at all, in which case it is necessary to resort to artificial means. One plan is to stuff a calf-skin

---

[1] This remarkable beast was a long time in the possession of Mr. Oswell, who, I believe, intended to bring it alive to England, but unavoidable circumstances prevented this distinguished traveller from carrying his plan into execution.

with hay or grass, and afterwards to place it on the ground for the cow to slobber over. Sometimes the adoption of the latter expedient gives rise to ludicrous scenes; for the cow when tenderly caressing her supposed offspring, has all at once got scent of the hay or grass, when, thrusting her snout into the skin, she has greedily devoured its contents!

The Damaras, as well as other nations, take great delight in having whole droves of cattle of the same colour. The Namaquas have a perfect mania for a uniform team. Bright brown is the favourite colour; and I myself have always found beasts of this hue to be the strongest and most generally serviceable. Dark brown oxen, with a yellowish streak along the back—by the Dutch designated 'geel-bak' —are also usually stout and enduring. Yellow, and more especially white, oxen are considered weak and unable to bear much fatigue or hardship.

The Damaras, as with almost every other people of Southern Africa, value their cattle next to their women, and take a pride in possessing animals that look high bred. The ox, in fact, forms the chief theme of the songs of the Damaras. They, moreover, rarely or never make use of a handsome animal as a beast of burden, but employ quiet, ugly bulls for such purposes. These have a buffalo look about them, and their horns, moreover, rarely attain to any size.

From their quick step, good feet, and enduring powers, the Damara cattle are much prized by the farmers of the Cape-Colony. The only drawback is their wildness, and immense size of their horns, which they sometimes use with fatal effect.

The day before we reached the Orange river, we fell in with a kraal of Hottentots, whom, to our great surprise, we found living in a locality altogether destitute of water!

The milk of their cows and goats supplied its place. Their cattle, moreover, never obtained water, but found a substitute in a kind of ice plant *(mesembryanthemum)*, of an exceedingly succulent nature, which abounds in these regions. But our own oxen, not accustomed to such diet, would rarely or never touch it. Until I had actually convinced myself—as I had often the opportunity of doing at an after period—that men and beasts could live entirely without water, I should, perhaps, have had some difficulty in realizing this singular fact.

On the 21st of August, we effected the passage of the Orange river in safety, at what is called the Zendlings Drift, or the missionary ford. We had no boat; and those of the men who could not swim were obliged to lay hold of the tails of the cattle, to which they pertinaciously clung. On gaining the opposite bank, which was very steep, the oxen, in climbing it, entirely submerged their charge, to the great delight and amusement of such of their companions as had landed at a more convenient point.

The Orange river was at this season almost at its lowest, yet it was a noble and highly picturesque stream. Looking eastwards, its aspect was particularly imposing. Its breadth at this point might have been from two to three hundred yards. The banks were on both sides lined with evergreen thorns, drooping willows, ebony trees, &c.; and the water forced its passage through a bold and striking gorge, overhung by precipices from two to three thousand feet high. But the country all round was desolate. The hills, which at some distant period had evidently been subject to volcanic eruptions, had a sunburnt and crumbling appearance, and were almost wholly destitute of vegetation. The soil, in the neighbourhood of the mountains, consisted of pure sand, and was covered with low and succulent shrubs, from which our cattle, hitherto accustomed to revel in the almost boundless savannahs of Damara-land, turned with disgust. The country for several weeks' journey in advance of us, was represented as of a similar nature.

We began now seriously to tremble for the poor beasts, which had already lost flesh. Upwards of two months' travelling had to be performed before we could reach our destination.

With the exception of that portion of Namaqua-land and Damara-land bordering on the coast, the part of the country I speak of has the most inauspicious appearance I ever saw. Its sterility arises probably from being situated near the limit, not only of the "thunder-rains," but of the regular rains, ("mist-rains," as they are called in the colony), and the consequent frequency of great droughts. Indeed, scarcely any rain falls here in some years.

CHAPTER XXVI.

GREAT NAMAQUA-LAND — ITS BOUNDARIES AND EXTENT — ITS RIVERS — NATURE OF THE COUNTRY — VEGETATION AND CLIMATE — GEOLOGICAL STRUCTURE — MINERALS — 'TOPNAARS' AND 'OERLAMS' — HOUSES — MYTHOLOGY AND RELIGION — TUMULI — WONDERFUL ROCK — CURIOUS LEGEND OF THE HARE — COMING OF AGE — THE WITCH-DOCTOR — AMULETS — SUPERSTITIONS — A NAMAQUA'S NOTION OF THE SUN — MARRIAGE — POLYGAMY — CHILDREN — BARBAROUS PRACTICE — LONGEVITY — SINGULAR CUSTOMS — ORNAMENTS — TATTOOING — ARMS — IDLE HABITS — FOND OF AMUSEMENTS — MUSIC AND DANCING — SPIRITS — MEAD — DOMESTIC ANIMALS.

HAVING now brought my narrative to a period when I am about to leave Great Namaqua-land, it may be well to say a few words of this country, its inhabitants, their manners and customs, &c.

The portion of Africa known as Namaqua-land is divided into two distinct parts, viz., Little and Great Namaqua-land. By the former is understood the territory (now British) between the Orange river and about the 31st degree of latitude on the south. By the latter, the country between the last-named river and Damara-land, its eastern boundary being the Kalahari desert; whilst on the west it is washed by the billows of the Atlantic ocean.

Great Namaqua-land covers a surface of no less than one hundred and twelve thousand geographical square-miles,[1] with, probably, a population of scarcely thirty thousand souls, or less than four persons to the square-mile. Excepting the great Sahara itself, there is, perhaps, not a country in the world, of equal extent, so scantily peopled, so destitute of water, so dismal, and so generally barren and useless. It is truly a 'region of curses.'

The coast-line of Great Namaqua-land, like that of Damara-land, consists of a dreary, sandy waste, extending in places from thirty to forty miles into the interior—in others to a hundred or more—and is, with very few exceptions, uninhabitable.

Some of the rivers, such as the Kuisip, and others of little importance, empty themselves into the Atlantic; but the larger portion run in an easterly direction, and are chiefly tributaries to the Fish-river. This remarkable watercourse, which takes its rise in the most northerly limit of Great Namaqua-land, finally joins the Orange river about three or four days' journey from where the latter finds an outlet into the sea—thus intersecting the country throughout its entire length.

Great Namaqua-land is characterised by immense sandy plains, traversed by hill and rock, and thickly strewn with quartz, which reflects a dazzling and perplexing light. Two to three days' journey south of Rehoboth, the dense thorny bush, so peculiar to Damara-land, ceases, and, with the exception of a few mimosas along the water-courses, and occasional ebony trees, the arboreous vegetation is scanty and stunted. For more than six months of the year, it is scorched by an almost vertical sun. The rains, which are always

---

[1] Or about 148,000 English square miles. The area of Damara-land is about 29,000 English square miles.

accompanied by heavy thunder, are periodical and very partial. In its northern portion, the wet season sets in at the same time as in Damara-land; but in a southerly direction, the rains are later and more uncertain; and, as has been said in the last chapter, little or none falls about the lower course of the Orange river and the neighbourhood. The springs (which are often either hot or salt) are indifferent and scantily distributed. The periodical water-courses, therefore, afford the chief supply.

The Namaquas, as well as the Damaras, are loud in their complaints that less rain falls now than half a century back. Indeed, the numerous ancient beds of rivers in the vast sandy plains, and the deeply-scored slopes and sides of the now 'sunburnt' and crumbling hills, clearly indicate that almost the whole country north of the Orange river, as far as Europeans have penetrated from the Cape side, has, at some former period, been much more abundantly watered. In some parts, the destruction of forests, which are well known to retain and condense vapoury particles, may partly account for such atmospheric changes; but in this region we must look for other causes.

In a geological point of view, Great Namaqua-land presents many interesting features. Between the Orange river and Walfisch Bay, beginning at the sea-side, three distinct terrace-like risings of the country are recognized. Besides the granite, which is the prevailing rock, great masses of quartz are met with, either, as aforesaid, scattered over its surface, or filling up the large gaps and fissures occasioned by ancient eruptions. Iron and sandstone, and slate formations, are also not uncommon.

At some remote period, this land must have been subjected to volcanic agencies; and though not one of these has taken place in the memory of the present generation, rumbling noises underground and tremors of the earth are of frequent occurrence. The existence of hot water springs; the confusion of the fantastically and curiously-shaped hills— "the strata bending and dipping from the perpendicular to the horizontal, and in others extending in a straight line from one hill to another"—bear ample testimony to its volcanic nature. The presence, moreover, of vast quantities of minerals is a further evidence of its igneous character. Tin, lead, iron, and copper ore is often met with. I have had specimens of the latter mineral in my possession containing from forty to ninety per cent of pure metal. At eight to ten days' journey with 'ox waggon,' east of the missionary station, Bethany, meteoric iron is found in apparently inexhaustible quantities. I have seen lumps, of several hundred weights, brought from thence, so pure and malleable that the natives converted it into balls for their guns, &c., without any previous application of fire. As Great Namaqua-land becomes better known, it is more than probable that it will be found equally prolific in minerals—if not more so—as Little Namaqua-land, where, of late, extensive and valuable mines have been brought to light.

The term Hottentot, and Namaqua, have probably originated with Europeans, since neither is found in the native language. The Hottentots of these regions may be divided in two great branches, viz., the 'Topnaars,' and the 'Oerlams.' With the latter is generally understood the newcomers, and the semi-civilized; but the real signification of the term is doubtful. Some conjecture the 'Oerlam' to be a corruption of the Dutch word 'o'erland,' or overland, that is, people who have come overland. Be this as it may, the Namaqua-Hottentots consider it as a compliment to be addressed as 'Oerlam.' 'Topnaar,' on the other hand, signifies the First, the Highest, the Great, or those who originally inhabited Great Namaqua-land, and they view with considerable jealousy the progress and superiority of the 'Oerlams,' whom they justly consider as intruders.

The northern Namaquas are divided into numerous tribes, each under petty chiefs. The principal of these are Jonker Afrikaner, Cornelius, Amral, Zwartbooi, Jan Boois, William Fransman, Paul Goliath, David Christian, and Bondel Zwartz.

The Namaquas dwell in small round huts, made on the same principle as those of the Damaras, and covered with mats composed of rushes, which are prepared in the following manner.—A quantity of the inner bark of the mimosa is collected and dried. When wanted for immediate use, the required portion is put into hot water and softened. Each member of the family then fills his mouth with as much of the fibre as it can hold, and chews it until it becomes quite pliable, when it is at once converted into strings by the rude process of twisting it on the naked leg. A large quantity is in this manner manufactured in an incredibly short time. The rushes are then cut to the desired length, and laid out on the ground singly, and in a row, when holes are made— at intervals of about two inches—through each rush, and the string in question passed through them by means of a bone or thorn needle. The ends of the rushes, however, are secured more strongly by back-stitches. These mats serve a double purpose. In warm weather they are open and airy, whilst, being of a porous texture, a shower closes them, and after a while they become proof against the most deluging rains.

When they remove their habitations, these mattings and the framework of the hut, which consists of semicircular boughs, are packed on oxen. Their household utensils, such as calabashes, milk-pails, pots, &c., are suspended to the boughs, and in the midst of all this confusion is often seated the good dame of the house, surrounded by her promising offspring.

It has been asserted by travellers, and others, that the Namaquas have not the slightest idea of a Superior Being, or of a life hereafter. Yet they believe in Heitjeebib, or Heitjekobib, whom they consider to have the power to grant or withhold them success and prosperity. But whether Heitjeebib is a deity, a goblin, or merely a deified ancestor, I shall not presume to say. At all events, they affirm he exists in the graves of all deceased people; and whenever a Hottentot passes a burial-place, he invariably throws a stone, a bush, or other token of offering and affection, on the tomb, pronouncing the name of Heitjeebib, and invoking his blessing and protection in his undertakings. From being thus constantly added to, these heaps often attain a great size. They are found throughout the country (I have observed them even in Damara-land), and frequently in situations perfectly 'stoneless,' from which it may be inferred that the natives carry the materials a long distance. Captain Harris mentions having seen similar heaps amongst the Matabili, but was unable to account for their presence. The Hottentots have an indistinct notion that they came from an easterly direction, and it is possible that the stone tumuli found by the traveller may have something to do with this tradition.

The natives in these parts have a strange tale of a rock, in which the tracks of all the different animals indigenous to the country are distinctly visible; moreover, that man and beast lived here together in great amity, but one day, from some unknown cause, their Deity appeared unexpectedly and dispersed them. I never had the good fortune to obtain a sight of this marvellous rock. Mr. Moffat, who makes mention of a similar story prevailing among the Bechuanas, was equally unsuccessful. "Once I heard a man of influence," says the reverend gentleman, "telling his story on the subject. I, of course, could not say that I believed the wondrous tale; but very mildly hinted that he might be misinformed; on which he swore, by his ancestors and his king, that he had visited the spot, and paid a tax to see the wonder; and that, consequently, his testimony was indubitable."

The Namaquas have the following singular superstition with regard to the hare, which no adult is allowed to eat. The legend involves the sublime Christian doctrine of immortality.

Once upon a time, the moon called the hare, and commanded him to convey to man the following message:—"As I die and am born again,[1] so you shall die and be again alive." The hare hastened to obey; but, instead of saying, "As I die, and am born again," he said, "As I die, and am *not* born again." On his return, the moon inquired what words he had conveyed to mankind; and, on being informed, the luminary exclaimed—"What! have you said to man, 'As I die and am *not* born again, so you shall die and not be again alive!'" And with this he hurled a stick at the hare, with such force as to split open his lips, which is the cause of the peculiar formation of this animal's mouth. The hare quickly betook himself to flight, and is said to be flying to the present day. The old Namaquas used to say:—"We are still enraged with the hare, because he has brought such a bad message, and we will not eat him."

On the occasion of a youth coming of age, or rather when becoming a 'man,' there is great rejoicing. From that day forward, he is forbidden to eat the hare, or even to come in contact with the fire where this animal has been qrepared. Should he transgress this command, he is not unfrequently

---

[1] When speaking of the moon, the Namaquas do not say, like ourselves, that it rises and sets, but that 'it dies and is born again.'

banished from his werft; though, on paying a fine, he may again be admitted to the community. He is, moreover, no longer permitted to 'suck the goats.'[1]

The Namaquas, like almost all nations who are sunk in barbarism, have great faith in sorcery; and male and female witch-doctors equally play conspicuous parts. These impostors are supposed to have the power to procure rain, to restore the sick to health, to discover the cause of a person's death, and to perform other miracles. They are crafty creatures, and know how to take advantage of the popular ignorance. Even civilized men have been deceived by their wiles. Their principal stipulation before they exercise any of their arts is to have some animal slaughtered, which they prescribe according to their fancy, and to the wealth of their patients. Mr. Moffat tells us that a stout ox might be a cure for a slight cold in a chieftain, while a kid would be a remedy for a fever among the poor, from whom there could be no chance of obtaining anything greater.

The Namaqua witch-doctor is called *kaiaob*, or *kaiaobs*, if a woman. On being called to the sick-bed, after having examined the patient, he or she generally declares that the ailment is caused by a great snake (toros) having fired an arrow into the stomach. The sorcerer operates by feeling this part of the body, and by a good squeezing endeavours to coax the illness away. Another approved plan is to make a small incision on the body about the place where the cause of the disease is supposed to lurk, and to suck it out. The production of a snake, a frog, an insect, or the like, is frequently the result. Eyebrecht solemnly declared that he once was an eye-witness to such an operation on a woman at Jonker's place. When the witch-doctor arrived, a sheep was

---

[1] It is a practice among the young Namaquas to hold a goat between the knees, and draw the milk directly from the teats of the animal into their own mouths.

killed, and the sinews of the back were cut out and rolled up into a small ball, which the patient was made to swallow; the remainder of the animal, of course, being appropriated to the sorcerer's own stomach. A few days afterwards, the wizard returned, and cut some small holes in the abdomen of the patient, on which a small snake escaped, then a lizard, numerous other animals following.

To become a witch-doctor of any importance, a person is required to be instructed by one previously well versed in the mysteries of the black art. He must begin his lessons by swallowing animal poison, be bitten by venomous reptiles, or have poison inoculated into his body. A cap, a handkerchief, or, any sort of. clothing worn by such a person until it has become perfectly saturated with filth, is considered the most infallible cure for all kinds of diseases, poisonous bites, &c. On emergences, a corner of this treasure is washed, and the dirty-water thus produced is given to the patient— beast or man—to drink. The chief, Amral, assured me that he possessed a cap of this kind, with which he had effected innumerable cures. "It is sure," he said, "to cause relief when nothing else is of any avail." The witch-doctors have also other disgusting methods of effecting cures.

Like most of the tribes in Southern Africa, the Namaquas have great faith in amulets, which consist, as usual, of the teeth and claws of lions, hyænas, and other wild beasts; pieces of wood, bone, dried flesh and fat, roots of plants, &c.

When a chief died, it was formerly customary to call the whole tribe together, and to give a grand feast in honour of the occasion. The fat, and all the choice parts of the slaughtered animals, were preserved for the son of the deceased, who was to succeed his father in the chieftainship.[1] The raw

---

[1] After a great hunt, it was also the custom to reserve for the chief the best pieces of the different kind of game which had been killed, such as the breast of the eland, the hump of the rhinoceros, and so forth; the rest being divided amongst the tribe.

fat was placed on his head, and worn until it became dry, when it was transferred to some crone, who carefully preserved it as a much-prized amulet.

During his journeyings in Great Namaqua-land, Sir James Alexander was told by the natives, that the Bush-women have it in their power to change their forms into lions, hyænas, and other beasts of prey. The following legend illustrates this superstition:—

"Once on a time, a certain Namaqua was travelling in company with a Bushwoman carrying a child on her back. They had proceeded some distance on their journey, when a troop of wild horses (zebras), appeared, and the man said to the woman, 'I am hungry; and as I know you can turn yourself into a lion, do so now, and catch us a wild horse, that we may eat.'

"The woman answered, 'you'll be afraid.'"

"'No, no,' said the man. 'I am afraid of dying of hunger, but not of you.'

"Whilst he was speaking, hair began to appear at the back of the woman's neck, her nails assumed the appearance of claws, and her features altered. She set down the child.

"The man alarmed at the change, climbed a tree close by, while the woman glared at him fearfully; and, going to one side, she threw off her skin petticoat, when a perfect lion rushed out into the plain. It bounded and crept among the bushes towards the wild horses; and, springing on one of them, it fell, and the lion lapped its blood. The lion then came back to where the child was crying, and the man called from the tree, 'Enough! enough! Don't hurt me. Put off your lion's shape. I'll never ask to see this again.'

"The lion looked at him and growled. 'I'll remain here till I die,' exclaimed the man, 'if you don't become a woman again.' The mane and tail began to disappear, the lion went towards the bush where the skin petticoat lay: it was slipped on, and the woman in her proper shape took up the child. The man descended, partook of the horse's flesh, but never again asked the woman to catch game for him."

On the death of a person, some of his cattle (the richer the deceased, the more numerous the animals), are killed, and a banquet is given to his relations and friends. On these occasions the poor beasts are suffocated. Ordinarily, and when intended for food alone, animals are dispatched by some sharp-cutting instrument. The flesh, never eaten raw, and not often when roasted, is usually served up when boiled.

The ideas of a Namaqua as to the formation and rotary motion of the heavenly bodies, if not very profound, are unquestionably very original. "The sun by some of the people of this benighted land," says an enterprising traveller, "is considered to be a mass of fat, which descends nightly to the sea, where it is laid hold of by the chief of a white man's ship, who cuts away a portion of tallow, and, giving the rest a kick, it bounds away, sinks under the wave, goes round below, and then comes up again in the east."

When a man feels a desire to enter the matrimonial state, he goes to the father of the woman on whom he has settled his affection, and demands her in marriage. If the parent be favourable to the match, the affair may be considered as settled. An ox or a cow is then killed outside the door of the bride's home, and the ceremony is over.

Polygamy is practised without limitation. If a man become tired of his wife, he unceremoniously returns her to the parental roof, and however much she (or the parents) may object to so summary a proceeding, there is no remedy.

Widows are left to shift for themselves.

They neither cradle nor circumcise their children, which they are said to name in the following singular manner. No man nor woman has more than one name, which is retained even after marriage. If a daughter be born, she assumes the name of her father, whilst a boy would be called after his mother, with very little alteration. I never could understand the reason of this.

Within the memory of the present generation, a barbarous practice prevailed, of leaving old and disabled people to perish far away from the dwellings of men. A slight fence was raised round the 'living-dead,' and a small supply of water was placed at his side, when he was abandoned to his fate. Mr. Moffat, during his wanderings in Namaqualand, saw one of these wretches (a woman); and on inquiring the cause of her being thus deserted, she replied:—" I am old, you see, and no longer able to serve them (referring to her grown-up children). When they kill game, I am too feeble to help in carrying home the flesh; I am incapable of gathering wood to make fire; and I cannot carry their children on my back as I used to do."

The Namaquas may be said to be long-lived, for individuals have been known to reach the advanced age of ninety, and even one hundred, years. This is the more remarkable, when the very wretched life they lead is taken into consideration.

The Namaquas have a singular custom both amongst themselves and with regard to strangers, which consists in the *adoption* of a 'father' and a 'mother.' This practice is so widely observed, that few who come in contact with the several tribes are able to avoid it. Almost every European trader, indeed, possesses in each village, which he is in the habit of frequenting, either a so-called 'father' or 'mother.' But the custom is a most inconvenient one—to the traveller, at least—for he may be pretty sure that, as soon as this near degree of consanguinity is established between himself and a Namaqua, he will be asked for a horse or an ox, or it may be for the very coat upon his back, which, as in duty bound, he is expected to hand over to 'papa' or 'mamma,' as the case may be. The poor son, it is true, has also the privilege of demanding anything that may captivate his fancy. But since a native is usually more forward and importunate than a European, the bargain, as a rule, is generally a losing one to the latter.

When two Namaquas are talking together, and one is relating a story, the listener repeats the last words of the speaker, even if he should know as much of the matter as his informant. For instance: if a man begin his recital by saying:—"As I walked along the river, a very large rhinoceros rushed suddenly upon me." "Rushed suddenly upon me," echoes the auditor. "He was very fat." "Very fat," the other ejaculates, and so forth.

The Namaquas are fond of ornamenting their persons profusely with brass, iron, and copper, but more especially with small beads of various colours. A kind of black, dull bead, manufactured by themselves, is particularly esteemed. A quantity of resin is procured, which they melt and mix with powdered charcoal, and, during the process of cooling, it is diligently kneaded, until, being converted to the consistency of gum, it is drawn out into long, narrow bars. Again it is gently heated over a slow fire, when small bits are detached and worked between the fingers till they assume the desired shape. Their patterns of bead-work are by no means devoid of taste.

These people tattoo themselves, and also anoint and besprinkle their bodies with a profusion of grease and powders.

The latter are of several kinds, and are chiefly obtained from the leaves of plants of the *croton* and *diosma* families. These powders are called 'buku,' by the Namaquas, and are much esteemed, more especially the kind procured south of the Orange river, which has a very agreeable and aromatic scent.

The sole arms of the Namaquas of the present day are guns. Their original weapons, which consisted of the bow and arrow, the assegai, and an immense shield (made out of an entire, single-folded ox-hide), are now rarely seen.

The Namaquas are an excessively idle race. They may be seen basking in the sun for days together, in listless inactivity, frequently almost perishing from thirst or hunger, when, with very little exertion, they may have it in their power to satisfy the cravings of nature. If urged to work, they have been heard to say: "Why should we resemble the worms of the ground?" A few may occasionally be seen employing themselves in making neat little camp stools, and in repairing guns, for which they have a certain aptitude. Jonker Afrikaner—be it said to his honour—is by far the most industrious Hottentot that I have yet seen.

They are excessively fond of diversions, more especially music and dancing. They do not, however, distinguish themselves by grace in their movements, nor do they even possess that dexterity and flexibility of limb that the Ovambo ladies —at the expense of our peace of mind—exhibited at King Nangoro's *court ball*.

They understand and practise the art of distilling spirits. When a certain kind of berry, of a sweet and agreeable taste, is ripe, large quantities are collected and put into a skin-bag to ferment. On being sufficiently advanced, they are deposited in a large pot and boiled, and the steam drawn off into another vessel joined to it by an old gun-barrel. The liquor is then allowed to settle for a few days, and becomes so strong and intoxicating that a small glass or two is sufficient to upset any man's reason not previously accustomed to it. I have seen the natives become perfectly maddened by its effect.

They also make a kind of mead (a favourite drink with the ancient northmen) which is a pleasant and refreshing beverage, and unless partaken of to excess, is comparatively harmless.

The domestic animals of the country, are the cow, the sheep, the goat, and the dog. The sheep is highly prized by them, so much so that at one time (before the introduction of tobacco) it was more thought of than anything else—even than women! The original breed of Namaqua cattle is nearly extinct. The southern tribes still possess it, though more or less mixed with that of the colony and Damaraland. In shape and size the Namaqua cattle approach nearer the European breed than to that indigenous to the countries north of them. They are of moderate size, very compact, and have short, but stout horns (usually curved inwards), with rather large hoofs.

CHAPTER XXVII.

LEAVE THE ORANGE RIVER—ARRIVAL AT KOMAGGAS—GARDENING AND AGRICULTURE—THE AUTHOR STARTS ALONE FOR THE CAPE—COLONY HORSES—ENMITY OF THE BOERS TO 'BRITISHERS'—DUTCH SALUTATION—THE AUTHOR MUST HAVE BEEN AT TIMBUCTOO, WHETHER OR NO—HE ARRIVES AT CAPE-TOWN—CUTS A SORRY FIGURE—IS RUN AWAY WITH—A FEAST OF ORANGES—GHOST STORIES—CATTLE AUCTION—HANS AND JOHN ALLEN PROCEED TO AUSTRALIA—PREPARATIONS FOR JOURNEY TO THE NGAMI—DEPARTURE FROM THE CAPE.

ON the 25th of August we left the inhospitable banks of the Orange river. After rather more than a week's slow travel, through dreary and uninteresting tracts of land covered by a deep, yielding, sandy-soil, bearing a dwarfish vegetation, we arrived at Komaggas, also a Rhenish missionary station. The Rev. Mr. Weich now officiated here.[1] The congregation consists of a promiscuous collection of Hottentots, and the offspring of other dark-coloured natives.

Komaggas is picturesquely situated, and well supplied

---

[1] This institution was founded by the Rev. Mr. Schmelen. In 1830, during the administration of Sir Lowry Cole, it received, by charter, an extensive grant of territory from the British government at the Cape. On that memorable occasion, the zealous missionary presented to the governor a translation of the four Gospels in the Namaqua tongue.

with water. Gardening is brought almost to perfection; and, notwithstanding the dryness of the atmosphere, corn is cultivated with success in the neighbourhood. Indeed, the best wheat in the west part of the colony, I am informed, is grown here. But its cultivation is attended with much labour, since it can only be raised on the summit of hills (which retain moisture longer than the lowlands), rising not unfrequently several thousand feet above the sea.

Except at the station, and one or two other spots, the extensive grounds are scantily watered, and ill-adapted for grazing. During our visit, numbers of cattle were dying from starvation. The region is, moreover, in some seasons infected by diseases fatal to beasts of pasture, and these maladies, of late years, have been of so destructive a character as nearly to exterminate the cattle. Indeed, many of the Bastards and Hottentots, who chiefly inhabit these parts, and who were formerly living in great abundance, are reduced to beggary from this cause.

I now determined to leave Hans, and proceed in advance to Cape-Town, with a view of making arrangements about the sale of the cattle, and the intended expedition to the Ngami. As we were now in a locality where horses might be obtained, I procured three or four of these animals without delay, partly for cash and partly for cattle. The rate of exchange was from five to ten oxen, according to the qualities of the horse; or, if money, 100 rixd. (£7 10.) A first-rate hack might be purchased for £10, though, of course, high-bred horses were more expensive.

The Cape-Colony horse is a wonderful beast. He is supposed to be of Spanish descent, but, of late years, has been much crossed by various breeds. Without any pretension to beauty, he is, perhaps, unrivalled in docility, hardiness, and endurance. In eight days (one of which was devoted to rest) I rode, accompanied by a Hottentot servant, from near Komaggas to Cape-Town—a distance of upwards of four hundred miles by road—thus averaging fifty miles per day. On an after occasion, I remember to have performed upwards of ninety miles at a very great pace, only once or twice removing the saddle for a few minutes. And be it borne in mind that the animals were young, indifferently broken in, unshod, and had never been stall-fed.

A most striking instance of the extraordinary endurance of Colony horses, occurred a few years ago in Great Namaqua-land. The animal in question belonged to a son of the Hottentot chief, Zwartbooi, who one day, whilst hunting in an open tract of country, fell in with a troop of eleven giraffes, to which he immediately gave chase, and the whole of which he rode down and shot in succession. But the immense exertion was too much for the gallant creature, whose life was thus sacrificed.

This remarkable horse was well known throughout Great Namaqua-land, and is said to have been quite mad with excitement when he observed a wild animal. He only ceased to pursue when the game was either killed, or no longer in sight.

The Colony horses, with a little training, answer admirably for either hunting or shooting. They may be taught to remain stationary for hours together by merely turning the bridle over their heads resting the extremities of the reins on the ground. They seldom trot; the usual pace is a canter, and occasionally an amble.

So much has already been said and written on the Cape-Colony, its sturdy boers, its soil, its production, and so forth, that it would be superfluous to add anything further. Suffice it to mention a few of the most remarkable incidents of my journey.

Soon after leaving Komaggas, my horse—a young half-trained stallion which had only been ridden thrice—shied, and, rearing on his hind legs, came to the ground on his back with sudden violence. Providentially, the soil was soft and yielding, and although I sustained his whole weight for a few seconds, I escaped with no worse consequence than a tight squeezing.

After leaving Komaggas, the homesteads of the boer became daily more numerous. Riding up, one morning, to a house, with a view of procuring some bread and flour, I was greeted with the following civil address—" Daar komt weder die verdoomde Engelsman,"—that is, "There comes again the cursed Englishman." Though I had heard much of the aversion these men entertain for all that is British, and their coarse language in general, I certainly had not expected that they would have carried their animosity so far. Walking straight up to the individual that had thus accosted me, I said, in as good Dutch as I could muster—" My good friend, in my country, when a stranger does us the honour to pay us a visit, before even asking his errand or his name, much less abusing him, we invite him to our table; and, when he has quenched his thirst and satisfied his hunger, we may probably inquire whence he comes or where he goes." And with this I leapt into the saddle. The fellow clearly felt the rebuke; for, on seeing me turn my horse's head away, he endeavoured to persuade me to stop. But his rude salutation had quite spoilt my appetite.

As a rule, however, though frequently coarse and abrupt in their language and conversation, they are undeniably hospitable; and when a person can converse with them in their own language, and accommodate himself to their manners and peculiarities, they are excellent fellows, as I have often since experienced. To several of their customs, nevertheless, the stranger will find some difficulty in reconciling himself.

In these localities, on meeting a wayfaring man, the Dutch boer invariably thus accosts him:—"Good day! Where do you come from? Where are you going? Are you married? How many children have you?"—and so forth. If you should be so unfortunate as not to have entered into the marriage state, he is astonished beyond measure, and looks upon you with something like contempt.

Like most people who are novices in a foreign language, I committed, at first, sad mistakes, and many a joke and laugh originated at my expense. Once, indeed, my awkwardness cost me the loss of a supper, of which I stood greatly in need, having ridden some fifty miles in the course of the day, without tasting food of any description. In the Dutch language, 'danken' signifies a direct refusal; but, not being aware of this, I interpreted it in the very reverse sense, as meaning, 'If you please.' As often, therefore, as I repeated the ominous word, so often had I the mortification of seeing the smoking dishes pass by me!

Refreshing myself, one afternoon, at a comfortable farm-house, the worthy host inquired whence, and how far I had journeyed. Having made a rough calculation in my own mind, I told him the approximate distance. No sooner had I done so, than he clasped his hands together, and, turning to his wife, exclaimed, in the utmost amazement—"Gracious heavens! the man has been in Timbuctoo!" "No, my good friend, not quite so far," I remarked. But he became too much absorbed in the novel idea, and, without attending to me, he went on to say—"Yes, indeed, the man has been at Timbuctoo." I again took the liberty to remonstrate, when his brother, who was also present, ejaculated—"Yes, brother, you are right. Timbuctoo!—ah! eh?—yes! Let me see,

Timbuctoo. Ah, I remember to have read that it is situated at the end of Africa, in a place where you can see nothing but sand." Once more I attempted to explain, but to no purpose. Right or wrong, I must have been at Timbuctoo. I secretly wished I had been there.

Finding they apparently knew more about my travels than I did, I left them to themselves to discuss the merit of the journey; and, diving into the eatables which had been liberally spread before me, I did ample justice to their hospitality.

On the 22nd of September I reached Cape-Town, where my appearance afforded no little delight and amusement to the mob, who shouted merrily after me, "Look at the jockey! ha! ha! ha!" My dress was certainly highly picturesque. An old English hunting-cap—a present from a friend—adorned my head. The striped jacket that I wore, now well bleached with sun and rain, had shrunk to such a degree as to reach only a few inches down my back; and as for sleeves, they just covered the elbows, the rest having been left on the 'Wacht-een-bigte' bushes. My nether garments, consisting of a pair of moleskin trousers, were on a par with my jacket, for they hardly reached to the calf of my leg; and to complete the 'turn out,' my 'veld' shoes were of untanned leather, and so sunburnt as to resemble bricks. And as Cape-Town at that time could boast of no 'Moses and Son,' or 'Silver and Co.,' it was only by degrees, and exploring the different shops, that I was able to remodel my dress.

I lost no time in advertising our cattle; and, having secured a good auctioneer, and made some other arrangements, I again set off to join my party.

Just as I left Cape-Town, my horse, which was excessively shy, took fright, and started off at a rate which would have 'taken the shine' out of even John Gilpin's runaway steed. In the attempt to stop him, the bit (a very substantial one), broke, and in an instant I was at the animal's mercy. Finding myself in an awkward predicament, and being desirous to shorten the race as much as possible, I unhesitatingly gave him both spur and whip, and, as a consequence, ditches, walls, and fences, were leapt and passed at a fearful rate, to the great danger of myself and those I encountered. I do not profess to be skilled in horsemanship, my experience as an equestrian being very small. It was, therefore, as much as I could do to keep my seat. Nevertheless, I had the good fortune to escape unhurt; for after awhile, my steed became exhausted, and pulled up of his own accord.

I found Hans in good health. The Dutch boers had once or twice behaved rudely; but the Dane's herculean appearance and independent manner quickly cooled their ire, and he was allowed to pass unmolested. He told his adventures with graphic effect and racy humour.

Oranges, which are very abundant in these parts, were beginning to ripen. One day, some of our Damaras expressed a wish to taste the enticing fruit; and being supplied with a shilling, they started off. In a short time they brought back no less than two hundred oranges. They had scarcely finished a dozen or two, however, before the effect became irresistible. The acidity of the fruit at this time of the year was so great that it acted with the force of gun-cotton; and, after having a 'good blow-out,' they were so disordered, as to be unable to taste food for several successive days. Indeed, they were effectually cured of their orange mania

At the bivouac-fire I was often entertained with ghost-stories. John, our waggon-driver, who seemed fully to believe in apparitions, was the chief narrator.

"Ghosts," said he, "abound in and about the neighbourhood of the Cape. At times they appear in the shape of dogs;

at others in that of human beings. Once, late at night, I was coming from Simon's Bay, when the oxen all of a sudden stopped short, and would have darted right into the bush had I not been quick to turn them. Just then, nothing could be seen; but presently, a large, white dog, with a chain round the neck, appeared. He passed us slowly without injuring us in any way, and shaped his course over a cross road, when we continued our journey. At another time I met the 'spook' (ghost), in the form of a very tall black man, accompanied by a large dog of the same colour.

"Frequently when returning late at night to my master's place, while yet at a distance, I have seen the whole yard and dwelling-house splendidly illuminated, but, on coming to the spot, all was gone.

"As a protection to the garden, my master had erected a hut, where men slept at night. After a while, however, the place became so haunted that the watchmen fled, and slept anywhere they could in the bush. The 'spooks' were seen continually to promenade up and down the walks arm-in-arm, taking an occasional peep into the house.

"In dark nights, a ghost would sometimes appear at the head of the team, and, laying hold of the thong attached to the leading ox, would conduct the cattle out of their proper course—I being totally unconscious of the proceedings at the time.

"Again: I would hear waggons and carriages coming along the road at a brisk pace, and, whilst making way for them to pass, I found, to my astonishment, that the vehicles were already far a-head of us."

On the 18th of October, and when within a day's ride of Cape-Town, we disposed of our cattle by public auction.

Owing to the great distance we had brought them, and the scarcity of pasturage during the latter part of the journey, our cattle had become very lean; and although they were in themselves an exceedingly fine lot, their want of condition neither suited the butcher nor the grazier. In their emaciated state, indeed, it would require fully a year before they would become acclimatised and re-fattened, in which interval, and before getting accustomed to their new pasturage, many would probably die. They scarcely averaged £2 per head. The cows sold almost the best—not on account of the milk they yielded, for that was little or nothing, but simply because, strange to say, they were exempted from a peculiar disease (*strangury*), which kills the oxen in these parts. The boers are in consequence obliged to make use of cows for agricultural purposes.

It is customary on these occasions to give a banquet to the purchasers, who chiefly consist of Dutch farmers; and if the cattle are known to be fit for slaughter, the butchers of the metropolis also come in for a share. A large quantity of wine is supposed to be necessary to facilitate the sale. Fortunately, this kind of liquor is very cheap; and though a person may have to entertain from fifty to one hundred people for two days together, the expense of such festivities rarely exceed seven or eight pounds sterling.

Our hands being now free, the first object to which we turned our attention, was to secure a vessel to carry us back to Walfisch Bay. There happened just then to be none at the Cape; but we were promised one within a certain period. In the meantime, we occupied ourselves in making the needful purchases, &c.

I also made excursions into the neighbourhood. Amongst other interesting places, I visited, in company with Mr. Bain (the distinguished South African geologist) the famous pass, called, after my kind host, Bain's Kloof, through which the road leads across the Drakenstein mountains from the village of Wellington to the district of Worcestershire. The vignette below is a view of a certain part of the pass designated

DACRE'S PULPIT.

Dacre's pulpit, and has been selected from the portfolio of an accomplished friend in Cape-Town.

We had nearly finished our arrangements when the news arrived at the Cape of the extraordinary successes met with at the Australian gold-diggings, and the same mania, though not quite to the same extent, which had turned the people's heads all over the world, took possession of the inhabitants of this colony. Every available vessel was bought up or chartered for the 'diggings.' I began seriously to apprehend that this would deprive us of the craft we had engaged. Indeed, the owner did actually sell her, but, fortunately, placed another at our disposal, the alteration, however, causing us very great delay.

Though the loss, at this period, of the assistance of Hans would have been grievous and irreparable, I thought it my duty to explain to him the respective advantages of remaining with me and going to Australia. By adhering to the trading, he would be pretty sure to secure a fair income annually, whilst by adopting the other plan, he might have the chance of realizing a fortune in the course of a year or two. I urged that if he felt at all inclined to try his luck at the 'diggings,' he should not hesitate; for, in that case, I would take charge of his goods and dispose of them as if they were my own. Hans evidently appreciated my well-meant intentions, but generously refused to do anything that was not in strict accordance with my own wishes. However, I could not take advantage of such an offer in his position, but told him to think the matter well over by himself and to be entirely guided by his own inclination.

After much hesitation, Hans finally came to the determination to migrate to Australia; and John Allen having also expressed a wish to accompany him, I drew up an agreement between them of such a nature that they might dissolve partnership if they wished, without detriment to either. With regard to myself and Hans, we agreed to share each other's fortunes (though far apart) bad or good.

Matters having been thus far settled, I immediately arranged about the passage of the two adventurers; provided them with a supply of every article necessary for such an expedition, and nearly one hundred pounds sterling in ready money. This change in our original plans proved of great inconvenience to me, inasmuch as we had already sunk every available shilling of our small capital in the intended expedition to Walfisch Bay. However, it was all successfully arranged, and in the early part of January, 1853, they took their departure.

Thus once more I was alone. I could not help reflecting on the difficulties of my position. Two of the best men that, perhaps, ever set foot on African soil, with whom I had shared hardships and privations of no trifling character, had left me to seek their fortunes in remote climes. On me alone, then, devolved the task of watching over and improving the united interest of myself and Hans. Another duty, not less urgent, claimed my attention—namely, that of solving the grand geographical problem—the discovery of a route from the west coast to the Lake Ngami.

On mentioning my trying position to some Cape friends, they coolly advised me to dispose of my goods and return to Europe. I turned in disgust from the proposal, which only served to urge me to renewed exertions. My spirits rose in proportion to the difficulties.

Immediately on the departure of Hans and John Allen, I hastened to attend to my own affairs. I was tolerably well supplied with everything but servants, and instruments for taking astronomical observations. After much search and many bargains, I succeeded in getting together a very fair set of the latter, consisting of a large, good-working sextant, a box-sextant for taking angular bearings, two artificial horizons, (one of coloured plate glass mounted in brass, with levelling screws, and another for mercury), an excellent azimuth-compass, one or two good pocket-compasses, three boiling-point thermometers for ascertaining heights of places above the level of the sea, two telescopes, one for common field-work, and the other large enough for occultations, a chronometer watch, and two ordinary watches. Mr. Maclear, the Royal Astronomer at the Cape, kindly assisted me in selecting most of the above instruments. He, moreover, took a great deal of pains in adjusting them, and shewing me their use, though, I fear, I almost wore out his patience, for I was excessively stupid in this respect. But I trust the result has proved that his labour was not altogether thrown away.

Shortly after our arrival at the Cape, I had been fortunate enough in securing the services of an old acquaintance, Timbo, who had safely returned from St. Helena, where he left Mr. Galton. He proved invaluable to me. To his charge my dogs and native servants were confided, and they throve wonderfully under his management.

I had intended to send two or three Damaras with Hans to Australia; but one day, previous to his departure, they came to me in great tribulation, and said that they did not want to go any further, but wished to return with me to their own land. If such was really their intention, it became my duty to gratify them; but I could not help feeling a little vexed, for since no one but Timbo could speak their language, I strongly suspected that he had influenced their decision. With a view of ascertaining the fact, I called him, and told him my opinion; but he stoutly denied the charge, adding, "Suppose, master, me was to take a horse from the stable in the Kaap to Wynberg, or to any other strange place, and then leave him to himself, surely he would return whence he came; and so it is with the natives." I was struck with the sagacity of the remark, and said no more about the matter.

Timbo had procured a passage from St. Helena in the *Birkenhead* man of war, and on the voyage he got acquainted with an English lad, George Bonfield, aged sixteen. A mutual attachment sprung up between the shrewd Ethiopian and the youthful Saxon; and, in a short time, the former was the means of indirectly saving the life of the latter. On the arrival of the vessel at the Cape, the boy requested permission to land, in order to enjoy the society of his swarthy friend. This was granted, on condition that he should re-join the vessel at Simon's Bay.

Whilst doubling the southern extremity of Africa, the

unfortunate *Birkenhead* struck, and, as is well known, was totally lost, with almost all hands on board.

Timbo took every care of the boy, whose life had thus been saved. He put him to school, and afterwards secured him a berth with a tradesman in Cape-Town. Finding that the youth was anxious to see something more of the world, and to add to his store of knowledge, I took him into my employ. He accompanied me to the Great Lake, and when, in the course of the journey, I became ill, and crippled by wounds inflicted by wild animals, his presence and tender care greatly relieved and soothed my sufferings.

On Timbo's recommendation, and from possessing a smattering of Portuguese, I engaged a Mozambique liberated slave, of the name of Louis; but he turned out the filthiest, laziest, most sensual, and most useless man I ever came across. Just as I was about to engage him, he said—"Of course, master give me my washing and ironing." "My good fellow," I replied, "has Timbo not explained to you the sort of country we are going to? You must thank your stars if you get water enough to wash your face, much less your clothes. And, if you happen to get a sufficiency for the latter purpose, you will certainly have to cleanse your own garments. In the wilderness, according to an old saying, 'every man is his own washerwoman.'"

A young Hottentot, whom I engaged as waggon-driver for the journey, ran into debt, and shuffled his cards so cleverly, that I did not become aware of the circumstance until the day fixed for our departure, when there was of course no time to look for another driver, and I had no alternative left but to pay his liabilities.

The last of my servants, also a Hottentot and a waggon-driver, known as 'old Piet,' was, however a most excellent and well-behaved man. He had been, it is true, in the habit of getting drunk, but, once out of the Cape, he proved himself a hard-working, honest and faithful fellow, and has never since left my service.

Finding that a Mr. Reid, whose acquaintance I had made in Great Namaqua-land, and who had been very kind and attentive to me when I was laid up by fever, was about to undertake a trading excursion to Walfisch Bay, I gladly availed myself of the opportunity thus afforded, of dividing between us the expenses of a vessel; a considerable sum was accordingly saved to me.

At last, after many difficulties and delays, we were ready; and on the 16th of January, having embarked in the schooner *Flying Fish*, we unfurled our sails and bade farewell to Cape-Town, where, during a second stay, I had enjoyed much kindness and hospitality.

NEGRO BOY.[1]

[1] The above wood-cut is a portrait of a negro youth, born and bred at the Cape. He has been shopping, and is returning home with the various articles entrusted to his charge.

CHAPTER XXVIII.

ARRIVAL AT WALFISCH BAY—ATROCITIES OF THE NAMAQUAS—MR. HAHN—HIS PHILANTHROPY—AUTHOR DEPARTS FOR RICHTERFELDT—SHOOTS A LION—LIONS UNUSUALLY NUMEROUS—PIET'S PERFORMANCES WITH LIONS—THE LION A CHURCH-GOER—BARMEN—EIKHAMS—KAMAPYU'S MAD DOINGS AND CONSEQUENCES THEREOF—KAMAPYU IS WOUNDED BY OTHER SHAFTS THAN CUPID'S—AUTHOR VISITS CORNELIUS, WHERE HE MEETS AMRAL AND A PARTY OF GRIQUA ELEPHANT HUNTERS—REACH REHOBOTH—TAN'S MOUNTAIN—COPPER ORE—JONATHAN AFRIKA—A LION SUPS ON A GOAT—A LION BESIEGES THE CATTLE.

We had an excellent run to Walfisch Bay, and reached it on the 23rd of the month in which we left the Cape. In the afternoon, I landed the horses, but very nearly lost the best. The halter having slipped off his head, he was making straight for the sea, and was well nigh exhausted before we could again secure him. The same night, I rode over to Scheppmansdorf; but the darkness was so profound that I was unable to see the track or hold any course. It was by the merest accident that I stumbled upon the house, to the great surprise of my old friends, the Bam family, whom I found well, but not so comfortably lodged as when I saw them last—the Kuisip having swept away their dwelling-house and out-buildings.

From the worthy missionary I learnt much both to please and grieve me. The Namaquas had, as usual, been pillaging the Damaras, and were dealing death and desolation around them. It was no longer considered safe even for white men to remain. Indeed, the Namaquas had already attacked Richterfeldt. Early one morning, a horde of these marauders suddenly appeared, and carried off all the cattle belonging to the people of the station. Not satisfied with this, they fired several shots into the dwelling-house, though, fortunately, without effect. Mrs. Rath and children were laid up by 'eye-sickness,' and Mr. Schöneberg, who had arrived the day previously, and who was in a very weak state from the effects of a recent severe illness, was almost frightened out of his senses by the sudden and unexpected onset.

On Mr. Rath walking up to the barbarians to remonstrate with them on their brutal conduct, they seized and flogged him most severely. A Damara, who was at his side, they shot dead. In consequence of this attack, Messrs. Rath and Schöneberg were daily expected to leave their stations, and to remove to Mr. Bam's place.

On the other hand, I heard that a party of Bechuanas had been visiting Jonker Afrikaner, and it was supposed they had crossed the Kalahari desert. This was gratifying intelligence, because if these natives had been able to pass through such dreaded regions, I might also humbly hope to do the same.

On my return to the Bay, I found almost all my goods, and those of my friend, Mr. Reid, safely landed; and, with the assistance of Mr. Bam's oxen, everything was quickly transferred to the station. This was scarcely effected, when the Rev. Messrs. Kleinschmidt and Hahn arrived from the Cape. The latter had been on his road to Europe to pay a visit to his family, and make some arrangements respecting the education of his chidren. But his heart bled for the wretched condition of this benighted land; and, at immense sacrifice, he returned with the view of endeavouring once more to bring about a reconciliation between the Namaquas and the Damaras.

Next to the love and worship which we owe to our Creator, must be ranked the love of our own species. This Divine doctrine recalls those beautiful lines by Leigh Hunt:—

> "ABOU BEN ADHEM (may his tribe increase!)
> Awoke one night from a deep dream of peace,
> And saw, within the moonlight in his room,
> Making it rich, and like a lily in bloom,
> An angel writing in a book of gold:—
> Exceeding peace had made Ben Adhem bold,
> And to the presence in the room he said,
> 'What writest thou?'—The vision raised its head,
> And, with a look made of all sweet accord,
> Answered, 'The names of those who love the Lord.'
> 'And is mine one?' said Abou. 'Nay, not so,'
> Replied the angel. Abou spoke more low,
> But cheerly still; and said, 'I pray thee, then,
> Write me as one that loves his fellow-men.'
>
> The angel wrote, and vanished. The next night
> It came again with a great wakening light,
> And show'd the names whom love of God had bless'd,
> And lo! BEN ADHEM'S name led all the rest."

All Mr. Hahn's exertions and painstakings, however, were in vain. Jonker was inexorable. He flatly told him there was no occasion for missionaries, since they themselves were quite capable of managing the affairs of the country. This proved the death-blow to the Damara mission; for though Messrs. Schöneberg and Rath continued their labours for some time afterwards, they were finally compelled to desist.

On leaving Great Namaqua-land the preceding year, I placed two teams of waggon-oxen under the charge of my friend, William Zwartbooi, to be kept ready for emergences. I now lost no time in sending people to fetch them down; but the distance was great, and I could not expect them for several weeks to come. Through my interference, Mr. Bam kindly furnished Mr. Reid with a sufficiency of trained oxen for his own conveyance, at a very moderate cost, which enabled him to start for the interior with scarcely any delay.

Whilst waiting for my own cattle, I busied myself with arranging my baggage, sketching plans for the future, eating naras, and now and then mounting my steed to chase the ostrich.

On the 9th of February, Mr. Rath arrived, and, seeing my dilemma, kindly proposed to place some of his oxen at my disposal as far as Barmen. I gratefully accepted the disinterested offer, and having obtained a few more oxen from the Namaqua chief, Jacob, at Scheppmansdorf, I prepared to commence my journey with one of the waggons, leaving the other to follow as soon as my cattle arrived. Rehoboth having been appointed as the place of *rendezvous*, I started.

My course, as on former occasions, lay by Tincas, Onanis, and Tjobis—places well known to the reader. I saw a good deal of game, but was too much pressed for time to stop and shoot. Until we reached Richterfeldt, little or nothing of interest occurred. William and Bonfield, in rambling about the hills one day, stumbled upon a lion, and it being the first time they had ever seen the dreaded beast in his native state, they became almost petrified with fear.

I also had an opportunity of shooting one of these animals. Whilst one day pursuing some gemsboks, a lion unexpectedly sprang out of a bush within forty or fifty paces of me. The brute's sudden appearance somewhat startled me, but I had so often been baulked in my attempts to get a shot at lions that I only hesitated for a moment. Accordingly, the lion having turned round to look at me, I took a deliberate aim at his forehead and fired; and, as good luck would have it, with deadly effect. Indeed, so accurate was my aim that it almost split his skull in two, and, as a matter of course, killed him on the spot.

My prize proved a full-grown male; but his hide was so much worn and torn, that I did not deem it worth the trouble of preservation.

Lions had been unusually numerous and daring during the year. Mr. Rath's waggon-driver, Piet, a mighty Nimrod, and his two foster-sons, had killed upwards of twenty in the course of a few months. And many and wonderful were their escapes from these animals.

One night, the old man was awakened by a peculiar noise outside his door, which was constructed so as to shut in two parts. The lower division was closed, but the upper was left open on account of the oppressive state of the atmosphere. Quietly taking up his gun, Piet stole softly to the door, expecting to meet with a hyæna, as he knew that one of these beasts was in the habit of harassing the goat-kids, which, for better security, he had kraaled against the wall of the house. His amazement, however, was great, when, instead of a hyæna, a lion stood before him. Without losing his presence of mind, he poked the muzzle of his piece against the animal's head and blew out its brains.

Again: Riding along one morning in a very weak state, having just recovered from a severe fever, a lion suddenly rushed at him. The ox became frightened, and threw the old man. One of his feet was caught in the stirrup; but, fortunately, the 'veld' shoe slipped off. "I know," said the veteran hunter, "I was thrown, and that I got on my legs again, but in what manner is quite a mystery to me to this day. I called, as loud as my feeble voice permitted, to my people to bring a gun, the lion always getting nearer and nearer, until he stood within arm's length. I once or twice tried to pull out my pistol or my sword-knife, which, as you know, I usually carry about with me, but in my anxiety I missed them. My jacket was lying just in front of me on the ground, but the brute had one of his paws on it. I felt desperate, however, and, pulling it forcibly away, struck the lion on the head, when he grinned and growled terribly, and I expected every moment he would tear me to pieces. At this juncture, my Damara, who fortunately had heard my cries of distress, came running up with my gun. Taking the piece from the man, I fired at the lion, who had retreated a few paces, where he sat quietly looking at me. I don't know whether I hit him, for what with the sudden fright, and my weak constitution, I felt very unsteady. Be that as it may, it had, at all events, the effect of scaring him away, for, at the report of the gun, he instantly betook himself to cover."

On another occasion, when the missionary waggon was on its road to Walfisch Bay, a lion sprang unexpectedly into the midst of the sleeping party, which was bivouacking, at the time, on the banks of the Kubakop river. One of Piet's sons, who was present, picked up his gun from the ground; but, in order to prevent the dew from injuring it, he had wrapped his waistcoat round the lock, and, in the hurry, he was unable to disengage the garment. Finding, however, that the lion was just about to lay hold of him, he held out the piece and fired at random, but fortunately with deadly effect.

Once a lion found his way into the church at Richterfeldt! The alarm being given, the Damaras, assegai in hand, rushed to the spot, and, seizing him by the tail and ears, dragged him bodily out of the sacred edifice. The poor brute was actually dying from starvation, and offered but a very feeble resistance. I saw his skin.

At Barmen I was obliged to leave Mr. Rath's cattle; but by the assistance of Mr. Hahn's waggon-driver, who, on reasonable terms, lent me half-a-dozen first-rate oxen, I was able to prosecute my journey. On arriving at Eikhams, I met my friend Reid, who had been very successful in the disposal of his stock-in-trade. I saw Jonker; but, though he was civil and obliging, the constant forfeiture of his word had disgusted me, and I felt compelled to treat him with great coolness and reserve.

Before leaving Eikhams, an accident occurred that might have ended seriously. A half-cast native lad, whom Eyebrecht had placed at my disposal, was the occasion of it. Though a shrewd youth, he was cursed with a passionate temper. The Namaquas had been teasing him for some time, when, suddenly unfolding his clasp-knife, he threatened to stab the nearest man, but was quickly deprived of the deadly instrument. His blood was up, however; and, seeing my rifle standing against the wall of the old church, he made a rush for it, and was about to discharge the contents into one of his tormenters, when, throwing myself hurriedly between the contending parties, I fortunately prevented the catastrophe. Being now convinced that a storm was brewing, I quickly pushed the boy through the door of the building, and placed myself resolutely at the entrance.

Notwithstanding the Namaquas would not hesitate to shoot any of their slaves for the smallest offence, they consider such an act, on the part of one of the subjected race against his master, to be of so atrocious a character, that they would undoubtedly have torn the lad to pieces, had I not been present. As it was, they rose to a man, and swore they would have his life. The boy, on his part, instead of betraying any symptoms of fear, was foaming with rage; and, had I permitted it, would unhesitatingly have attacked the whole party.

Finding that I was determined to foil them of their victim, they turned their ire on me. I quietly told them that the lad was in my employ, and that, if they left him alone, I would duly investigate the matter, and, should I find him guilty, would punish him severely. But, if they chose to take the law into their own hands, they must look to the consequences, for they should only pass to the youth over my body. This somewhat cooled their rage, and, after much parleying, the matter was finally and peacefully settled.

Many a time since has the same boy, by the violence of his temper, placed me and himself in the most critical positions, and I often marvelled that he was not killed. At last he received a severe lesson. Having one day, coquetted with some Kalahari women, the indignant husband or parent sent him off with two poisoned arrows, one of which pierced his nose, and the other transfixed his arm. For a short time he suffered agonies, but escaped with his life.

Excepting his passionate temper, he was an excellent fellow—honest, willing, obliging, industrious, enduring, but, above all, an inimitable 'tracker.' Indeed, in this respect he surpassed the bushmen. Many a weary mile have I trodden under his able guidance, and many a wild beast have I laid low by his assistance. His sight was also remarkable. I rather pride myself on my experience as a woodsman, and usually proved a match for the natives; but this youth beat me hollow. My men called him Kamapyu—a most appropriate name, since it signified *hot water*. I was at last compelled to part with him, which I did with considerable reluctance. I rewarded his services, which had proved invaluable to me, by a variety of things, besides sufficient cattle to buy him half a dozen wives, an acquisition which, next to carnivorous food, is the greatest bliss of a savage.

After my departure from Jonker's, I directed my steps towards Cornelius. On taking leave of this chief the previous year, I promised forthwith to return with a supply of goods, provided he and his people behaved themselves satisfactorily. In order to save time, I dispatched a messenger to acquaint him with my approach, as also to request him to call his tribe together and urge them to bring such cattle as they desired to dispose of. My wish was attended to; for, on arriving at the werft, I found about two hundred head of cattle waiting for me, which, after some little bargaining, I secured in the course of two days. I had the misfortune, however, to lose a small portion of this number, which broke through the kraal in the night, and were never again heard of. I strongly suspect they were stolen by the original owners. I had also the mishap to get my telescope spoiled. Being, probably, smitten by the lustre of the metal, the mischievous Namaqua lads extracted the object glass, which could be of no earthly use to them, except as an ornament.

About this time two of my horses died of the 'horse-sickness.' One still remained, and though a remarkably fleet animal, was so shy as to be useless as a hunter. He was the same that ran away with me at Cape-Town. The natives offered to buy him at a great price; but I had made up my mind that, rather than go without him, I would run the risk of losing him by the fearful distemper in question. However, he lived to see the Lake, where I finally disposed of him.

Some days after my arrival at Cornelius' werft, my old friend, Amral, made his appearance. He was accompanied by a party of Griquas,[1] from whom I learnt much to interest me.

In the hope of meeting with elephants, they had crossed the Kalahari direct from their own country, but had suffered great privations; for, though from all appearances, water must have been abundant in the rainy season, the desert was fearfully dry when they passed through it. They had occasionally been as much as nine consecutive days without a drop of water, but sustained their own lives, and those of their quadrupeds, by sucking and eating the wild gourd, which, fortunately, covered the waste in great abundance. To lessen the bitterness of the juice, they first cooked or roasted the fruit.

The party, which consisted of no less than forty-seven waggons, had penetrated to within a few days of the Lake Ngami, but not finding elephants, they retraced their steps. A certain portion of the country they had visited was infested by the 'tsetse,' by whose poisonous bites they had lost some of the cattle and horses. The "horse-sickness" also prevailed.

I engaged, as Bechuana interpreter, one of the Griquas, who had visited the Lake by the ordinary route (*viâ* Kuruman). He spoke of the inhabitants as civil and hospitable, but warned me against the Dutch farmers, should I fall in with any. I was well aware of their troublesome disposition; but of course made due allowance for the exaggerations of an individual belonging to a nation who are sworn enemies to the boers. The Griquas supposed that Ngami might be reached in nine days from Tunobis (the farthest point to the eastward reached by Mr. Galton about a year and a half ago), and said that two or three fountains existed on the road.

---

[1] Descendants of Dutch farmers and Hottentot women; and hence also called Bastards.

On the 17th of March I found myself at Rehoboth, having in little more than a month, with borrowed oxen, passed over several hundred miles of country, and obtained by barter about three hundred head of cattle. I felt rather proud of the performance. My other waggons, which I had ordered to take the Kuisip route, had not yet arrived. I felt disappointed, and was unable to account for the delay, since want of oxen could not have been the cause, the missionaries having kindly and promptly sent me more than one team. Indeed, Onesimus had started, with upwards of forty well-trained beasts, several weeks previously to my reaching the station, and I began to fear that some evil had befallen them.

Whilst abiding their forthcoming, I busied myself in mapping the country, and exploring the neighbourhood. Close to the station rose some conspicuous masses of granite (on Mr. Galton's map erroneously termed limestone), interspersed with large quantities of glittering quartz. From the highest peak I obtained a fine and extensive view of the surrounding country. The beautiful table-mountain of Tans, visible from many points, stood out in bold relief against the western horizon. In a clear atmosphere it may be distinguished at an immense distance. Thus, it can be discerned at Onanis, from the top of 'Wit-water' range, at Rehoboth, and even considerably to the south on the Fish river.

Sir James Alexander, in his journey to Walfisch Bay from the Orange river, climbed Tans mountain, and considered its elevation to be about 4,000 feet; but he does not say whether above the plain or the level of the sea. Be that as it may, however, I do not think either estimation correct. Mr. Vollmer, who once, with great labour, crossed the table of Tans in his own waggon, informed me that its western aspect, or side facing the Kuisip, is very steep and high, but the eastern slope is gradual, and not a great deal elevated above the plain.

The rocks all about Rehoboth are strongly impregnated with copper, and specimens of the ore, of a very productive quality (forty to ninety per cent.), are occasionally found. I presented Mr. Reid with several pieces, giving him permission to use them as he thought fit. I advised him, however, to get them analysed by Mr. Schmieterleuv, whom I knew to be a straightforward man; but he preferred to subject them to his own friend, Dr. G——. After about a year's absence, I met Mr. Reid again, and, on asking him what advantage he had derived from the copper I gave to him, he replied, "None whatever. Dr. G—— declared the specimens were worthless. Yet, not long afterwards, he went into partnership with a certain merchant on the strength of these identical specimens." So much for friendship!

Captain Zwartbooi's people had started off to Damara-land under pretext of looking out for fountains; but the sequel proved it was solely with a view of stealing cattle. The example set them by Jonker, Cornelius, and others, was too strong to be longer withstood.

One evening, Jonathan Afrika presented himself at the station. I had already, at Barmen, seen this man, who was of Bechuana extraction, but had been brought up amongst civilized people. A shrewder fellow I never came across. He bore an excellent character throughout the country. When he first arrived, he accompanied Mr. M——, the trader, in whose service he suffered much privation.

Jonathan, who soon afterwards entered into my service, was a man of great courage, and an excellent marksman. He had shared many a hunting exploit with his friend Hans, and had made numerous lions bite the dust.

On one occasion, Jonathan was riding leisurely along, when suddenly, a short distance in advance of him, a fine lion rushed out of the bushes. Throwing himself quickly off the ox, he gave chase to the beast, calling out loudly: "Nay, stop a little. To day we must, indeed, talk with each other." Whether the lion thought he could not escape, or that he considered his dignity concerned, I shall not presume to say; but, at all events, he stopped to look at his pursuer. No sooner, however, had he turned his head, than a well-directed ball entered one of his eyes and laid him low in an instant.

After waiting at Rehoboth for about a week, I had the satisfaction to see my men and waggon arrive in safety. The cause of the delay had been the nature of the road, the greater part of which consisted of a succession of sand ridges, as bad as those at Scheppmansdorf. The oxen were good, and more than sufficient to do the work; but from want of yokes, they could only make use of twelve at a time.

The men had also been much plagued by lions. One fine moonlight night, just as they had unyoked at the base of a small sand-hill, one of these animals appeared immediately above. After having eyed them for a moment, he dashed in amongst the goats, and before the men could get their guns in order, he was out of harm's way with one of the quadrupeds.

At another time, a lion made a rush at the cattle when at pasture, who fled precipitately into a defile, where, not finding an outlet, they faced about and confronted their fierce antagonist. The beast evidently dreaded the forest of bristling horns; for, after having paced to and fro at the entrance of the pass the best part of the night, keeping cattle and men in great tribulation by his savage growls, he slunk off towards morning.

CHAPTER XXIX.

DISPATCH CATTLE TO THE CAPE—TERRIBLE THUNDER-STORM—TREES STRUCK BY LIGHTNING—THE NOSOP RIVER—A COMET—THE AUTHOR NEARLY POISONED—SOME OF THE MEN ABSCOND ; THEY RETURN TO THEIR DUTY—BABEL-LIKE CONFUSION OF TONGUES—GAME ABUNDANT—AUTHOR SHOOTS A GIRAFFE—MEET BUSHMEN—UNSUCCESSFUL ELEPHANT HUNT — SUFFERINGS FROM HUNGER — TUNOBIS — GAME SCARCE—AUTHOR AND STEED ENTRAPPED—PIT-FALLS—THE MEN TURN SULKY—PREPARATIONS FOR DEPARTURE FROM TUNOBIS— VICIOUS PACK-OXEN—CONSEQUENCES OF EXCESSIVE FATIGUE—THE JACKAL'S HANDY-WORK—TRACKS OF ELEPHANTS—MORE PIT-FALLS —LOSS OF THE ANGLO-SAXON LION AND THE SWEDISH CROSS—REACH GHANZÉ.

ON the 1st of April I dispatched my cattle (three hundred and sixty in number) to the Cape, in charge of old Piet, Thomas Gibbons, William, and two or three Damaras. The first-mentioned was well accustomed to a large drove of oxen, and was the only one of the party in whom I had any confidence. Under such circumstances, it was, perhaps, natural that I should feel some misgivings about their safe arrival. But I placed my trust in that same Providence who had hitherto watched over the lonely stranger, firm in the conviction that, whatever befel me or my property (both of which I was about to risk in the cause of humanity and civilization), would be for the best.

Fearing, from experience, that waggons would be only an incumbrance, and impede the dispatch, if not defeat the success, of my expedition to the Ngami, I parted with them. As I knew, however, that the road as far as Tunobis was practical for wheel-carriages, I borrowed an old battered vehicle for the occasion, intending to send it back with Eyebrecht. Thence I purposed pursuing the journey with pack-and-ride oxen. This, though the most eligible plan, subjects the traveller to much hardship and inconvenience, from exposure to the inclemency of the weather, and the very small stock of provisions, &c., that can be conveyed.

Up to this period the men had worked well and willingly; but the day on which I bade farewell to the hospitable missionary roof (5th of April), Timbo became sulky and expressed a wish to return to the Cape, from which I had some difficulty in persuading him. It was the first time I had real cause for being dissatisfied with the man, but not the last.

Four days after this little difficulty was got over, it came on to rain so tremendously, that it seemed as if we were going to have another deluge. For three days and as many nights, it continued to pour down with scarcely any intermission. The scriptural expression, "The windows of heaven were opened," might indeed have been here realized. During the last twelve hours the thunder and lightning were truly appalling, and perfectly stunned and blinded us. Peal after peal, flash after flash, followed in rapid succession — re-echoed and reflected from a hundred peaks. Trees were broken short off or torn up by the roots by the violence of the wind.

> "———————————The clouds,
> From many a horrid rift, abortive pour'd
> Fierce rain with lightning mix'd, water with fire
> In ruin reconciled ; nor slept the winds

Within their stony caves, but rush'd abroad
From the four hinges of the world, and fell
On the vexed wilderness, whose tallest pines,
(Though rooted deep as high), and sturdiest oaks,
Bow'd their stiff necks, loaden with stormy blast
Or torn up sheer."

The men's tent, which was secured with numerous strong straps to the side of the waggon, was carried bodily away, and men and quadrupeds were literally swimming in the torrent, which, rushing down with irresistible fury from the slopes of the hills swept over our camping ground. The poor dogs howled from fear and suffering. Every moment I expected to see the waggon capsized by the blast, or, what was worse, struck by lightning, as we had somewhat incautiously encamped under a kameel-doorn boom, which is one of the most certain of conductors. Indeed, nearly two-thirds of the full-grown trees of this kind are found splintered by the electric fluid.

So completely did this deluge saturate and swamp the locality, that for two days after the rains had ceased we were unable to move; yet such is the partial operation even of such thunder-storms as we had just endured, that, after travelling a day or two further to the eastward, we all but perished from thirst, and the vegetation was parched and sunburnt!

Our route lay through a country similar in character to that travelled over by Mr. Galton and myself, about a year and a half previously, in our journey to the eastward—namely, large sandy plains, richly covered with fine grass and brushwood, with occasional clusters of kameel-thorn trees. Water was very scarce.

From the number of bleached bones of rhinoceroses, giraffes, and other wild beasts scattered about, it was evident that game had at one time been abundant in these parts; but the introduction of fire-arms amongst the Namaquas had either put an end to the animals, or scared them away to less peopled haunts. With the exception of hyænas and jackals, beasts of any size were scarce.

In about a fortnight we reached the Nosop river, near to its junction with the Black Nosop. The two streams, when united, flow under the common name of Nosop; and, though nothing is known of the course of this river three days south of Wesley Vale *(see map)*, it is believed ultimately to make its way to the Orange river. Indeed, the fact of fish having been found in the pools at Elephant Fountain, of similar kind to those inhabiting the Garieb (the Orange) river, strengthens the supposition.

I had ordered Eyebrecht to meet me on the Nosop, and I found him in company with a handsome Griqua girl, whom he had married according to the fashion of the Namaquas. The union bade fair to be a fruitful one, for the happy couple were already blessed with an infant. The face of the tawny-complexioned husband was beaming with paternal pride and satisfaction. He was living with his father-in-law (Jan Zaal), a great hunter, with whom I also took up my quarters for a short time. The people were exceedingly kind to me, and remarkably clean and neat in all their household arrangements. Besides, I enjoyed an unlimited supply of sweet and sour milk, both of which I greatly relished.

During my stay on the Nosop, I observed for several nights a remarkable comet. On the last of April, about eight o'clock in the evening, when about to set, the latitude being 23° S., it bore 296° by compass.

Having engaged my host's son, Klaas Zaal, to accompany me as a waggon-driver as far as Tunobis, whence he and Eyebrecht were to return, I was again on the move on the afternoon of the 4th of May. For a day or two, we followed the right bank of the white Nosop, and then crossed over to the other branch, where, in order to explore the road before us, we rested a couple of days.

Having proceeded one morning in search of game, I became very hungry; and, observing an inviting bean-looking fruit, I ate greedily of it; but it nearly cost me my life. I was seized with giddiness, vomiting, and racking pains, and arrived in a staggering and bewildered state at our camp, completely exhausted. I then learnt that the pulse I had eaten, was, in a raw state, highly deleterious; but, if cooked, could not alone be eaten with impunity, but was really beneficial.

Almost from my first entrance into the country, thinking that I might one day be obliged to live on Bushman diet, I partook eagerly of every root, bulb, berry, &c., that grew wild about the country; but always (with the exception of the above instance) took the precaution first to ascertain from the natives its properties. I derived benefit from this plan; for when ordinary food failed me, I could at all events contrive to exist for a time on this rude fare.

On returning one day to the camp from a fatiguing hunt, I found that all my Damaras had absconded. I was astonished and vexed beyond measure; for the greater part had been long in my employ and had proved themselves very faithful. One of them had, only the day previously, been telling me that unless I drove him forcibly away, he would never abandon me, but would share my fortune whether good or bad. I soon discovered that Timbo had caused the defection. I had appointed him head-man of the servants; but he being dark complexioned, the Damaras did not like to be ruled by one so much resembling themselves.

In the first burst of anger, I declared I would do without them, and that I would punish them severely on my return.

A moment's reflection, however, convinced me that both for my own sake, and by way of example to the remainder of the men, it was necessary, if possible, to bring them back to their duty. Eyebrecht was accordingly dispatched on this errand. After several days' absence, he returned with the runaways; and as they looked penitent, I thought it best to pass the offence quietly over, and say nothing.

At Twass, the head quarters of Lambert, Amral's eldest son—a chief of even greater importance than his father—I was joined by Piet, the Griqua, who was to accompany me to the Lake in the capacity of interpreter. He knew the Bechuana language tolerably well, and, as a matter of course, spoke Dutch fluently. Onesimus also knew a smattering of this last tongue, and was perfect in the Damara and Namaqua. Louis was pretty well versed in Portuguese, and the different dialects of the countries bordering upon the settlements about the Mozambique-channel. Personally, I could make myself understood in more than one European language; and this Babel-like confusion was completed by Timbo's *patois*.

The preceding year, when our steps were pointed in the same direction, as at present, we travelled on the summit of the low range of hills which take their rise near to Twass, extending eastward. We were then on saddle-oxen; but from what we saw of the country we deemed it nearly impracticable for waggons. I therefore determined to strike through the woods at the base of the hills in question, or along the valley intervening between them and another mountain range running in the same direction. The soil proved exceedingly soft and yielding, and the bushes harassing; yet this new route was preferable to the other.

We saw a good deal of game, chiefly of the larger kinds; but the animals were wary, and I shot badly. My horse was so unsteady as to be of little or no use. His speed was great; he was a match for the swiftest antelope; but when I fired from his back, he was very apt to start on one side. If his rider, at such times, was not on his guard, the chances were in favour of his being dismounted. One day, Eyebrecht begged eagerly to be allowed to try his hand on the giraffes, which abounded in this locality. His request was granted, and I lent him my horse, though we well knew what would be the result. After nearly a whole day's absence, he returned, when the men hailed him with shouts of laughter, as his appearance too plainly indicated his misfortunes. But, notwithstanding his flushed face and torn and soiled dress, he stoutly denied having been thrown. It so happened, however, that the very next day we passed a spot where he had been chasing a herd of giraffes, and where we could distinctly see the marks of how the scared horse had been dragging Eyebrecht along the ground for a considerable distance.

On arriving at Elephant-Kloof, we had better success. My first prize consisted of a magnificent giraffe, which dropped dead to the first shot—the only instance I recollected of killing this animal outright with a single bullet. I never before or since (excepting, perhaps, a cow-elephant) saw so fat an animal. The flesh was delicious, and I thought my men would kill themselves by gorging. Indeed, Bonfield became seriously ill, and, for a whole week, was unable to take nourishment of any description, not even coffee. Everything he tried to swallow was instantly rejected. At one time, I became apprehensive for his safety. My Griqua guide also got indisposed from feeding too heartily on an oily ostrich.

From the midst of abundance, we were—or rather I was—soon reduced to the other extreme. When half way to Otjiombindè, we encountered some Bushmen, who persuaded me to go in search of elephants, which they said abounded at no great distance. A person might visit the place they frequented, and come back the same day. Having hastily made a few arrangements, I set out; but, foolishly relying on their statements, provided myself with only one small slice of raw flesh, which, after a while, in the full anticipation of a quick and successful return, I gave to the half-starved 'children of the desert.' I was sadly out of reckoning, however; for, instead of it being merely a few hours to the water in question, we travelled a whole day, at a brisk pace, before reaching our destination.

We were now at the beginning of the cold season, and the nights had already attained a very low temperature. The day had been oppressively hot; we had journeyed rapidly; and, in the hurry, I had come away without my coat. As evening set in, I felt a deadly chill stealing over me; and though we found fuel, I deemed it necessary to do with as little fire as possible, for fear of alarming the elephants, should they make their appearance. Thrusting my head into a bush, and bundling the rest of my body in as small a compass as was possible, I spent a long and comfortless night.

At break of day we were stirring. On arriving at the water, which was not far distant from our bivouac, we had the satisfaction to discover the fresh tracks of elephants, but out of the troop that had visited the place, there was only one bull. His tracks were of course selected in preference to the rest; but though we followed them perseveringly till near sunset, all our endeavours to come up with the animal proved vain.

Hungry, disheartened, and exhausted, we retraced our steps to the bivouac, were we spent another still more cheerless night. Two days had now elapsed without my having tasted a morsel of food, nor did I obtain any until I reached my own people at the expiration of the third day.[1]

During the last twelve hours, I am free to confess, I was almost ravenous enough to eat my shoe-soles, and probably might have done so had time and opportunity permitted to boil them down to a jelly. Contrary to custom, the field we had traversed, was destitute of eatables of any sort. Once, indeed, I observed a small antelope; but the animal only seemed to mock our sufferings; for, before I could level my piece, he vanished. Seeing the Bushmen try to appease their hunger with a bitter, woody substance, I could not resist the temptation to taste it, though warned of the consequences. But scarcely had I masticated the first mouthful, before I was seized with tormenting nausea and sickness.

From our great success on a former occasion at Tunobis, I expected to find full employment for my rifle, on my arrival there. But, alas! now that we stood so much in need of animal food, not a wild beast was to be seen. At first, one might almost be led to imagine that the amazing number of animals congregated here, less than two years before, must be either killed or driven altogether away from the locality; but this was not the case. Water was still to be found in the vleys and pools at some distance; and until these were exhausted, wild animals were little likely to visit a spot where they were subject to constant persecution.

One or two rhinoceroses, however, occasionally visited the fountains, as appeared by their tracks. These I determined to watch, whilst I dispersed my men over the adjoining country in search of game. One night, a huge animal came wad-

---

[1] On accidentally mentioning my fast to Captain Sturt, the distinguished Australian traveller, he assured me it was a mere trifle to what he himself had once suffered, having been six and a half consecutive days without nourishment of any kind!

dling along; but though I lodged a ball in its body, it was to no purpose. The men were equally unsuccessful, and returned, after several days' absence, half starved, and consequently as ravenous as wolves. They had encountered several rhinoceroses, zebras, &c.; but they only wounded or mangled the poor beasts. It seemed as if every gun, mine included, had been bewitched.

Tunobis, as often stated in the preceding pages, was the furthest easterly point which Galton and myself had attained in our journey towards the Ngami. Every inch of the ground a-head was now unknown, to Europeans at least. The Bushmen, it is true, had furnished us with some information; but it was either too vague to be relied upon or not applicable to the course I intended to pursue. Knowing nearly the position of the Lake, I was anxious to take as straight a line as possible; but on consulting the few natives hereabout, they declared that were I to do so it would be certain destruction to myself and cattle, inasmuch as the 'field' in that direction was one howling wilderness, totally destitute of water. By travelling southward, however, for a few stages along the sandy and dry watercourse of Otjiombindè, I should, they said, run no risk. I was quite at a loss to know how far I could depend on their information; but Piet, the interpreter, who had crossed the Kalahari in the beginning of the rainy season, having corroborated their story, I no longer hesitated to follow their advice.

Before finally quitting Tunobis, an incident occurred which bade fair to finish my career in this world. Cantering along one day in the bed of the river Otjiombindè, with a view of ascertaining its course, I all at once found myself on the very verge of a pit-fall! but it was too late, for at the moment I was about to rein in my horse, down we both went together, with a fearful crash, through the light net-work of sticks and grass that covered it, to the bottom of the gulf, which could not have been less than ten feet in depth, though happily without either of us breaking our necks!

This pit-fall was specially intended for the giraffe, which abounded hereabout, and was very different in construction from those in use for elephants, rhinoceroses, and other large animals, for instead of a single cavity, it was divided into two compartments, separated from each other by a wall of earth. Though I never before knew the meaning of this peculiar arrangement, it was soon explained. My horse having recovered somewhat from his surprise, and the stunning effects of the fall, plunged violently forward, and endeavoured to leap the wall in question; but he only got his fore quarters over it, and the depth of the hole preventing him from touching the ground either with his fore or hind feet, his whole weight rested on his belly; and thus suspended between earth and heaven, he became totally helpless.

Seeing that the poor animal could not possibly live long in this position, and that I was too far from camp to return for assistance, I unhesitatingly sprang back into the pit, from which I had just extricated myself, and placing my shoulders under his chest (my feet resting against the side of the pit to give me a better leverage), I exerted all my strength, and succeeded in pushing him back into the compartment in which he had been originally deposited. Finding that he was about to renew the plunge, I seized the bridle with my left hand and held his head forcibly down, whilst with my right hand, and by the aid of a stick that I picked up, I scraped away the soil on one side of the pit so that it became in a degree an inclined plane; with my feet I also so far levelled the wall that it formed a kind of platform. This matter being arranged, I laid myself on my back on the edge of the pit and pulled stoutly at the bridle. The horse understood me, for with a violent jerk of his body, he sprang on to the platform, and next to the inclined plane, where for a moment he nearly lost his equilibrium, but at last successfully cleared the abyss.

The poor brute was so sensible of the danger he had escaped, that, on finding himself on firm ground, he uttered a wild, half-suppressed neighing, or rather scream, and continued to tremble violently for several minutes. On examining him, I found he had sustained no farther injury than the loss of a few inches of skin and a quantity of hair. As for myself, I escaped with a violent twist of the neck, which inconvenienced me slightly for a few days.

PIT-FALLS.

Almost all the tribes of Southern Africa avail themselves of pit-falls (often on a most gigantic scale) for the capture of game. These traps, or rather, these lines of pit-falls, are either constructed in the shape of very obtuse triangles, open at the base and gradually tapering to a point, where a single, double, or treble row of pits are dug, into which the game is driven by shouts and yells; or they are formed in the shape of a crescent—often miles in extent—usually shutting out a valley or defile, with pits at every fifty or a hundred paces apart, artfully concealed with grass, sand, &c., the intervening spaces being planted and filled up with stout palisades, closely interwoven with boughs and branches of thorn-trees.

The Hill-Damaras are remarkable for the perseverance and industry they exhibit in the construction of game-pits. From want of proper tools, the trees have first to be burnt down and then carried on men's shoulders to their destination, and when we add to this that the task is frequently executed in the most arid districts — the haunts of the gemsbok, the eland, the koodoo, and other tenants of the wilds, who are capable of existing more or less without water for long periods—it is easy to imagine the labour and fatigue of the process.

On counting over the different articles of my baggage, I found that at least nine or ten oxen would be required to carry them, in addition to those necessary for myself and men to ride upon. Almost all my cattle were young, and only half broken-in, and there was scarcely time for further training. To save all trouble, I felt inclined to push on with the old waggon; but, for more than one reason, the idea was quickly abandoned. I worked night and day, but was much harassed. Through carelessness, the hyænas were allowed to devour the skins intended for pack-'riems' and divers minor articles. The men were lazy, stubborn, and ill-humoured; and I was kept constantly on the rack by their annoyances. One day I was obliged to resort to the very unusual measure of flogging Onesimus, who by this time thought himself too civilized to need correction. Indeed, they were all more or less of this opinion, and wanted their dismissal. Having always been kind and considerate towards my men—too much so, perhaps—I felt disgusted at their ingratitude, and exclaimed, rather passionately—"Yes, go cowards! go and tell your friends that you have left your master in the desert to the mercy of wild beasts and savage men: go and exult. Your conduct shall not prevent me from persevering in my plans." On more mature consideration, however, they thought better of it, and again returned to their duty with a good will.

After many delays and the most strenuous exertions, everything was at length in readiness for a start. Before setting off, I wrote to some of my friends at the Cape, and also a letter or two to Europe, entrusting them to Eyebrecht, who returned forthwith to Walfisch Bay.

At noon of the 14th of June, we assembled our oxen and began to pack; but, though we laboured till our heads turned giddy and our arms were paralyzed, we made but slow progress. No sooner had we finished arranging the burthen of one ox, than another threw off his pack. It is utterly impossible for those who have never had ocular demonstration of this kind of work with half-wild cattle, to understand the difficulty, and imagine the ludicrous scenes that take place. I have already given a faint sketch of the process of training oxen, from which the reader may glean some notion of the obstacles to be surmounted—bearing in mind, at the same time, that, instead of a single ox, we had ten to load, besides those on which we were mounted, and which were not the most manageable.

At last, we were off; but the day was then so far advanced, that we were unable to accomplish more than seven or eight miles before we found it necessary to make a halt, and to bivouac for the night. We were so thoroughly knocked up with the severe labour of the day, that, after having hastily removed the packs from the vicious beasts, we literally dropped to sleep where we stood—not one of the party giving a thought as to food, fire, water, or covering, of each and all we stood greatly in need.

On returning to consciousness, the following morning, the first object that met my half-sleepy gaze was a jackal, busily engaged examining our baggage. Having no gun within reach, I threw a handful of sand at the impudent fellow, on which he saluted me with a mocking laugh, and slowly retreated. But had I then been aware of the full extent of his mischievous propensities, he should certainly not have escaped so easy. The brute had, indeed, devoured one of the 'riems,' with which we secured the packs on the oxen. Nothing could possibly have been more unfortunate; the thong was, at that time, worth its weight in gold. We had ten oxen to pack, and only nine 'reims!' Here, then, was a fine opportunity for a man to exert his ingenuity. It was totally out of the question to divide any of the remaining straps, for they were short and narrow enough already, and they must be of a certain length and solidity in order to serve the purpose effectually. At length, however, and after much searching, patching, and splicing, a very indifferent substitute was produced, and we were again *en route*—though not before I had, for the fiftieth time, vowed dire vengeance against the whole race of jackals.

This day (May 15th), we proceeded alternately in the bed and on the borders of the Otjiombindè river. The soil consisted of fine, white sand, reflecting a light dazzling and painful to the eyes, whilst it was soft and yielding to the feet. The grass was still green and very plentiful, and the vegetation, in general, was rank. We passed several vleys containing small quantities of muddy water, alive with loathsome reptiles; and, in some places, the wallowing of elephants and rhinoceroses had converted it into a substance not unlike a mass of well-kneaded dough, heaving with insect life, and tinted and variegated by the stains of larger animals. Yet we drank, or rather gulped, it with avidity!

We encountered also a vast number of 'sand-wells,' varying from one to three fathoms in depth, with an average diameter at the top of twenty feet. The construction of these pits indicated great perseverance and skill, and had evidently been formed by a pastoral people possessed of large herds of cattle. No European would ever have dreamt of looking for water in such localities, since it usually lay ten feet below the surface of the ground, which gave no indication whatever of its presence. Not having been used or kept in repair for many a long year, several were partially filled with sand, but the greater portions were still in tolerable order. They contained no standing water, but plenty of moisture; and, by inserting a reed—the plan adopted by the Bushmen when the liquid will not flow—enough to quench a person's thirst was generally obtained. Elephants had been at work in many, but were clearly disappointed.

About sunset we came to a large vley where a troop of elephants had evidently only a short time previously been enjoying themselves. This circumstance put my men on the *qui vive*; and my Griqua interpreter, who was one of the most chicken-hearted of beings, took good care to magnify the danger of encountering these animals at night. He declared that it was absolutely necessary to come to a halt; but this did not suit my purpose at all. I assured my men that elephants, if left unmolested, were very timid and civil beasts, and that, no doubt, if we met them, and only gave them room to pass, they would in all probability, treat us with equal courtesy. This, having in some degree quieted their apprehensions, we proceeded till about nine o'clock, when we unloaded the tired oxen and camped for the night. As for

CHASING THE ELAND.

London, Hurst & Blackett, 1856.

ourselves, though much fatigued, we took the precaution to provide security from all skulking night-prowlers. By a roaring fire, and over a hearty supper, we forgot the miseries of the day; and, in the firm anticipation of success, cheerfully resigned our weary limbs to sleep.

At an early hour the next morning, we were on the move. The air being cool, we proceeded briskly. About noon some Bushmen were observed digging roots; but they only allowed us to approach within shouting distance. We managed, however, to hold some little conversation with them, and learnt that water was not far off. They warned us to proceed with caution, as the whole river-bed in advance was undermined with pit-falls. And true enough, for, before being aware of it, we found ourselves entrapped in a maze of yawning chasms, down some of which, bipeds and quadrupeds went together in the most amicable confusion. However, being partially prepared for the event, and travelling at a slow pace, we escaped with a few bruises. To prevent a recurrence of the mischief, a man or two proceeded in advance, and unmasked the remainder. They were constructed on the same principle as the one into which I had a short time previously been so unceremoniously precipitated.

At two o'clock p.m., we came to a halt by a well of clear, good water. Within gun-shot of this place was a 'salt-lick,' much frequented by wild animals, such as rhinoceroses, giraffes, gemsboks, koodoos, elands, gnoos, &c.; but I preferred to devote the ensuing night to rest and astronomical observations, rather than lying in ambush for game.

At an after period I had some good sport in this locality; as also some spirited chases after elands, which, as well as the animals themselves, are admirably represented on the accompanying plate. But space prevents me from entering into details.

The Otjiombindè, without materially taking us out of our direct route, had thus far befriended us; but if I wished to reach the Lake, it was now out of the question any longer to follow this river, as hence it pursued too southerly a course. According to the advice of the Bushmen, therefore, we now left it to the right, and struck out in a northerly direction through an intensely dense 'Wacht-een-bigtje' (thorn-jungle). After a few hours' travel, 'we packed-off' to the eastward of some dilapidated limestone pits; but though they contained water, from the depth of the cavities, and the difficulty of access to them, it occupied the men several hours to supply the wants of our small herd of cattle. The next stage —a short one—we slept without water.

In the course of the following day's march we had traversed dense brakes which annoyed us excessively, for the thorns, not only tore our flesh and clothes, but subtracted several articles of value from the pack-saddles. Amongst other losses, I had to bewail that of two magnificent flags— the British and the Swedish—which had been expressly made for, and presented to, me by my kind friend, Mr. Letterstedt, the Swedish Consul-General at the Cape, and which I hoped to have unfurled on the shores of the far-famed Ngami. All my efforts to recover these valued standards proved fruitless, some hyænas having probably swallowed the Anglo-Saxon Lion and the Swedish Cross.

At dusk, after having been ten hours in the saddle, we reached a famous place called Ghanzé, where we pitched our camp.

CHAPTER XXX.

GHANZÉ—SPOTTED HYÆNA—THE RHINOCEROS—WHERE FOUND—SEVERAL SPECIES—DESCRIPTION OF RHINOCEROS—SIZE—APPEARANCE—AGE—STRENGTH—SPEED—FOOD—WATER—THE YOUNG — AFFECTION—SENSES — DISPOSITION — GREGARIOUS—INDOLENCE—DOMESTICATION—FLESH—HORNS—THE CHASE—MR. OSWELL'S ADVENTURES WITH RHINOCEROSES—A CROTCHET—WHERE TO AIM AT THE RHINOCEROS—DOES NOT BLEED EXTERNALLY WHEN WOUNDED—GREAT NUMBERS SLAIN ANNUALLY.

GHANZÉ, according to the interpretation of my Griqua, signifies very large, and yet very small. Absurd as this explanation may appear, there is, nevertheless, some aptness in it. The 'very large' means that, from the moisture of the ground, there is an indication of much water, whilst the real quantity is trifling. Ghanzé is a peculiar and dreary-looking place, consisting of an extensive hollow, with innumerable small stones scattered over its surface, and on one side fenced by a natural limestone wall, three to five feet in height. The whole is hemmed in with thorn-coppices, intersected by numerous foot-paths, the work of those huge creatures, the elephant and the rhinoceros, who have probably wandered here for ages in undisputed sway. Here and there an 'iron' tree, the mythological progenitor of the Damaras, stands majestically forth, shooting its wide-spreading branches high into space.

Ghanzé, it would appear, has been long known to the Bechuanas and the Griquas. A party of the latter, I was told, reached it many years previously to my arrival in a despairing state, having been obliged to abandon their waggons in the Kalahari. The body of men from whom I obtained my interpreter had also visited it. It had even been frequented by Europeans. An English traveller, Moyle, crossed the desert in safety, and arrived at Ghanzé in 1852, on a trading and hunting expedition. From this place he was guided by Bushmen to Great Namaqua-land, whence he retraced his steps home. The year after this, he again crossed the desert, though under unfavourable circumstances—having, with the exception of two horses, lost all his beasts of burden; as also his servants, some of whom died from want.

Almost the first animal I saw at this place was a gigantic 'tiger-wolf,' or spotted hyæna, which, to my surprise, instead of seeking safety in flight, remained stationary, grinning in the most ghastly manner. Having approached within twenty paces, I perceived, to my horror, that his fore paws, and the skin and flesh of his front legs had been gnawed away, and that he could scarcely move from the spot. To shorten the sufferings of the poor beast, I seized my opportunity and knocked him on the head with a stone; and, catching him by the tail drove my hunting knife deep into his side. But I had to repeat the operation more than once before I could put an end to his existence. I am at a loss how to account for his mangled condition. It certainly could not have been from age, for his teeth were good. Could it be possible that from want of food he had become too weak for further exertions, and that, as a last resource, he had attacked his own body? Or was he an example of that extraordinary species of cruelty said to be practised by the lion on the hyæna, when the latter has the insolence to interfere with the monarch's prey?[1]

Fortune once again favoured us; for, in the course of the few days we remained at Ghanzé, several rhinoceroses were shot, affording an abundance of provision. These animals were very numerous, but rather shy. One night I counted twenty defiling past me, though beyond reach. The cause of so unusual a number being seen together was as follows:— In the early part of the night, one or two were approaching the water, but, having winded me, they kept walking restlessly round the place, grunting and snorting most viciously. This had the effect of putting those who arrived later on their guard, and they soon joined company.

Of all the South African animals, not the least curious, perhaps, is the rhinoceros. He inhabits a large portion of the African continent—such localities, at least, as are suitable to his habits. Formerly, as before mentioned, he was common even in the immediate vicinity of Cape-Town; but, owing to constant persecution, is now rarely met farther to the southward (I speak of the west coast) than about the twenty-third degree of latitude. In the interior, however, the tribe is still very numerous. "On one occasion," says Captain Harris, in a private letter, "whilst walking from the waggons, to bring the head of a koodoo that I had killed about a mile off, I encountered twenty-two rhinoceroses, and had to shoot four of them to clear the way."

The rhinoceros is, moreover, an inhabitant of Bengal, Siam, China, and other countries of Asia; as also of Java,

---

[1] It is asserted by more than one experienced hunter, that when the hyæna proves troublesome, the lion has been known to bite off all its feet, and, thus mutilated, leave the poor animal to its fate!

Sumatra, and Ceylon. But the three species[1] indigenous to this quarter of the globe would seem to be quite different from any yet found in Africa. Almost all the Asiatic species have an exceedingly coarse hide, covered with large folds, not unlike a coat of mail; whilst that of the African species is comparatively smooth. Two of the Indian rhinoceroses have only one horn, whereas all the African are provided with two.[2] The third Asiatic species, which is found in the island of Sumatra, resembles the African in having two horns, but in other respects differs considerably.

Though the rhinoceros is abundant in the interior of

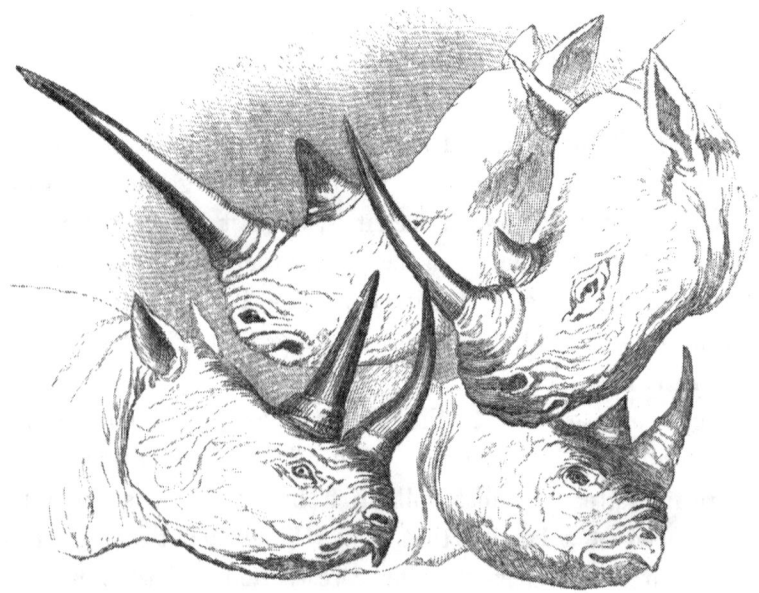

HEADS OF RHINOCEROSES.[3]

[1] *Rhinoceros Indicus, Rhinoceros Sondaicus,* and *Rhinoceros Bicornis Sumatrensis.*

[2] I have met persons who told me that they have killed rhinoceroses with three horns; but in all such cases (and they have been but few) the third, or posterior, horn is so small as to be scarcely perceptible.

[3] The above woodcut is a rough but characteristic outline of the heads of the four distinct species of rhinoceroses recognised as indigenous to Africa. The two lowest heads in the sketch are those of the 'black.'

Africa, it is described as far from numerous in Asia, and as less generally distributed than the elephant.

Four distinct species of rhinoceroses are known to exist in South Africa, two of which are of a dark colour, and two of a whitish hue. Hence they are usually designated the 'black' and the 'white' rhinoceros.

One of the two species of 'black'—the Borele, as it is called by the Bechuanas—is the common small black rhinoceros (*rhinoceros bicornis*); the other, the Keitloa (*rhinoceros Keitloa*), or the two-horned black rhinoceros, as it is also termed by naturalists. The latter differs from the Borele in being somewhat larger, with a longer neck; in having the horns of nearly equal length, with a lesser number of wrinkles about the head; and it is of a more wild and morose disposition. The upper lip of both (more especially in the Keitloa) is pointed, overlaps the lower, and is capable of extension. It is pliable, and the animal can move it from side to side, twist it round a stick, collect its food, or seize with it anything it would carry to its mouth. Both species are extremely fierce, and, excepting the buffalo, are perhaps the most dangerous of all the beasts in Southern Africa.

Of the white species, we have the common white rhinoceros (*rhinoceros simus*, Burch.), called Monoohoo by the Bechuanas, and the Kobaaba (*rhinoceros Oswellii*, Gray), or long-horned white rhinoceros.[1] It is with regard to their

---

[1] Only the horns of this species have been described by naturalists. Dr. Gray, of the British Museum, seems to be one of the first who drew attention to the Kobaaba as a distinct rhinoceros. In the 'Proceedings of the Zoological Society,' No. ccl. p. 46, the following details appear. They were obtained from a pair of horns (of which the woodcut in the next page is an excellent likeness) presented by Mr. Oswell to Colonel Thomas Steele, of Upper Brook Street:—

"The front horn is elongated and thick; but instead of being bent back, as is the general character of *R. bicornis*, or erect, as in *R. simus*, it is bent forwards, so that the upper surface is worn flat by being rubbed against the ground. The front horn is thirty-one inches long, flat, square, rough and fibrous in front, rounded and smooth behind. The hinder horn, eleven inches in length, is short, conical, and subquadrangular."

horns that the two species chiefly differ from each other; for whilst the anterior horn of the Monoohoo has an average

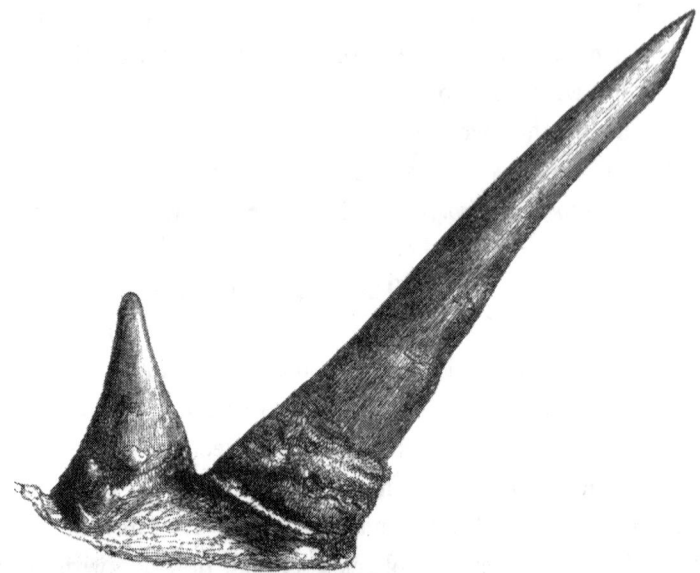

HORNS OF RHINOCEROS OSWELLII.

length of two or three feet, curving backward, that of the Kobaaba not unfrequently exceeds four feet, and is slightly pointed forward, inclining from the snout at about an angle of forty-five degrees. This rhinoceros is also the rarer of the two, and is only found in the more interior parts of South Africa.

The chief distinguishing characteristics of the white rhinoceros, are its superior size; the extraordinary prolongation of its head, which is not far from one-third of the whole length of the animal's body; its square nose (hence also designated 'square-nosed rhinoceros'), and the greater length of the anterior horns.

The 'black' and the 'white' rhinoceros, though so nearly allied to each other, differ widely in their mode of living, habits, &c. The chief sustenance of the former animal consists of the roots of certain bushes, which it ploughs up with its strong horn, and the shoots and tender boughs of the 'wait-a-bit' thorn; whilst the 'white' rhinoceros, on the contrary, feeds solely on grasses.

In disposition, also, there is a marked distinction between them; for whilst the 'black' is of a very savage nature, the 'white,' on the other hand, is of a comparatively mild disposition; and, unless in defence of its young, or when hotly pursued, or wounded, will rarely attack a man.

The body of the rhinoceros is long and thick; its belly is large, and hangs near the ground; its legs are short, round, and very strong; and its hoofs are divided into three parts, each pointing forward. The head, which is remarkably formed, is large; the ears are long and erect; its eyes small and sunk. The horns, which are composed of a mass of fine longitudinal threads, or laminæ, forming a beautifully hard and solid substance, are not affixed to the skull, but merely attached to the skin, resting, however, in some degree, on a bony protuberance above the nostrils. It is believed by many, that when the animal is at rest, the horns are soft and pliable, but that when on the move, they at once become hard and solid. Moreover, that it can, at will, turn the posterior horn, the other horn meanwhile remaining firm and erect. But there can scarcely be sufficient foundation for such notions.

In size, the African rhinoceros—the white species, at least—is only exceeded by the elephant. A full-grown male (*R. simus*) measures, from the snout to the extremity of the tail (which is about two feet), between fourteen and sixteen feet, with a circumference of ten or twelve. To judge from these data, and the general bulkiness of the body, it cannot weigh less than from four to five thousand pounds. In our 'bush-cuisine,' we reckoned one of these animals equal to three good-sized oxen.

The general appearance of the African rhinoceros is not unlike that of an immense hog shorn of his hair, or rather bristles; for, with the exception of a tuft at the extremity of the ears and the tail, it has no hair whatever. And, as if in mockery of its giant form, its eyes are ludicrously small; so small, indeed, that at a short distance they are imperceptible. Altogether, what with its huge body, mishapen head, ungainly legs and feet, and diminutive organs of vision, the rhinoceros is the very image of ugliness.

I have no data that would enable me to determine the age of this animal; but if we are to judge from the length of time that the horns require to be perfected, and supposing the animal to continue to grow in the meanwhile, it may be safely conjectured that he is one of the most long-lived of beasts. Indeed, it is probable he attains the age of one hundred years.

In strength, the rhinoceros is scarcely inferior to the elephant. Of its prodigious power, sufficient evidence was shown in the manner in which it charged the missionary waggon, as mentioned at page 35 of this volume. It is on record, moreover, that the rhinoceros, which Emanuel, King of Portugal, sent to the Pope in the year 1513, destroyed, in a paroxysm of fury, the vessel in which he was transported.

Ungainly and heavy as the rhinoceros looks, it is, nevertheless, so exceedingly swift of foot—at least, as regards the black species—" that a horse with a rider," to quote the words of Gordon Cumming, " can rarely manage to overtake it." The testimony of Captain Harris is to the like effect; for, when speaking of the chase of this animal, and after telling us that it is most difficult to kill, he says :—" From its clumsy appearance, one would never suppose it could dart about as it does, like lightning."

The food of the rhinoceros consists entirely, as mentioned, of vegetables, shoots of trees, grasses, &c. It is fond of the sugar-cane, and eats all kinds of grain;[1] but it does not seem to be a voracious feeder. Indeed, it would appear to be somewhat fastidious in the selection of its food, in search of which it wanders far and wide.

Water is indispensable to the rhinoceros, and, even if his usual haunts be distant from the fountain, he seeks it at least once in the course of the twenty-four hours, as well to quench his thirst, as to wallow in the mud, with which his body is frequently encrusted—leaving to the thirsty traveller nothing but a mass of well-kneaded dough.

FŒTUS OF RHINOCEROS KEITLOA.

Little seems to be known of the breeding habits of this animal; whether it lives in monogamy, or has a plurality of wives, and so forth. It appears certain, however, that the female only produces one young at a birth, and that too at considerable intervals. During the first month, the young rhinoceros exceeds not the size of a large dog, with the merest indication of horns. A complete and full-grown fœtus of *R. Keitloa* that I once obtained measured thus:—

[1] The Asiatic specimen in the Zoological Gardens, Regent's Park, is fed on clover, straw, rice, and bran. His daily allowance is one truss of straw, three-quarters of a truss of clover, one quart of rice, half a bushel of bran, and twenty to twenty-four gallons of water.

		ft.	in.
Length of body (from tip of nose, over the head, and along the back) to insertion of tail		3	6
Length of tail		0	10
Circumference of body behind shoulder		2	4
,, neck		1	6
,, head (across the eyes)		1	8
Height at the shoulder		2	1
Length of head between ears and eyes		0	$4\frac{1}{2}$
Breadth ,, ,, ,,		0	4
,, ,, ,, eyes (corner nearest nostrils)		0	7

At the age of two years, the horn is said to be not more than an inch long; at six years old, it is nine or ten inches long, and grows, as seen in the white species, to the length of three or four feet.

The rhinoceros is a very affectionate mother, and guards her offspring with the tenderest care. The young, in its turn, clings doatingly to its dam; and, even for a day or two after the latter has been killed, the calf is frequently found alongside the carcase. Several instances of the kind have come under my personal notice, and many others are to be found in the records of African travellers and hunters.

The sense of hearing and smell of this animal is most acute. I have had numerous opportunities of testing both these qualities. Even when feeding, lying down, or obeying any passing demand of nature, he will listen with a deep and continued attention until the noise that has attracted his attention ceases. He 'winds' an enemy from a very great distance; but, if one be to leeward of him, it is not difficult to approach within a few paces.

His sight, on the other hand, is not good. From the peculiar position of his eyes—which are deep set in the head—and his unwieldy horns, he can only see what is immediately before him.

The 'black' species, as before said, are of a very sullen and morose disposition. They are, moreover, subject to sudden paroxysms of unprovoked fury, rushing and charging with inconceivable fierceness animals, stones, bushes—in short, any object that comes in their way.

Seen in his native wilds, either when browsing at his leisure, or listlessly sauntering about, a person would take the rhinoceros to be the most stupid and inoffensive of creatures; yet, when his ire is roused, he becomes the reverse, and is then the most agile and terrible of animals.

Colonel Williamson speaks of a rhinoceros in India whose ferocity was such as to render the roads impassable, by attacking travellers, or those who passed near his haunts; and he relates an attack upon a sporting company by the same animal, in the close of the year 1788, as generally known to the army and residents of the district. "Two officers belonging to the troops cantoned at Dinapore, near Patna, went down the river towards Monghyr, to shoot and hunt. They had encamped in the vicinity of Derrzapore, and had heard some reports of a rhinoceros having attacked some travellers many miles off. One morning, just as they were rising, about daybreak, to go in quest of game, they heard a violent uproar; and, on looking out, found that a rhinoceros was goring their horses, both of which, being fastened by their head and heel with ropes, were consequently unable either to escape or resist. Their servants took to their heels, and concealed themselves in the neighbouring jungle; and the gentlemen had just time to climb up into a small tree not far distant, before the furious beast, having completed the destruction of the horses, turned his attention to their masters. They were barely out of his reach, and by no means exempt from danger, especially as he assumed a threatening appearance, and seemed intent on their downfal. After keeping them in dreadful suspense for some time, and using some efforts to dislodge them, seeing the sun rise, he retreated to his haunt; not, however, without occasionally casting an eye back, as with regret, at leaving what he wanted the power to destroy."

But the rhinoceros is not dangerous to man alone—all the beasts of the forest dread him, and none venture to attack this truly formidable animal. The lion, if they chance to meet, slinks out of his way. Even the elephant, should they encounter, retreats, if possible, without hazarding an engagement. Major Lally stated to the author of 'Oriental Sports,' that he once witnessed, from a distant hill, a most desperate battle between a large male elephant and a rhinoceros, in which the former was worsted and fled. Amral told me, that one day, whilst himself and party were engaged in pursuit of an elephant, a black rhinoceros suddenly appeared amongst them, charging madly both beasts and men, several of whom had narrow escapes from being gored by the animal.

The rhinoceros will also fight his own species. One night, when at the 'skärm,' I saw four huge beasts engage each other at the same time, and so furious was the strife, and their gruntings so horrible, that it caused the greatest consternation amongst my party, who was encamped some little way off. I succeeded after a while in killing two of them, one of which was actually unfit for food, being quite rotten from wounds received on previous occasions, and, probably, under similar circumstances.

The rhinoceros, though it cannot strictly be called a gregarious animal, and though most commonly met with singly or in pairs, would seem to be of a somewhat social disposition. Indeed, as many as a dozen have been seen pasturing and browsing together.

The rhinoceros is nocturnal in his habits. At the approach of dusk he commences his rambles, and, if not disturbed, generally visits the pool at an early hour of the evening; afterwards, he not unfrequently wanders over a great extent of country. Soon after sunrise, he seeks repose and shelter against the heat, under some friendly mimosa, or the projecting ledge of a rock, where he spends the day in sleep, either stretched at full length or in a standing position. Thus seen from a distance, he may easily be mistaken for the fragment of a rock.

The Asiatic species is frequently kept in confinement, but, though generally tractable, his morose and savage nature makes him rather dangerous. The least provocation often puts him into a tempest of passion, when he will not hesitate to destroy his best friend. In his rage, he will jump about, and leap to a great height, driving his head furiously, and with incredible swiftness, against the partitions of his place of confinement. Three or four specimens are at the present day alive in England.

The flesh of the rhinoceros varies greatly in quality. That of the 'black' species, from its leanness, and the animal feeding on the 'wait-a-bit' thorn-bushes, which gives it an acrid and bitter flavour, is not over-esteemed. That of the white, on the other hand, whose sustenance consists of grass, which imparts to it an agreeable taste, coupled with its usual fatness, is greatly sought after by natives and colonists. Indeed, the flesh of this animal seems always to have been in repute in the Cape-Colony. Kolben, when speaking of it, says: "The flesh of a rhinoceros, which I have often eaten with a great deal of satisfaction, is not so sinewy as some writers have represented."

The horns of the rhinoceros, which are capable of a high polish, are a valuable article of commerce. At the Cape, this commodity fetches half as much as ordinary elephant ivory. It is extensively used in the manufacture of sword handles, drinking cups, ramrods for rifles, and a variety of other purposes. In Turkey the rhinoceros-horn is much esteemed, more especially such as have a reddish tint about the grain. These, when made into cups, the Turks believe to have the virtue of detecting poison.

"The horns of the rhinoceros," says Thunberg, "were kept by some people, both in town and country, not only as rarities, but also as useful in diseases, and for the purpose of detecting poison. As to the former of these intentions, the fine shavings of the horns taken internally were supposed to cure convulsions and spasms in children. With respect to the latter, it was generally believed that goblets made of these horns in a turner's lathe would discover a poisonous draught that was put into them, by making the liquor ferment till it ran quite out of the goblet. Such horns as were taken from a rhinoceros calf were said to be the best, and the most to be depended upon."

"The horn of the rhinoceros," Kolben tells us, "will not endure the touch of poison. I have often been a witness to this. Many people of fashion at the Cape have cups turn'd out of the rhinoceros-horn. Some have them set in silver, and some in gold. If wine is pour'd into one of these cups, it immediately rises and bubles up as if it were boiling; and if there be poison in it, the cup immediately splits. If poison be put by itself into one of those cups, the cup, in an instant, flies to pieces. Tho' this matter is known to thousands of persons, yet some writers have affirm'd that the rhinoceros-horn has no such virtue. The chips made in turning one of those cups are ever carefully sav'd, and return'd to the owner of the cup; being esteem'd of great benefit in convulsions, faintings, and many other illnesses."

The chase of the rhinoceros is variously conducted in Southern Africa. One of the most approved plans is to stalk the animal, either when feeding or reposing. If the sportsman keep well under the wind, and there be the least cover, he has no difficulty in approaching the beast within easy range, when, if the ball be well directed, the prey is usually killed on the spot. With a little precaution, this kind of sport may be conducted without greatly endangering a person's safety.

But by far the most convenient way of destroying this animal, is to shoot him from the 'skärm' as he comes to the pool to quench his thirst. In this manner I have myself killed several scores of rhinoceroses.

Occasionally he is also taken in pit-falls, which are constructed in pretty much the same manner as those for the capture of elephants, and other large game.

He is not often pursued on horseback, and chiefly because his speed and endurance are such that it is very difficult to come up with and follow him—to say nothing of the danger attendant on such a course. Many a hunter, indeed, has thereby endangered his life.

"Once, as I was returning from an elephant chase," said Mr. Oswell to me, one day, in conversation, "I observed a huge white rhinoceros, a short distance a-head. I was riding a most excellent hunter—the best and fleetest steed that I ever possessed during my shooting excursions in Africa—at the time; but it was a rule with me never to pursue a rhinoceros on horseback, and simply because this animal is so much more easily approached and killed on foot. On this occasion, however, it seemed as if fate had interfered. Turning to my after-rider, I called out — 'By Heaven! that fellow has got a fine horn! I will have a shot at him.' With that, I clapped spurs to my horse, who soon brought me alongside the huge beast, and the next instant I lodged a ball in his body, but, as it turned out, not with deadly effect. On receiving my shot, the rhinoceros, to my great surprise, instead of seeking safety in flight, as is the habit of this generally inoffensive animal, suddenly stopped short, then turned sharply round, and, having eyed me most curiously for a second or two, walked slowly towards me. I never dreamt of danger. Nevertheless, I instinctively turned my horse's head away; but, strange to say, this creature, usually so docile and gentle—which the slightest touch of the reins would be sufficient to guide—now absolutely refused to give me his head. When at last he did so, it was too late; for, notwithstanding the rhinoceros had only been walking, the distance between us was so inconsiderable, that by this time I clearly saw contact was unavoidable. Indeed, in another moment, I observed the brute bend low his head, and, with a thrust upwards, struck his horn into the ribs of the horse with such force as to penetrate to the very saddle on the opposite side, where I felt its sharp point against my leg. The violence of the blow was so tremendous as to cause the horse to make a complete somersault in the air, coming heavily down on his back. With regard to myself, I was, as a matter of course, violently precipitated to the ground. Whilst thus prostrated, I actually saw the horn of the infuriated brute alongside of me; but, seemingly satisfied with his revenge, without attempting to do further mischief, he started off at a canter from the scene of action. My after-rider having by this time come up, I rushed upon him, and, almost pulling him off the horse, leapt into the saddle; and, without a hat, and my face streaming with blood, was quickly in pursuit of the retreating beast, which I soon had the satisfaction to see stretched lifeless at my feet.

"My friend, Captain Vardon, by whom I was accompanied on this journey, soon after joined me, and, seeing my head and face covered with blood, at first imagined me to be mortally hurt or dying. However, with the exception of a blow on the skull, occasioned by the stirrup-iron, which laid my head open a few inches, I received no further injury. But the horse was killed on the spot."

Again:—"On another occasion, as I was bending my steps towards my camp on foot, I espied at no great distance two rhinoceroses of the species Keitloa. They were feeding, and slowly approaching me. I immediately couched and quietly waited their arrival; but though they soon came within range, from their constantly facing me, I was unable to fire, well knowing the uselessness of a shot at the head. In a short time, they had approached so close that, on account of the exposed nature of the ground, I could neither retreat nor advance, and my situation became highly critical. I was afraid to fire; for, even had I succeeded in killing one, the other would, in all likelihood, have run over and trampled me to death. In this dilemma, the thought struck me, that on account of their bad sight I might possibly save myself by trying to run past them. No time was to be lost; and, accordingly, just as the leading animal almost touched me, I stood up and dashed past it. The brute, however, was much too quick for me, and before I had made good many paces, I heard a violent snorting at my heels, and had only time to fire my gun at random into his head, when I felt myself impaled on his horn.

"The shock stunned me completely. The first return to consciousness was, I recollect, finding myself seated on one of my ponies, and a Caffre leading it. I had an indistinct notion of having been hunting; and, on observing the man, I asked quickly why he was not following the track of the animal, when he mumbled something to the effect that it was gone.

"By accident I touched my right hip with my hand, and on withdrawing it, was astonished to find it clotted with blood. Yet my senses were still so confused, and the side so benumbed, that I actually kept feeling and working the wound with my fingers. Whilst trying to account for my strange position, I observed some of my men coming towards me with a cartel, and on asking them what they were about, they cried out that they had come to fetch my body, having been told that I was killed by some animal. The truth now for the first time broke upon me, and I was quickly made aware of my crippled condition. The wound I had received was of a very serious character, and, though it ultimately healed, it left scars behind which no doubt will remain to the day of my death."

We are fond of the marvellous. It is generally received as a fact that the hide of the rhinoceros is impenetrable to a bullet, or even to an 'iron ingot,' as a certain writer quaintly expresses it. But this is just as idle a notion, as regards the African species, at least, as that entertained respecting the softness and pliability of the animal's horns; for a common leaden ball will find its way through the hide with the greatest facility. It is true one should be near the brute; for, though I have known a rhinoceros killed at the distance of a hundred yards, it is an exception to the rule. Indeed, beyond thirty or forty paces one cannot make sure of the shot. Under all circumstances, a double charge of powder is desirable.

Though a common leaden ball may do the work well enough, I would not recommend it. The best metal is spelter, which has almost the hardness of iron, with all the weight of lead; but it is often difficult to procure. For want of a better, two-thirds lead and one-third solder answers the purpose very well.

The most deadly part to aim at is just behind the shoulder; a ball through the centre of the lobes of the lungs is certain to cause almost instantaneous death. From the very solid structure of the head, the great thickness of the hide on that part, the position of the horns, the smallness of the brain,[1] a shot in the head rarely, or never, proves fatal. The same may be said of the breast.

However severely wounded the rhinoceros may be, he seldom bleeds externally. This is attributable in part, no doubt, to the great thickness of the hide, and its elasticity, which occasions the hole caused by the bullet nearly to close up; as also from the hide not being firmly attached to the body, but constantly moving. If the animal bleed at all, it is from the mouth and nostrils, which is a pretty sure sign that it is mortally stricken, and the chances are it will be found dead within a short distance.

The number of rhinoceroses destroyed annually in South Africa is very considerable. Of this, some idea may be formed, when I mention that Messrs. Oswell and Vardon killed, in one year, no less than eighty-nine of these animals; in my present journey, I, myself, shot, single-handed, nearly two-thirds of this amount.

[1] Sparrman says that the cavity containing the brains of a rhinoceros that he shot was only six inches long, and four high, and of an oval shape. On being filled with peas, it was found to hold barely one quart; a human skull, measured at the same time, did not require much less than three pints to fill it.

CHAPTER XXXI.

DEPARTURE FROM GHANZE — NECTAR IN THE DESERT — DIFFICULTY IN FINDING WATER — ARRIVE AT ABEGHAN — UNSUCCESSFUL CHASE — A 'CHARM' — HOW TO MAKE THE UNDRINKABLE DRINKABLE — AN ELEPHANT WOUNDED AND KILLED — BOLD AND COURAGEOUS DOG — KOBIS — AUTHOR SEIZED WITH A SINGULAR MALADY — MESSENGERS DISPATCHED TO THE CHIEF OF THE LAKE NGAMI — A LARGE TROOP OF ELEPHANTS — AUTHOR KILLS A HUGE MALE — LIONS AND GIRAFFE — AUTHOR'S HAIR-BREADTH ESCAPES:—FROM A BLACK RHINOCEROS; FROM A WHITE RHINOCEROS; FROM TWO TROOPS OF ELEPHANTS; HE SHOOTS A COUPLE OF HIS ADVERSARIES — WHERE TO AIM AT AN ELEPHANT.

HAVING enjoyed a good deal of shooting, and feasted ourselves and Bushmen on rhinoceros flesh to our hearts' content, we left Ghanzé on the 23rd of June. The first portion of the country through which our road led was very thorny; but the bush gradually opened, and we journeyed with more ease.

In the early part of the day after our departure, I caused my horse to be saddled, and rode off to look for water. About noon, I reached a hollow, of a similar nature as Ghanzé, but on a smaller scale. I thought I perceived indications of the existence of water; and, having 'hobbled' the steed, went in search of it. The elephants, however, had so trampled the place that, though I could not doubt of water being there, I soon found that it was only to be had by a vast deal of labour.

Whilst reflecting on what was best to do, whether to remain and clear out the pit, or to push on in hopes of finding another watering-place, I observed several small birds flying in and out at a small crevice in the limestone-rock. Running to the spot, I discovered a narrow, circular aperture, about two feet broad, and perhaps twice as much in depth, with something at the bottom reflecting light. Taking for granted that it was water which thus shone, and being tormented with thirst, I leapt into the hole, and greedily swallowed a large quantity. I was too eager to be able to distinguish its taste; but, having somewhat slaked my burning thirst, my palate resumed its function, and I thought I had never experienced so abominable a flavour. Imagine my horror, when, taking a small portion in the hollow of my hand and holding it up to the light, I found I had been drinking *blood*, mixed with the refuse of some wild animal! I shall never forget the loathing I felt on making this discovery; and, though my stomach was presently relieved of its nauseous contents, I long retained a qualmish sensation. The mystery was, however, cleared up. On a more close examination of the aperture in question, it was found that a herd of zebras had, like myself, been looking for water, and, in so doing, one of them had fallen in, and been found and killed by the Bushmen. Hence the blood and offal of the unfortunate animal.

As soon as the men arrived with the cattle, every person who could be spared was employed in cleaning out the hole where I had at first seen indications of water. Large fragments of rock, which the bulky forms of elephants and other gigantic animals had pushed into the cavity, were removed after immense exertions. Occasionally, in displacing a firmly-imbedded stone or piece of wood, the pure liquid would gush forth with great vigour, and we flattered ourselves that we had found the 'eye' of a spring; but the next instant all our hopes vanished. After eight or nine hours' hard work, our best endeavours to discover any steady supply of water proved abortive. The little we *did* obtain—sufficient for the horse and dogs—was of such questionable quality, that, thirsty as we were, it was with the utmost repugnance we could prevail on ourselves to swallow a few mouthfuls.

At break of day the next morning, we renewed our labours, but with no better success. I now became anxious for the safety of the cattle, which began to show symptoms of distress. Mounting my horse, and guided by two active Bushmen, I rode briskly in the direction of the Lake, giving orders to my men to continue their exertions during the remainder of the day; but, should they not succeed in obtaining a sufficiency of drink for the cattle by the next morning, they were to follow on my tracks.

I had ridden long. The sun had already sunk below the tree-tops, and yet no water. The Bushmen, however, gave me to understand by signs that it was not far off, and the number of wild-beast-tracks gave weight to their assertion. At last, the noisy chattering of guinea-fowls, the cooing of doves, and the screams of paroquets, broke on my ear, and indicated a more favourable vicinity. Putting spurs to my horse, I struck into a large 'game path;' and just as the sun was sinking below the horizon, I came alongside a large sheet of clear water. I felt truly thankful, and only wanted my own people and cattle to complete my happiness. This place, according to my interpreter, was called Abeghan.

At dark, I tied up my horse some little distance from the water, cut him an ample supply of grass with my hunting knife, and, having struck a light for the Bushmen, and given them, as a reward for their services, the piece of flesh we carried with us, I shouldered my rifle and proceeded to the fountain with a view of procuring something for the larder. It was a glorious night. The sky was dark, but studded with innumerable twinkling stars reflected in the watery mirror below. For some fifty paces, the locality was tolerably free from bushes; and, on one side, the prospect extended nearly a quarter of a mile through an avenue lined on either side with noble Damara 'parent trees.' Elsewhere the darkness was impenetrable. Silence, like that of the sepulchre, reigned in this remote solitude, relieved, at long intervals, by the hyæna and the jackal lapping the water, and the distant grunting of the rhinoceros. The latter, however, took care not to come within range of the rifle.

At the return of daylight, having then been already twenty-four hours without food, I felt very hungry, and hastened back to the Bushmen to see whether they had left any of the flesh I had given them; but I might as well have searched the dens of ravenous wolves as the lair of these starved 'children of the desert.' Indeed they looked very crestfallen when I announced my bad luck.

Fearing my men might possibly delay in following me, I wrote a few hurried lines in my note-book, and tearing out the leaf, handed it to one of the guides with the intimation that he must hasten back whence he came. But having never seen a piece of paper before, he received it at first with caution, and, taking it between two of his fingers, began blowing on it, thinking probably it was a kind of 'charm' for better luck. Seeing me smile, he took courage and blew still harder. This was too much, and I burst into a roar of laughter, in which I was heartily joined by my tawny friend. However, after numerous signs and gestures, I made him comprehend my wishes, and off he started to meet the caravan.

After another twelve hours' fasting and waiting, and just as it was getting dark, I had the satisfaction to see the whole party arrive safely. They had succeeded in procuring enough water for almost all the oxen.

To guard against thirst by the way, the men had brought two wooden kegs of water from the last halting-place. Seeing Timbo about to take his fill from one of the vessels in question, I observed to him that there was surely no longer any necessity to partake of such villanous stuff. He nevertheless drank, exclaiming, "Master, the water is capital!" "Nonsense," I ejaculated sceptically, "you don't mean to say that that abominable fluid is good." "Well," he rejoined, "if master won't believe me, he better try it himself." Less from any faith in what he said, than from curiosity, I did taste it, and, truly enough, it was 'capital.' Even the smell had vanished. Everybody agreed in praising its excellence. I could not account for so great a marvel, but supposed that under the influence of the sun the water had undergone some chemical change. In the course of twelve hours, four gallons of turbid water had, without any apparent cause, been converted into a fluid as bright and sweet as was ever drawn from fresh spring.

On leaving the pestiferous fountain, I entrusted young Bonfield with my watch, in order that he might ascertain the number of hours they were on the road. On again meeting the lad, he told me in a flurried manner that he thought there was something the matter with the 'piece,' as it would not go properly. The truth at once flashed across me. In winding it up, he had forcibly pushed it the wrong way, and thus made it useless. I cannot describe my feelings on ascertaining this fact. My chronometer, and another watch, had some time previously ceased to act. This was my last time-piece. I had no longer the means of going on with my observations. Latitudes I could still manage; but as for longitudes, the most important part, it was out of the question—at least, I thought so at the time. I had indulged in the hope of being able to settle the position of the Lake.

I was totally unacquainted with the mechanism of a watch; but necessity has no law; and, as a last chance, I determined to pull it to pieces, in order to ascertain the cause of its stopping. Twice I did so, and twice I successfully put it together, but it would not go properly. I dissected it a third time, but was even less fortunate than before, for the chain snapped in two places. Nothing daunted, however, I procured a very fine, well-dried gut, with which I tried to splice it; but it is easy to imagine the result. I believe at that moment I would have freely given the best half of what I possessed in this world—and that, perhaps, after all, was not much—for a good strong watch.

The second night after my arrival at Abeghan, and when lying in wait near the water for wild animals, I was surprised by three huge bull-elephants, whose approach had been so silent that, before I was aware of their presence, they were within ten paces of me. I was ambushed in a very exposed place, but nevertheless stoutly held my ground, and, taking a steady aim at the foreleg of the leader, fired. As he wheeled about I saluted him with the contents of the second barrel. He gave a loud shriek, and, curling up his trunk, trotted quickly away. The next day we followed many a weary mile on his track. He had separated from the rest; but we were unable to overtake him. Some time afterwards, however, I heard of his death. The Bushmen brought the tusks.

The same evening, I shot a couple of rhinoceroses. One of them, on receiving my ball, made a headlong charge, and was so close upon me that, to avoid actual contact, I threw myself backwards, and fell to the ground. He then ran a few hundred yards, when he came to a stand. At break of day, my men went on his trail. He had still strength enough to make a dash at them, and would probably have laid hold of some of them, had not a small bitch (half-terrier and half-bull dog), called 'Venus,' (in derision of her ugliness) caught the enraged animal by the lower lip, where she stuck with such tenacity that the rhinoceros, with all his fury, was unable to shake her off. She only relinquished her hold when her huge antagonist was fairly laid prostrate by a ball.

But the sagacity of this favourite dog was as great as her courage. Being now in a game country, all sorts of beasts of prey abounded, more especially jackals, which might be seen running about by dozens. In order not to frighten the elephants and other large animals, we were in the habit of encamping some little way from the water to which Miss 'Venus' regularly resorted to bathe and drink. On perceiving a jackal, she instantly crouched, looking very timid. 'Reynard,' mistaking her posture as an indication of fear, and probably thinking that, from her diminutive size, she would prove an easy conquest, boldly approached his supposed victim. But he had reckoned without mine host; for the instant the cunning dog found her antagonist sufficiently near, she leapt like a cat at his throat, and once there, the beast had no chance. She then returned to camp, where her contented looks and bloody jaws soon attracted the attention of the men, who immediately went on her track, and brought the jackal, who was valued on account of his fur.

Having dried some of the flesh of the rhinoceroses, and given the rest to the hungry Bushmen, who had already began to flock round us, we set out for Kobis, which we reached after less than two hours' journeying. This place, owing probably to heavy rains at no very distant period, was a magnificent sheet of water (a glorious sight to our thirsty imagination), swarming with geese and ducks. From the number of well and freshly-trodden paths, we conjectured it to be the great stronghold of game—nor were we disappointed. I, therefore, determined to devote a few days here to shooting, and selected my camp with caution and to the best of my judgment.

I had not been long settled in my new quarters, when some Bushmen made their appearance, carrying bundles of reeds (intended as shafts for their arrows) which they had brought from the Lake Ngami, or 'Tlannis,' as they called it in their language. They had been five days on the road; but said it might be reached in two. This was cheerful news. But I was nearly foiled in my plans on the threshold of the object of my ambition.

Having late one night, with much danger and difficulty, succeeded in despatching an enormously large white rhinoceros, I fell asleep towards morning, overpowered by the exertion and fatigue of several previous nights' watching. I was awakened by a smarting sensation a little below the left knee; and when I reached my people, the pain had become intolerable. I was compelled to go to bed immediately. The next day the affected part was much inflamed. The skin became so tender that I could not bear even the touch of my linen; and when little George applied (though with the tenderest care) the lotion I had prescribed, I screamed with anguish. No position suited me. If I was compelled to change, which could only be effected by another person's assistance, the movement was agonizing.

Apprehending that my illness might be of some duration, and knowing but too well the character of savages, I deemed it advisable to dispatch one or two of my men with a few trifling presents to Lecholètébè, the chief of the Bechuanas and the other people who inhabited the borders of the Lake

Ngami, to inform him of my arrival in his neighbourhood and the motive of my journey. Timbo, and Piet the Griqua, were selected to carry out my wishes.

Whilst anxiously awaiting their return, we once more ran short of flesh. I possessed a few sheep, it is true, but I was afraid to kill them, not knowing what the future had in store for me.

I therefore dispersed my men over the surrounding country; but though they met with game in abundance, from mismanagement and bad shooting, they were unable to bag a single animal.

One evening I desperately resolved to go to the water myself in the hope of succeeding better. Accordingly I ordered my servants to prepare a 'skärm,' and to carry me there, taking the chance of being run over or gored by elephants or rhinoceroses; for in my disabled state, it was impossible, should any animal charge, to get out of its way. Seeing my helpless condition, the men remonstrated, but I was resolved to go, and fortune favoured me.

I had patiently waited till nigh morning without seeing anything but hyænas and jackals. I believe these creatures knew I would not hurt them, for they approached within a very few paces, staring and laughing at me in the most impudent manner. I threw gravel-pebbles at them, but this only served to increase their mockery. I could stand it no longer, but hurled my camp-chair at their heads, when they quickly betook themselves to flight.

Scarcely had they made their exit, than I heard the heavy tramp of elephants. At this sound, my heart beat violently; but it was only momentarily. The next instant, I recovered my self-possession. Pushing my gun gently over the 'skärm,' I quietly waited (without daring to think of my poor leg) the approach of the giants. Nearer and nearer they came; their steps were more distinct and measured; confused forms were seen advancing amongst the trees. Gradually they assumed shape; and, lo! suddenly a huge elephant stood out in bold relief against the sky line; then another, and another; till the ground became alive with their numbers. There must have been at least fifty. They hesitated for a moment, but then came swiftly on by a broad path, at right angles to, and within a dozen feet of, my place of concealment. I scarcely dared to breathe. The leader stood conspicuously forth from the rest, and, as a matter of course, I selected him for a mark. Having allowed the huge creature to pass a few paces beyond me, so as to have an opportunity of a second shot, I gave a low whistle which instantly arrested the attention of the brutes, who, partially raising their huge ears, and describing with their trunks eccentric circles through the air, seemed anxiously to inquire the cause of the strange noise. This was my opportunity; and, in an instant, the forest resounded with the report of the gun. Curling up his trunk, the stricken animal uttered a faint cry, and, turning sharply round, staggered back whence he came. It was clear the wound he had received was mortal; but to make more sure, I gave him the contents of my second barrel, though, apparently, without effect. Having reached the skirts of the wood, he tottered, and plunging violently forward, came heavily to the ground.

I had eagerly watched the scene; and now, strange to relate, that the danger and excitement was over, I was seized with a violent tremor. After a time, however, when my nerves had become somewhat composed, I pushed down part of the enclosure, and, though crippled, crawled on all fours up to the carcass. Having ascertained that life was extinct, I scrambled on to the back of the defunct elephant, where, like a schoolboy, I seated myself in triumph.

By this time, the day began to dawn. Being within hearing of the camp, and feeling chilly, I shouted to my people to bring some fire. But, though I received no answer, I could distinctly hear them in earnest conversation, as if discussing some weighty matter. I shouted again and again, but with no better success. Being convinced they must have heard me, I was puzzled and vexed at not receiving a reply. At last, after having waited fully a quarter of an hour, I observed a number of flickering lights—resembling so many will-o'-the wisps; and soon afterwards I was joined by my men. The mystery of their unaccountable silence to me was presently explained. It appeared that on first hearing my shouts, which they took to be cries of distress, they were struck with fear and astonishment; and, as the shouts proceeded from a rather different quarter to that where they had left me on the previous evening, they were led to suppose that some savage beast had carried me away. Their own loud talking, it seemed, had arisen in debating in what manner they could best assist me. I could not help saying to myself—" How brave and considerate !"

There was now no want of flesh, and the result was great rejoicings. The report of my success spread like wild-fire, and the animal was scarcely cold before scores of hungry Bushmen—like so many vultures—had assembled to participate in the feast. Before noon, with the exception of the sternum, the head, and some of the larger bones, every vestige of the giant beast had disappeared. The way in which the Bushmen gorge on the carcass of elephants is very disgusting; and the process of cutting it up, in which they show no little method and dexterity, is nearly equally so.

Elephants, rhinoceroses, gnoos, zebras, &c., were now shot almost nightly. Giraffes were not very numerous in this neighbourhood, but occasionally they made their appearance at the pool, when I managed to get a shot.[1]

Late one evening, in another part of the country, I had badly wounded a lion, and at an early hour on the succeeding morning was following the bloody tracks of the beast, in the hope of putting an end to his career. Presently, we came upon the 'spoor' of a whole troop of lions, as also that of a solitary giraffe. So many tracks confused us; and whilst endeavouring to pick out from the rest those of the wounded lion, I observed my native attendants suddenly rush forward, and the next instant the jungle re-echoed with shouts of triumph. Thinking they had discovered the lion we were in pursuit of, I also hurried forward; but imagine my surprise, when emerging into an opening in the jungle, I saw, not a dead lion, as I expected, but five living lions (two males and three females), two of whom were in the act of pulling down a splendid giraffe, the other three watching, close at hand, and with devouring looks, the deadly strife. The beautiful illustration facing the title-page of this volume is an exact representation of this most interesting incident.

The scene was of so imposing a nature that, for the moment, I forgot I carried a gun. The natives, however, in anticipation of a 'glorious gorge,' dashed madly forward, and, with the most piercing shrieks and yells, compelled the lions to beat a hasty retreat.

When I reached the giraffe, now stretched at full length on the sand, it made a few ineffectual attempts to raise its neck; its body heaved and quivered for a moment, and the next instant the poor animal was dead. It had received

---

[1] It was my intention to introduce at length the history of this animal; but being (as already alluded to in a preceding chapter) confined as to space, I must, though reluctantly, abandon the idea.

several deep gashes about the flanks and chest, caused by the claws and teeth of its fierce assailants. The strong and tough muscles of the neck were also bitten through.

All thought of pursuing the wounded lion was now out of the question. The natives remained gorging on the carcass of the cameleopard until it was devoured. A day or two afterwards, however, I had the good fortune to fall in with my royal antagonist, and finished him without much difficulty.

At Kobis, and the neighbourhood I enjoyed shooting to perfection.[1] But I had many hair-breadth escapes from elephants and rhinoceroses.

One fine moonlight night, when snugly ensconced in my 'skärm,' and contemplating the strange, but picturesque scene before me, my reverie was interrupted by the inharmonious grunting of a black rhinoceros. He was evidently in bad humour, for, as he emerged from amongst the trees into more open ground, I observed him madly charging anything and everything that he encountered, such as bushes, stones, &c. Even the whitened skulls and skeletons of his

[1] The accompanying plate represents one of those numerous and exciting scenes that I have witnessed at night, at the water, when lying in ambush for game. There is one fact—a fact that has hitherto escaped the attention of the African sportsman—connected with this illustration that makes it particularly interesting, and which induced me to designate it 'The Approach of Elephants.' The animals are just appearing above the distant hill. If the spring or pool, as the case may be, be of small extent, all the animals present will invariably retire from the water as soon as they are aware of the presence of the elephants, of whom they appear to have an instinctive dread, and will remain at a respectful distance until the giants have quenched their thirst. Thus, long before I have seen, or even heard, the elephants, I have been warned of their approach by the symptoms of uneasiness displayed by such animals as happened to be drinking at the time. The giraffe, for instance, begins to sway his long neck to and fro; the zebra utters subdued, plaintive cries; the gnoo glides away with a noiseless step; and even the ponderous and quarrelsome black rhinoceros, when he has time for reflection, will pull up short in his walk to listen; then, turning round, he listens again, and, if he feel satisfied that his suspicions are correct, he invariably makes off, usually giving vent to his fear or ire by one of his vicious and peculiar snorts. Once, it is true, I saw a rhinoceros drinking together with a herd of seven male elephants; but then he was of the white species, and, besides, I do not believe that either party knew of each other's proximity.

THE APPROACH OF ELEPHANTS.

own species, lying scattered about on the ground, were attacked with inconceivable fury. I was much amused at his eccentric pastime; but, owing to the openness of the ground, and the quantity of the limestone thereabouts, which made objects more distinct, he was not easy of approach. However, after divesting myself of my shoes, and all the more conspicuous parts of my dress, I managed to crawl—pushing my gun before me—to within a short distance of the snorting beast. As he was advancing in a direct line towards me, I did not like to fire, because one has little chance of killing the rhinoceros when in that position. Having approached to within a few feet of me, his attention was attracted, and suddenly uttering one of those strange 'blowing' noises, so peculiar to the beast when alarmed or enraged, he prepared to treat me in a similar manner to the stones and skulls he had just so unceremoniously tossed about. Not a moment was to be lost; and, in self-defence, I fired at his head. I shall never forget the confusion of the animal on receiving the contents of my gun. Springing nearly perpendicularly into the air, and to the height of many feet, he came down again with a thump that seemed to make the earth tremble—then plunging violently forward (in doing which, he all but trampled on me), he ran round and round the spot for fully five minutes, enveloping every object in a cloud of dust. At last he dashed into the wood and was hidden from view. Not finding blood on his tracks, I had no reason to suppose he was much hurt. My notion is, the bullet struck his horn, partially stunning him with its jarring violence. Had my gun missed fire when he charged, it is more than probable, I should have been impaled.

Again: having on a certain night, stalked to within a few paces of a huge white rhinoceros (a female as it proved), I put a ball in her shoulder; but it nearly cost me dear—

for, guided by the flash of the gun, she rushed upon me with such fury that I had only time to throw myself on my back, in which position I remained motionless. This saved my life, for, not observing me, she came to a sudden halt just as her feet were about to crush my body. She was so near to me, that I felt the saliva from her mouth trickle on my face! I was in an agony of suspense, though, happily, only for a moment; for, having impatiently sniffed the air, she wheeled about, and made off at her utmost speed. I then saw, for the first time, that her calf was in company, and at once recognized the pair as an old acquaintance, and as specially vicious animals.

On another occasion, when the night was very dark, I crept to within a short distance of seven bull-elephants, and was endeavouring to pick out the largest, when I was startled by a peculiar rumbling noise close behind me. Springing to my feet, I perceived, to my surprise and alarm, a semi-circle of female elephants, with their calves, bearing down upon me. My position was critical, being between two fires, so to say, and I had no other choice than either to plunge into the pool, which could only be crossed by swimming, in the face of the male elephants, or to break through the ranks of the females. I adopted the latter alternative, but first fired at the nearest of the seven bulls; and then, and without a moment's delay, I rushed on the more open rank of the female phalanx, uttering, at the time, loud shouts. My cries caused a momentary panic amongst the animals, of which I took advantage, and slipped out between them, discharging my second barrel into the shoulder of the nearest as I passed her. No sooner, however, had I effected my escape, than the whole herd made a simultaneous rush at me, and trumpeted so shrilly as to cause every man at the camp, as I learnt afterwards, to start out of his sleep. Fortunately, the darkness prevented the beasts from following me; and, the jungle being close by, I was soon in safety. In my precipitate flight, however, I severely lacerated my feet; for, when stalking the elephants, I had taken off my shoes, that I might the better steal upon them.

When, after a while, I ventured out of my place of concealment, I found every thing quiet: only one solitary elephant remained. Having approached within a short distance, I could distinctly see him laving water on to his sides with his trunk. I immediately suspected he belonged to the troop of seven bulls, and was the one that I had fired at. Seating myself right across his path, I quietly watched his proceedings. After a time I saw him, as I thought, moving off in an opposite direction. But I was mistaken; for in an another instant his towering form loomed above me. It was too late to get out of his way; so, quickly raising myself on one knee, I took a steady aim at his fore leg. On receiving the ball, he uttered the most plaintive cries, and rushing past me, soon disappeared in the neighbouring forest. The next afternoon he was discovered dead within rifle-shot of the water. It had been a very successful night; for a fine female elephant had also fallen to my other shot.[1]

[1] I lost many noble beasts from the small calibre of my guns, which did not carry more than fourteen and seventeen balls respectively to the pound. This was more especially the case as regarded the elephants; and it was not until after a time, and when they had become scarce and shy, that I found out the way of bringing them down with any certainty at one or two shots. I found the best part to aim at (when shooting by night) was the shoulder, either behind or in the centre, near to the lower edge of the ear. Another good point, provided the gun be of large calibre, is to fire at the leg, which once broken, the animal, in almost every instance, is completely at the mercy of the hunter.

CHAPTER XXXII.

TIMBO'S RETURN FROM THE LAKE; HIS LOGIC; HE TAKES THE LAW IN HIS OWN HANDS—CALF OF AUTHOR'S LEG GOES ASTRAY—A TROOP OF ELEPHANTS—AUTHOR IS CHARGED BY ONE OF THEM, AND NARROWLY ESCAPES DEATH—HE SHOOTS A WHITE RHINOCEROS—HE DISABLES A BLACK RHINOCEROS—HE IS CHARGED AND DESPERATELY BRUISED AND WOUNDED BY THE LATTER—HE SAVES THE LIFE OF HIS ATTENDANT, KAMAPYU—AUTHOR AGAIN CHARGED BY THE RHINOCEROS, AND ESCAPES DESTRUCTION ONLY BY THE OPPORTUNE DEATH OF HIS ANTAGONIST—REFLECTIONS—HE STARTS FOR THE NGAMI.

AFTER about a week's absence, Timbo returned. I learned from him that, previously to his arrival at the Ngami, Lecholètébè, the chief had not, contrary to my expectations, been made aware of my approach; and the sudden appearance of strangers, therefore, created no small degree of surprise and consternation both to him and his people, who fled precipitately with their flocks.

Many years before, when my friends, the Damaras, extended their migrations to the neighbourhood of the Lake in question, the Bechuanas were in the habit of robbing them of their cattle. "How does it happen"—said Lecholètébè to Timbo—" that the Damaras are your servants? They are a mighty nation, rich in cattle, which I know well, because my father fought many a bloody battle with them. We invariably came off victorious, though often at the cost of numbers of our warriors, who were slain by the broad assegai of the Damaras. All is not right! Is your master richer than they?"

To this query Timbo logically replied, "No! my master no rich; master very poor; but master has something, and Damaras nothing; therefore, master more rich than Damaras."

Timbo then explained the way in which that tribe had been impoverished and nearly exterminated, as also the motives of our journey. On hearing all this, the apprehensions of the chief gradually subsided, and he became more communicative and friendly, urging Timbo to return to me without delay, and hurry on my departure, being anxious, as he said, for my arrival; he moreover hinted that he would forthwith send men to meet and assist us in our progress. But here ended his courtesy; for, subsequently, he allowed our party, whilst at his town, all but to starve. It seems a characteristic of black chieftains to be avaricious.

Previously to reaching Lecholètébè's residence, it was necessary to cross the Zouga, his town having been removed to the north side of the river, from fear, as it is said, of Sekomo, another Bechuana chieftain. When Timbo and his party were on their return to me, the natives refused to ferry them over the river without payment. "Me have no money," said Timbo; "but me soon make Caffres do it for nothing: me say, 'So you will not row me across!' And with that me lay hold of big stick, and me pitch into the rascals. Oh, master, such fun! me now get plenty of boats." "But were you not afraid of resorting to such severe measures?" I inquired. "Me frightened," he exclaimed; "no, me flog natives very well; it do them plenty good; the fellows too lazy to do work."

I now resolved to lose no more time, but to push on at once to the Lake. My leg had in some degree recovered its strength; but, unobserved by me, it had, received a somewhat ugly twist. Little George first drew my attention to the fact: "Sir," said he, "your leg has grown crooked."

"Crooked!" echoed I, somewhat angrily. "What do you mean?"

"Only," he wickedly replied, "the calf is nearly where the shin ought to be."

The boy's remark was not without foundation; but in time the leg assumed its proper shape.

Notwithstanding my anxious desire to reach the Ngami —the goal of my wishes—I determined, before finally leaving Kobis, to devote one more day, or rather night, to the destruction of the denizens of the forest. But the adventure nearly terminated fatally; and the night of the 15th of July, will ever be remembered by me as one of the most eventful epochs of my life; for, in the course of it, I was three several times in the very jaws of death, and only escaped destruction by a miracle.

From the constant persecution to which the larger game had of late been subjected at Kobis, it had become not only scarce, but wary; and hearing that elephants and rhinoceroses still continued to resort to Abeghan, I forthwith proceeded there on the night in question. Somewhat incautiously I took up my position—alone, as usual —on a narrow neck of land dividing two small pools; the space on either side of my 'skärm' being only sufficient for a large animal to stand between me and the water. I was provided with a blanket, and two or three spare guns.

It was one of those magnificent tropical moonlight nights, when an indescribably soft and enchanting light is shed over the slumbering landscape; the moon was so bright and clear that I could discern even a small animal at a considerable distance.

I had just completed my arrangements, when a noise that I can liken only to the passage of a train of artillery, broke the stillness of the air; it evidently came from the direction of one of the numerous stony paths, or rather tracks, leading to the water, and I imagined it was caused by some waggons that might have crossed the Kalahari. Raising myself partially from my recumbent posture, I fixed my eyes steadily on the part of the bush whence the strange sounds proceeded; but for some time I was unable to make out the cause. All at once, however, the mystery was explained by the appearance of an immense elephant, immediately followed by others, amounting to eighteen. Their towering forms told me at a glance that they were all males. It was a splendid sight to behold so many huge creatures approaching with a free, sweeping, unsuspecting, and stately step. The somewhat elevated ground whence they emerged, and which gradually sloped towards the water, together with the misty night-air, gave an increased appearance of bulk and mightiness to their naturally giant structures.

Crouching down as low as possible in the 'skärm,' I waited with beating heart and ready rifle the approach of the leading male, who, unconscious of peril, was making straight for my hiding-place. The position of his body, however, was unfavourable for a shot; and, knowing from experience that I had little chance of obtaining more than a single good one, I waited for an opportunity to fire at his shoulder, which, as before said, is preferable to any other part when shooting at night. But this chance, unfortunately, was not afforded till his enormous bulk towered above my head. The consequence was, that, while in the act of raising the muzzle of my rifle over the 'skärm,' my body caught his eye, and, before I could place the piece to my shoulder, he swung himself round, and, with trunk elevated and ears spread, desperately charged me. It was now too late to think of flight, much less of slaying the savage beast. My own life was in imminent jeopardy; and seeing that, if I remained partially erect, he would inevitably seize me with his proboscis, I threw myself on my back with some violence; in which position, and without shouldering the rifle, I fired upwards at random towards his chest, uttering, at the same time, the most piercing shouts and cries. The change of position in all human probability saved my life; for, at the same instant, the trunk of the enraged animal descended precisely on the spot where I had been previously couched, sweeping away the stones (many of a large size) that formed the fore part of my 'skärm,' like so many pebbles. In another moment his broad fore-feet passed directly over my face.

I now expected nothing short of being crushed to death. But magine my relief, when, instead of renewing the charge he swerved to the left, and moved off with considerabe rapidity—most happily without my having received other injuries than a few bruises, occasioned by the falling of the stones. Under Providence, I attribute my extraordinary escape to the confusion of the animal caused by the wound I had inflicted on him, and to the cries elicited from me when in my utmost need.

Immediately after the elephant had left me I was on my legs, and, snatching up a spare rifle lying at hand, I pointed at him, as he was retreating, and pulled the trigger; but, to my intense mortification, the piece missed fire. It was matter of thankfulness to me, however, that a similar mishap had

MORE CLOSE THAN AGREEABLE

London, Hurst & Blackett 1855.

not occurred when the animal charged; for had my gun not then exploded, nothing, as I conceive, could have saved me from destruction.

During this incident, the rest of the elephants retreated into the bush; but by the time I had repaired my 'skärm' they re-appeared with stealthy and cautious steps on the opposite side of the pool, though so distant that I could not fire with any prospect of success. As they did not approach nearer, I attempted to stalk them, but they would not allow me to come to close quarters; and after a while moved off altogether.

Whilst pondering over my late wonderful escape, I observed, at a little distance, a huge white rhinoceros protrude his ponderous and mis-shapen head through the bushes, and presently afterwards he approached to within a dozen paces of my ambuscade. His broadside was then fully exposed to view, and, notwithstanding I still felt a little nervous from my conflict with the elephant, I lost no time in firing. The beast did not at once fall to the ground, but from appearances I had every reason to believe he would not live long.

Scarcely had I reloaded when a black rhinoceros of the species Keitloa (a female, as it proved) stood drinking at the water; but her position, as with the elephant in the first instance, was unfavourable for a good shot. As, however, she was very near me, I thought I was pretty sure of breaking her leg and thereby disabling her; and in this I succeeded. My fire seemed to madden her: she rushed wildly forward on three legs, when I gave her a second shot, though apparently with little or no effect. I felt sorry at not being able to end her sufferings at once; but as I was too well acquainted with the habits of the rhinoceros to venture on pursuing her under the circumstances, I determined to wait patiently for daylight, and then destroy her with the aid of my dogs. But it was not to be.

As no more elephants, or other large game appeared, I thought after a time it might be as well to go in search of the white rhinoceros, previously wounded; and I was not long in finding his carcase; for my ball, as I supposed, had caused his almost immediate death.

In heading back to my 'skärm,' I accidentaly took a turn in the direction pursued by the black rhinoceros, and by ill luck, as the event proved, at once encountered her. She was still on her legs, but her position, as before, was unfavourable. Hoping, however, to make her change it for a better, and thus enable me to destroy her at once, I took up a stone and hurled it at her with all my force; when, snorting horribly, erecting her tail, keeping her head close to the ground, and raising clouds of dust by her feet, she rushed at me with fearful fury. I had only just time to level my rifle and fire before she was upon me; and the next instant, whilst instinctively turning round for the purpose of retreating, she laid me prostrate. The shock was so violent as to send my rifle, powder-flask, and ball-pouch, as also my cap, spinning in the air; the gun, indeed, as afterwards ascertained, to a distance of fully ten feet. On the beast charging me, it crossed my mind that unless gored at once by her horn, her impetus would be such (after knocking me down, which I took for granted would be the case) as to carry her beyond me, and I might thus be afforded a chance of escape. So, indeed, it happened; for having tumbled me over (in doing which her head, and the forepart of her body, owing to the violence of the charge, was half buried in the sand), and trampled on me with great violence, her fore-quarter passed over my body. Struggling for life, I seized my opportunity, and as she was recovering herself for a renewal of the charge, I scrambled out from between her hind legs.

But the enraged beast had not yet done with me;

DESPERATE SITUATION.

London, Hurst & Blackett, 1856.

Scarcely had I regained my feet before she struck me down a second time, and with her horn ripped up my right thigh (though not very deeply) from near the knee to the hip: with her fore feet, moreover, she hit me a terrific blow on the left shoulder near the back of the neck. My ribs bent under the enormous weight and pressure, and for a moment, I must, as I believe, have lost consciousness—I have at least very indistinct notions of what afterwards took place. All I remember is, that when I raised my head, I heard a furious snorting and plunging amongst the neighbouring bushes. I now arose, though with great difficulty, and made my way, in the best manner I was able, towards a large tree near at hand, for shelter; but this precaution was needless; the beast, for the time at least, showed no inclination further to molest me. Either in the *mêlée*, or owing to the confusion caused by her wounds, she had lost sight of me, or she felt satisfied with the revenge she had taken. Be that as it may, I escaped with life, though sadly wounded and severely bruised, in which disabled state I had great difficulty in getting back to my 'skärm."

During the greater part of the conflict I preserved my presence of mind; but after the danger was over, and when I had leisure to collect my scattered and confused senses, I was seized with a nervous affection, causing a violent trembling. I have since killed many rhinoceroses, as well for sport as food; but several weeks elapsed before I could again attack those animals with any coolness.

About sunrise, Kamapyu, my half-caste boy, whom I had left on the preceding evening, about half a mile away, came to the 'skärm' to convey my guns and other things to our encampment. In few words, I related to him the mishap that had befallen me. He listened with seeming incredulity; but the sight of my gashed thigh soon convinced him I was not in joke.

I afterwards directed him to take one of the guns and proceed in search of the wounded rhinoceros, cautioning him to be careful in approaching the beast, which I had reason to believe was not yet dead. He had only been absent a few minutes, when I heard a cry of distress. Striking my hand against my forehead, I exclaimed—"Good God! the brute has attacked the lad also!"

Seizing hold of my rifle, I scrambled through the bushes as fast as my crippled condition would permit; and, when I had proceeded two or three hundred yards, a scene suddenly presented itself that I shall vividly remember to the last days of my existence. Amongst some bushes, and within a couple of yards of each other, stood the rhinoceros and the young savage; the former supporting herself on three legs, covered with blood and froth, and snorting in the most furious manner; the latter petrified with fear—spell-bound, as it were—and riveted to the spot. Creeping, therefore, to the side of the rhinoceros, opposite to that on which the boy was standing, so as to draw her attention from him, I levelled and fired, on which the beast charged wildly to and fro without any distinct object. Whilst she was thus occupied I poured in shot after shot, but thought she would never fall. At length, however, she sank slowly to the ground; and, imagining that she was in her death agonies, and that all danger was over, I walked unhesitatingly close up to her, and was on the point of placing the muzzle of my gun to her ear to give her the *coup de grace*, when, to my horror, she once more rose on her legs. Taking a hurried aim, I pulled the trigger, and instantly retreated, with the beast in full pursuit. The race, however, was a short one; for, just as I threw myself into a bush for safety, she fell dead at my feet, so near me, indeed, that I could have touched her with the muzzle of my rifle! Another moment and I should probably have been impaled ou her murderous horn, which, though short, was sharp as a razor.[1]

When reflecting on the wonderful and providential escapes I recently experienced, I could not help thinking that I had been spared for some good purpose, and my heart was lifted in humble gratitude to the Almighty who had thus extended over me His protecting hand.

The second day after the scenes described, my bruises began to show themselves; and on the third day they were fully developed, giving my body a black and yellow hue. So far as I was aware, none of my bones were broken; but burning and agonizing pains in the region of the chest were clearly symptomatic of severe internal injury. Indeed, at first, serious apprehensions were entertained for my life. After great suffering, however, I recovered; and, as my shooting mania had by this time somewhat cooled down, my whole thoughts were bent on seeing the Ngami. Though my frame was quite unequal to bear fatigue, my spirit would not brook longer delay.

With the assistance of my men, I therefore mounted my steed, on the 23rd of July, and was off for the Lake, leaving my hunting spoils, and other effects, under the care of the Bushman-chief at Kobis.

---

[1] The black rhinoceros is, under all circumstances, as already mentioned, a morose and sulky beast. The one in question was unusually savage, as she had probably a young sucking calf. We did not see the latter, it is true, but assumed such to be the case from the beast's teats being full of milk. It is most likely that her offspring was of too tender an age to accompany her, and that, as not unfrequently happens, she concealed it amongst the bushes when about to quench her thirst at the pool.

CHAPTER XXXIII.

START FROM KOBIS—MEET BECHUANAS—FALSE REPORT—WONDERFUL RACE OF MEN—THE BAOBOB TREE—THE NGAMI—FIRST IMPRESSIONS OF THE LAKE—REFLECTIONS—EXPERIENCE SOME DISAPPOINTMENT—REACH THE ZOUGA RIVER AND ENCAMP NEAR IT—INTERVIEW WITH CHIEF LECHOLÈTÉBÈ—INFORMATION REFUSED—IMMODERATE LAUGHTER—PRESENTS TO THE CHIEF—HIS COVETOUSNESS—HIS CRUELTY—FORMIDABLE DIFFICULTIES—AUTHOR PERMITTED TO PROCEED NORTHWARDS.

Our first day's march from Kobis lay through an exceedingly dense 'wait a-bit' thorn-coppice, crossed in every direction by numerous paths of rhinoceroses and elephants. The soil consisted of soft and yielding sand, which made travelling very fatiguing. The second day, at an early hour, we arrived at a fine vley of water, where I was met by a number of Bechuanas (amongst whom were some of the leading men of the tribe) waiting to conduct me to Lecholètébè, who had given them orders to render me any assistance I might require. Whether this was from courtesy, or to serve his own purposes, I am uncertain; though, from what I afterwards saw of the chief, I am inclined to think it was entirely from selfish motives.

The men in question belonged to a tribe called Batoana,

residing on the shores of the Lake Ngami. They were remarkably fine-looking fellows, stout and well built, with Caffre features, and longish hair. Their appearance, indeed, was not unlike that of the Damaras. One and all were armed with a shield (oblong in form, and made of a single fold of ox-hide), and a bundle of assegais of various descriptions, each provided with several barbs. What with these formidable weapons, and their martial bearing, the aspect of these savages was imposing and warlike. They wore few or no ornaments.

By a liberal supply of tobacco and flesh, we soon became excellent friends; but all my endeavours to elicit information about the country, were fruitless. They merely shrugged their shoulders, urging as an excuse their ignorance of such matters; they said, however, that their chief would, no doubt, satisfy my curiosity on these points.

We bivouacked at the vley, where a great number of Bushmen—friends and relatives of those at Kobis—also happened to be encamped. Just as I had retired to rest, and whilst watching with interest the animated features and gestures of our new friends, the Bechuanas, who, by a glorious fire, were regaling themselves with the pipe and the 'flesh pots,' Bonfield came running up to me in great haste, saying:—" Please, sir, the Bushmen tell us that Sebetoane, having heard of our coming, had sent a message to Lecholètébè with orders to dispatch people to waylay and kill us, and that these were the very individuals to whom the task was entrusted!"

Being myself by this time pretty well used to similarly absurd and unfounded stories, and knowing that I had nothing to fear, I took no notice of the communication, but again retired with as much unconcern as if I had been in a civilized country. This, however, was far from the case with my men, for the following morning I learnt that their anxiety had kept them awake during the greater part of the night, and that some had actually packed up their things, intending to steal away secretly.

The next morning proved the groundlessness of the report. The Bushmen, we found, had fabricated the story as a means of prolonging my stay amongst them, in the anticipation of obtaining an occasional gorge from the spoils of the chase. The low cunning of this people is only equalled by their credulity. To them, no tales can be too ridiculous and absurd for belief. For instance, my Bushmen guides amused me by relating one evening that a tribe of black people had just taken up their abode a little in advance of us, "whose stomachs rested on their knees, and whose whole aspect was of the most unnatural and ferocious character."

About noon on the same day we were again *en route*. Instead of feeling our way by the zig-zag tracks made by rhinoceroses and other wild beasts, our guides now took us a straight cut across the country, which was densely wooded.

The 'wait-a-bit' thorns were extremely harassing, tearing to ribbons our clothes, carosses, and even pack-saddle bags, made of strong ox-hide. Notwithstanding the wooded character of the country, it affords excellent pasturage; and the numerous old wells and pits found between Tunobis and the Ngami, clearly indicate that these regions have, at no very remote period, been largely resorted to by some pastoral people.

I hoped to reach the Lake by the evening; but sunset found us still at a distance from the object of our enterprize. We encamped in a dense brake, near to which were several gigantic baobob[1] trees, the first we had seen; the stems of

---

[1] 'The baobob,' says Mr. Livingstone, ' the body of which gives one the idea of a mass of granite, from its enormous size, yields a fruit about the size of a quart bottle;

FIRST VIEW OF THE LAKE.

some we judged to be from forty to sixty feet in circumference. Finding abundance of fuel, the wood was soon illumined by numerous watch-fires, around which, besides my own party, were grouped many a merry and laughing savage, each with his shield planted as a guard behind him. Altogether, the scene was striking and picturesque.

The return of daylight found us again on the move. The morning being cool and pleasant, and our goal near, the whole party was in high spirits, and we proceeded cheerily on our road. I myself kept well a-head in hope of obtaining the first glimpse of Ngami. The country hereabout was finely undulated; and in every distant vale with a defined border I thought I saw a lake. At last, a blue line of great extent appeared in the distance, and I made sure it was the long-sought object; but I was still doomed to disappointment. It turned out to be merely a large hollow in the rainy season filled with water, but now dry and covered by saline incrustations. Several valleys, separated from each other by ridges of sand, bearing a rank vegetation, were afterwards crossed. On reaching the top of one of these ridges, the natives, who were in advance of our party, suddenly came to a halt, and, pointing straight before them, exclaimed—"Ngami! Ngami!" In an instant I was with the men. There, indeed, at no very great distance, lay spread before me an immense sheet of water, only bounded by the horizon—the object of my ambition for years, and for which I had abandoned home and friends, and risked my life.

The first sensation occasioned by this sight was very curious. Long as I had been prepared for the event, it now

the pulp between the seeds tastes like cream of tartar, and it is used by the natives to give a flavour to their porridge.' Mr. Green writes me that plants have been raised in England of the baobob from seeds brought home by his son, Frederick Green, who is at present treading in my tracks in the interior of South Western Africa. For further details of the baobob, see 'Saturday Magazine' for the year 1832.

almost overwhelmed me. It was a mixture of pleasure and pain. My temples throbbed, and my heart beat so violently, that I was obliged to dismount, and lean against a tree for support, until the excitement had subsided. The reader will no doubt think that thus giving away to my feelings was very childish; but "those who know that the first glimpse of some great object which we have read or dreamt of from earliest recollection is ever a moment of intensest enjoyment, will forgive the transport." I felt unfeignedly thankful for the unbounded goodness and gracious assistance, which I had experienced from Providence throughout the whole of this prolonged and perilous journey. My trials had been many; but, my dearest aspirations being attained, the difficulties were all forgotten. And here I could not avoid passing my previous life in review. I had penetrated into deserts almost unknown to civilized man—had suffered the extremity of hunger and thirst, cold and heat—and had undergone desperate toil, sometimes nearly in solitude, and often without shelter during dreary nights in vast wildernesses, haunted by beasts of prey. My companions were mostly savages. I was exposed to numerous perils by land and by water, and endured torments from wounds inflicted by wild animals. But I was mercifully preserved by the Creator through the manifold dangers that hovered round my path. To Him are due all homage, thanksgiving and adoration.

After feasting my eyes for a while on the interesting scene before me, we descended from the higher ground towards the Lake, which we reached in about an hour and a half. But, though we breathed a fresher atmosphere, no perfumed or balmy scents, as might have been anticipated on the borders of a tropical lake, were wafted on the breeze.

Whether my expectations had been raised to too high a pitch, or that the grandeur of this inland sea, and the luxuriance of the surrounding vegetation, had been somewhat exaggerated by travellers, I must confess that, on a closer inspection, I felt rather disappointed. In saying this, I must admit having visited it at a season of the year little favourable to the display of its grandeur. But, if I am not mistaken, its discoverers, Messrs. Oswell, Livingstone, and Murray, saw it under no more auspicious circumstances. The eastern extremity, however, the only portion ever seen by the gentlemen in question, certainly possesses superior attractions to the western, or where I first struck upon the Ngami.

The Lake was now very low; and at the point first seen by us, exceedingly shallow. The water, which had a very bitter and disagreeable taste, was only approachable in a few places, partly on account of the mud, and partly because of the thick coating of reeds and rushes that lined the shore, and which were a favourite resort of a great variety of waterfowl. Many species, new to us, were amongst them; but we had no time to spare for approaching the birds.

We twice bivouacked on the south border of Ngami before coming in sight of Lecholètébè's residence, situated on the north bank of the river Zouga, and at a short distance from where its waters separate themselves from the Lake.

I had accomplished the journey from Kobis in five days. With unencumbered oxen, it might, with some exertion, be made in half this time.

Lecholètébè requested me to pitch my tent in his immediate vicinity; but feeling fatigued, and well knowing the inconvenience of being in too close proximity to the natives, we encamped on the south side of the Zouga.

I determined to pay my respects to the chief at an early hour on the following morning. To make a favourable impression on the mind of savages at the first interview, is of great importance, as much of their future good-will towards one depends on this; and scarcely anything propitiates them more than outward show.

Accordingly, at the contemplated hour, I donned my best apparel, which consisted of jacket and trousers of fine white-duck a handsome red velvet sash, lined with silk of the same colour, and a gold-embroidered skull-cap.

The two last articles of dress were a memento of a dear female friend, and I had pledged myself to wear them on the first *grand* occasion.

Having crossed the Zouga river, a few minutes' walk brought me to Batoana-town, the capital and residence of Lecholètébè. I found the chief seated on a wooden stool, in the midst of forty or fifty of his followers, drinking coffee within a stout semi-circular palisading. He was attired in a half-European and half-barbarous costume; his lower extremities were immersed in a pair of wide mole-skin trousers; he had encased his feet in socks and 'veld' shoes, whilst from his shoulders depended gracefully a very handsome jackal caross. This latter, however, he almost immediately exchanged for waistcoat and jacket.

Piet the Griqua, and a Bechuana man, whom a trader (then at the Lake) had kindly placed at my disposal, were my interpreters. After the first salutations were over, I explained to the chief the motives of my visit, the friendly wishes of the British Government at the Cape, and so forth. He listened to my story with apparent attention, and in profound silence, eyeing me the whole time suspiciously. But he asked no question, nor did he venture any remark.

Having conveyed to him all I had to say, I prepared to depart. Previously, however, to taking leave, I requested him to have the goodness to give me some information about his country, to which he abruptly replied—

"I know nothing at all!"

"Is there, then," I said, "none of your people who can furnish me with some account of it?"

"No," was his immediate answer.

I was annoyed, but felt the necessity of concealing my vexation; and, soon after rising, I said: "Well, Lecholètébè, perhaps, when we become better acquainted you will be more communicative. In the meantime, when it suits you, come over to my encampment and have a chat, and, may be, you will find something there to captivate your fancy."

I had no occasion to say this twice, as I too soon found to my cost. Unlike our fat friend, king Nangoro, who had the *courtesy* to make us wait about three days before he condescended to see us, the Bechuana chief could scarcely restrain his curiosity for as many hours.

When he arrived, I was busy preparing some skins of birds and snakes, which caused no small amount of jesting amongst his followers. One fellow, more inquisitive and impertinent than the rest, approached close to me, and, seizing one of the reptiles by the tail, held it up before the multitude, which were now thronging my tent to inconvenience, and, addressing to it some unintelligible words, the whole assembly burst out into a deafening roar of laughter. Indeed, the mirth became so outrageous as to throw the party into convulsions, many casting themselves at full length on the ground, with their hands tightly clasped across their stomachs as if in fear of bursting, whilst their greasy cheeks became furrowed with tears trickling down in streams. Fancy, reader, a *royal cortége* prostrated in the dust by laughter! Although this merriment was, no doubt, at my expense, the sight more amused than annoyed me.

As soon as the noise had subsided, I brought forward my presents for the chief, consisting of beads, knives, tobacco, snuff, steel-chains, rings, blue calico, red woollen caps, and trinkets of various kinds. Without deigning even a look of satisfaction, Lecholètébè silently distributed the goods amongst the principal of his men who were grouped around him, reserving, apparently, nothing to himself. This being done, he looked anxiously round, from which I inferred that some ungratified desire was still on his heart. Nor was I deceived; for all at once he inquired whether I had not brought him some powder and lead, which he might barter for ivory. I told him that I had some; but, firstly, it was not more than I myself wanted; and, secondly, I was prohibited by the British Government at the Cape from disposing of either arms or ammunition, and that I could not think of disobeying these orders.

At this declaration his countenance fell, and I saw clearly that he was very much annoyed. But I was prepared for his displeasure; and, by opportunely placing in his hand a double-barrelled pistol, which I had previously been informed he coveted excessively, and which I begged him to accept as a memento of my visit, his visage soon beamed with delight and satisfaction, and we became excellent friends.

When Europeans first visited the Lake, they were, I am told, liberally entertained by Lecholètébè; but whatever civility he might have shown to strangers in former times, much cannot be said in favour of his hospitality at the present day. During my whole stay at the Lake, I never received from him so much as a handful of corn, or a cup of milk. On the contrary, *he*, whilst we ourselves were almost starving, was in the habit of begging food daily from *me*.

If any thing takes his fancy,—no matter what—it may be the shirt you wear—he has no scruple in asking you for it at once. Upon your refusal, he will, perhaps, leave you for a time, but is sure to return and renew his request with the greatest pertinacity, never ceasing his solicitations till, by his vexatious importunity, he has succeeded in getting the object of his desire—a line of policy, the success of which, he seems fully to understand.

The arrival of several waggons at the Lake, at the same time, puts him in the highest glee. On these occasions, he never fails to make his rounds, craving bread from one, sugar from another, coffee from a third, meat from a fourth, and so on.

The traders, however, know how to take advantage of this weakness in his character, and often make him pay dearly for such articles as may captivate his fancy; for instance, I have known a man to get a good-sized bull-elephant tusk for three common copper drinking-cups![1]

Lecholètébè possesses great power over his people, when he chooses to exercise it; but I am inclined to think their subjection is attributable more to superstition, and the force of custom, than to any real regard for his person. Generally speaking, he is not of a cruel disposition. But that he holds human life in very light estimation, the following incident, which came under my own immediate notice, serves to show.

Having lately bought some horses, two Bushmen were ordered to take charge of them; but unfortunately, by their neglect, one of the animals fell into a quagmire, and was suffocated. Being afraid to tell the truth, they reported to the chief that the horse had died from the effects of the bite of a snake. On hearing this, Lecholètébè questioned the men as to the part of the body wounded by the reptile, and being told that it was in the head, he ordered the man to lead him to the place, that he might see for himself. On arriving at

[1] When the lake was first discovered, a man told me that he obtained, in exchange for a musket, twelve hundred pounds of ivory, worth, at the least, £240 sterling!

the spot, he at once saw how the case stood, and told the Bushmen that the animal had not died from the bite of a snake, but was evidently choked in the mud, to which they confessed, as there was no longer any chance of concealing the truth. Without further question or remark, the chief ordered the halter of the dead horse to be loosened, and the hands and feet of the Bushmen to be secured with it. This being done, they were thrown into the mud, alongside the dead quadruped, where, of course, they soon miserably perished, Lecholètébè coolly exclaiming: "There, now mind the horse!"

Another instance of the little value he sets on human (rather *Bushman*) life, I have upon good authority. A Bushman lad, who had long been successfully engaged in sheep-stealing, was at length detected, and, as a punishment for his crimes, was tied to a tree, and practised upon with guns at the long distance of two hundred paces.

The object I had now chiefly in view was to visit a place called Libèbé, situated considerably to the north of the Lake, not so much to see the country, as to collect information in regard to the mighty waters (part of which are tributaries to the Ngami) lately brought to light in that remote region; as also to ascertain if any water communication existed with the sea. But many difficulties were in the way. My people refused almost to a man to accompany me; and as our agreement only bound them as far as the Ngami, I could not compel them to go on. The parts that I should have to pass through are infected with fevers fatal to human life; and then, again, the tsetse fly abounds, which, from the ravages it causes amongst cattle, renders travelling by land almost impossible.

The only way left was to penetrate northwards by water, if practicable; but here again I found serious impediments. I had no boat of my own, and Lecholètébè (like all native chiefs) was known to be particularly hostile to any attempt to pass beyond his territory. Not the most alluring promises of presents and rewards had yet succeeded in inducing him to assist any one in this matter. Consequently I could not expect that he would treat me differently, the rather as I was really not in a position to offer him a bribe of any value. It being a darling scheme of mine, however, to penetrate to Libèbé, I was determined on carrying it out if possible.

Accordingly, I seized the first favourable opportunity of broaching the subject to the chief, and requested he would furnish me with men and canoes. To my great astonishment, but no less delight, and without the slightest objection, he agreed to my proposal. As, however, I could not flatter myself that I had produced a more favourable impression than any other traveller, I suspected deceit of some kind; and the sequel proved I was not mistaken in my conjecture.

CHAPTER XXXIV.

THE NGAMI — WHEN DISCOVERED — ITS VARIOUS NAMES—ITS SIZE AND FORM—GREAT CHANGES IN ITS WATERS—SINGULAR PHENOMENON—THE TEOGE RIVER—THE ZOUGA RIVER—THE MUKURU MUKOVANJA RIVER—ANIMALS—BIRDS—CROCODILES—SERPENTS—FISH.

At an early period of the present century rumours had reached Europeans of a vast lake in the interior of South Africa; but for a very long time its existence continued to be involved in mystery, and travellers and hunters were unavailingly expending their resources and energies to solve the grand problem.

The cause of all these failures was chiefly to be found in the desert and inhospitable regions which lie between the explorers and the supposed lake, commonly known as the Kalahari desert. Towards the close of 1849, however, and when the hope of our being able to overcome this apparently insurmountable barrier was almost extinguished, the great object was accomplished by the persevering exertions of Messrs. Oswell, Livingstone, and Murray, and the existence was made known of a fine fresh-water lake in the centre of South Africa.

This important and highly interesting discovery at once opened a new and extensive field for the inquiries of the geographer and the naturalist, and gave a fresh impulse to the enterprising and speculating spirit of the colonists of Southern Africa. The lake was described as a magnificent sheet of water, abounding in fish and hippopotami, and the country around as well stocked with elephants, and other large game, whilst the vegetation was said to be on the most luxuriant scale. The discovery excited very considerable interest.

The Lake goes with the natives by different names—all of which are more or less appropriate—such as *Inghàbé* (the giraffe); *Noka ea Botlètle* (lake of the Botletle); *Noka ea Mokoròn* (lake of boats); and *Ngami*, or *The* Waters. As the last designation is the one by which the Lake is best known to Europeans, I will retain it throughout the remainder of this narrative.

As before said, on taking a nearer survey of the Lake, I experienced some disappointment as to its attractions. It is, however, indisputably a fine sheet of water; but in size is somewhat overrated, the estimation of its length alone being at one time considered no less than one hundred miles, and the width about fifteen or sixteen. The misconception may thus, perhaps, be accounted for. In the first instance, no person, to the best of my belief, has ever yet been quite round it; secondly, the shores—with the exception of the south and west side—are low and sandy, and in hazy weather cannot easily be distinguished; and, lastly, I am inclined to think that the discoverers mistook its length for its breadth, for, according to Cooly, " The travellers beheld with delight the fine river, and the Lake extending out of sight to the north and west." Again, my friend Mr. Frederick Green, who visited the Lake shortly after its discovery, thus states, in his manuscript journal, the impression he experienced on first viewing it.

"The day after reaching the town of Batoani, we took a ride to view the Lake. From the southern side, we could trace the opposite shore some ten or twelve miles, but beyond that distance, and to the westward, we could not, even with the aid of a telescope, discern any sign of land—only a blue horizon of water. In a subsequent journey, however, and when travelling along its southern shores, I found that the opposite strand could always be seen. When first viewing it, we were not, as we then thought, looking across, but *lengthwise*."

The whole circumference is probably about sixty or seventy geographical miles; its average breadth seven miles, and not exceeding nine at its widest parts. Its shape, moreover, as I have represented it in the map, is narrow in the middle, and bulging out at the two ends; and I may add, that the first reports received many years ago from the natives about the Lake, and which concurred in representing it of the shape of a pair of spectacles, are correct.

The northern shore of Ngami is low and sandy, without a tree or bush, or any other kind of vegetation within half-a mile, and more commonly a mile. Beyond this distance, (almost all round the lake) the country is very thickly wooded with various sorts of acacia indigenous to Southern Africa, the Damara 'parent tree,' a few species of wild fruit trees, and here and there an occasional baobob, which raises its enormous head high above the highest giant of the forest. The southern coast of the Lake is considerably elevated, and the water is so closely fringed by extensive belts of reeds and rushes, that it is only accessible in a few places, or where the native cattle have broken through these natural defences. The west shore of the Lake is also somewhat raised, though the water is very shallow; but it deepens considerably towards its eastern extremity.

The Ngami must have undergone very considerable changes at different periods. The natives have frequently pointed out to me places, now covered with vegetation, where they used to spear the hippopotamus. Again, there are unmistakeable proofs of its having been at one time of smaller dimension than at present; for submerged stumps of trees are constantly met with. This is not, I believe, to be attributed to the upheaving, or to the sinking of the land, but that, in all probability, the Lake was originally of its present size, or nearly so, when a sudden and unusually large flood poured into it from the interior, which, on account of the flatness of the country, could not be drained off as quickly as it flowed in, but caused the water to rise above its usual height, which, remaining in that state some time, soon destroyed the vegetation.

Before the Lake was known, and when only rumours had reached us of its existence, the natives spoke of its waters as retiring daily to 'feed.' But I am rather inclined to think they pointed to a singular phenomenon that I observed when navigating its broad waters, which I then attributed to the wind, though, on consideration, I suspect it was more likely to have arisen from the effects of the moon's attraction.

When navigating the Lake, we were in the habit of landing every night, to bivouac, always taking the precaution to unload the most important articles of our baggage. The canoes were then pushed in shore as far as the shallowness of the water would permit, and left to themselves, perhaps, as far as two hundred yards from *terra firma*. On remonstrating with the boatmen for not better securing our little flotilla, they replied that any further precautions were unnecessary, inasmuch as the water (which had already begun to ebb) would shortly recede and leave the canoes dry on the beach. I felt sceptical; but, nevertheless, allowed them to have their own way. In the course of the night, it fell calm (a fresh breeze had been blowing during the day) and next morning we found that what the boatmen had predicted was fulfilled; the canoes were as far from the water, as, on the preceding evening, they had been from the shore.

From the time that the wind fell, the water began slowly to return, and about nine o'clock in the morning, it was at its usual height, and the canoes floated once more without any effort on our side.

The Lake is fed by the Teoge at its north-west extremity. The river never, perhaps, much exceeds forty yards; but it is deep, and, when at its greatest height, contains a large volume of water. Its annual overflow takes place in June, July, and August, and sometimes even later. The source of the Teoge is as yet unknown, but it is supposed to be very distant. It may, probably, have its rise on the same high table-land as the Quanza, and other streams of importance. The main course of the Teoge is N.W., but it is so serpentine that, in thirteen days when I ascended it, travelling, on an average, five miles per day, and reckoning two and a quarter miles to the hour, I only made about one degree of latitude due north of the Lake. As far as I proceeded, however, it was navigable with smaller craft; for only in three places that I can remember, did I find less than five feet of water, and, generally speaking, the depth was considerable. It must be recollected, however, that it was then at its greatest height.

Though that portion of the Teoge ascended by me is narrow, I am told that, on approaching its source, it widens considerably (one of the many curious points in African geography); and the country on both sides is often inundated to a very great extent, frequently having the appearance of an endless lake, thickly overgrown with reeds and rushes, and dotted with islets covered with beautiful trees and shrubs.

At its eastern extremity, the Ngami finds an outlet (the only one) in the fine and stately Zouga. This river, near to Batoana-Town, where it escapes from the Lake, is about two hundred yards wide; and, from its gentle flow, appears at rest, the motion of the stream being imperceptible to the eye. Indeed, it is asserted by some—and should it be found correct, it certainly would be a most extraordinary fact—that the waters of the Zouga are, at one time of the year, forced back into the Lake by a branch of the Teoge (*see map*), which river thus not only feeds the Lake at its N.W. extremity, as has been already stated, but at the E. as well. From the very imperfect development of the watercourses in these parts, I do not think this impossible.

The Zouga continues to run in an easterly direction from the Lake for nearly a month's journey, or a distance of about three hundred miles, taking all the windings into account, when it is lost in an immense marsh or sand-flat,[1] called, by some, Great Reed Vley. It is a perfect sea of reeds (with occasional openings), and affords a favourite resort to innumerable herds of buffaloes.

About twenty miles before the Zouga ceases to flow, it expands into a lake, two to four miles broad, and about twelve or fifteen in extent. During the dry season, this river presents "a series of pools with dry spaces between."

The vegetation all along its course is varied and luxuriant, and in some places the scenery is quite charming;

---

[1] Many are of opinion that this river continues to flow subterraneously, and that it ultimately finds an outlet into the sea on the east coast. It is by no means uncommon in African geography—and we have in England an instance of it in the Mole—to find a river suddenly disappearing, and as unexpectedly re-appearing at some little distance.

the banks of the river being often, to the very water's edge, covered with majestic trees of beautiful and dense foliage. The baobob is particularly conspicuous, attaining, not unfrequently, round its stem, a girth of from sixty to seventy-five feet. "The banks," says Mr. Livingstone, in a letter to a friend, " are beautiful beyond any we had ever seen, except, perhaps, some parts of the Clyde * * * The higher we ascended the river, the broader it became, until we often saw more than one hundred yards of clear deep water between the broad belt of reed which grows in the shallower parts. * * * One remarkable feature in this river is, its periodical rise and fall. It has risen nearly three feet since our arrival; and this is the dry season. That the rise is not caused by rains, is evident, from the water being so pure. Its purity and softness increased as we ascended towards its junction with the Tamanakle, from which, although connected with the lake, it derives its present increased supply. The people could give no reason for the rise of the water, further than that a chief, who lives in a part of the country to the north, called Mazzekiva, kills a man annually, and throws his body into the stream, after which the water begins to flow."

Before closing my remarks on the rivers of the Lake, I must beg to draw the attention of the reader to a circumstance, which may prove of the most vital interest to the civilization and commerce of these regions. It is as follows :—

About two days west of the Teoge, two rivers are reported to exist. The one is a small branch of the Teoge, and is supposed, after meandering through the desert for a couple of days, to lose itself in a marsh. The second (and to which I particularly desire to draw notice) is of larger dimensions, though, near to its source, only periodical. In its course, however, it is fed by fountains—not an uncommon thing in Africa; and it soon increases to a constantly running stream. In due time, it becomes a mighty river, flowing slowly through the country of several black nations, and ultimately discharging itself into the sea. This is the statement of a party of Griquas, who travelled in this direction in search of elephants. I should, perhaps, have hesitated to give credit to their account, had it not, on more than one occasion, been corroborated. Whilst on our visit to the Ovambo, we inquired, as mentioned, if they were not aware of any permanently running river in their neighbourhood, to which they immediately and unhesitatingly replied in the affirmative. "The Cunenè," they said, "was only four or five days foot-journey distant from them;" but added, "that it was not to be compared with a river called Mukuru-Mukovanja, that comes out of Ovatjona-land (clearly the Bechuana country), of which the Cunenè is only a branch." This valuable and interesting information was confirmed by the Hill-Damaras.

Again, when Mr. Galton and myself, distant only some eight or ten days' journey from the Lake, were obliged to retrace our steps, on account of excessive drought, we were informed by the Bushmen, of the existence of a large river to the north, coming from Bechuana-land, and running westward. They further added, that another small river comes from the same direction, but is soon lost in the sand, or terminates in a marsh. Now, excepting that the latter is a branch of the Teoge (instead of having its source in the Làke, in common with the large river, as they asserted) their account may be said to have been substantiated.

From these statements, the existence of a river, in all probability of great magnitude, and perhaps navigable to its very source, or nearly so, is so far authenticated that I have had no hesitation in laying it down on my map. Assuming that the Teoge and the Mukuru-Mukovanja run parallel, though in contrary directions, at the distance from each other of two or three days' journey, as I was informed by the Griquas above mentioned, there exists an almost uninterrupted navigation of several hundred miles, affording a comparatively easy transport to the sea-coast of the produce of a rich and fertile interior.

A great variety of animals are found in the Lake regions, more especially in the vicinity of the rivers,[1] such as elephants, rhinoceroses, buffaloes, giraffes, koodoos, pallahs, &c., as also two new species of antelopes, the nakong and the leché, both of which are well represented on the accompanying plate.

The leché bears some resemblance to the pallah, but is altogether a larger animal. In size, indeed, it almost equals the water-buck (*aigocerus ellipsiprymnus*), and the horns are very similar to those of the male of that beast. The general colour of the skin is a pale brown; chest, belly, and orbits, white; and front of legs dark brown. The fur (which in the young animal is long, soft, and often curly) of the adult is short and 'adpressed.' The upper part of the nape and withers are provided with a small whorl of hair. The tip of the tail (slender at the base) is adorned with a tuft of black hair.

The leché is a species of water-buck; for though not actually living in water, he is never found any distance from it. When pursued, the leché unhesitatingly plunges into the water, however deep. Great numbers are annually destroyed

---

[1] Dr. Livingstone informs us that on the first discovery of the Zouga, its banks literally swarmed with wild animals, and that in the course of three years no less than nine hundred elephants were killed. However, from the persecution to which the game is constantly exposed, and the introduction of fire-arms, the number of animals has rapidly decreased, and what remain are wild and wary.

NAKONG AND LECHÉ.

London, Hurst & Blackett, 1856.

by the Bayeye, who convert their hides into a kind of rug for sleeping on, carosses, and other articles of wearing apparel.

To the best of my belief, the nakong has never been described by naturalists.[1] Unfortunately, the materials I possessed, and which would in some degree have enabled me to supply this deficiency, were left behind in Africa. Through the kindness of Colonel Steele, an opportunity has been afforded me of inspecting one or two heads of the nakong, as also a caross (brought from the Lake Ngami by Mr. Oswell), made out of pieces of the skins of this animal. But they are all so imperfect, that to attempt anything like a scientific description would be ineffectual; the more so, perhaps, as I only once had an opportunity of viewing a pair of nakongs, and that was at a distance. Suffice it, therefore, to say that the general colour of the animal is a subdued brown, darkest on the back, and on the front of head and legs. Beneath, it is of a lighter hue—almost ash-coloured. On each side of the rump, as also on the inside of the legs, if I remember rightly, there is a whitish line or patch. The hair of the skin, which is much used by the natives for carosses, is long and coarse.

---

[1] Dr. Gray, of the British Museum, to whom I submitted an imperfect skin, and a sketch of the head, of the nakong, is unable to determine its exact nature, but seems inclined to consider it identical with the *tragelaphus eurycerus*—the broad-horned antelope—of which specimens of horns and heads have been brought from the Bight of Biafra, on the west coast of Africa. In the 'Proceedings of the Zoological Society,' No. 250, p. 47, the following details appear:—

'Head, pale brown. Broad band before the eyes, and two large spots on cheeks, chin, and front of upper lip, white. Horns elongate, thick, scarcely bent forward at the tip. Throat with long black hairs.'

Again, from a head in Mr. Warwick's collection:—

'The horns are very similar to those of *t. angasii*, but the head is considerably larger, nearly as large as that of the koodoo, and the horns are thicker and larger; they are twenty-seven inches long in a straight line from base to tip, and nine inches in circumference at the base. The hair of the head is also paler and more uniformly coloured, and with very large white spots on the cheek, much larger than those of the koodoo or of *t. angasii*. The throat has a distinct mane of blackish rigid hairs. The muffle is very like that of *t. angasii*, and larger than that of the koodoo. The skull is imperfect; it has no appearance of any suborbital pit or slit.'

The horns are black, very like those of the koodoo; and, in the adult animal, would appear to attain to an equal, if not larger, size. Before they are much developed, there is scarcely any indication of spiral turns, and they are then not unlike the horns of goats.

The nakong is a water-buck. By means of its peculiarly long hoofs (which are black), not unfrequently attaining a length of six to seven inches, it is able to traverse with facility the reedy bogs and quagmires with which the Lake country abounds—localities only fit for the feathery tribe. When at the Ngami, I offered very tempting rewards to the natives if they would bring me this animal either dead or alive; but they protested, that though they frequently kill the nakong by pit-falls and spears, it was not then possible to gratify my wishes, as, at that season, the beast dwelt almost entirely in muddy and watery localities, where any attempt to follow it would be certain destruction to a man.

Hippopotami abound on the northern side of the Ngami, and more especially towards its north-west extremity, or to the right of where the Teoge river enters the Lake.

Otters are not uncommon in the rivers and the Lake. They appear to be of the same species as with us, but present great variety of colour. The fur is good and much sought after.

If the quadrupeds of the Lake Fauna are numerous and varied, the *aves* class is no less rich and abundant. In our first journey through Damara-land, I had made such a complete collection of its birds and insects, that I almost despaired of obtaining anything new and interesting; but here I found at once an unexplored and almost unlimited field for the naturalist. Unfortunately, I was not in a state to be able to benefit, to any extent, by its abundance and variety, which I regret exceedingly.

The aquatic birds were particularly numerous and varied. A friend, who visited the Lake, assured me that here, and on the Zouga, he had, at one time and another, killed specimens of no less than nineteen species of ducks and geese. One of the latter varieties is not larger than a common teal, but clothed in the most brilliant plumage. The herons and water-hens vie with the duck-tribe in numbers and gaudiness of plumage. During a hurried journey up the Teoge, I procured, in a short time, herons of upwards of ten distinct species, besides several different kinds of storks, cranes, &c.

The Lake and its rivers swarm with crocodiles. During the cold time of the year, they resort to deep water, where they remain in a state of comparative inactivity; but on the approach of the hot season they again come forward, and may be seen lying in great numbers along the banks, basking in the noonday sun, and looking exactly like so many logs of wood. I have often surprised them in this position; and, if not too close, they have invariably feigned to be asleep. The instant, however, that I have raised my gun, or even merely pointed towards them, they have plunged into the deep like a shot.

They are said occasionally to attain a gigantic size; but no authenticated instance has come to my knowledge of any specimen being killed which measured above fifteen or sixteen feet, though I have heard it asserted that they sometimes reach double that length.

The crocodile chiefly lives on quadrupeds, which he lies in wait for, and destroys when coming to drink; but he is said never to devour his prey before the flesh has arrived at a state of putrefaction.

When in its native element, the power of this animal must be enormous; for if the testimony of the inhabitants is to be relied on, he not unfrequently succeeds in destroying the buffaloe, which they say he accomplishes by seizing the beast by the muzzle and dragging him into deep water, where he suffocates him. This being done, he hauls his victim back to the shore, and, pushing the carcase above water-mark, watches over it until it has become *nicely* tainted, when he commences his feast.

From the moist and swampy nature of the ground about the Lake and the rivers, snakes, as may well be supposed, are numerous; but, though they at times attain a gigantic size, they appear very harmless, being often destroyed by the natives, who devour them with great relish. I never myself saw a specimen exceeding seven or eight feet in length, but procured skins measuring fully three times that size. The Bushmen assured me that they not unfrequently surprise these monsters when asleep and gorged, and that on such occasions it was not unusual to dispatch them with a blow on the head from the knob-kierie. These snakes feed chiefly on birds and smaller quadrupeds.

The finny tribe was also pretty numerous; but my stay at the Lake was of too short a duration to collect much information on this head. I saw and tasted many different kinds, some of which were most excellent eating, and had a rich and agreeable flavour. The only ones, however, which I remember had any likeness to northern fishes were a sort of perch, and one or two barbel kinds.

CHAPTER XXXV.

THE BATOANA—GOVERNMENT—ELOQUENCE—LANGUAGE—MYTHOLOGY—RELIGION—SUPERSTITION—THE RAIN-MAKER—POLYGAMY—CIRCUMCISION—BURIAL—DISPOSITION OF THE BECHUANAS—THIEVISH PROPENSITIES—DRESS—GREAT SNUFF-TAKERS—SMOKING—OCCUPATIONS—AGRICULTURE—COMMERCE—HUNTING AND FISHING.

THE people who dwell on the shores of the Lake are, as before said, called Batoana,[1] under the rule of Lecholètébè. They are a small tribe of that large family of 'Blacks' known as Bechuanas, who, as a whole, are probably the most widely distributed and the most powerful of all the dark-coloured nations in Southern Africa. The Batoana have not been long dwellers in the Lake regions; they came as conquerors under Lecholètébè's father. Having dispossessed the aborigines, they reduced them to a state of slavery, giving them a name corresponding to their condition, viz., *Bakoba* or *Makoba*, that is 'serfs.' These people, however, style themselves Baÿeye, or 'Men;' and, by that appellation, I shall hereafter call them.

In giving a general description of the manners and cus-

[1] Some of the notions entertained of these people before the existence of the Ngami was known to Europeans are curious and amusing. Captain Messum, in an article in the Nautical Magazine on 'the exploration of Western Africa,' says that he had heard the inhabitants of the Lake regions represented as monsters with only one eye in the centre of the forehead, and feeding on human flesh, as the giants of old used to take their breakfasts. 'A baby was nothing; they swallowed it whole.'

toms, religious rites, superstitions, &c., of the Bechuanas—the parent stock as shown of the Batoanas—I shall also have described those of the latter tribe; for though they may differ in some respects, they agree in the main.

THE BECHUANA PICHO.

"The government of the people is at once both monarchical and patriarchal, and comparatively mild in its character. Each tribe has its chief or king, who commonly resides in the largest town, and is held sacred from his hereditary right to that office. A tribe generally includes a number of towns or villages, each having its distinct head, under whom there are a number of subordinate chiefs. These constitute the aristocracy of the nation, and all acknowledge the supremacy of the principal one. His power, though very great, and in some instances despotic, is, nevertheless, controlled by the senior chiefs, who, in their *pichos* or *pitshos* (their parliament, or public meetings), use the greatest plainness of speech in exposing what they consider culpable or lax in his government. An able speaker will sometimes turn the scale even against the king. * * * These assemblies keep up a tolerable equilibrium of power between the chiefs and their king; but they are only convened when it is necessary to adjust differences between tribes—when a predatory expedition is to be undertaken—or when the removal of a tribe is contemplated; though occasionally matters of less moment are introduced."[1]

The language used by the natives on public occasions, and more especially by the chiefs, is often powerful, eloquent, shrewd, and fluent, and would do honour to the best educated European. Take the following speech as an example, which contains the address of the famous Basuto king, Mosheshe, to his people, when congratulating them on the happy event of having received three worthy missionaries amongst them:—

"Rejoice, you Makare and Mokatchani!—you rulers of cities, rejoice! We have all reason to rejoice on account of the news we have heard. There are a great many sayings among men. Among them some are true, and some are false; but the false have remained with us, and multiplied—therefore, we ought to pick up carefully the truths we hear, lest they should be lost in the rubbish of lies. We are told that we have all been created by one Being, and that we all spring from one man. Sin entered man's heart when he ate the forbidden fruit, and we have got sin from him. These men say that they have sinned; and what is sin in them is sin in us, because we come from one stock, and their hearts and ours are one thing. Ye Makare have heard these words, and you say they are lies. If these words do not conquer, the fault will lie with you. You say you will not believe what you do not understand. Look at an egg! If a man break it, there comes only a watery and yellow substance out of it; but if it be placed under the wing of a fowl, a living

[1] Moffat.

thing comes from it. Who can understand this? Who ever knew how the heat of the hen produced the chicken in the egg? This is incomprehensible to us, yet we do not deny the fact. Let us do like the hen. Let us place these truths in our hearts, as the hen does the eggs under her wings; let us sit upon them, and take the same pains, and something new will come of them."

The language of the Bechuanas (the plural of Mochuana, a single individual) is called Sichuana—an adjective implying anything belonging to the nation. It is exceedingly soft and mellifluous, owing to their being few syllables that end with a consonant. The only exceptions are 'nouns in the ablative case, plural verbs, verbs definite, and the interrogatives *why*, *how*, and *what*, all of which end with the ringing n.'

The first acquaintance of Europeans with the Bechuanas, dates from an early period of the history of the Cape Colony. There is reason to believe that this nation once extended as far as the Orange River; but at the present day, none of the tribes are found beyond the 28th parallel of south latitude.

The Bechuanas (as already mentioned in the history of the Damaras) believe that they originally sprang from a cave, said to exist in the Bakone country, where the footmarks of the first man may still be seen in the rock.

If we are to credit the testimony of some missionaries, the Bechuanas have no notion of a Superior Being. It is a strong argument in favour of this hypothesis, that no word in their language properly denotes God. Speaking of these people, Mr. Moffat says:—"I have often wished to find something by which I could lay hold on the minds of the natives; an 'altar to the unknown God;' the faith of their ancestors, the immortality of the soul; or any religious association. But nothing of this kind ever floated in their minds. 'They looked on the sun with the eyes of an ox.' To tell the greatest of them that there was a Creator, the Governor of the heavens and earth—of the fall of man, or the redemption of the world—the resurrection of the dead, and immortality beyond the grave, was to tell them what appeared to be more fabulous, extravagant, and ludicrous, than their own vain stories about lions, hyænas, and jackals. To tell them that these (referring, of course, to the different elements of our creed) were articles of our faith, would extort an interjection of superlative surprise, as if they were too preposterous for the most foolish to believe."

"'What is the difference?' said a native one day to the writer just quoted, pointing to his dog, 'between me and that animal? You say I am immortal, and why not my dog or my ox? They die; and do you see their souls? What is the difference between man and beast? None, except that man is the greater rogue of the two!'

"They could not see that there was anything in our customs more agreeable to flesh and blood than in their own; but would, at the same time, admit that we were a wiser and a superior race of beings to themselves. For this superiority, some of their wise heads would try to account; but this they could only do on the ground of our own statement, that God made man.

"A wily fellow, who was the oracle of the village in which he dwelt, once remarked, after hearing me enlarge on the subject of creation, 'If you verily believe that one Being created all men, then, according to reason, you must also believe that, in making white people, he had improved on his work. He tried his hand on Bushmen first, and he did not like them, because they were so ugly; and their language like that of frogs. He then tried his hand on the Hottentots; but these did not please him either. He then exercised his power and skill, and made the Bechuanas, which was a great improvement; and at last he made the white people. Therefore,' exulting with an air of triumph at the discovery, 'the white people are so much wiser than we are in making walking-houses (waggons), teaching the oxen to draw them over hill and dale, and instructing them also to plough the gardens, instead of making their wives do it, like the Bechuanas.'"

Dealers in the black art are numerous amongst the Bechuanas, who place the most implicit confidence in the sayings and prescriptions of the wizards. This applies more especially to those persons who devote themselves to the study of 'rain-making.'

The rain-maker possesses an influence over the minds of the people superior even to that of their king, who is likewise compelled to yield to the dictates of these 'arch-officials.' They are, in general, men of natural talent and ingenuity. Indeed, it is probable that, in the full consciousness of their superiority, they are emboldened to lay the public mind prostrate before their mysteries. Being, moreover, usually foreigners, they take good care to magnify prodigiously their feats abroad. Each tribe has one rain-maker, and sometimes more. The wizards are also doctors; and, at times, they assume the office of sextons by superintending the disposal of the dead, it being generally believed that the ceremonies practised by these impostors have some influence over the watery treasures floating in the skies. It not unfrequently happens that the rain-maker prohibits the usual form of interment, and, perhaps, orders the dead to be dragged to a distance to be devoured by beasts of prey.

Mr. Moffat, in his "Missionary Labours and Scenes in Southern Africa," has given, at some length, a very striking account of one of these rain-makers, which amply illustrates the immense influence exercised by them over the ignorant and superstitious mind, as also the craft and ingenuity of the men themselves, in order to effect their purpose. It is in substance as follows :—

Having for a number of years experienced severe droughts, the Bechuanas at Kuruman held a council as to the best measures for removing the evil. After some debate, a resolution was passed to send for a rain-maker, of great renown, then staying among the Bahurutsi, two hundred miles N.E. of the station. Accordingly, commissioners were dispatched, with strict injunctions not to return without the man; but it was with some misgivings as to the success of their mission that the men started. However, by large promises, they succeeded beyond their most sanguine expectations.

During the absence of the ambassadors, the heavens had been as brass, and scarcely a passing cloud obscured the sky, which blazed with the dazzling rays of a vertical sun. But, strange to relate, the very day that the approach of the rain-maker was announced, the clouds began to gather thickly, the lightning darted, and the thunder rolled in awful grandeur, accompanied by a few drops of rain. The deluded multitude were wild with delight; they rent the sky with their acclamations of joy; and the earth rang with their exulting and maddening shouts. Previously to entering the town, the rain-maker sent a peremptory order to all the inhabitants to wash their feet. Scarcely was the message delivered, before every soul, young and old, noble and ignoble, flew to the adjoining river to obey the command of the man whom they imagined was now collecting, in the heavens, all his stores of rain.

The impostor proclaimed aloud that this year the women must cultivate gardens on the hills, and not in the valleys, for the latter would be deluged. The natives, in their enthusiasm, saw already their corn-fields floating in the breeze, and their flocks and herds return lowing homewards by noon-day from the abundance of pasture. He told them how, in his wrath, he had desolated the cities of the enemies of his people, by stretching forth his hand and commanding the clouds to burst upon them; how he had arrested the progress of a powerful army, by causing a flood to descend, which formed a mighty river, and stayed their course. These, and many other pretended displays of his power, were received as sober truths, and the chief and the nobles gazed on him with silent amazement. The report of his fame spread like wildfire, and the rulers of the neighbouring tribes came to pay him homage.

In order to carry on the fraud, he would, when clouds appeared, command the women neither to plant nor sow, lest the seeds should be washed away. He would also require them to go to the fields, and gather certain roots and herbs, with which he might light what appeared to the natives mysterious fires. Elate with hope, they would go in crowds to the hills and valleys, collect herbs, return to the town with songs, and lay their gatherings at the magician's feet. With these he would sometimes proceed to certain hills, and raise smoke; gladly would he have called up the wind also, if he could have done so, well knowing that the latter is frequently the precursor of rain. He would select the time of new and full moon for his purpose, aware that at those seasons there was frequently a change in the atmosphere. But the rain-maker found the clouds in these parts rather harder to manage than those of the Bahurutsi country, whence he came.

One day, as he was sound asleep, a shower fell, on which one of the principal men entered his house to congratulate him on the happy event; but, to his utter amazement, he found the magician totally insensible to what was transpiring. "Hela ka rare! (halloo, by my father!) I thought you were making rain," said the intruder. Arising from his slumber, and seeing his wife sitting on the floor, shaking a milk-sack, in order to obtain a little butter to anoint her hair, the wily rain-maker adroitly replied, "Do you not see my wife churning rain as fast as she can?" This ready answer gave entire satisfaction; and it presently spread through the length and breadth of the town, that the rain-maker had churned the shower out of a milk-sack.

The moisture, however, caused by this shower, soon dried up; and, for many a long week afterwards, not a cloud appeared. The women had cultivated extensive fields; but the seed was lying in the soil as it had been thrown from the hand; the cattle were dying from want of pasture; and hundreds of emaciated men were seen going to the fields in quest of unwholesome roots and reptiles, while others were perishing with hunger.

All these circumstances irritated the rain-maker very much, and he complained that secret rogues were disobeying his proclamations. When urged to make repeated trials, he would reply—"You only give me sheep and goats to kill; therefore, I can only make goat-rain; give me fat slaughter oxen, and I shall let you see ox-rain."

One night, a small cloud passed over, and a single flash of lightning, from which a heavy peal of thunder burst, struck a tree in the town. Next day, the rain-maker and a number of people assembled to perform the usual ceremony on such an event. The stricken tree was ascended, and roots and ropes of grass were bound round different parts of the trunk. When these bandages were made, the conjuror deposited some of his nostrums, and got quantities of water handed up, which he poured with great solemnity on the wounded tree, while the assembled multitude shouted "Pula! pula!" The tree was now hewn down, dragged out of the town, and burned to ashes. Soon after, the rain-maker got large bowls of water, with which was mingled an infusion of bulbs. All the men of the town were then made to pass before him, when he sprinkled each person with a zebra's tail dipped in water.

Finding that this did not produce the desired effect, the impostor had recourse to another stratagem. He well knew that baboons were not very easily caught amongst rocky glens and shelving precipices, and, therefore, in order to gain time, he informed the men that, to make rain, he must have a baboon. Moreover, that not a hair on its body was to be wanting; in short, the animal should be free from blemish. After a long and severe pursuit, and with bodies much lacerated, a band of chosen runners succeeded in capturing a young baboon, which they brought back triumphantly and exultingly. On seeing the animal, the rogue put on a countenance exhibiting the most intense sorrow, exclaiming, "My heart is rent in pieces!—I am dumb with grief!" Pointing, at the same time, to the ear of the baboon that was slightly scratched, and the tail which had lost some hair, he added, "Did I not tell you I could not bring rain if there was one hair wanting?"

He had often said, that, if they could procure him the heart of a lion, he would show them he could make rain so abundant that a man might think himself well off to be under shelter, as when it fell it might sweep whole towns away. He had discovered that the clouds required strong medicines, and that a lion's heart would do the business. To obtain this, the rain-maker well knew was no joke. One day it was announced that a lion had attacked one of the cattle outposts, not far from the town, and a party set off for the twofold purpose of getting a key to the clouds and disposing of a dangerous enemy. The orders were imperative, whatever the consequences might be. Fortunately, the lion was shot dead by a man armed with a gun. Greatly elated by their success, they forthwith returned with their prize, singing the conqueror's song in full chorus. The rain-maker at once set about preparing his medicines, kindled his fires, and standing on the top of a hill, he stretched forth his hands, beckoning to the clouds to draw near, occasionally shaking his spear, and threatening them with his ire should they disobey his commands. The populace believed all this, and wondered the rain would not fall.

Having discovered that a corpse, which had been put into the ground some weeks before, had not received enough water at its burial, and knowing the aversion of the Bechuanas to a dead body, he ordered the corse to be taken up, washed, and re-interred. Contrary to his expectation, and horrible as the ceremony must have been, it was performed. Still the heavens remained inexorable.

Having exhausted his skill and ingenuity, the impostor began to be sorely puzzled to find something on which to lay the blame. Like all of his profession, he was a subtle fellow, in the habit of studying human nature, affable, acute, and exhibiting a dignity of mien, with an ample share of self-complacency, which he could not hide. Hitherto, he had studiously avoided giving the least offence to the missionaries, whom he found were men of peace, who would not quarrel. He frequently condescended to visit them, and in the course of conversation would often give a feeble assent to their opinions as to the sources of that element over which he pretended to have sovereign control. However, finding all his wiles unavailing to produce the desired result, and notwithstanding the many proofs of kindness he had received from the missionaries, he began to hint that the reverend gentlemen were the cause of the obstinacy of the clouds! One day it was discovered that the rain had been prevented by Mr. Moffat bringing a bag of salt with him from a journey that he had undertaken to Griqua-town. But, finding on examination that the reported salt was only white clay or chalk, the natives could not help laughing at their own credulity.

From insinuations he proceeded to open accusations. After having kept himself secluded for a fortnight, he one day appeared in the public fold and proclaimed that he had at last discovered the cause of the drought. After keeping the audience in suspense for a short time, he suddenly broke forth, "Do you not see," he asked, "when clouds cover us, that Hamilton and Moffat look at them? Their white faces scare them away, and you cannot expect rain so long as they are in the country." This was a home stroke. The people became impatient, and poured forth their curses against the poor missionaries, as the cause of all their sorrows. The bell, which was rung for public worship, they said, frightened the vapours; the prayers even came in for a share of the blame. "Don't you," said the chief one day rather fiercely to Mr. Moffat, "bow down in your houses, and pray and talk to something bad in the ground?"

But to shorten a long story: after exposing the missionaries to much risk and danger by his insinuations and accusations, the tables were turned in their favour. The rain maker was now suspected; his gross impositions were unveiled, and he was about to pay the penalty of death—the well merited reward for his scandalous conduct—when Mr. Moffat generously interfered, and, through his presence of mind and humanity, succeeded in saving the life of one who had so often threatened his own, and who would not have scrupled to take it, could he thereby have served his purpose. Death, however, soon overtook him, for he was eventually murdered amongst the Bauangketsi nation.

Mr. Moffat concludes his remarks on the career of this notable rain-maker by the following observation:—

"It is a remarkable fact that a rain-maker never dies a natural death. I have known some, and heard of many, who had, by one means or other, fallen a prey to the fury of their disappointed employers; but, notwithstanding this, there was no want of successors. There is not one tribe whose people have not imbrued their hands in the blood of these impostors, whom they first adore, then curse, and, lastly, destroy."

Polygamy exists to almost unlimited extent. A man may have as many wives as he chooses, provided he can pay for such privilege the usual fees, which vary according to the wealth of the husband.

Like the Damaras, the Bechuanas practise circumcision. From an early age upwards, even to manhood, the males are circumcised. Children, however, born of parents previously to their having been operated upon, cannot inherit regal power. The ceremony being performed, the youth is anointed, and at once assumes the character, air, and dress of a man. He is also considered fit to carry arms.

The females have also their 'religious' festival about the same age as the boys; and, for a certain period, are under the tuition of matrons, who indoctrinate them in all the duties of wives—passive obedience being especially inculcated. As a last ordeal, they are made to carry a piece of heated iron, in order to show that their hands are fit for labour. They are then lubricated with grease; the lower part of their hair is shaven off, and the remainder profusely bedaubed with a paste of butter and sebilo (dark, shining ochre). They now adopt the usual female dress. "Raised thus, from comparative infancy to what they consider womanhood, they view themselves with as much complacency as if they were enrobed in the attire of a daughter of an eastern potentate. They have reached nearly to a climax in their life, for they expect soon to be married; to be a mother they consider the chief end of a woman's existence."

The Bechuanas generally bury their dead. The ceremony of interment, &c., varies in different localities, and is influenced by the rank of the deceased; but the following is a fair specimen of the way in which these obsequies are managed.

On the approaching dissolution of a man, a skin, or net, is thrown over the body, which is held in a sitting posture, with the knees doubled up under the chin, until life is extinct. A grave is then dug—very frequently in the cattle-fold—six feet in depth, and about three in width, the interior being rubbed over with a certain large bulb. The body, having the head covered, is then conveyed through a hole, made for the purpose in the house and the surrounding fence, and deposited in the grave in a sitting position, care being taken to put the face of the corpse against the north. "Portions of an ant-hill are placed about the feet, when the net which held the body is gradually withdrawn. As the grave is filled up, the earth is handed in with bowls, while two men stand in the hole to tread it down round the body, great care being taken to pick out everything like a root or pebble. When the earth reaches the height of the mouth, a small twig or branch of an acacia is thrown in, and on the top of the head a few roots of grass are placed. The grave being nearly filled, another root of grass is fixed immediately over the head, part of which stands above ground. When this portion of the ceremony is over, the men and women stoop, and with their hands scrape on to the little mound the loose soil lying about. A large bowl of water, with an infusion of bulbs, is now brought, when the men and women wash their hands and the upper part of their feet, shouting 'Pùla! pùla!' (Rain! rain!) An old woman, probably a relation, will then bring the weapons of the deceased (bow, arrows, war-axe, and spears); also grain and garden seeds of various kinds; and even the bone of an old pack-ox, with other things. They finally address the grave, saying, 'These are all your articles.' The things are then taken away, and bowls of water are poured on the grave, when all retire, the women wailing—'Yo! yo! yo!' with some doleful dirge, sorrowing without hope."

"The ancients were of opinion that the face was always the index of the mind. Modern physiognomists have gone a step farther, pretending, that a fine form, perfect in all its parts, cannot contain a crooked or an imperfect mind." Judging the mind of a Bechuana by such a rule, it would not be pronounced deficient in talent. Nor is it. But, though the Bechuanas are a very superior race of men, they frequently conceal cunning and duplicity under an open and dignified exterior. Any act, no matter how disgraceful, if attended with success, will make them perfectly happy. "The Bechuana character is frank and sociable, which, however, does not appear to rise from benevolence of disposition, so much as from a degree of etiquette, and habits arising from relationship and docility." Like most barbarians, their political wisdom consists in duplicity and petty cunning; and their ordinary wars are merely predatory incursions upon weaker neighbours, for the purpose of carrying off cattle with as little exposure as possible of their own lives.

They are exceedingly vindictive and revengeful; but if the injured party be propitiated with gifts, and the enemy acknowledge the error of his doings, apparent cordiality and unanimity generally succeed to the most inveterate hatred.

From the king to the slave, theft is a prevailing vice with the Bechuanas; and, from what I have seen of them, I am confident that the wealthiest and the most exalted amongst them would not hesitate to steal the shirt off one's back, could he effect it without being compromised. Their pilfering habits know no bounds; and they carry on the game with much dexterity. When grouped about our camp fires, I have known them to abstract the tools with which we have been working; nay, indeed, the very knives and forks from our plates. Once, they actually took the meat out of the pot, as it was boiling on the fire, substituting a stone! They will place their feet over any small article lying on the ground, burying it in the sand with their toes; and, if unable to carry it away at the time, they return to fetch it at a more convenient period.

I have suffered cruelly from their thievish propensities. When at the Lake, they deprived me of almost the whole of my wardrobe, besides numerous other articles. Not liking to make a disturbance, and knowing the uselessness of complaining, I bore my misfortunes for a time with patience; but there is a limit to everything. Finding one morning, that a bag, containing no less than forty pounds of shot (a most invaluable treasure to me) had disappeared in a mysterious manner, I could no longer restrain my rage. We tracked the thief to the water; but here, of course, all our efforts to follow him farther were frustrated. I then proceeded direct to the Chief, and represented to him, in the strongest colours, the abominable conduct of his people, who robbed me with impunity under his very eyes, adding, that their behaviour was the more flagitious, as I had loaded both him and his men with presents, and treated them with undeviating kindness. To my astonishment and disgust, he laughed outright in my face, and told me that he could not control his men in this respect. Indeed, his own relations would play him the same trick.

"So much the more disgraceful to you," I remarked; adding, "that he might rest assured I would take good care to tell my countrymen of the villanous conduct of the people at Lake Ngami."

"Well," he replied, "I really cannot assist you in this matter, but will give you wholesome advice—and my authority for acting on it; that is, to hang on the nearest tree the first man you catch stealing."

He said this with so much coolness, indifference, and good humour, that I could not, vexed as I was, refrain from smiling; and, half reconciled, I turned away from him, exclaiming, "Well, Lecholètébè, you are an incurable rogue!"

That the people really did purloin articles from their own chief, I had an instance when at the Lake. Entering a trader's hut one day, I observed some beautiful hippopotamus teeth, and on inquiring how he had become possessed of them, he replied, "why, Lecholètébè has just asked the same question. They were stolen from the chief by his own uncle this very morning, who sold them to me as his individual property, not above half an hour ago."

The attire of the Bechuanas is scanty enough. Those, however, who have had much intercourse with Europeans, begin to adopt their mode of dress; but the women, contrary to custom, are very tenacious of their peculiar toilet, apparently preferring the garb of mother Eve. The appearance of the ladies is masculine and far from prepossessing. Their figures are usually short, stout, and clumsy, which is still farther increased by the vast numbers of beads worn by the more wealthy, which hang in cumbrous coils round the waist and neck. Their wrists, arms, and ankles, moreover, are encircled by wrings of copper, iron, and brass, of various forms and sizes. They delight in finery; and, besides the decoration of their own persons, they profusely ornament their skin, shirts, and cloaks—the whole being bedaubed with masses of fat and red ochre. 'Their naturally woolly hair is twisted in small cords, and matted with the above substances into apparently metallic pendules, which being of equal length, assume the appearance of a skull-cap or inverted bowl of steel.'

Notwithstanding the Bechuanas acknowledge us to be a superior race to themselves, they have no hesitation to pronounce many of our habits and customs both clumsy and troublesome. They laugh at us for putting our legs and arms into bags, and using buttons for the purpose of fastening bandages round our bodies, instead of suspending them as ornaments from the neck, or hair of the head. Once initiated in the use of these things, however, they are but too glad to benefit by them. To wash the body, instead of lubricating it with grease and red ochre, seems to them a disgusting custom; and cleanliness about one's food, house, bedding, &c., often creates their mirth and ridicule.

The Bechuanas are great snuff-takers, and they indulge in the luxury to excess. Sharing the contents of your snuff-box with a stranger is almost the greatest compliment that can be paid to him. Knowing their propensity in this respect, I brought with me a large supply; but, on my arrival at the Lake, was astonished to find that they scarcely deigned to look at it. I soon discovered the cause of their singular abstinence, which arose simply from the article not being sufficiently pungent. Unless it forces tears into their eyes, they look upon snuff as worthless.

The way in which the Bechuanas themselves manufacture snuff is singular enough. A piece of tobacco being presented to a man, two stones are forthwith procured, between which the weed is carefully ground, and, when of sufficient fineness, a quantity of wood-ash is added, which, to their nostrils, constitutes the very perfection of snuff. When the amalgamation of the ingredients is perfected, every one present presses eagerly forward to have a pinch. Each fills the palm of his hand with the mixture, and scoops it into the nose with a peculiarly shaped iron or ivory spoon, hung round the neck, drawing every grain leisurely up into the nostrils in such abundance as to force big tears into the eyes, thus proving the extent of the enjoyment. 'Worse than barbarian would that man be esteemed who would wantonly interrupt a social party so employed.' Their greasy fingers constitute their handkerchiefs on such occasions, and their faces, after one of these 'snuff-floods,' may not inaptly be likened to a dewy and furrowed field. Their snuff-boxes are either the kernel of the palm-fruit, hollowed out, or a diminutive gourd; and, like the ladles, are suspended round the neck, though sometimes they are secured to the arm above the elbow.

The Bechuanas smoke; but it can hardly be said to be a fashionable vice among them. This is, at least, as regards the men, for the women, on the contrary, are inveterate smokers—a habit (as already mentioned when speaking of the Hill-Damaras) often productive of serious bodily disorders.

The occupations of the men consist chiefly in going to war, hunting, preparing fur and skins for carosses, milking the cows, &c.; whilst those of the women are by far the heaviest — namely, the erection of houses, collecting and bringing fuel, tilling, sowing, reaping, thrashing and grinding the corn, — not to mention the heavy task of rearing a family. While cultivating the ground, I have often seen a woman, with one or two babies fastened to her back, under a scorching sun. Yet, notwithstanding all these exhausting and galling duties, they would be amazed were a person to tell them that a state of 'single blessedness' would be preferable to that of being the drudge of a haughty and indolent husband.

"While standing near the wife of one of the grandees," writes Mr. Moffat, "who, with some female companions, was building a house, and making preparations to scramble, by means of a branch, on to the roof, I remarked that they ought to get their husbands to do that part of the work. This set them all into a roar of laughter. Mahuto, the queen, and several of the men drawing near, to ascertain the cause of the merriment, the wives repeated my—to them—strange and ludicrous proposal, when another peal of mirth ensued. Mahuto, who was a sensible and shrewd woman, stated that the plan, though hopeless, was a good one, as she often thought our custom was much better than theirs. It was reasonable that woman should attend to household affairs, and the lighter parts of labour; while man, wont to boast of his superior strength, should employ his energy in more laborious occupations; adding, she wished I would give their husbands medicine to make them do the work."

The Bechuanas, who inhabit the shores of the Ngami, are rich in sheep and goats, but possess comparatively few horned cattle. Like other tribes of that nation, they are excessively fond of their oxen, but more particularly prize their cows, which scarcely anything can induce them to part with. Indeed, they will readily give ivory, when plentiful, in exchange for cows.

Gardening and agriculture are much practised by the Bechuanas. These occupations are conducted in nearly a similar manner as that described amongst the Ovambo. The vegetables and the grain are also very much the same.

The only marketable articles, as yet ascertained at the

Lake, are ostrich feathers, furs and skins of various sorts, rhinoceros-horns, and ivory (elephant and hippopotamus). The staple articles of exchange are beads, and more especially ammunition. Clothing is as yet but very little in demand, the people not being sufficiently advanced in civilization to care for such a luxury. Even beads are not sought after with the avidity they used to be, such quantities having of late been exported to the Lake country, that (to use a vulgar, but very emphatic expression of Lecholètébè) " the women," who chiefly wear beads, " grunt under their burdens like pigs." No visitor, however, should be entirely without them. All large beads are useless. Small beads of the following colours, pink, dull-white, light-green, brick-coloured, light-blue, dark-blue, and yellow, are chiefly in demand.

The Bechuanas of the Lake are fond of the chase, and almost daily parties are sent out to provide for the chief's table. But, though possessed of a great number of fire-arms, few of the men have as yet attained any proficiency in their use. By far the greater portion of animals slain are obtained by means of pit-falls dug by the Bushmen and the Bayeye along the banks of the rivers. As many as thirty to forty pit-falls may be seen extending in one continuous line.

Though the finny tribe is pretty numerous in the Lake and its rivers, none of the Bechuanas take the trouble to catch them. The conquered race, the Bayeye, however, are very expert and industrious fishermen.

CHAPTER XXXVI.

DEPARTURE FOR LIBÈBÉ—THE CANOE—THE LAKE—REACH THE TEOGE—ADVENTURE WITH A LECHÉ—LUXURIOUS VEGETATION—EXUBERANCE OF ANIMAL LIFE—BUFFALOES—THE KOODOO—HIS HAUNTS—PACE—FOOD — FLESH — HIDE — DISPOSITION — GREGARIOUS HABITS—THE CHASE.

As Lecholètébè proved true to his word, with regard to providing me with men and boats, I was able, after only a few days stay' at the Lake, to proceed on my exploring tour to the north. To the last moment, however, the chief and his people endeavoured to dissuade me from the attempt, urging, amongst other reasons, the enormous windings of the Teoge, which would prevent me from reaching my destination for many months; as, also, the great number of hippopotami, which they represented as the most savage and voracious of beasts.

I did not give much credit to the story of these men, not having the least faith in their word. I told them, that with regard to the sinuosities of the stream, I hoped to overcome that difficulty by patience; and as to the sea-cows, if they really were such monsters as described, I assured them I was quite confident that my black followers (pointing to the boatmen), to whom they were accustomed, would be first swallowed, which would give me time to escape. With this rude joke, which highly pleased my untutored audience, I stepped into the canoe, and waving my hand, in token of leave to my men and the chief, I launched forth on the Zouga.

The canoe in which I embarked (and they are all somewhat similarly constructed) was but a miserable craft. It consisted of the trunk of a tree, about twenty feet long, pointed at both ends, and hollowed out by means of fire and a small hatchet. The natives are not at all particular as to the shape of the canoe. The after part of some that have come under my notice, would form an angle of near forty-five degrees with the stem! Nevertheless, they were propelled through the water by the Bayeye (my boatmen were of that nation) with considerable speed and skill.

The 'appointments' of the canoe, consist of a paddle and a pole, ten to twelve feet in length. The paddle-man sits well in the stern, and attends mostly to the steering; whilst his comrade, posted at the head of the canoe, sends her along, by means of the pole, with great force and skill.

The natives, however, rarely venture any distance from the shore in their frail skiffs. It was said that they had made several attempts to cross the widest part of the Lake, but had never succeeded. A party, consisting of ten or twelve canoes, hazarded the experiment a few years previous to its discovery by Europeans, but were not again heard of, from which it was concluded that they had been overtaken by a storm, and perished. After about an hour's paddling, the broad expanse of the Lake lay before me, glittering in all the beauty and softness produced by reflection of the warm rays of a tropical sun. It was, indeed, a luxury, after so much travelling in the burning desert, to able, at last, to float upon

"The glassy, cool, translucent wave;"

and the pleasure was increased by my partiality to water—an element with which I became familiar in the early stages of boyhood, and on which I have spent some of my happiest days.

As I felt the cool breeze fanning my cheeks, new life seemed to stir within me, and my heart beat high with joyous excitement.

Our party, at starting, consisted of only three or four canoes; but, as we proceeded on the voyage, the number increased, and ultimately amounted to about a dozen.

In consequence of the frail structure of our craft, and the boatmen's tenacity in keeping near the shore, we were two days in getting from the Zouga to the western extremity of the Lake, although, in reality, it is only one good day's voyage. It was not, therefore, until the third day that we reached the chief entrance of the mouth of the Teoge (for here the river spreads out into several branches), where there is a bar. The water was so low on it that although the stream was fast rising at the time (August), we were forced to draw the canoes across it by main force. It is true we might have avoided the inconvenience by proceeding a mile or two to the westward, where a channel exists that is said to be navigable at all seasons.

Our voyage across the Lake was attended with no incident worth recording; but on reaching the point just mentioned, I had a little adventure with a leché, hundreds of which might be seen grazing and sporting amongst the shallows and the numerous little islets of the Teoge.

I had gone in advance of my party in the hope of

obtaining a shot; but, though I met with vast numbers of animals, the openness of the ground, prevented me from getting within range. Being quite tired by my severe, but fruitless exertions, I was resting on the rifle, contemplating the novel and striking scene,—the Lake with its broad blue waters—its finely wooded shores—the varied and vast herds of animals—the Teoge with its numerous little channels and sedgy shores—when I saw, a little a-head of me, two magnificent stag lechés approaching each other, evidently with no friendly intentions. I was right in my conjecture; for in a few seconds afterwards they were engaged in combat. Taking advantage of this lucky incident, I approached, unperceived, within a dozen paces, when I quickly dropped on one knee and took a deliberate aim at the shoulder of the nearest; but, just as I pulled the trigger, he received a violent thrust from his antagonist, which made him swerve to one side, and the consequence was, that the ball, instead of piercing his heart, merely smashed one of his hind legs. The animals, nevertheless, were so intently engaged, that, notwithstanding the report of the gun, and the wounded state of one of them (he probably attributed this to his adversary), they did not observe me. Throwing aside the rifle, I drew my hunting knife, and, thus armed, rushed upon the combatants. Just, however, as I was about to bury the fatal weapon in the flank of one of the animals, they both suddenly became aware of me, and fled precipitately. The wounded beast at once made for the river, which was hard by, and though it was running very swiftly at this point—perhaps not less than four or five miles an hour—he plunged into the water.

Not being then aware of the aquatic habits of this species of antelope, I was very much astonished, and for a while thought the beast would surely be carried away by the violence of the current and drowned. But I was soon undeceived; for he struck bravely out for the opposite shore, his course being marked with streaks of crimson. On gaining the bank, he gave one glance behind him, shook his bloody and drizzling coat, and made off. I was determined, however, not to be beaten; and, as I had nothing on but a pair of trousers and a flannel shirt, I threw myself, as I was, into the stream, and soon succeeded in reaching the opposite bank, when I at once started in pursuit.

In this way, swimming and wading alternately, several rivulets, swamps, and dykes were crossed and re-crossed; but, for a long time, the result was doubtful. At last, however, the poor animal slackened his pace, staggered and lay down, but again proceeded, though apparently with pain and difficulty. Seeing this, I redoubled my exertions, and having succeeded in turning him towards the Lake, I drove him right into the water, which was here shallow, and where he several times stuck fast in the mud. I now felt sure of my quarry; and having approached sufficiently near, I seized him by the wounded leg, and severed the tendon at the knee joint. The struggle between us now became severe. On trying to lay hold of his horns, which were most formidable weapons, with the intention of cutting his throat, he struck out with so much violence, as to upset me, and I was nearly smothered with mud and water. But the poor creature's course was run. His loss of blood and crippled state soon enabled me to put an end to his miseries. He was a noble old stag—the finest antelope of the species that I ever shot, and they were many; he well rewarded me for all my exertions.

After passing the bar at the mouth of the Teoge, the depth of the water increased, and the current flowed with less velocity—from two to three miles per hour, I sould say.

For the first few days' journey, the country presented a rather dreary and monotonous appearance, being frequently flooded for many miles; thus converting the land on both sides into extensive reedy marshes, only occasionally relieved by a pleasant group of the date and the fan-palm. The banks were in many places so low, that when bivouacking on shore, we often slept in the water. Even where the banks rose a few feet above the surface, they were entirely undermined by the stream; and if a stick was thrust through, water immediately appeared in the hole. Fuel was exceedingly scarce, and could only be purchased from the natives (thinly scattered along its banks) who not unfrequently brought it from a very great distance.

ASCENDING THE TEOGE.

On the fourth day, the landscape assumed a more pleasing aspect; the banks of the river became higher, and were richly covered with a rank vegetation. There was the fan-palm, the date, the black-stemmed mimosa, the wild and wide-spreading sycamore, the elegant and dark-foliaged moshoma, and a variety of other beautiful, often to me new, trees; many yielding an abundance of palatable and nourishing fruit. Timbo, who accompanied me, recognised no less than six or seven kinds of fruit-trees, indigenous to the east coast of Africa, and the adjacent countries. The arboreal scenery, indeed, in some places exceeded in beauty anything that I have ever seen. I could have spent days under the shade of some of these ornamental trees resounding at times with the wild notes of birds, whilst in the distance might be seen herds of the finest of the antelope tribe. Yet common prudence forbids the traveller to tarry. When the stream, after the annual overflow, begins to subside, noxious effluvia are emitted, carrying death along with them. Such is the climate of Africa!

Animal life was almost on a par with the exuberant vegetation. Rhinoceroses, hippopotami, buffaloes, sassabys, hartebeests, pallahs, reed-bucks, lechés, &c., were constantly seen; and every day some game animal or other was shot. Thus I was able to support and satisfy our large and hungry party, now consisting of fifty or sixty individuals.

One fine afternoon, we came to a place where the tracks of buffaloes were unusually numerous; and, having hitherto seen little of that animal, I determined to halt for a day or two, in the hope not only of becoming better acquainted with it, but of having good sport. The surrounding scenery, besides, was attractive, which was an additional inducement to devote a short time to rest and amusement.

The first night that I passed at a 'skärm,' was a failure, in respect of game, owing, probably, to my being to windward of the point whence the buffaloes were likely to come, who, getting scent of me from a distance, did not venture to approach my place of concealment. A small herd of these animals, however, came within range of Timbo, whom I had also placed in ambush some little way from me; but, as usual, he missed, and they all went off unhurt.

Returning to camp the following morning, the natives, on hearing of our ill luck, looked so hungry and unhappy withal, that although I stood greatly in need of rest and refreshment, I again shouldered my rifle, and started off in search of game.

On this occasion, I was accompanied by about a score of natives. A couple of pallahs, and a koodoo, were soon bagged; but a noble sassaby that we met with, got off unscathed.

Afterwards, we searched long without finding anything; but the numerous tracks of buffaloes testified that this part of the country was a favourite haunt of those animals. At last, we came to the skirts of a dense thicket; and, peering amongst the bushes, I presently espied several dark objects on the ground, which at once struck me must be buffaloes. Placing my finger on my lips, as a sign that silence was required, and pointing in the direction of the dark objects, I whispered the word 'onja,' meaning buffaloe. Not the presence of his Satanic Majesty could have caused greater consternation amongst my followers; for no sooner was the magic word uttered, than one and all of them wheeled about, and made a headlong retreat. One of the men was carrying a heavy rifle of mine, and wishing to get possession of it, I followed in their footsteps. But this made bad worse; for seeing me also running, and thinking the enemy was at their heels, they redoubled their pace; nor did they stop until at a most respectful distance from the thicket. It was really absurd to see us thus endeavouring to outrun each other.

Having, at length, overtaken the men, and secured my rifle, I returned to the spot whence I had first observed the suspicious objects; but though I approached to within a dozen paces of them, I was unable, from the denseness of the cover, to make out their identity.

A tree was hard by; and, in the hope of obtaining a better view, I at once ascended it. But in this matter I was disappointed; for even when thus elevated, I could see no better than from the ground. As the only mode left me of satisfying my doubts, I now fired into the midst of the dark objects in question; but not a living thing stirred. For a moment, I fancied I must have been in error, and that what I had taken for animals, were neither more nor less than huge stones. However, to set the point at rest, after reloading, I sent a second ball in the same direction as the first; and this time to some purpose; for at the report of the gun, up sprung to their feet, four magnificent male buffaloes; and after tossing their heads proudly, and sniffing the air for a moment, they broke cover in good style, and, to all appearance, unhurt. I never saw them again.

Following leisurely on their tracks, in order to ascertain whether any of the beasts were hurt, a herd of buffaloes—at least two hundred in number—suddenly rushed past us with the violence of a tornado, breaking down and crashing every thing that opposed their headlong career; and raising so great a cloud of dust as nearly to conceal their dark forms from view. I fired into the midst of them, at random, and had the satisfaction to see a cow drop to the shot.

The report of the rifle brought the whole herd almost immediately to a stand; and, facing round, they confronted us in one dark mass. Taking advantage of a tree at some little distance a-head, I stalked to within about one hundred and fifty paces of this formidable phalanx. Resting the gun on a branch, I took a steady aim at the leading bull; but, though I very distinctly heard the bullet strike him, he did not flinch in the slightest degree.

One of the natives having by this time mustered courage to steal up to me with my rifle, I fired a second time, though at another of the herd, but with no better result. Six several times, at the least, did I repeat the dose; and, though on each occasion the ball told loudly on the animal's body, neither it, nor any one of the herd (strange as it may appear) budged an inch! They seemed to be chained to the spot by some invisible power, eyeing me all the while with an ominous and sinister look. Their strange and unaccountable bearing, puzzled me beyond measure. I expected every instant to see them charge down upon me. But even had this happened—though I am free to confess I felt anything but comfortable—my personal safety would not, perhaps, have been much endangered, as by ascending the tree against which I was leaning, I should have been out of harm's way. However, I was not driven to this extremity; for, whilst about to ram down another ball, the whole herd suddenly wheeled about, and, with a peculiar shrieking noise, tails switching to and fro over their backs, and heads lowered almost to the ground, they made off at a furious pace.

On proceeding to the spot where the buffaloes had been standing, I observed large patches of blood on the ground, and felt convinced that both the animals at which I had fired must have been severely, if not mortally, wounded. We followed their tracks for a considerable distance, but saw no more of them. From information received from the Bushmen at a subsequent period, however, there is little doubt that both perished.

The night closing in, I determined on once more lying in ambush. I waited long in vain; but at last I observed a solitary buffaloe—an immense bull—slowly and cautiously approaching my hiding-place, stopping every now and then to listen. When so near the 'skärm' as almost to touch it, I pulled the trigger, but, to my great annoyance, the gun snapped. On hearing the click, the animal wheeled about, and hurriedly retreated; but, after proceeding about forty paces, he suddenly halted, and, turning partially round, exposed his broadside. Having, in the interim, put on another cap, I took advantage of his favourable position, and again pulled the trigger. This time I succeeded in placing a bullet well in the beast's shoulder. The instant he received the shot, he leaped high into the air, and then plunged violently forward. Immediately afterwards I heard a deep moaning in the direction he had taken—an unmistakeable sign that he was mortally hurt. Nevertheless, what with the severe lesson I had recently received from the black rhinoceros, and the well-known savage nature of a wounded buffalo, I did not think it prudent to follow him. The next morning, however, search was made, when he was found dead within less than a hundred yards of my 'skärm,' the ball having pierced his heart.

Koodoos were also occasionally seen and killed. Of all that varied and beauteous form of animal life, to be found in the boundless woods and plains of tropical South Africa, the koodoo is unquestionably the most distinguished for elegance and gracefulness, united with strength. The height of the male at the shoulder is about four feet. The general colour of his body is a 'rufous grey,' marked with several white bars over the back and croup. The male carries his exquisitely formed head, ornamented with ponderous spiral horns of about three feet or more in length, very erect, which gives him an air of nobility and independence. The koodoo, in short, is a perfect picture; and 'when standing broadside on, is decidedly one of the grandest looking antelopes in the world.'

The koodoo is not uncommon throughout the more wooded

THE KOODOO.

London, Hurst & Blackett. 1856.

districts of Damara-land; but from its leading a very secluded life, it is not so often seen as others of the antelope tribe. His favourite haunts are the stony slopes of hills, overgrown with brushwood. In localities not much frequented by man, however, and in the early part of the day, he may be seen in more open ground, on the outskirts of woods, borders of vleys, and banks of rivers.

His gait is very graceful; but his pace, which consists of a moderately fast gallop, is less elegant. When pursued, he clears with considerable agility, bushes, stones, and other minor obstructions that may oppose his course, his leaps being often of very considerable extent.

His food consists chiefly of leaves, buds, and the young shoots of trees and bushes. He seems capable of going a very long time without water, and only occasionally frequents the pool.

The koodoo produces only one young at a time.

His flesh, when in good condition, is excellent, and the soup, or *bouillon*, made from it is delicious. The marrow extracted from the bones is highly prized by the natives, who deem it better than that obtained from any other animal. They, consequently, devour it greedily, and often without any kind of preparation.

The hide of the koodoo is greatly valued, as well by the hunter as the colonist. It is rather thin, but exceedingly tough and pliable, and will stand more wear and tear than any other hide of the same substance. It is chiefly used for shoes, lashes of whips, thongs, straps, and harness in general. A koodoo hide, well prepared according to the custom of the country, is worth from twenty to thirty shillings; and, being much in request amongst the farmers, is no despicable article of commerce for home-consumption.

The koodoo is naturally of a shy and timid nature; but

the male, when hotly pressed or wounded, will not unfrequently face about, and even attack his pursuer.

This species of antelope is gregarious, though seldom seen in large herds, five or six being the usual number. The males are frequently met with singly.

As already seen, when taken young, this animal is easily domesticated, and becomes very tame. Notwithstanding, to the best of my belief, no specimen has ever been brought to this country alive.

From the koodoo's secluded habits, fewer of these animals are killed—as regards Damara-land, at least—than any other species of antelope indigenous to Southern Africa. He is sometimes hunted on horseback; and if a hunter has the good fortune to meet with one in a favourable and open locality, there is no great difficulty in running it down; but as the animal holds, for the most part, to hilly and stony ground, and such as is wooded withal, the chase—even if successful—usually proves an arduous one.

The preferable course is to hunt it on foot. Stalking the koodoo was a favourite pursuit of mine, and many a noble stag have I thus laid low. But, on account of the wooded nature of the country it inhabits, the difficulty of approaching, unperceived, within gunshot is very considerable, and it is greatly increased by Nature, who, with her usual wonderful provision, has provided the koodoo with the most exquisite sense of hearing. Its large, prominent ears apparently act as a kind of focus, against which any unusual noise or sound is quickly arrested in its progress.

The Bushmen have a way of their own of hunting the koodoo, viz., by running it down, not by speed of foot, but by gradually exhausting it. When a hunt of this kind is decided on, a number of these people assemble, armed with assegais, &c. Having started the animal, one of the party takes up its 'spoor' at a quick pace, the rest following more leisurely. On feeling fatigued, the leading man drops behind his comrades, and the next in order takes up the pursuit, and so on, until they secure the prize. Sometimes this is effected in the course of a few hours; but it happens, also, that the chase lasts for a whole day, or even longer. All depends on the ground. If stony or rocky, the men have an immense advantage over the animal, who, under such circumstances, soon becomes foot-sore, lies down repeatedly, and after a while, is found unable to rise, when he is quickly despatched. The women and children carry water on these occasions for the hunters, so that, should the animal prove very enduring, his pursuers may not be necessitated to give up the chase for want of that indispensable necessary.

CHAPTER XXXVII.

TSETSE FLY—CONFINED TO PARTICULAR SPOTS—ITS SIZE—ITS DESTRUCTIVENESS—FATAL TO DOMESTIC ANIMALS—SYMPTOMS IN THE OX WHEN BITTEN BY THE TSETSE.

DURING my hunting excursions along the Teoge, I encountered, for the first time, that most extraordinary of insects, the tsetse (*glossina morsitans*, Westw.)[1] Among the several scourges to which the traveller is subjected in the South African wilderness, one of the greatest is this insect; not, it is true, as to the wayfarer's own person, for he himself escapes almost unscathed, but as regards the horses and cattle.

The tsetse is found chiefly in the bush, or amongst the reeds; but rarely in the open country. It is confined to particular spots, and is never known to shift its haunts. Thus, cattle may be seen grazing securely on one side of a river, whilst the opposite bank swarms with the insect. Should the natives, who are well acquainted with localities frequented by the fly, have occasion to change their cattle-

---

[1] For a scientific description of this insect, see 'Proceedings of the Zoological Society,' No. ccxvii.

posts, and are obliged to pass through tracts of country where it exists, they choose, I am told, a moonlight winter's night; as, during the hours of rest in the cold season, it does not bite.

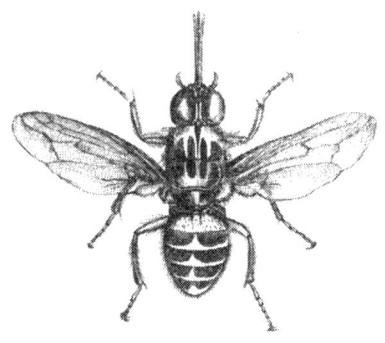

TSETSE FLY.

In size the tsetse is somewhat less than the common blue fly that settles on meat; but its wings are longer. Yet, though so small and insignificant in appearance, its bite carries with it a poison equal to that of the most deadly reptile. Many is the traveller who, from his draught-oxen and horses having been destroyed by this pestiferous insect, has not only had the object of his journey completely marred, but his personal safety endangered by the loss of his means of conveyance.

Very lately, indeed, a party of Griquas, about twenty in number, who were elephant-hunting to the north-west of the Ngami, and who were provided with three waggons and a large number of trek, or draught-oxen, lost, prior to their return to the Lake, all their cattle by the bite of the tsetse. Some horses brought with them to further their sport, shared a similar fate.

The very same year that this disaster happened to the Griquas, a party of Englishmen, amongst whom was my friend, Mr. Frederick Green, attempted to reach Libèbé; but they had only proceeded seven or eight days' journey to the north of the Ngami, when both horses and cattle were bitten by the fly in question, and the party were in consequence compelled to make a hasty retreat. One of the number, I am told, was thus deprived of as many as thirty-six horses, excellent hunters, and all sustained heavy losses in cattle.

There are large tribes which cannot keep either cattle or sheep because the tsetse abounds in their country. But it is only fatal to domestic animals, as wild animals feed undisturbed in parts infested by the insect. Yet many of them, such as oxen and buffaloes, horses and zebras, dogs and jackals, &c., possess somewhat the same nature. Moreover, it bites man, and no danger follows. The sensation experienced has not inaptly been likened to the sting of a flea.[1] The problem to be solved is, what quality exists in domestication which renders domestic animals obnoxious to this poison? "Is man not as much a domestic animal as a dog? Is it the tsetse at all which kills the animal?"

Captain Vardon, of the Indian army, one of the earlier pioneers of the more interior parts of Southern Africa, was amongst the first to decide the point; for he rode his horse up a hill infested by tsetse, and in twenty days his doubts were removed by the death of his horse.

According to the statement of the celebrated explorers, Messrs. Oswell and Livingstone, who were severe sufferers by the tsetse, the following symptoms are observed in the ox when bitten:—the eye runs, the glands under the throat swell, the coat loses it gloss, there is a peculiar flaccidity of

---

[1] When allowed to settle on the hand of a man, all it is observed to do is to insert its proboscis a little farther than seems necessary to draw blood. It then partially withdraws the dart, which assumes a crimson hue. The mandibles now appear to be agitated; the shrunken body swells; and, in a few seconds, the insect becomes quite full, and quietly abandons its prey.

the muscles generally, and emaciation commences, which proceeds unchecked until — perhaps months after the bite — purging supervenes, and the animal perishes of exhaustion. Some die soon after the bite is inflicted, especially if they are in good condition, or should rain fall; but, in general, the process of emaciation goes on for many weeks. In some cases, the animals become blind before they die.[1]

"From what I have seen of the tsetse," writes Mr. Oswell to me, "I believe that three or four flies are sufficient to kill a full-grown ox. We examined about twenty of ours that were bitten and died, and the appearances were *similar* in all. On raising the skin, we perceived a glairy appearance of the muscles and flesh, which were much wasted. The stomach and intestines were healthy; heart, lungs, and liver, sometimes all, but invariably one or the other, much diseased. The heart in particular attracted our attention. It was no longer a firm and muscular organ, but collapsed readily on compression, and had the appearance of flesh that had been steeped in water. The blood of the whole carcass was greatly diminished in quantity. Not more than twenty pints (a small pail full) were obtained from the largest ox, and this thick and albuminous; the hands, when plunged into it, came out free of stain. The poison would seem to grow in the blood, and, through the blood, affect the vital organs.

"A curious feature in the case is, that dogs, though reared on milk, die if bitten,[2] while calves, and other young *sucking* animals, are safe as long as they *suck*. Man, and all the wild animals, escape with impunity. Can the poison be alkaline, and neutralized by the acid?"

[1] 'One of my steeds,' says Gordon Cumming, 'died of the tsetse. The head and body of the poor animal swelled up in a most distressing manner before he died; his eyes were so swollen that he could not see; and, in darkness, he neighed for his comrades who stood feeding beside him.'

[2] A dog, reared on the meat of *game*, may be hunted in tsetse districts in safety!

CHAPTER XXXVIII.

THE CROCODILE—AN ENGLISHMAN KILLED BY ONE OF THESE MONSTERS —THE OMOROANGA VAVARRA RIVER — HARDSHIPS — BEAUTIFUL SCENERY—LECHOLÈTÉBÈ'S TREACHERY—THE REED-FERRY.

As we journeyed up the Teoge, we frequently observed crocodiles, basking in the sun in the more secluded parts of the river. One day, whilst trying to trace a wounded antelope, I nearly trod on one of these monsters who was fast asleep. My foot was already descending on his tail before I was aware of him. Without daring to move, I gently raised the rifle to my shoulder, and with a well-directed ball behind the ear killed him on the spot.

One does not often hear of crocodiles in these parts seizing on human beings when immersed in water, which would seem to prove that these animals are 'man-eaters' from the compulsion of hunger, rather than from habit. Indeed I have been assured by several persons that there is little danger of being attacked, provided one makes a great noise previously to entering the water. Accidents, however, do occur. Only a few years ago an English gentleman, Mr. R——, was carried off by one of these horrid creatures.

He and his companion, Mr. M——, who told me the sad story, had encamped on the banks of the Zouga; and, as a number of water-fowl were seen disporting themselves on the stream, Mr. R—— proceeded there in the hope of obtaining a shot. He soon succeeded in killing several, and amongst the rest a muscovy duck; but he was unable to secure it for want of a boat.

Whilst looking about for a canoe, he observed a fine antelope approaching; and, running quickly towards the waggon, which was hard by, he called out to his men to bring him a rifle. On his return to the river, he found that the antelope had escaped. He then proceeded towards the spot whence he had shot at the duck, which was still floating on the surface. His companion having by this time joined him, he expressed his determination to possess the bird at any cost, and that he would swim after it. He confessed, however, that he felt some doubt about the safety of such a proceeding, adding that he had once been witness to the death of a man who was seized and destroyed by a shark alongside his own boat. Notwithstanding this (his own) opinion of the risk he was about to incur, and the warning of his friend, he undressed and plunged into the stream. Having swam a little distance, he was observed to throw himself on his back, as if startled at some object beneath him; but in another moment, he was pursuing his course. When, however, he was about to lay his hands on the bird, his body was violently convulsed; and throwing his arms on high, he uttered a most piercing shriek, after which he was seen to be gradually drawn under the surface, never to re-appear!

On the ninth day after we had entered the Teoge, we left the principal channel and passed into the Omoroanga (little river) Vavarra. This rivulet is merely one of those small branches of the main stream (formed by its overflowing its banks) so frequently met with, and which usually rejoin it after a day or two. The Omoroanga Vavarra is only navigable with canoes when the Teoge is at its greatest height, and even then the navigation is of the most intricate description. The boatmen, many of whom were born and bred in the neighbourhood, constantly lose their way. We passed two nights on the Omoroanga, during which time we were exposed to much inconvenience and hardship.

Lecholètébè had placed two canoes at my disposal; but the rascally boatmen had by this time so filled them with their own things that no place was left for me. The consequence was, as the country was one succession of swamps, lakes, rivulets, and quagmires, I found myself early and late immersed in water, sometimes swimming, at others wading up to my neck. Indeed, from the time that I left my camp on the Zouga, to my return to it, a period of about a month, I scarcely knew what it was to have a dry thread about me. The only time I could partially dry my clothes was at night along the bivouac-fire; but then I had to lie down wet. It would have been ruinous to any constitution not previously inured to hardships of all kinds.

But I was compensated for what I lost in comfort by the beauty of the surrounding scenery. Wherever the soil was raised a few feet above the surface of the water, it was covered by a rich and majestic vegetation.

At length, and after about twelve days voyaging, we reached a large village where the great chief of the Bayeye resided. This was a charming spot, and one to which the most skilful artist would have had some difficulty in doing justice. Located on a small island, about two hundred feet long, by one hundred in breadth, the village consisted of somewhat more than a hundred houses, standing in the midst of a beautiful group of elegant fan-palms, and some gigantic wild fruit trees. At the foot of the werft, in a semicircle, the clear transparent Teoge wound its meandering course. On every side, as far as the eye could reach, lay stretched a sea of fresh water, in many places concealed from sight by a covering of reeds and rushes of every shade and hue; whilst numerous islands, spread over its surface, and adorned with rich vegetation, gave to the whole an indescribably beautiful appearance. This was particularly the case at sunrise and sunset, when the luxuriant vegetation received additional charms by the brilliant, but softened, rays of a tropical sun.

I had been given to understand by Lecholètébè that the chief at whose werft I had now arrived, was to have provided me with other men and other boats. To save time, as also in accordance with the men's own wishes, I sent my principal guide and others to inform the chieftain of my coming, requesting him to get everything ready; but on reaching the place, the following day, I found, to my utter astonishment, that he, with all his people, had set out that very morning to hunt the sea-cow; and no one could, or rather would, inform me when the great man was likely to return.

It now occurred to me that I was deceived; and my suspicions at once fell upon Lecholètébè. Still hoping I might be mistaken, I waited patiently for several days, but to no purpose. In the meantime, the women of the village had secretly informed Timbo, who, as usual, was a great favourite with the sex, that their husbands would to a certainty not return for a month; and that, even then, I could not expect to receive any assistance from them. I felt excessively mortified at being thus basely duped, and at once called on the only man left in the place, who, I was informed, was the chief's brother, and ordered him to tell me, without prevarication, the real state of the case. As I had suspected, Lecholètébè was at the bottom of the affair. The man declared he had no orders to furnish me with men and boats, but that, if I insisted on proceeding, he was to give a guide to the next tribe, whence I was to find my way to Libèbé as well as I could, well knowing that such an arrangement was quite incompatible with my designs.

It is impossible to describe my feelings at being thus baffled; as, from the success that had hitherto attended me, I had sanguinely hoped it would have been in my power fully to carry out all my plans. Here I was, in the midst of an inundated country of unknown extent, without men, without conveyances, without provisions—in short, without anything necessary for such an expedition. Indeed, I was so completely at the mercy of the natives that I could not stir a step without their assistance. Nevertheless, rather than be thus foiled, I determined to risk the utmost, and directed the promised guide to appear without delay, declaring my intention of proceeding to Libèbé on foot. But it was quite clear they had resolved not to let me pass beyond them; for, though I waited several days more, the man was not forthcoming.

Finding remonstrances unavailing, I had no alternative but to retrace my steps; and, accordingly, I requested the temporary chief to prepare the canoes to convey me back to the Lake. This highly delighted and gratified the wily savage.

Mortified and annoyed at the shameful manner in which I had been treated, I was, nevertheless, glad to have come thus far. I had learnt much in this short time (a summary of which will be given in the following chapters), which I could not have done had I remained at the Lake, to say nothing of the beautiful, diversified, and novel scenery which almost daily presented itself to the view—which alone was a sufficient reward for my troubles and anxieties.

REED-FERRY.[1]

[1] The above woodcut represents a native in the act of ferrying himself across the river on nothing but a bundle of reeds, with sidings and uprights of the same light materials. It is a most ingenious contrivance, and, in localities where wood is scarce, answers the purpose admirably.

CHAPTER XXXIX.

THE BAYEYE—THEIR COUNTRY; PERSONS; LANGUAGE; DISPOSITION; LYING AND PILFERING HABITS—POLYGAMY PRACTISED AMONGST THE BAYEYE—THEIR HOUSES; DRESS; ORNAMENTS; WEAPONS; LIQUORS; AGRICULTURE; GRAIN; FRUITS; GRANARIES—HUNTING—FISHING—NETS—DISEASES—THE MATSANYANA—THE BAVICKO—LIBÈBÉ.

FOR a considerable distance to the northward of the chief's werft, the banks of the Teoge are inhabited by Bayeye, and a few scattered Bushmen, all acknowledging Lecholètébè as their chief. Cooley supposes that these people came originally from the west coast, and that they have been established in their present abode for a long period. Formerly, and before their subjugation by the Bechuanas, they must have possessed a large territory; and, even now, the country they occupy is of considerable extent, consisting, as I believe, of one continued plain, intersected by rivers, with extensive marshes. The banks of the rivers are, in general, very low; but wherever they rise a few feet above the level of the water, they are shaded by a rank and wild vegetation. The trees are of a gigantic size, having their stems and branches interwoven with beautiful parasitical plants and creepers.

In person, feature, and complexion, the Bayeye appear closely allied to the Ovambo and the Hill-Damaras.

The language of the Bayeye bears considerable resemblance to the Ovaherero; and has, moreover, some affinity with the dialects of the east coast, though two or three 'klicks' would seem to indicate a Hottentot origin.[1]

The Bayeye are of a merry and cheerful disposition, and, like my friends, the Damaras, are the happiest of creatures, provided they have a pot full of flesh and a pipe. These elements of human felicity are not, however, peculiar to savages, as may be seen in the following stanza of an old song, often chanted by our English rustic forefathers:

> "What more can any man desire,
> *Nor* sitting by a good coal fire,
> And on his knee a pretty wench,
> And on the table a bowl of punch?"

In one respect the English clown has an advantage over the barbarian of South Africa, inasmuch as the latter does not appear to make any stipulation in favour of a female companion.

The Bayeye are much given to lying and pilfering, and are as suspicious as they are deceitful. As an instance of their thievish propensities, I may mention that, when ascending the Teoge, they deprived me gradually of almost the entire stock of articles of exchange, consisting chiefly of beads. These things constituted my only money, and being

---

[1] As perhaps many of my readers are interested in philology, I may mention that in the 'Geographical Journal' of this year I have introduced a short vocabulary of the Bayeye language. The words, though necessarily few in number, have been selected with a view to their utility, and consist chiefly of those denoting family relations, names of the different parts of the body, familiar objects, numerals, &c. I have at the same time given the corresponding terms in the Otjiherero (Damara) and the Chjlimanse (a tribe inhabiting the country west of the Portuguese settlement on the east coast), to show the striking analogy existing between these languages. The nations here mentioned occupy a narrow strip of territory extending obliquely across the continent, from the west coast almost to that of the east.

well aware that without it I should not be able to get on, I determined to recover my property at all hazards. But, before proceeding to extremes, I was anxious to acquire positive proofs of the guilt of my treacherous companions. Accordingly, I ordered my own men to mark carefully the different parcels. As soon as the canoes arrived at night at the appointed rendezvous (we ourselves, as I have mentioned, were walking) we hastened to the shore, and, whilst Timbo was ransacking the baggage, I stationed myself at the head of the canoe in order to prevent the crew from landing until we had ascertained if any pilfering had taken place during our absence.

Scarcely had my servant opened the first pack, before he exclaimed, "Oh, yes, master, the rascals have been there sure enough!" Immediately stepping up to the native who was in charge of the canoe, I presented my gun, on cock, at his head, threatening to blow out his brains if he did not instantly produce the stolen goods. A scene of the utmost confusion now took place. The men appeared at first inclined to be hostile, many seizing their arms, whilst the women were running to and fro, crying and howling in a manner which baffles all description. However, I was determined, come what would, to have my property back, and I quietly told them that their menaces should be of no avail, for the first individual who attempted to molest me would, to a certainty, be a dead man. And, to give effect to my threat, I added, with a significant look at the gun, that they well knew I was not much in the habit of missing my mark. Conceiving that I was in earnest, they thought better of the matter, and in a few seconds I had half a dozen of them at my feet, begging I would spare their lives, and promising that if I would not mention the circumstance to their paramount chief, Lecholètébè, they would forthwith restore the missing articles.

Being but too glad to recover my property on such easy terms, I declared myself satisfied, warning them, however, of the consequences of any future attempt on their part to steal, as I should certainly not again trouble myself about inquiring who was the thief, but would simply shoot the first man I came across. This had the desired effect; for they not only left my property untouched for the future, but treated me with far more civility than they had hitherto manifested.

The men, excepting when hunting and fishing, in which pursuits they show great activity, usually lead a very idle life at home. All the drudgery falls on the women, who till the ground, reap, and afterwards cleanse and grind the corn, &c.

Respecting their mythology and religion I am so much in the dark, that it would not be worth while to communicate to the reader the little I know. It is always difficult to obtain information on these subjects from savages; and, besides, it requires both time and a knowledge of their language. This applies also, though not to as great extent, to their superstitious notions, which are numerous, and, as may well be supposed, often ridiculous.

Polygamy prevails amongst the Bayeye, and one not unfrequently finds the more wealthy consoling themselves with half a dozen wives.

They live in large round huts, covered with matting made of rushes, and constructed in the same manner as those of the Namaquas.

The men have adopted, as in many other things, the dress of their conquerors, the Bechuanas, which consists simply of a piece of skin, broad in front, tied round the waist, with a tassel attached to it on each side falling down over the hips; and, in addition to this, they wear a skin, or light caross, which they accommodate to the body according to the state of the weather.

The women dress very much like those of the Damaras, viz., with a short skin skirt, which, as well as their own persons (when they can afford it) is profusely bedecked with beads and various brass, copper, and iron ornaments. But the plate facing this page will give a far better idea of the appearance, attire, &c., of these people than can be conveyed in words.

They are fond of the dance, which is a mimic representation of the playful sports and courtships of the different wild animals surrounding them.

The only weapons in use amongst the Bayeye are light javelins, having sometimes two or three barbs. In addition to this, the elders of the nation carry a shield, nearly oval in form, made of a single fold of ox-hide; but they have only become acquainted with this mean of defence since they were subdued by the Bechuanas. To the want of shields, they entirely attribute their own defeat.

With regard to their habits, customs, manners, &c., much of what has already been said of the Bechuanas may be applied to the Bayeye—a natural consequence of subjugation.

Like most dark-coloured nations, they are addicted to intoxicating liquors. They understand how to brew beer, on which they frequently become inebriated.

The men are inveterate snuff-takers, and the women 'dacka'-smokers.

In former times the Bayeye possessed numerous herds of cattle; but these passed into the hands of the Bechuanas upon their assuming the mastery over the country. They are permitted, however, to rear a few goats, which they do less for the sake of the milk and flesh than for the skins, which are converted into sleeping rugs, and carosses for wear. They also keep a few barn-door-fowls, but apparently of a very ordinary breed.

BAYEYE.

London, Hurst & Blackett, 1856.

They derive their chief subsistence from the produce of the soil, which is fertile, yielding the necessaries of life in abundance, and with little labour. A month or two before the rainy season, the ground for cultivation is selected, cleared and slightly worked by a small short hoe, the only agricultural implement I have seen used by the Bayeye in tilling. After the first heavy rains, they begin to sow the corn, of which there are two kinds indigenous to the country, namely, the common 'Caffre,' and another sort, very small-grained, and not unlike canary-seed—a description which is akin, as I am informed, to the 'badjera' of India. This is more nutritious than the other, and, when well ground, makes excellent flour. Tobacco, calabashes, water-melons, pumpkins, beans, and small peas are also grown, as well as different kinds of edible earth-fruits, of which the oiengora (motu-o-hatsi, of the Bechuanas, I believe) may be mentioned in particular. This is a sort of bean, having its pods under ground. It is well known to the Mosambiques; is extensively grown by the black population in Mauritius; and is, I am told, no uncommon article of importation at the Cape of Good Hope.

Moreover, the country, as before said, produces a variety of wild fruit-trees, which serve no less to beautify the scenery, than to afford good and wholesome sustenance to the inhabitants. Amongst the most handsome and useful trees, the moshoma stands, perhaps, pre-eminent. On account of the great height, the straightness of the trunk, and the distance at which it begins to branch out, the fruit can only be gathered when it falls to the ground. It is then exposed to the sun for some time, and, when sufficiently dried, is put into a hollow piece of wood (a sort of mortar) and pulverized. It is fit for use at any time, by simply mixing it with water, when it is not unlike honey in appearance, and has a sweet agreeable flavour. Strangers, however, must use it cautiously at first;

for, if eaten in any large quantity, it is apt to derange the stomach. The moshoma invariably grows on the banks of rivers, or in their immediate neighbourhood, and may, with the greatest facility, be conveyed down the Teoge to the Lake. The Bayeye use the timber extensively for canoe-building, and in the manufacture of utensils. I found the moshoma growing in Ovambo-land, and I am also given to understand that it is common throughout the countries west of the Portuguese settlements on the east coast.

The Bayeye store their corn and other products of the soil, in large baskets, not unlike those of the Ovambo, manufactured from palm leaves, and other fibrous and tenacious substances.

The Bayeye are fond of hunting; and as the country abounds in game, the spoils of the chase contribute materially to the support of the people. They are, moreover, expert fishermen. They either strike the fish with a barbed spear, or, more commonly, capture them in nets. These are made from the fibrous stalks of a species of aloe, which is found in abundance throughout the countries of the Namaquas, Damaras, the Ovambo, and others lying to the eastward, but only grows to perfection about the Teoge. The fibres are of great tenacity, apparently stronger and more flexible than hemp, though requiring less labour and attention in its growth and manufacture. Could this plant be naturalised, it would, no doubt, prove a valuable acquisition to any country. I believe the nets are also occasionally manufactured from fibrous and tenacious leaves, rushes, and grasses. The meshes are knotted the same way as in Europe.

From the humid nature of the country, the Bayeye, although generally speaking, a healthy race, suffer at times from rheumatism, and other similar affections. Ophthalmia is also of frequent occurrence; and many of the natives bear marks of the small-pox. Like the Lake district, the Teoge and the surrounding country is visited by a dangerous fever, which carries off many of the natives.

North of the Bayeye country, we find the Matsanyana; but I have not been able to ascertain whether these people form a distinct nation.

Still farther north, that is, beyond the Matsanyana, we hear of the Bavicko (or Wavicko) nation, whose capital is called Libèbé, from which also the chief derives his name. The Griquas, whom I mentioned when speaking of the watersheds of the Lake, and whom I met and conversed with on the subject, say that the country about Libèbé is flat and thickly overgrown with bush, occasionally relieved by large isolated trees, and that the Teoge is there of great width and studded with beautiful islands, on which the natives chiefly dwell.

The Bavicko are represented as an industrious and honest people of agricultural habits. Their mode of dress resembles that of the Moviza (a great trading nation in the interior of the east coast, and west of the Portuguese settlement). Timbo, who was well acquainted with the appearance of the Moviza, on hearing a description of the Bavicko, mistook them for the former nation. The latter have some slight knowledge of metallurgy. Iron they procure easily and in abundance from their neighbours; but, from all I can gather, this ore does not seem to be indigenous to their own country.

Libèbé appears to be the centre of a great inland trade. Amongst other tribes that repair here for the purpose of commerce are the Mambari, a race probably resident in the vicinity of the new Portuguese settlement, Little Fish Bay. A strong argument in favour of this supposition is, that the

Griquas, lately alluded to, and who found a party of these men at Libèbé, were informed by them, that their tribe was visited by two different white nations: by one of them—meaning probably the Portuguese—chiefly for the purpose of purchasing slaves; by the other, most likely the English or Americans, to obtain, by barter, ivory and other valuable productions of the country. The Mambari bring to Libèbé, as articles of exchange, blue and striped cotton, baize, beads, and even cattle.

Again, we find the Ovapangari and Ovapanyama also visiting Libèbé for trading purposes. These nations, as before mentioned, occupy the country north of Ovambo-land. On our visit to the latter in 1851 (Galton's expedition), we found the tribes above-named likewise trading with the Ovambo. The Bavicko have, moreover, intercourse with Sebetoane, Lecholètébè, and others.

CHAPTER XL.

DEPARTURE FROM THE BAYEYE WERFT—THE REED-RAFT—THE HIPPOPOTAMUS — BEHEMOTH OR HIPPOPOTAMUS —WHERE FOUND — TWO SPECIES—DESCRIPTION OF HIPPOPOTAMUS—APPEARANCE—SIZE—SWIMS LIKE A DUCK—FOOD—DESTRUCTIVE PROPENSITIES OF THE ANIMAL—DISPOSITION—SAGACITY—MEMORY—GREGARIOUS HABITS—NOCTURNAL HABITS—DOMESTICATION—FOOD—FLESH—HIDE—IVORY—MEDICINAL VIRTUES.

AFTER about a week's stay at the Bayeye werft, I was once more launched on the Teoge, and only regretted that my course did not lie to the north instead of to the south. My departure afforded a fresh proof of the rascality of the Bayeye. As previously mentioned, according to the injunctions of Lecholètébè, I was to have two canoes at my disposal; but, on the day in question, the natives unceremoniously deposited me on a raft composed solely of reeds! When I first saw the unshapely mass, I could not help smiling; and it was not until I had set my people the example that they ventured to embark.

This primitive raft, which is in general use amongst the Bayeye, either for hunting purposes or for descending the Teoge and other rivers, is exceedingly simple in its construction. All one has to do is to cut the reeds (the different species of palmyra, from their buoyancy, are peculiarly well adapted to the purpose) just above the surface of the water, and to throw them in layers, crosswise, until the heap is of sufficient size to support the party. No binding of any kind is requisite; but fresh layers of reeds must occasionally be added to the raft, as, from the constant pressure at the top, the reeds get soaked, and the air contained in them displaced by water. A stout pole is placed upright in the centre of the mass, to which is attached a strong and long rope. When the voyagers wish to land, this rope is taken ashore by one of the men in the canoe that is always in tow or on board the raft, and secured to a tree, or other firm object.

No small recommendation to the reed-raft, is the extreme facility and ease with which it can be constructed. In the course of an hour, three or four men can put one together of sufficiently large dimensions to support themselves and baggage.

This mode of conveyance, though inconvenient enough, is well worthy the traveller's attention, and more especially in localities where suitable wood for the construction of a common raft, is difficult to procure—anywhere, in short, where boats or canoes are not obtainable. It must be borne in mind, however, that the reed-raft is only available where the current is in one's favour.

Though I was at first much disconcerted at the appearance of our very primitive looking craft, I soon got accustomed to it, and it proved far more comfortable than might have been supposed. It was much safer, moreover, than our own canoes, one or two of which we obtained shortly after our departure. No efforts were made to steer or propel the raft, which was left entirely to the stream. As soon as we were caught by some projecting reed-bed—and this was of frequent occurrence—the raft immediately swung round and thus disengaged itself; but when we came in contact with trees overhanging the river, we were more inconvenienced; for before we could get clear of them, ourselves and baggage were at times nearly swept into the water. In this manner, nevertheless, and without serious accident, we accomplished about one hundred and fifty miles in nine days, entirely by the force of the current, which rarely exceeded two miles an hour.

Whilst descending the Teoge, we met several parties of natives in pursuit of the hippopotamus; the men were embarked on rafts similarly constructed as our own. But, before describing the manner in which the chase is conducted by these people, it may be proper to say a few words regarding the natural history of the above animal.

"Behold now behemoth which I made with thee; he eateth grass as an ox: his bones are as strong pieces of brass; his bones are like bars of iron: he lieth under the shady trees, in the covert of the reed and fens. The shady trees cover him with their shadow: the willows of the brook compass him about. Behold he drinketh up a river; he trusteth that he can draw up Jordan into his mouth. He taketh it with his eyes; his nose pierceth through snares."

The above grand and figurative language of the book of Job, seems particularly applicable to the hippopotamus, whom most people believe to be identical with the behemoth of the sacred writer. Indeed, in his 'Systema Naturæ,' Linnæus ends his description of the hippopotamus with calling it the '*Behemot Jobi.*'

The hippopotamus is generally distributed in the large rivers and lakes of Africa, from the confines of the Cape Colony to about the 22nd or 23rd degree of north latitude.

It is found in none of the African rivers that fall into the Mediterranean, except the Nile, and in that part of it only which runs trough Upper Egypt, or in the fens and lakes of Ethiopia. It is, however, receding fast before civilization. It inhabits both fresh and salt water.

Formerly, there is every reason to believe, it existed in parts of Asia; but the species is now extinct on that continent.

There are said to be two species of hippopotami in Africa, namely, the *hippopotamus amphibius*, and the *hippopotamus Liberiensis*—the latter being described as very much the smaller of the two; but, to the best of my belief, I never fell in with it.

The hippopotamus is a most singular-looking animal, and has not inaptly been likened to a " form intermediate between an overgrown hog and a high-fed bull without horns and with cropped ears." It has an immensely large head. Ray says the upper mandible is moveable, as with the crocodile. Each of its jaws are armed with two formidable tusks; those in the lower, which are always the largest, attain, at times, two feet in length. The inside of the mouth has been described by a recent writer as resembling " a mass of butcher's meat." The eyes—which Captain Harris likens " to the garret windows of a Dutch cottage "—the nostrils and ears, are all placed nearly on the same plane, which allows the use of three senses, and of respiration, with a very small portion of the animal being exposed when it rises to the surface of the water. The size of its body is not much inferior to that of the elephant; but its legs are much shorter—so low, indeed, is the animal at times in the body, that the belly almost touches the ground. The hoofs are divided into four parts, unconnected by membranes. The skin, which is of nearly an inch in thickness, is destitute of covering, excepting a few scattered hairs on the muzzle, edges of the ears, and tail. The colour of the animal, when on land, is of a purple brown; but when seen at the bottom of a pool, it appears altogether different—viz., of a dark blue, or, as Dr. Burchell describes it, of a light hue of Indian ink.

When the hippopotamus is enraged, its appearance is most forbidding and appalling, and I am not surprised to hear of people losing their presence of mind on being suddenly brought into contact with the monster, whose horrible jaws, when fully distended, afford ample *accommodation* for a man.[1]

The size of the *H. amphibius* is enormous. The adult male attains a length of eleven or twelve feet, the circumference of its body being nearly the same. Its height, however, seldom much exceeds four-and-a-half feet. The female is a good deal smaller than the male, but in general appearance the sexes are nearly alike.

The following dimensions of the female hippopotamus at the Zoological Gardens, Regent's Park, may enable those who are curious in the matter to form some notion of the progressive growth of the animal—at least, in a state of confinement—when young:—

	On its arrival, July 22, 1854.	At present, Jan. 1856.
From nose to tip of tail	8ft. 4in	„ 10ft. 1in.
Circumference of body	7 1	„ 8 9
Height at shoulder	3 5	„ 3 10

The hippopotamus, when in the water—I won't say its 'native element,' for it seems to belong as much to the land as the deeps—swims and dives like a duck, and, considering its great bulk and unwieldiness of form, in a manner perfectly astonishing. When on *terra firma*, however, what with its

---

[1] In an old painting at Hampton Court representing the Last Judgment, the mouth of the hippopotamus is said to be figured as the entrance of 'the place of the wicked.'

dumpy legs and the weight they have to support, its progress is anything but rapid.

> "The hippopotamus, amidst the flood
> Flexile and active as the smallest swimmer,
> But on the bank ill-balanced and infirm."

Even were the beast to charge—provided the locality was tolerably open—a man would have no great difficulty in getting out of its way. It is seldom met with at any considerable distance from water, for which it instantly makes when disturbed.

The hippopotamus is an herbaceous animal. Its chief food, in the selection of which it appears rather nice, consists of grass, young reeds, and bulbous succulent roots.

When the hippopotamus is located near cultivated districts, it is very destructive to plantations of rice and grain. Mr. Melly, in his description of the Blue and White Nile, informs us that the inhabitants of a certain island found themselves so plagued by these animals, that they were obliged to apply for troops to drive them away, which was responded to by a hundred soldiers being dispatched in pursuit of the marauders. Mr. Burckhardt, again, in his travels in Nubia, tells us that in Dongola, the 'barnick' (the Arabic name for hippopotamus) is a dreadful torment, on account of its voracity, and the want of means, on the part of the natives, to destroy it. During the day it remains in the water, but comes on shore at night, destroying as much by the treading of its enormous feet as by its voracity.

The ravages of the hippopotamus would appear to be an old grievance; for Sir Gardener Wilkinson, when speaking of the ancient Egyptians, says:—" Though not sô hostile to man as the voracious crocodile, it was looked upon as an enemy, which they willingly destroyed, since the ravages it committed at night in the fields occasioned heavy losses to the farmer."

Naturalists and others represent the hippopotamus as of a mild and inoffensive disposition. It may be so in regions where it is unacquainted with man; but from the numerous unprovoked attacks made by these animals on voyagers, and the very great dread entertained of them by the Bayeye, who, so to say, live amongst them, I am inclined to believe they are not quite such harmless animals as we are given to understand. In ascending the Teoge, I saw comparatively little of them, and used almost to ridicule the natives on account of the timidity they showed when these beasts made their appearance. But on my return journey, I very frequently encountered the hippopotamus. More than once I narrowly escaped with life, and found that the men had good reason to fear a contest with this truly formidable animal.

In regions not much visited by the European hunter and his destructive companion, the fire-lock, the hippopotamus appears as a comparatively fearless animal, not unfrequently abiding the approach of man, whom he apparently surveys with a curious and searching look, as much as to say: 'Why this intrusion upon my native haunts, which I have enjoyed in undisturbed tranquillity from time immemorial?' But man is cruel, and by his relentless persecutions, a nature, once so unsuspicious and confiding, is soon changed to that of the most timid and circumspective, causing the animal to take instant refuge in the water on hearing the least noise.

The sagacity of the hippopotamus is very considerable. Indeed, if we are to credit the testimony of Plinius, the cunning and dexterity of this beast is so great that, when pursued, he will walk backwards in order to mislead his enemies. "The habits of the animal," says Dr. Andrew Smith, "are opposed to our becoming intimately acquainted with it; yet, from what has been noticed of its adroitness in guarding against assailants, in avoiding pits dug purposely to entrap it, in conducting its young both in and out of the water, and in migrating from localities which it may have discovered are not to be longer held without serious danger to others not exposed to such inconveniences—even though to reach those it may require to make long journeys—are all evidences that it is far from the stupid animal it has been frequently described."

It is asserted that if a hippopotamus be shot dead just after calving, the offspring will immediately make for the water, an element which it has never yet seen!

Its memory is also considered good. "When once a hippopotamus," says the author just quoted, "has been assailed in its watery dwelling, and injured from incautiously exposing itself, it will rarely be guilty of the same indiscretion a second time; and though its haunts may not again be approached by hunters till after a long period has elapsed, it will survey such approaches, and perform the movements necessary for its respiration with a degree of caution, which clearly shows that it has not forgotten the misfortunes to which an opposite course had exposed it."

The hippopotamus is gregarious, and is usually found in troops of from five or six, to as many as twenty or thirty. It is amusing to watch these animals when congregated; to see them alternately rising and sinking as if impelled by some invisible agency; in the while snorting most tremendously, and blowing the water about in every direction. At others, they will remain perfectly motionless near the surface, with the whole, or part, of their heads protruding. In this position, they look, at a little distance, like so many rocks.

The hippopotamus is a nocturnal animal, and seldom or never feeds except during the night. He usually passes most part of the day in the water; but it is somewhat doubtful if this be not rather from necessity than choice. Indeed, in more secluded localities, one most commonly sees it reclining in some retired spot:—"He lieth under the shady trees, in the covert of the reeds and fens. The shady trees cover him with their shadows, the willows of the brook compass him about." Or it may be under shelter of an overhanging dry bank; or, at least, with its body partially out of the water. I have not unfrequently found the animal in this situation, and once shot an immense fellow while fast asleep with his head resting on the bank of the river.

When from fear of enemies, the hippopotamus is compelled to remain in the water throughout the day, it takes the shore on the approach of night in order to feed. Just as it emerges into the shallows, it has the peculiar habit of performing some of the functions of nature, during which it keeps rapidly thumping the surface of the water with its stumpy tail, thereby creating a very great noise. I have known from twenty to thirty hippopotami thus occupied at once; and, to add to the din, they would at the same time grunt and bellow to such a degree as to deprive our party of the rest, that exhausted nature but too well needed.

During the nocturnal excursions of the hippopotamus on land, it wanders at times to some distance from the water. On one occasion the animal took us by surprise, for, without the slightest warning, it suddenly protruded its enormous head within a few feet of our bivouac, causing every man to start to his feet with the greatest precipitation, some of us, in the confusion, rushing into the fire and upsetting the pots containing our evening meal.

The hippopotamus would seem to be easily domesticated. We may judge so at least from the fine specimens now in the Zoological Gardens, Regent's Park, which are as manageable as most of the larger animals of that magnificent establishment. Though these are the first living specimens that ever found their way into England, the ancient Romans (who, during their conquests in Northern Africa, became acquainted with the hippopotamus) held them in captivity. This may be safely inferred; for, "on a medal of the Emperor Philip,

MEDAL.

or rather of his Queen Otacilla Severa, is (as seen in the above wood-cut) a very striking likeness of a young, and, perhaps, hungry hippopotamus, designed by some Wyon of the day. This is, perhaps, the earliest *good* figure of the creature; and its representation on such a place shows in what estimation, as a novelty, it was held."

For the information of the curious in these matters, I may mention, that the food of the *larger* of the hippopotami now in the Regent's Park Gardens, when first shipped at Alexandria, in 1850, and when yet comparatively a 'baby,' consisted of the milk of two cows and three goats. This quantity, however, until supplemented with Indian corn-meal, was found insufficient to satisfy his voracity. On his arrival at the gardens, 'oatmeal was substituted for Indian corn; and the change, with an extra supply of milk, seemed to give the gigantic infant great satisfaction.' By degrees vegetable diet was supplied instead of milk; and, at the present day, the animal is fed on clover, hay, corn, chaff, bran, mangle-wurzel, carrots and white cabbage. The three last-named vegetables constitute his most favourite food. On this (1cwt. being his daily allowance) he thrives wonderfully, a proof of which is, that since his arrival (he then weighed about one thousand pounds) he has increased more than a ton in weight.

The flesh of the hippopotamus is highly esteemed, and with justice, for it is very palatable. The tongue is reckoned a delicacy; and the fat ('speck,' as it is termed by the colonists) is very excellent, and forms a capital substitute for butter. In general, both flesh and fat of wild animals have a peculiar, and often strong flavour, but that of the hippopotamus is an exception.

The hide is also in much request, and forms no mean article of commerce in the Cape colony. As already mentioned, it is chiefly converted into 'shamboks.' In Northern Africa the hide is used as whips for the dromedary; as also for punishing refractory servants. The ancient Egyptians employed it largely in the manufacture of shields, helmets, javelins, &c.

But the most valuable part of the hippopotamus is its teeth (canine and incisors), which are considered greatly superior to elephant-ivory, and when perfect, and weighty— say from five to eight pounds each—have been known to fetch as much as one guinea per pound. It is chiefly used for artificial teeth, for which purpose it is particularly well adapted, since it does not readily turn yellow, as is frequently the case with elephant-ivory; as also for instruments, knife-handles, and a variety of other purposes.

Medicinal virtues are attributed to certain parts of the body of the hippopotamus. According to Thunberg, the *processus mamillaris* of this animal is an effectual remedy for the stone and gravel; and "the fat"—says Kolben—"is reckoned an excellent thing against a surfeit and a redundancy of humours in the body."

CHAPTER XLI.

THE BAYEYE HARPOON THE HIPPOPOTAMUS—THE HARPOON DESCRIBED—HOW THE CHASE OF THE HIPPOPOTAMUS IS CONDUCTED BY THE BAYEYE—HOW IT WAS CONDUCTED BY THE ANCIENT EGYPTIANS—THE SPEAR USED BY THEM—FEROCITY OF THE HIPPOPOTAMUS—KILLED BY GUNS—FRIGHTFUL ACCIDENT—THE DOWNFALL.

On the Teoge, and other rivers to the northward of Ngami, the natives are accustomed to harpoon the hippopotamus in a somewhat similar manner as that practised with the whale. I will endeavour to describe the process, which, singularly enough, has never to my knowledge been done by any traveller.

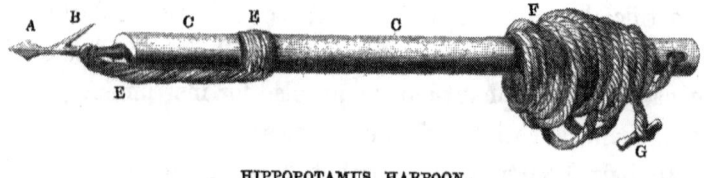

HIPPOPOTAMUS HARPOON.

The harpoon (of iron), A, is, as seen in the above diagram, short and strong, and provided with a single barb, B. The shaft, or handle, C C, consists of a stout pole from ten to twelve feet in length, by three or four inches in thickness.

At the inner end of the shaft, C C, is a socket for the reception of the harpoon, A; which is farther secured to the shaft (at about one-third from the socket) by a number of small cords, E E.[1] These cords, when the animal is struck, and a strain consequently comes upon them, relax, so as to allow the harpoon to slip out of the socket, though, of course, it still remains attached to the shaft. To the other extremity of the handle is fixed the harpoon-line, F, which is strong, and of considerable length; and to the end of this a 'float' or 'buoy,' G.

From the weight of the shaft, the harpoon is seldom or never hurled at the hippopotamus, but is held by the harpooner, who drives it either vertically or obliquely into the body of the animal.

Sometimes the chase is conducted with canoes alone; at others, in connection with a 'reed-raft,' similarly constructed to that recently described. We will suppose the latter plan is adopted. At the appointed time, the men assemble at the rendezvous; and after everything has been duly arranged, and the canoes, needed for the prosecution of the hunt, drawn up on the raft, the latter is pushed from the shore, and afterwards abandoned entirely to the stream, which propels the unwieldy mass gently and noiselessly forward.

Hippopotami are not found in all parts of the river, but only in certain localities. On approaching their favourite haunts, the natives keep a very sharp look-out for the animals, whose presence is often known by their snorts and grunts, whilst splashing and blowing in the water, or (should there be no interruption to the view) by the ripple on the surface, long before they are actually seen.

---

[1] The object of having the connecting line to consist of a number of small cords, instead of a single stout one, is to reduce the chance of its being severed by the teeth of the hippopotamus.

As soon as the position of the hippopotami is ascertained, one or more of the most skilful and intrepid of the hunters

THE REED-RAFT AND HARPOONERS.

stand prepared with the harpoons; whilst the rest make ready to launch the canoes, should the attack prove successful. The bustle and noise caused by these preparations gradually subside. Conversation is carried on in a whisper, and every one is on the *qui-vive*. The snorting and plunging become every moment more distinct; but a bend in the stream still hides the animals from view. The angle being passed, several dark objects are seen floating listlessly on the water, looking more like the crests of sunken rocks, than living creatures. Ever and anon, one or other of the shapeless masses is submerged, but soon again makes its appearance on the surface. On, on, glides the raft with its sable crew, who are now worked up to the highest state of excitement. At last, the raft is in the midst of the herd, who appear quite unconscious of danger. Presently, one of the animals is in

HIPPOPOTAMUS HARPOONED.

immediate contact with the raft. Now is the critical moment. The foremost harpooner raises himself to his full height to give the greater force to the blow, and, the next instant, the fatal iron descends with unerring accuracy in the body of the hippopotamus.

The wounded animal plunges violently, and dives to the bottom; but all his efforts to escape are unavailing. The line, or the shaft, of the harpoon may break; but the cruel barb, once imbedded in the flesh, the weapon (owing to the thickness and toughness of the beast's hide) cannot be withdrawn.

As soon as the hippopotamus is struck, one or more of the men launch a canoe from off the raft, and hasten to the shore with the harpoon-line, and take a 'round turn' with it about a tree, or bunch of reeds, so that the animal may either be 'brought up' at once,[1] or, should there be too great a strain on the line, 'played' (to liken small things to great) in the same manner as the salmon by the fisherman. But if time should not admit of the line being passed round a tree, or the like, both line and 'buoy' are thrown into the water, and the animal goes wheresoever he chooses.

THE SPEAR.

The rest of the canoes are now all launched from off the raft, and chase is given to the poor brute, who, so soon as he comes to the surface to breathe, is saluted with a shower of light javelins, of which the above wood-cut is a sample. Again he descends, his track deeply crimsoned with gore. Presently—and perhaps at some little distance—he once more appears on the surface, when, as before, missiles of all kinds are hurled at his devoted head.

[1] The accompanying plate represents a hippopotamus in this position.

When thus beset, the infuriated beast not unfrequently turns upon his assailants, and either with his formidable tusks, or with a blow from his enormous head, staves in, or capsizes the canoes. At times, indeed, not satisfied with wreaking his vengeance on the craft, he will attack one or other of the crew, and, with a single grasp of his horrid jaws, either terribly mutilates the poor fellow, or, it may be, cuts his body fairly in two!

The chase often lasts a considerable time. So long as the line and the harpoon hold, the animal cannot escape, because the 'buoy' always marks his whereabout. At length, from loss of blood or exhaustion, Behemoth succumbs to his pursuers.

It is a remarkable fact that almost the same method of securing the hippopotamus, as that just described, was adopted by the ancient Egyptians.[1]

"The hippopotamus," says Diodorus, "is chased by many persons, each armed with iron javelins. As soon as it makes its appearance at the surface of the water, they surround it with boats, and closing in on all sides they wound it with blades, furnished with iron barbs, and having hempen ropes fastened to them, in order that, when wounded, it may be let out, until its strength fails it from loss of blood."

The many drawings relating to the chase, &c., of the hippopotamus, to be found on the sculptures and monuments of Thebes, would seem to prove that the ancient Egyptians greatly delighted in this kind of sport. One of these representations is shown on the opposite page, and has been borrowed from that valuable work, 'The Manners and Customs of the Ancient Egyptians,' by Sir Gardner Wilkinson, who thus explains the very interesting illustration.

---

[1] In some parts of ancient Egypt the hippopotamus was worshipped. It is also said to have been a representation of Typho (in connection with the crocodile) and Mars. According to Plutarch, it 'was reckoned amongst the animals emblematic of the Evil Being.'

"The chasseur is here in the act of throwing the spear at the hippopotamus, which he has already wounded with three

other blades, indicated by the ropes he holds in his left hand; and having pulled the animal towards the surface of the water, an attendant endeavours to throw a noose over its head, as he strikes it for the fourth time. Behind him is his son, holding a fresh spear in readiness: and in order that there should be no question about the ropes belonging to the blades, the fourth is seen to extend from his hand to the shaft of the spear he is throwing. The upupa, heron, and other birds are frightened from the rushes as the boat approaches; and the fish, with a young hippopotamus, seen at the bottom of the water, are intended to show the communication of the fenny lake with the Nile."

"The spear they used on these occasions was evidently of a different construction from that intended for ordinary pur-

poses, and was furnished, as Diodorus observes, with a rope for letting out the wounded animal, in the same manner as practised by the modern Ethiopians;[1] there was sometimes another line fastened to the shaft, and passing over a notch at its upper end; which was probably intended to give the weapon a great impetus, as well as to retain the shaft when it left the blade. The rope attached to the blade was wound

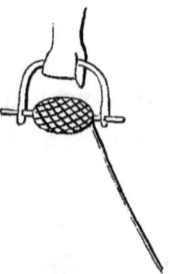

upon a reel, generally carried by some of the attendants. It

[1] Sir Gardner Wilkinson informs us further, that the inhabitants at Sennar still follow up the practice of their ancestors, and, like them, prefer chasing it in the river to an open attack on shore.

was of very simple construction, consisting of a half ring of metal, by which it was held, and a bar turning in it, on which the line or string was wound."

Again: "This weapon," alluding to the harpoon, "consisted of a broad flat blade, furnished with a deep tooth or barb at the side, having a strong rope of considerable length attached to its upper end, and running over the notched summit of a wooden shaft, which was inserted into the head or blade, like a common javelin. It was thrown in the same manner; but, on striking, the shaft fell, and the iron head alone remained in the body of the animal, which, on receiving a wound, plunged into deep water, the rope having been immediately let out. When fatigued by exertion, the hippopotamus was dragged to the boat, from which it again plunged, and the same was repeated till it became perfectly exhausted; frequently receiving additional wounds, and being entangled by other nooses, which the attendants held in readiness, as it was brought within their reach."

To return. If the hippopotamus' hunt, as just described by me, was conducted altogether from the reed-raft, one's personal safety would be little, or not at all, endangered; for, on account of the great size, buoyancy and elasticity of the raft, the animal, however wickedly inclined, could neither 'board,' nor capsize it. But when one pursues him in a canoe —though far the most exciting way—the peril, as shown, is considerable. One morning, when descending the Toege, we met a party of hippopotami hunters, one of whose canoes had been upset by one of those animals, whereby the life of a man was sacrificed. Indeed, similar mishaps are of constant occurrence on that river.

Our own safety, moreover, was considerably jeopardized by a hippopotamus. One afternoon, about an hour before sunset, I sent a canoe, with several men, in advance to look out for a bivouac for the night, and to collect fuel. They were scarcely out of sight, when an immense hippopotamus, with its calf, rushed out from amongst the reeds, where she had been concealed, and, passing under our raft, almost immediately afterwards made her appearance on the surface of the water. Upon seeing this I lost no time in firing; but, though to all appearance mortally wounded, we lost sight of her at the time. A few minutes afterwards, however, on coming to a bend of the river, we fell in with the canoe that had been sent on, bottom uppermost; and found, to our great consternation, that the wounded beast, in going down the stream, had caught sight of the canoe, and instantly attacking it, had, with one blow of her head, capsized it. The men saved themselves by swimming, but all the loose articles were either lost or spoiled by the water. Fortunately for me, however, I had taken the advice of the Bayeye to remove the most valuable of my things, such as books, instruments, &c., to the raft previous to the canoe leaving.

Innumerable instances, showing the ferocity of the hippopotamus, are on record. "Lieutenant Vidal," says Captain Owen, in his Narrative of Voyages, and when speaking of the river Temby, "had just commenced ascending this stream in his boat, when suddenly a violent shock was felt from underneath, and in another moment a monstrous hippopotamus reared itself up from the water, and, in a most ferocious and menacing attitude, rushed, open-mouthed, at the boat—and, with one grasp of its tremendous jaws, seized and tore seven planks from her side; the creature disappeared for a few seconds, and then rose again, apparently intending to renew the attack, but was fortunately deterred by the contents of a musket discharged in its face. The boat rapidly filled, but, as she was not more than an oar's length from the shore, the crew succeeded in reaching it before she sank. The keel, in all probability, touched the back of the animal, which, irritating him, occasioned the furious attack; and, had he got his upper-jaw above the gunwale, the whole broadside must have been torn out. The force of the shock from beneath, previously to the attack, was so violent that her stern was almost lifted out of the water, when the midshipman steering was thrown overboard, but, fortunately, rescued before the irritated animal could seize him."

In justice, however, to the poor hippopotamus, who, in these parts, has, already, earned for itself a sufficiently bad name for ferocity, one must not attribute the whole of the casualties that occur on the Teoge, to *wilful* attacks on the part of the animal; for, owing to the narrowness of the stream, it doubtless, at times, happens that, on coming to the surface to breathe, it accidentally encounters a canoe, and in its fright, or it may be in playful frolic, upsets it.

The colonists, and others, who are possessed of guns, most commonly shoot the animal from the shore; and this is not a matter of any great difficulty, for when it comes to the surface, either to breathe, or for amusement, " a single shot through, or under the ear," as Captain Harris truly says, "is fatal to the Behemoth." If there are several 'gunners,' and they station themselves on opposite sides of the pool where the hippopotami are congregated (in which case, the animals, when rising to the surface, invariably come within range of one or other of the party) great slaughter may be committed.

Should the hippopotamus be killed outright, it usually sinks; but in about half a day reappears at the surface; and, in order eventually to secure the carcase, it is only necessary to keep a sharp look-out in the stream below.

Shooting the hippopotamus from the shore, is attended with but little danger. Accidents, however, do, at times, occur.

"A native," says Mr. Moffat, "with his boy, went to the river to hunt sea-cows. Seeing one at a short distance below an island, the man passed through a narrow stream to get nearer to the object of his pursuit. He fired, but missed; when the animal immediately made for the island. The man, seeing his danger, ran to cross to the opposite bank of the river; but before reaching it, the sea-cow seized him, and literally severed his body in two with its monstrous jaws.

Various devices are resorted to by the natives of Southern Africa to destroy the hippopotamus. At times, he is entrapped in pit-falls. But the most ingenious plan, and which will be readily understood by the accompanying wood-cut, is by means of the downfall, which the natives would seem to practise with considerable success.

A is behemoth. B, a downfall, consisting of a log of wood. C C, stones attached to the downfall, to increase its weight. D, the harpoon affixed to the lower end of the downfall. E, a tree, or, in lieu of it, an artificial support of about twenty-five feet in height. F F, a line attached to the downfall, which, after having been passed over a branch of the tree or artificial support, crosses horizontally the path-way that the hippopotamus is in the habit of frequenting during his nocturnal rambles. When the animal (which, from the shortness of his legs, lifts his feet but little from the ground) comes in contact with the line, secured on either side of the path by a small peg, it at once snaps, or is disengaged by means of a trigger. The liberated downfall instantly descends, and the harpoon is driven deep into the back of the beast, who, wounded and bloody, rushes with pain and fury to the nearest water, where he shortly dies. His death is sometimes hastened by the iron being poisoned.

THE DOWNFALL.

CHAPTER XLII.

RETURN TO THE LAKE — THE AUTHOR STARTS FOR NAMAQUA-LAND TO PROCURE WAGGONS—NIGHT ADVENTURE WITH A LION—DEATH OF THE BEAST—SUFFERINGS OF THE AUTHOR.

AFTER about a month's absence, I returned in safety to the Lake, and was delighted to find that affairs were going on prosperously at my camp. My men, however, complained much of the begging and pilfering of the natives. They had also been greatly annoyed by Lecholètebè, who was one of the first persons I encountered on my arrival. I had long been puzzling my brains how I could most effectually pay off the chief for his treachery, and had resolved to assume an angry and dissatisfied air; but a glance at his smooth, sly, smiling face was sufficient to mollify every feeling of resentment; and when, with the most innocent look, he inquired if I had seen Libèbé, and if I felt satisfied with the trip in general, my anger was turned into mirth, and I burst into a hearty laugh. This was all my cunning friend wanted: he seemed like one resting complacently on a profound sense of his own merits, and waiting to receive the thanks and praises which he felt to be his due.

When stopped so unexpectedly in my exploring career by the artifices of Lecholètébè, I made up my mind to return forthwith to the Cape, partly for the purpose of obtaining a fresh outfit, and partly to procure boats suitable to navigate the Ngami and its water-sheds, and then return to the Lake to follow up my discoveries. But it was not to be.

As the reader will probably remember, I reached the Ngami by means of pack-and-ride oxen; but I had found this mode of travelling so exceedingly inconvenient, that I almost dreaded a renewal of it. Moreover, my collection of ivory, specimens of natural history, curiosities, &c., had by this time so increased, that I found my few remaining half-broken-in cattle altogether inadequate to the task of conveying me and my stores to the Cape. A waggon had become absolutely necessary; and the only possible way of obtaining one was to return to Namaqua-land, where, should my man Eyebrecht not have such a vehicle at my disposal, I was in hope of being able to borrow one from the natives. To ensure dispatch, although I stood sadly in need of rest and quiet, I determined on undertaking the journey.

After about a week's stay at Batoana-town, I set out for Namaqua-land on the 10th of September, accompanied by only one man, leaving Timbo in charge of the camp in my absence.

Before I returned to the Lake, and was fairly on my way home, four months had elapsed; but though this portion of my travels was not devoid of interest, the volume has already swelled to such a bulk, that I must content myself with relating merely one striking incident that befel me, and a few general remarks.

Journeying in a very lonely part of the country, and only accompanied by a single native, I arrived, one day, at a fountain, situated in a defile between some craggy rocks. The water issued from different parts amongst these cliffs, forming little pools here and there; and though the place was difficult of access, elephants, and other large game, were in the habit of flocking to the water nightly. As the stony nature of the ground afforded excellent 'ambuscades,' and being much in want of provision, I determined to watch the pools in question, for a night or two.

The first night was a failure; but in the second, I succeeded in killing a white rhinoceros. After this, though I watched long and well, nothing appeared, and at last sleep overtook me. How long I slumbered I know not; but on a sudden I thought, or dreamt, that I was in danger. From much night-watching, my hearing and sight had gradually acquired such an acuteness, that, even in sleep, I was able to retain a certain consciousness of what was passing around me; and it is probable that I was indebted to this remarkable faculty for the preservation of my life on the present occasion. At first, I could not divest myself of fear; and, for a while, my senses were too confused to enable me to form any accurate notion of the imagined danger. Gradually, however, consciousness returned, and I could distinctly hear the breathing of an animal close to my face, accompanied by a purr like that of a cat. I knew that only one animal existed in *these parts*, capable of producing the sound; and at once I came to the conclusion that a lion was actually stooping over me.

If a man had ever cause for dread, I think I certainly had on this occasion. I became seriously alarmed. My first impulse was to get hold of my gun, which was lying ready cocked immediately before me, and the next to raise myself partially from my reclining position. In doing so, I made as little noise as possible; but slight though it might be, it was sufficient to attract the notice of the beast who uttered a gruff kind of growl, too well known to be misunderstood. Following with my eyes the direction of the sound, I endeavoured to discover the lion, but could only make out a large dark mass looming through the night-mist. Scarcely knowing what I was about, I instinctively levelled my gun at the beast. My finger was on the trigger; for a moment I hesitated; but, by a sudden impulse, pulled it, and the next instant the surrounding rocks rang with the report, followed by roarings from the beast, as if in the agonies of death. Well knowing what a wounded lion is capable of, and how utterly helpless I was, I regretted my rashness. The wounded beast, who at times seemed to be within a few paces of the 'skärm,' and at others at some little distance, was rolling on the ground, and tearing it up, in convulsive agonies. How long this struggle between life and death lasted is hard to say, but to me it appeared an age. Gradually, however, and to my great relief, his roars and moans subsided, and after a while ceased altogether.

Dawn at length appeared; but it was not until after some time, and then with much caution, that I ventured to ascertain the fate of the lion, who, to my great satisfaction, I found dead within fifty yards of my place of concealment. The beast was of an average size; but, unfortunately, the hyænas and jackals had played sad havoc with his skin.

Some time previously, my men, Eyebrecht and Klaas Zaal, had also shot a lion in this identical spot; but owing to his fearful growls, whilst dying, they thought it best to decamp at once without ascertaining his fate.

During the four months that I was absent from my men, I travelled either alone or accompanied by a single native, sometimes on foot, and at others on horse-back or ox-back, over upwards of a thousand miles of country, parts of it emulating the Sahara in scarcity of water and general inhospitality.

Tongue is too feeble to express what I suffered at times. To say nothing of narrow escapes from lions and other dangerous beasts, I was constantly enduring the cravings of hunger and the agonies of thirst. Occasionally, I was as much as two days without tasting food; and it not unfrequently happened that in the course of the twenty-four hours I could only once or twice moisten my parched lips. Sometimes I was so overcome by these causes, coupled with bodily fatigue, that I fainted. Once both my steed and myself (as seen in the sketch below) dropped down in the midst of a sand-plain, where we remained a long time in a state bordering on unconsciousness, and exposed to all the injurious effects of a tropical sun. I would at times pursue my course with a pained and listless step, scarcely knowing what I was about, and staggering like a drunken man. "This," says Captain Messum when speaking of the hardships he had undergone in a short tour into the

AUTHOR AND STEED BROKEN DOWN.

interior of the west coast, " was the pleasure of travelling in

Africa. It requires the endurance of a camel and the courage of a lion."

SIGNAL STATION AT CAPE-TOWN.

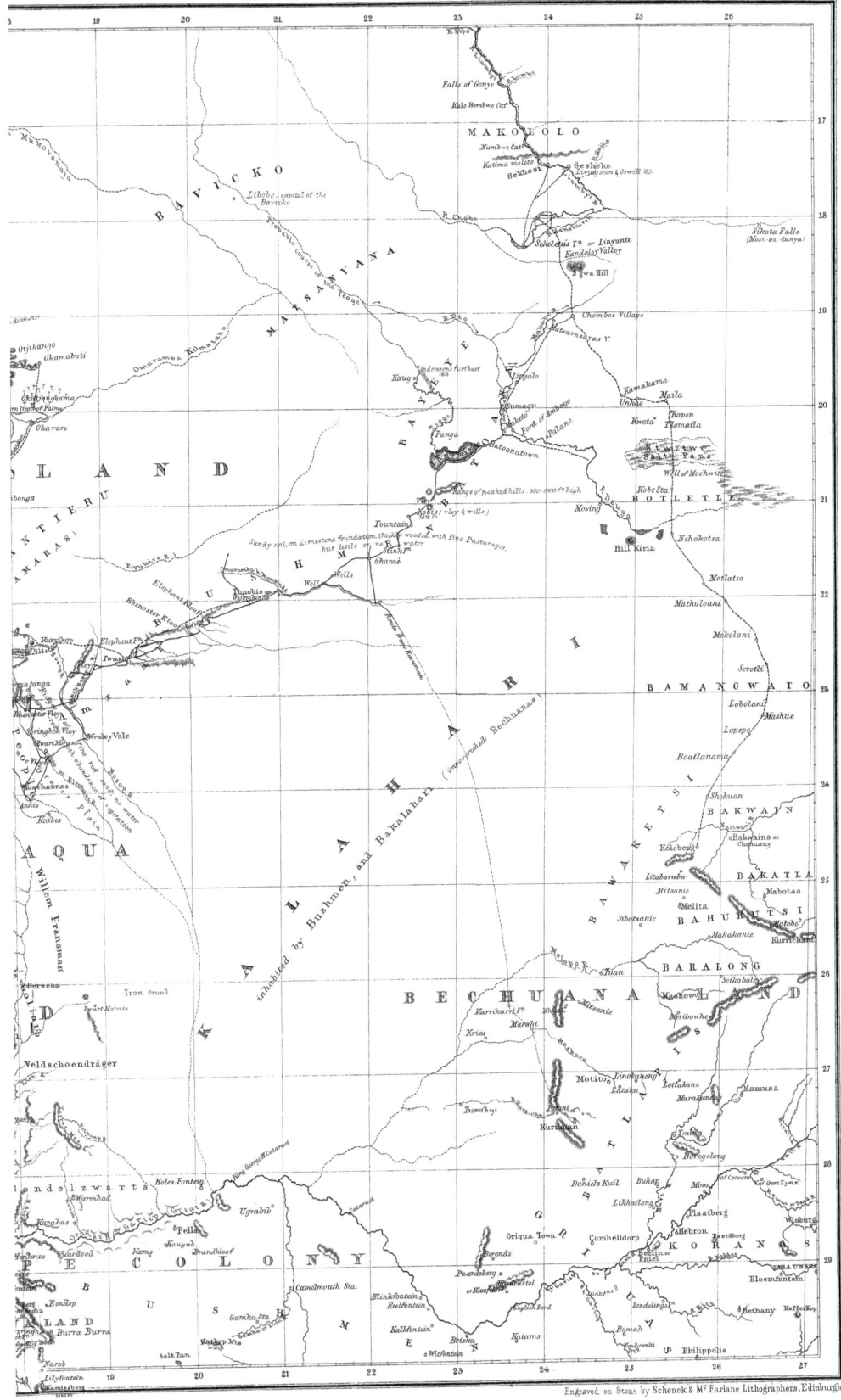

GENERAL INDEX.

A.

Aamhoup, the, a periodical river, 312; splendid mirage at, *ib.*

Abeghan, a watering-place, 404; the author shoots a large bull elephant there, 407

Afrika, Jonathan, 363; his adventure with a lion, 364

Allen, John, 58; enters Mr. Galton's service, *ib.*; his adventure on the banks of the Swakop, 271; falls sick of a fever, 310; emigrates with Hans to Australia, 347

Amral, a Namaqua chieftain, 330

Amulets, great faith of the South African natives in, 179, 330

Ana, the, a species of acacia, 27, 45; its fruit nutritious food for cattle, *ib.*

Animals, domestic, of the Ovambo, 202; of the Damaras, 232; of the Namaquas, 336; of the Bechuanas, 472; of the Bayeye, 502

Antelopes, Author stalking, in company with lions, 212

Archery, the Ovambo inferior to the Damaras in, 185

Articles of barter of the Ovambo, 173

B.

Baboon Fountain, 170

Bahurutsi, the natives at Kuruman send ambassadors to a rain-maker residing amongst the, 459

Bain, Mr., the distinguished South African geologist, 345

Bam, Mr., slight results of his missionary efforts amongst the Namaquas, 27; his wonderful escape from a rhinoceros, 35

Baobob tree, the, 430, 442

Barmen, its aspect and situation, 99; ill suited for an encampment, 119; return to, 216; second departure from, 246

Basutos, the famous king of the, 455

Batoana, the, a Bechuana tribe, 428; their appearance and manners, 429; their government, 454; their Pichos, *ib.*

Bayeye, the, expert fishermen, 473

Beads, in request with the South African tribes, 204; kinds most esteemed, *ib.*, 334, 473

Bean, a species of white, used as an antidote for snake bites, 305; the Author falls sick from eating a bean-looking fruit, 369

Bears, affecting story of two, 2

Bechuanas, the, their language, 456; first acquaintance of Europeans with, *ib.*; their want of religious ideas, *ib.*; wizards numerous amongst, 458; hold a council at Kuruman, as to the best means of removing a severe drought, 459; practise circumcision, 465; festivals attending the age of puberty, *ib.*; funeral ceremonies, 466; vindictiveness, *ib.*; theft a prevailing vice amongst, 468; attire, 469; great snuff-takers, 470

Beer, 195, 502

Bees, wild, frequently make their nests in the giant dwellings of the Termites, 132; their disposition unusually quiet and forbearing, *ib.*

Berry, delicious, 141

Bethany, a Rhenish missionary station, 314

Bill, a Damara lad, in the Author's service, loses himself in the bush, 213

Blacksmiths, 205

Boers, the, on the Trans-vaal river, 10; Sir Harry Smith's opinion of, 11; an uncivil one, 340

Bonfield, George, 349; spoils the Author's watch, 406

Boom-slang, the (or tree-snake), 303

Borele, a species of rhinoceros, 387

Buffaloes, following the tracks of, 481; proof against bullets, 483

GENERAL INDEX.

Buphaga Africana, the sentinel bird, 214
Bushmen; a few met with near Omuvereoom, 155; Lake Omanbondè, called Saresab in their language, *ib.*; a few met with near Baboon Fountain, 170; and at Otjikoto, 182; legend of a Bushwoman changing herself into a lion, 331; some met with returning from Lake Ngami, 409; their manner of hunting the koodoo, 486
Bush-ticks, deadly effects of the bite of, 20
Bustard, the large, very abundant at Schmelen's Hope, 130; the flesh good eating, 131
Buxton Fountain: origin of its name, 97

C.

Caffre-corn, the, 189, 503
Cameleopards; a troop of them seen near Omanbondè, 164; one shot, *ib.*
Canoe, description of a Bayeye, 475
Cape-Cross, a vessel supposed to be wrecked at, 124, 134
Cape-Town, 6; varieties of the human race encountered in its streets, 7; sensation caused by the Author's appearance in, 342
Caracal, the, 129; its fur warm and handsome, *ib.*; supposed medicinal virtues of the skin, *ib.*
Caravan, 179; caravan route, 183
Chikor'onkombè, chief of an Ovambo trading caravan, 174; his residence, 188; desertion of, 209
Christmas in the Desert, 112
Cobra-di-capella, the, common in the Cape Colony, 301; a remarkable escape from one, 302
Cockatrice, the, Damara's account of, 301
Cold weather, 150, 186, 309
Comet, the Author observes a remarkable, 368
Cornelius, chief of a powerful tribe of Namaquas, 286
Cow, the Damara, 318
Cunenè, a river of Africa; its discovery and subsequent mysterious disappearance, 206; the Ovambo often extend their trading excursions to, 207; attempt of Mr. Galton's party to visit it frustrated, 208; the Ovambo's account of, 447

D.

Dacre's pulpit, 346
Damara-Land only partially inhabited, 220; the seasons there the reverse of those in Europe, *ib.*; reptiles numerous in, 300
Damaras, the, beautifully formed, 49; not strong, *ib.*; complexion and symmetrical shape of the women, 50; clothing, ornaments, weapons, 51; divided into two large tribes, 52; carry firebrands at night, 85; one struck dead by lightning, 101; believe that all men of a light complexion are their enemies, 104; entirely a pastoral people, 114; their notions respecting property in land, 115; cruelly treated by the Namaquas, 122; the flesh of the leopard, hyæna, and other beasts of prey eaten by the poor, 128; a Damara's opinion of his countrymen, 138; addicted to telling falsehoods, 139; their method of cooking and eating, 147; villages, 156; their immorality, 176; eight Damara women surprised and put to death by Bushmen, 210; general reflections on, 217; whence they came, 218; their conquests, *ib.*; attacked by the Namaquas, 219; their own ideas respecting their origin, 221; their chief deity, *ib.*; their tribes, *ib.*; have great faith in witchcraft, 222; a fire always kept burning before the hut of their chief, 223; curious customs respecting food amongst the, 224; the women marry at much the same age as those in Europe, *ib.*; customs on the occasion of a girl's betrothal, 225; polygamy practised amongst, *ib.*; domestic habits, *ib.*; customs respecting the naming of children, *ib.*; bury their dead, 226; ceremonies on the death of one of the tribe, *ib.*; the law of succession amongst, 225, 228; ceremonies on the accession of a new chief, 229; fever and ophthalmia their prevailing maladies, *ib.*; milk their staple food, 230; fond of music and dancing, *ib.*; power of the chief, 231; rudiments of science amongst, *ib.*; value their cattle next to their women, 319
Dance, a, at Nangoro's residence, 196
Daviep, arrival at, 38; much frequented by lions, *ib.*
Dogs, miserable plight of the Namaqua, 285
Duikers, the (cormorants and shags): mode in which they obtain their food, 16

E.

Eggs, the, of the ostrich, 47; of the guinea-fowl, 82, 131
Eikhams, the residence of Jonker Afrikaner, 124; twilight at, 234; abundantly supplied with water, *ib.*; hot-spring in the neighbourhood of, *ib.*; history of the mission at, 235; terrific thunder-storm at, 284
Elands, spirited chase after, 381
Elephants, tracks of, 139; breed near to Omuvereoom, 154; combat between rhinoceros and, 162; unsuccessful hunt of, 168; Hans and Phillipus kill one, 174; the Author shoots a large bull-

elephant, 407 ; a midnight meeting with a troop of, 410 ; adventure with a herd of female elephants at Kobis, 416 ; a midnight spectacle of a magnificent troop of, 421
Elephant-Fountain, arrival at, 237 ; formerly a Wesleyan missionary station, *ib.*; chiefly inhabited by Hill-Damaras, *ib.*; nature of the country eastward of, *ib.*; return to, 241 ; abundance of game in its neighbourhood, 242
Elephant-Kloof, the Author shoots a magnificent giraffe at, 371
Erongo, a mountain famous for its peculiar formation, and as a stronghold of the Hill-Damaras, 107 ; about three thousand feet in height above the level of the plain, 113
Etosha, a sterile plain, 187 ; at times inundated, *ib.*
Euphorbia Candelabrum, use made of its poison by the Ovaherero and the Hill-Damaras, 81 ; fatal to the white rhinoceros, but harmless to the black species, *ib.* ; abundant at Okamabuti, 175
Eyebrecht, Mr., Jonker's right hand man, 236

F.

Fever, the Author attacked by, 309
Fig-tree, a gigantic one near Otjironjuba fountain, 153
Fire, the Author nearly destroyed by, 186
"Fiscaal," the, curious belief of the Cape people respecting, 67
Fish, 182
Fly, wasp-like, 44 ; the Author severely stung by one, *ib.*
Flying Fish, the, a schooner, 351
Foam, the, a small schooner chartered by Mr. Galton, for the voyage to Walfisch Bay, 12
Fowl, domestic, 202, 502

G.

Gabriel, his violent disposition, 68 ; dismissed at Barmen, 119 ; marks his subsequent career with violence and insolence, 135
Galton, Mr., starts for the Erongo Mountain, 107 ; obtains information from Jonker, 134 ; departs for England, 582
Gemsbok, the, first sight of, 43 ; death of one, 117 ; the Damaras feast on it, *ib.* ; description of, 279
Geological characteristics of Great Namaqua-land, 324
Ghanzé, arrival at, 382 ; description of, 383 ; departure from, 402
Giraffe, the ; one killed, 46 ; their marrow good eating, *ib.* ; troop of, 83 ; peculiar motion of, *ib.* ; troop of, 150 ; a splendid one pulled down by lions, 413

Giraffe-thorn, the, 27
Gnoo, a, chase after and death of, 106 ; stalking them in company with lions, 212
Grain, kind of, grown amongst the Ovambo, 189 ; the storing of, 202
Griquas, the Author meets with a party of, 361 ; one of them engaged as interpreter, *ib.* ; information derived from, 417 ; severe losses sustained by a party of, 489
Gross-beak, the social, 96
Guinea-fowls, an immense number at Onanis, 82 ; the flesh of the young tender and well flavoured, *ib* ; the best mode of shooting them, 83 ; their eggs excellent, 131
Guitar, 195

H.

Hahn, Mr., a missionary of the Rhenish Society, settled amongst the Damaras, 42 ; a Russian by birth, 101 ; his missionary labours, 102 ; his coadjutors, *ib.*, his fruitless efforts to bring about a reconciliation between the Damaras and the Namaquas, 121
Hans (Larsen), 56 ; a fine specimen of the true Northman, 57 ; his great strength, *ib.* ; an indefatigable sportsman, *ib.* ; enters Mr. Galton's service, 58 ; his character for being a good woodsman damaged, 151 ; meets with a little adventure, 245 ; enters into partnership with the Author, 272 ; goes into Damara-land to trade with the natives, 275 ; has an adventure with the Damaras, 276 : emigrates to Australia, 317
Hare, the, Namaqua superstition respecting, 328
Hareld, the (Arctic duck), mode in which it obtains its food, 16
Heat, effects of excessive, 37, 93
Heitjeebib, a deity worshipped by the Namaquas, 327
Hill-Damaras, the, 47 ; a kraal of, at Onanis, 79 ; cultivate dacka or hemp as a substitute for tobacco, *ib.*; unusual manner in which they smoke, 79 ; description of the pipe they use, 80 ; a kraal of, at the foot of Omuverecom, 153 ; probably the aborigines of Damara-land, 218
Hippopotamus, the, the actions and figure of, mimicked by a Damara, 156 ; visits Omanbondè, 161 ; one takes up his abode at Schmelen's Hope, *ib.*; abound on the northern side of Lake Ngami, 450 ; its supposed identity with the behemoth of Scripture, 509 ; where found, *ib.* ; two species in Africa, 510 ; description of, *ib.* ; its food, 512 ; ravages caused by, *ib.*; possessed of a good memory, 514 ; nocturnal excursions, 515 ; easily domesticated, *ib.* ; kept in captivity by the ancient Romans, 516 ; details re-

specting those in the Zoological Society's Gardens, in the Regent's Park, London, *ib.*; its most valuable parts, 517; manner in which the Bayeye harpoon, 518; drawings on the monuments and sculptures of Thebes relating to the chase of, 522; the Author's safety jeopardized by one, 525; instances of the ferocity of, 526; various devices for destroying, 527

History of Damara-land, 218

Hogs, found amongst the Ovambo, 190

Honey, wild, poisonous, 81

Horse, the Cape-Colony, 338; instance of the extraordinary endurance of, 339

Horse-sickness, the, 54; three mules and one horse perish of, *ib.*; its cause unknown, *ib.*; usually makes its appearance in the months of November and December, *ib.*; common throughout various parts of Southern Africa, 155

Hottentots, a small kraal of, 23; Frederick, their chieftain, and the alarum, 24; of Great Namaqua-land, 325

Hountop river, the, Author's party encamps near, 310; game abundant in the neighbourhood of, 311; an interesting atmospheric phenomenon at, 312

Houses, the Ovambo, 202; the Damara, 225; the Namaqua, 326; the Bayeye, 501

Hyæna, the, 117; called wolf by the colonists, 126; mode of setting spring-guns for, *ib.*; starling appearance of a spotted, 384

I.

Ice, 212, 309

Implements of husbandry, 45, 96, 203

Ivory, 203

J.

Jackal, a mischievous, 379

Ja Kabaka, the, a mountain, 139, 151

Jonker Afrikaner, 101, 105; a letter from, 118; his quarrel with Kahichenè, 121; an instance of his cruelty, 124; Mr. Galton sets out to visit, *ib.*: relations between him and William Zwartbooi,133; sends an express to Zwartbooi for his horses, *ib.*; promises to live in peace and amity with the Damaras, *ib.*; his first victories over the Damaras, 219; whence he came, *ib.*; gifts presented by Mr. Galton to, 235; the Author takes his portrait, 236; loses the greater part of his cattle, 245; his werft in the neighbourhood of Eikhams, 285; engaged in a cattle-lifting foray, 295; the Author upbraids him for his depredations, 297; his defence, 298

Justice, summary, 145

K.

Kachamaha, a powerful Damara chief, 295; the Author's visit to, 297

Kahichenè, a Damara chieftain, 115; immense number of oxen and sheep possessed by, *ib.*; his quarrel with Jonker Afrikaner, 121; meets the Author's party at Kotjiamkombè, 143; his appearance and manners, *ib.*; at variance with a tribe of Damaras under the rule of Omugunde,144; his summary treatment of thieves, 145; his kraal, 146; his death, 149

Kaiaob, the Namaqua witch-doctor, 329

Kamapyu, a half-caste native lad, 358

Kameel-doorn, the, 96; hardness of its wood, *ib.*; the social grossbeak constructs its nest in the branches of, *ib.*; groups of, 161

Klaas Zaal, engaged as a waggon-driver, 368

Kleinschmidt, Mr., 134, 293

Kobis, good shooting at, 414; adventure with a black rhinoceros there, *ib.*; with a white one, 415; and with a herd of female elephants,416; departure from,427

Kolbé, Mr., 102, 121, 133

Komaggas, a Rhenish missionary station, 337

Konyati, the, a mountain, 139

Koodoo, the; a young one caught and reared, 125: its tragic end, 126; description of, 484; the bushmen's manner of hunting, 486

Kotjiamkombè, a splendid vley, 142

Kuisip, the, a periodical stream, 26; swollen by heavy rains, 271

L.

Lambert, eldest son of Amral, a Namaqua chief, 370

Larvæ, locust, sudden appearance of at Schmelen's Hope, 135; conjecture respecting, 136; devoured by storks, *ib.*

Larsen (*vide* Hans)

Leché, the, a species of antelope, 448; the Author shoots one, 477

Lecholètébè, chief of the Batoanas: the Author sends presents to, 409; Timbo's interview with, 418; the Author visits, 434; his manner of receiving presents, 436; his greediness, *ib.*; his prompt mode of punishing his subjects, 438

Leopard, the, erroneously called tiger by the Dutch, 127: one seizes and wounds a favourite dog, *ib.*; pursued and slain, 128

Libèbé, the capital of the Bavicko, situated considerably to the north of Lake Ngami, 438; the Author determines to visit, *ib.*; the centre of a great inland trade, 505; visited by the Mambari, *ib.*

Lightning, a man killed by, 101

Lion, the; a daring and destructive one slain by Messrs. Galton and Bam, 25;

a horse and mule killed by lions, 39; panic caused by a troop of lions, 53; two met with on the banks of the Swakop, 84; narrow escape from, *ib.*; midnight interview with a, 88; one deprived of his prey, 90; one mistaken for a zebra, 105; one kills a goat, 107; pursued and slain, 110; the travellers serenaded by a whole troop of, 116; Mr. Galton confronted by one, 163; stalking antelopes in company with, 212; very numerous and daring in the neighbourhood of Zwart Nosop, 242; adventure with one at night, 243; story of the seizure of lion cubs, 248; troops of them in the neighbourhood of Tincas and Onanis, 273; a lion devours a lioness, 311; a fair shot at one, 356; Old Piet's adventures with, *ib.*; one finds his way into the church at Richterfeldt, 357; instances of their boldness, 365; unexpected meeting with five, 413; serious night adventure with one, 533

Locust, the, larvæ of, 289; immense masses of, *ib.*; their arrival a cause of rejoicing to the Bushmen, 291; how prepared as food, *ib.*

Locust-bird, the (*Spring-haan vogel*), 292

Louis, a Mozambique liberated slave, 350

M.

Mackintosh Punt, 156

Malays, the, religion and mode of life of, 7

Mambari, the, an African tribe, 505

Matsanyana, the, an African tribe residing north of the Bayeye, 505

Mimosa, the black-stemmed, found in the periodical water-courses, 81

Mirage, a remarkable, 17, 312

Missionaries; their exertions unavailing in Namaqua-land, 27; the natives very reserved on their first appearance in Damara-land, 102; prospect of their success at Schmelen's Hope disappointed, 121; arrival of the missionary ship, 251; decline of the mission at Rehoboth, 293; the Rhenish missionary station at Bethany, 314; blamed by the Bahurusti rain-maker as the cause of a severe drought, 464

Monoohoo, a species of rhinoceros, 387

Mortar, John; irritability his only fault, 69; a famous teller of stories, 70; his disappointment in the matter of soap manufacture, 241

Mosheshe, the famous Basuto king, 455

Mukuru-Mukovanja, a large river, 207; the Ovambos' account of, 447

Mules, the; one becomes exhausted and is left behind, 37; shortly afterwards killed by lions, 39; the travellers lay in a stock of mules' flesh, 40; the flesh of, not unpalatable, 42; worn out, 48; three killed by sickness, 54; escape, and are intercepted at Barmen, 124; again make off, and are not retaken, 125

Mummies, 182

Mushrooms, grow on the sides of the nests of the termites, 132

N.

Naarip, the, a sterile plain, 34, 36; travellers often lose their way on, 62; the Author's party suffers much from cold on, 64; affords a good road, 74; its pleasant appearance after rains, 273

Ngami, the, Lake, preparations for navigating, 5; failure of Mr. Galton and the Author to reach it, 238; the Author resolves to make another attempt, 240; first appearance of, 431; arrival at, 432; first information received by Europeans respecting, 440; different names by which it is known amongst the natives, 441; description of, *ib.*; Mr. Green's description of, 442; its shores, *ib.*; must have undergone very considerable changes at different periods, 443; the Author navigates, *ib.*; fed by the river Teoge, 444; finds an outlet at its eastern extremity in the Zouga, 445; a great variety of animals found in its neighbourhood, 448; hippopotami abound on the northern side of, 450; swarms with crocodiles, 451; snakes numerous on the shores, 452; fish, *ib.*; departure from, 532

Naitjo, an Ovambo man, 188

Nakong, the, a species of antelope, 448; description of, 449

Namaqua-land, Great, description of, 323; in a geological point of view, 324

Namaquas, the; their character, 27; their astonishment at the first waggons they saw, 28; treat the Damaras very cruelly, 122; usually very barbarous, 123; their respect for truth-tellers, 298; best mode of behaving towards, *ib.*; names of the chiefs of the Northern, 326; their habitations, *ib.*; their religious ideas, 327; their superstitions with regard to the hare, 328; have great faith in sorcery, 329; their neglect of widows, and cruel treatment of old and disabled persons, 333; their custom of adopting fathers and mothers, *ib.*; personal adornment, 334; excessively idle, 335; understand the art of distilling spirits, *ib.*; attack Richterfeldt, 353; ill-treat the missionaries, *ib.*

Nangoro, king of the Ovambo, 163; assists a Damara chief, 167; a messenger sent to, 186; interview with, 193; his personal appearance, *ib.*; his wives, 199

Naras, the, a delicious fruit, 21; its beneficial qualities, 22; where found, *ib.*

Nosop, the river, 368

O.

Obesity, equivalent to high treason amongst certain African tribes, 193
Oerlams, a branch of the Hottentot race, 325
Okamabuti, the residence of the Damara chief, Tjopopa, 167; the northern limit of Damara-land, 168; rank vegetation at, 175
Omanbondè, lake; Mr. Galton hears of, 104; surmises respecting its extent, 155; Mr. Galton's party makes preparation for spending some time on its shores, 156; arrival at, *ib.*; its insignificance, *ib.*; visited by hippopotami, 161; departure from, 164
Omatako, 137; its beautiful appearance, *ib.*; the river of, 138
Ombotodthu, a mountain, 146; remarkable for its peculiar red stone, *ib.*
Omoroanga Vavarra, the, a branch of the Teoge, 493
Omugundè, the chief of a tribe of Damaras, 144; slays several of Kahichenè's children, and keeps the others prisoners, *ib.*
Omukuru, the chief deity of the Damaras, 221
Omumborombonga, a tree, the supposed progenitor of the Damaras, 218
Omuramba-K'Omatako, a periodical river, 211; supposed to flow towards the Bechuana country, *ib.*
Omurangere, the holy fire of the Damaras, 223
Omutenna, a tributary to the Swakop, 48, 107
Omutjamatunda, a cattle post belonging to the Ovambo, 183; a copious fountain, 184; ducks and grouse numerous there, 185
Omuvereoom, the, a mountain, 139; distance between it and Omatako, 150; arrival at the southern extremity of, 151; extensive view from its summit, 154
Onanis, the residence of a kraal of very poor Hill-Damaras, 79; fine pasturages, 82; troops of lions seen at, 273
Ondangere, the vestal virgin of the Damaras, 223
Ondara, the, a species of serpent, 299; story of one, *ib.*
Ondonga, the country of the Ovambo, 187; arrival in, *ib.*; water and pasturage scarce, 190; departure from, 209
Onesimus, Zwartbooi's henchman; joins the Author's party, 135; is flogged, 377
Ongeama; native name for Lion, 107; cries of, 179
Onguirira, a species of animal resembling, but totally distinct from, the lion, 149
Ophthalmia, the Author attacked by, 288
Orange river, the, description of, 320
Oranges, a feast of, 343
Orukumb'ombura, 'rain-beggars,' the name given by the Damaras to columns of sand driven along by the wind, 220
Oryx, the, death of one, 117; the Damaras feast on it, *ib.*; description of, 279
Ostrich, the, omelet of the eggs, 47; the egg equal to twenty-four of the common fowl, *ib.*; numerous on the Naarip plain, 253; chase and capture of part of a brood of young ones, 254; interesting manœuvre of a parent ostrich, *ib.*; districts in which found, 255; types in other parts of the world, *ib.*; general appearance, *ib.*; its cry greatly resembles that of the lion, 256; its marvellous speed, *ib.*; food, *ib.*; power of enduring thirst, 257; season for breeding, *ib.*; period of incubation, 258; a peculiarity in regard to the eggs of the ostrich, 259; nature of the covering of the young birds, *ib.*; the flesh of the young ostrich palatable, 260; in estimation with the ancient Romans as an article of food, *ib.*; uses to which the egg-shells are applied, 261; ostrich feathers, *ib.*; the ostrich in a wild state, 263; its powers of digestion, 264: resemblance to quadrupeds, 265; modes in which it is captured, 267
Oswell, Mr., his chase of a rhinoceros, 397
Otjihako-tja-Mutenya, 187; sufferings from cold on, 209
Otjikango, the, name of a series of wells, 170, 179
Otjikoto fountain, 180; a wonderful freak of nature, 181; its remarkable cavern, 182; visited by a great number of doves, *ib.*; Bushmen reside near to it, *ib.*
Otjironjuba fountain, 153; departure from, 154
Otjombindè, 238
Otjruru, an apparition, 222
Otters, not uncommon in Lake Ngami, 450
Ovaherero, the: their mode of using tobacco, 81; tip their arrows with the poison of *euphorbia candelabrum*, *ib.*
Ovambo, the, a people of Africa, 163; first interview with, 171; their food, 172; arms, 173; effect of fireworks on, 194; musical instruments in use amongst, 195; their personal appearance, 196; their strict honesty, 197; no pauperism in their country, *ib.*; their national pride, 198; hospitality, *ib.*; staple food, *ib.*; morality amongst, 199; state of religion amongst, 200; their dwellings, 201; domestic animals, 202; farm implements, 203; their chief articles of export, *ib.*; have some slight knowledge of metallurgy, 204
Ovapangari, the, an African tribe, 207, 506
Oxen; invaluable in South Africa, 29; method of breaking in, 30; one charges Mr. Galton, 33; manner of guiding a

GENERAL INDEX.

saddle-ox, 59; can be made to travel at a pretty quick pace, *ib.*; training for the yoke, 66; vicious one ridden by Mr. Schöneberg, 94; become wild and unmanageable from their over-long rest, 116; several stolen from Mr. Galton's party, 144; extraordinary confusion amongst, and the cause of it, 214; curious custom when an ox dies at a chief's werft in Damara-land, 223; their instinctive power of catching the scent of humid winds and green herbage at a great distance, 244; instance of affection between two, 274; Author's adventure with a runaway, 277; the Author has an ugly fall from one, 297; superstition that they refrain from eating on Christmas-eve, 316; the Damara breed of, 317; the Bechuana breed of, *ib.*; the Namaqua breed of, 336

P.

Palm-trees, a large number seen, 164; description of a peculiar kind of fan-palm, 165; fruit of, 166, 189
Parrots, crested, 44, 46
Pelicans, 66; curious mode of flight, *ib.*
Phenomenon, 138
Phillipus, a Damara, joins the Author's party as a waggon driver, 135
Pichos, the (or parliaments), of the Bato-anas, 454
Pit-falls, for the capture of game, 376
Polygamy, 199, 225, 332, 465, 501
Population of the Ovambo country estimated, 190
Portuguese, 183
Puff-adder, the, 302; its manner of seizing its prey, *ib.*

R.

Rain-maker, the Bahurutsi, 459; murdered amongst the Bauangketsi nation, 465
Rains, the, begin as early as Sept. and Oct., 118
Rath, Mr., 48, 102, 115; his description of a track of a nondescript animal, 127
Rehoboth, a Rhenish missionary station, 134, 288; description of, 293; the rocks in its neighbourhood strongly impregnated with copper, 363
Religion, 200
Reptiles, numerous in Damara-land and Namaqua-land, 301; superstitions respecting, 303; antidotes used in Southern Africa for the bites of, 304
Rhinoceros, the; curious anecdote preserved in the archives of Cape-Town relating to a death of one, 9; Mr. Mr. Bam's story of his wonderful escape from one, 35; tracks of, *ib.*; one shot, 60; fall frequently on their knees when killed, *ib.*; curious anecdote, *ib.*; flesh not unpalatable, *ib.*; hide useful, *ib.*; discovery of a, 74; adventure in pursuit of one, 75; its escape, 77; combat between elephant and, 162; several shot at Ghanzé, 385; where found, *ib.*; four distinct species known to exist in South Africa, 387; distinctions between the black and the white rhinoceros, 388; appearance of, 390; food, 391; breeding, *ib.*; Colonel Williams's story respecting one, 393; conflicts with elephants, 394; the flesh and horns, 395; adventure with a black rhinoceros at Kobis, 414; with a white one, 415; the Author shoots a white one, 423; desperate adventure with a black one, *ib.*; method of chasing, 396; Mr. Oswell's stories respecting the chase of, 397
Richterfeldt, a Rhenish missionary station, reached, 48; water abundant, *ib.*; soil fertile, 49; when founded, *ib.*; return to, 86; bid a final farewell to, 116
Rifle, obtained in barter, 146; excellent weapon, 147
Rights of succession, 200, 225, 228
Ringel-hals, the, or ring-throat, a species of snake, 303
Roode Natie, the (or Red Nation), a powerful tribe of Namaquas, 286; their character, 287; Cornelius, their chief, *ib.*; their country, 288; few Damara slaves amongst them, *ib.*

S.

Salt-lick, a, 381
Sand Fountain, excursion to, 18; badness of its water, 19; its disagreeable guests, 20; its advantages, 21; general aspect of the country in the neighbourhood of, 23
Sand-wells, 380
Scarlet Flower, the, emotions on first seeing, 34; observe it again, 35
Scenery, striking, 168
Schaap-Steker, the, a species of snake, 303
Scheppmansdorf, Mr. Galton arrives at, 24; all the baggage safely deposited at, 25; description of, 26; first impressions of, 65; kind friends at, *ib.*; departure from, 73
Scheppman's Mountain; origin of its name, 95
Schmelen, Mr., a highly-gifted and enterprising missionary, 121
Schmelen's Hope; its situation, 120; origin of its name, 121; agreeable residence; abundance of game to be obtained there, 130; departure from, 142; return to, 216
Schöneberg, Mr., 93; his mishap, 94; his wailing, 95
Scorpions, a swarm of, 97; their fondness of warmth, 98; their bite poisonous, but rarely fatal, *ib.*

544 GENERAL INDEX.

Season, the rainy, in Ovambo-land, 202; in Damara-land, 220
Sebetoane, an African chief, false report respecting, 429
Serpent, tracks of an immense (the Ondara), 299; story of a, *ib.*
Serpent-stones, 306
Servants, described, 67; African travellers cannot be too particular in the selection of, *ib.*; become refractory, 119; adventure of one of them with an ox, 277; Damara servants abscond, 369
Shambok, the, 61 and 62
Shrike, a species of, 67; superstitious belief respecting, *ib.*
Smith, Dr. Andrew, 215; 513
Snake, a curious species of, 300; several species occasionally met with in Damaraland and Namaqua-land, 303; antidotes for the bites of, 304; numerous in and about Lake Ngami, 452
Snake-stone, the, 307
Snuff, manner in which the Bechuanas manufacture, 470
Spring, hot, at Barmen, 101; at Eikhams, 234; at Rehoboth, 293
'Spring,' Author's ride ox, 59
Spuig-Slang, the, or spitting snake, 303
St. Helena, John, officiates as head waggoner, 69; his extraordinary disposition, *ib.*; discourses on ghosts, 340
Steinbok, the: a young one taken and reared, 125; its tragic end, 126
Stewardson, Mr., 30
Stink-hout, a species of oak, 168
Sugar-cane, supposed to exist in many parts of Southern Africa, 189
Sun-stroke, Author receives one, 45; usual results of a, 46; the Author in danger of a second, 78
Sunrise, the, in the tropics, 37; often followed by intense heat, and sufferings thereon, *ib.*; a mule left behind, *ib.*
Superstition, a, with regard to oxen, 148
Swakop, the, first appearance of, 34; its cheerful aspect, *ib.*; the Author's party attacked by two lions on the bank of, 84; the Damaras flock with their cattle to, 246

T.

Table Mountain, 8; ascent by the Author of, 9
Tans Mountain, 362
Tent, the Author's, takes fire, 308
Teoge, the river, feeds Lake Ngami, 444; scenery along the banks of, 479; crocodiles observed on, 492
Termites, the: Schmelen's Hope swarms with, 131; their method of constructing their nests, *ib.*; encampment in the middle of a nest of, 140; instance of the fearful ravages they are capable of committing in an incredibly short space of time, 151
Textor-erythorhynchus, a parasitical insect-feeding bird, 215
Thirst, suffering from, 38; water not quenching thirst, *ib.*
Thorn-coppices, 183
Thunder-Storm, a, in the tropics, 100, 136, 366
Tiger-wolf (or spotted hyæna), 384
Timbo, a native of Mazapa, 70; carried into captivity by Caffres, 71; sold as a slave to the Portuguese, *ib.*; liberated by an English cruiser, *ib.*; his faithless spouse, *ib.*; his good qualities, *ib.*; his love of (native) country, 72; friendship between him and George Bonfield, 349; turns sulky, 366; the Author sends him to Lake Ngami, 409; his return, 418
Tincas, the mountain, 38; great stronghold and breeding-place of lions, *ib.*
Tincas, the river, 74
Tjobis, a river and tributary to the Swakop, 46
Tjobis Fountain, arrive at, 47, 83; depart from, 48, 83
Tjopopa, a great chief of the Damaras, 167; reach his werft, *ib.*; his character, 168; death of his mother, 175; his idleness and fondness for tobacco, 175, 176; his sensuality, 176; leaves Okamabuti, 210
Tobacco, great size of leaves of, 103; the Ovambo cultivate it, 189; buy sheep for, 210
Topnaars, a branch of the Hottentot tribe, 325
Toucans, 46
Trans-vaal river, the, rumours respecting the churlish conduct of the Boers on, 10
Travelling, by day injurious, 45, 48; by night preferable, but dangerous, 74; difficulties of African, 157
Trees, bearing an apple-looking fruit, 175, 118; enormous sized, *ib.*
Tsetse fly, the, where chiefly found, 488; description of, 489; poisonous nature of its bite, *ib.*; result of Captain Vardon's experiment on, 490; Mr. Oswell's examination of oxen bitten by, 491; wild animals unaffected by the poison of, 491
Tunobis, 238; days profitably and pleasantly passed there, 239; immense quantity of game in the neighbourhood of, *ib.*; the Author's misadventure at, 374
Twass, the head quarters of the Namaqua chief, Lambert, 370

U.

Usab, the, a striking gorge: we arrive at the, 73

V.

'Venus,' a small half-bred dog; her combat with a rhinoceros, 408; great sagacity of, *ib.*

Voet-gangers (*vide* larvæ)
Vollmer, Mr., 134

W.

Waggoner, John; his sulkiness and reluctance to work, 68; dismissed at Barmen, 119; his subsequent dishonest career, 134
Waggons, the, fourteen cwt. a good load for, 67; accident to, 169
Wait-a-bit Thorn, the, 152; great strength of its prickles, *ib.*; excessively troublesome, 382, 430
Walfisch Bay; the Author's party advised to select this place as a starting point for their journey into the interior, 11; arrival at the entrance of, 13; appearance of the coast as seen from, 14; description of, *ib.*; trading establishments there, *ib.*; frequented by immense numbers of waterfowl, 115; outrageous conduct of the crews of whaling and guano ships visiting, 247; extraordinary number of dead fish in, 249; the Author's second visit to, 352
Water, difficulty of obtaining, 315, 403
Water-courses, the periodical, afford the only really practicable roads, 118
Wenzel, Abraham, 68; his thievish habits, *ib.*; dismissed at Schmelen's Hope, 135
Whirlwinds, 220

Williams, John; results of his carelessness, 69
Willow-tree, the, in the neighbourhood of Omuvereoom, 151
Witch-Doctor, the Namaqua, 329
Witchcraft, Damaras have great faith in, 222; the Bechuanas have great faith in, 458
'Wolf,' 107
Wolves, or hyænas, 126
Women, Ovambo, 196; Damara, 224; Bayeye, 502

Z.

Zebra, melancholy wail of the, 89; the Author shoots one, 94; its flesh not very palatable, *ib.*; a lion mistaken for one, 105; the Author shoots one, 138
Zouga, a river which flows out of Lake Ngami, 419; runs in an easterly direction from Lake Ngami, for a distance of about three hundred miles, 445; vegetation along its course varied and luxuriant, *ib.*
Zwartbooi, William, a Namaqua chieftain, 132; relations between Jonker Afrikaner and, *ib.*; his territory, 133; assists us with servants, 135
Zwart Nosop, many pit-falls for game constructed in the neighbourhood of, 242
Zwart-slang, the, or black snake, 303

LATIN INDEX.

Acacia giraffæ, 27, 96
Aigocerus ellipsiprymnus, 448
Amadina squamifrons, 215
Behemot Jobi, 509
Buphaga Africana, 214
Canis mesomelas, 285
Chizoerhis concolor, 46
Columber canus, 303
Croton, 335
Diosma, 335
Euphorbia candelabrum, 81, 175
Felis caracal, 129
Francolinus adspersus, 36
Glossina morsitans, 488
Gryllus devastator, 289
Harelda glacialis, 16
Hippopotamus amphibius, 510, 511
    ,, Liberiencis, 510
Holcus Caffrorum, 172
Hyrax Capensis, 299
Lanius subcoronatus, 67

Loxia socia, 96
Naia haje, 303
Oryx Capensis, 279
  ,, beisa, 279
  ,, leucoryx, 279
Otis kori, 130
Processus mamillaris, 517
Python Natalensis, 299
Quercus Africana, 168
Rhinoceris bicornis, 387
    ,,   ,, Sumatrensis, 386
    ,, Indicus, 386
    ,, Keitloa, 387, 391
    ,, Oswellii, 387, 388
    ,, simus, 387, 389
    ,, Sondaicus, 386
Textor erythrorhynchus, 215
Tragelaphus Angasii, 449
    ,, eurycerus, 449
Trimerorhinus rhombeatus, 303
Vipera inflata, 302

THE END.

www.ingramcontent.com/pod-product-compliance
Lightning Source LLC
Chambersburg PA
CBHW060305230426

43663CB00009B/1596